New Directions in German Studies
Vol. 31

Series Editor:
IMKE MEYER
Professor of Germanic Studies, University of Illinois at Chicago

Editorial Board:

KATHERINE ARENS
Professor of Germanic Studies, University of Texas at Austin

ROSWITHA BURWICK
Distinguished Chair of Modern Foreign Languages Emerita,
Scripps College

RICHARD ELDRIDGE
Charles and Harriett Cox McDowell Professor of Philosophy,
Swarthmore College

ERIKA FISCHER-LICHTE
Professor Emerita of Theater Studies, Freie Universität Berlin

CATRIONA MACLEOD
Edmund J. and Louise W. Kahn Term Professor in
the Humanities and Professor of German, University
of Pennsylvania

STEPHAN SCHINDLER
Professor of German and Chair, University of South Florida

HEIDI SCHLIPPHACKE
Associate Professor of Germanic Studies,
University of Illinois at Chicago

ANDREW J. WEBBER
Professor of Modern German and Comparative Culture,
Cambridge University

SILKE-MARIA WEINECK
Professor of German and Comparative Literature,
University of Michigan

DAVID WELLBERY
LeRoy T. and Margaret Deffenbaugh Carlson University
Professor, University of Chicago

SABINE WILKE
Joff Hanauer Distinguished Professor for Western Civilization and
Professor of German, University of Washington

JOHN ZILCOSKY
Professor of German and Comparative Literature, University of Toronto

Volumes in the series:

Vol. 1. Improvisation as Art: Conceptual Challenges, Historical Perspectives
by Edgar Landgraf

Vol. 2. The German Pícaro and Modernity: Between Underdog and Shape-Shifter
by Bernhard Malkmus

Vol. 3. Citation and Precedent: Conjunctions and Disjunctions of German Law and Literature
by Thomas O. Beebee

Vol. 4. Beyond Discontent: "Sublimation" from Goethe to Lacan
by Eckart Goebel

Vol. 5. From Kafka to Sebald: Modernism and Narrative Form
edited by Sabine Wilke

Vol. 6. Image in Outline: Reading Lou Andreas-Salomé
by Gisela Brinker-Gabler

Vol. 7. Out of Place: German Realism, Displacement, and Modernity
by John B. Lyon

Vol. 8. Thomas Mann in English: A Study in Literary Translation
by David Horton

Vol. 9. The Tragedy of Fatherhood: King Laius and the Politics of Paternity in the West
by Silke-Maria Weineck

Vol. 10. The Poet as Phenomenologist: Rilke and the New Poems
by Luke Fischer

Vol. 11. The Laughter of the Thracian Woman: A Protohistory of Theory
by Hans Blumenberg, translated by Spencer Hawkins

Vol. 12. Roma Voices in the German-Speaking World
by Lorely French

Vol. 13. Vienna's Dreams of Europe: Culture and Identity beyond the Nation-State
by Katherine Arens

Vol. 14. Thomas Mann and Shakespeare: Something Rich and Strange
edited by Tobias Döring and Ewan Fernie

Vol. 15. Goethe's Families of the Heart
by Susan E. Gustafson

Vol. 16. German Aesthetics: Fundamental Concepts from Baumgarten to Adorno
edited by J. D. Mininger and Jason Michael Peck

Vol. 17. *Figures of Natality: Reading the Political in the Age of Goethe*
by Joseph D. O'Neil

Vol. 18. *Readings in the Anthropocene: The Environmental Humanities, German Studies, and Beyond*
edited by Sabine Wilke and Japhet Johnstone

Vol. 19. *Building Socialism: Architecture and Urbanism in East German Literature, 1955–1973*
by Curtis Swope

Vol. 20. *Ghostwriting: W. G. Sebald's Poetics of History*
by Richard T. Gray

Vol. 21. *Stereotype and Destiny in Arthur Schnitzler's Prose: Five Psycho-Sociological Readings*
by Marie Kolkenbrock

Vol. 22. *Sissi's World: The Empress Elisabeth in Memory and Myth*
edited by Maura E. Hametz and Heidi Schlipphacke

Vol. 23. *Posthumanism in the Age of Humanism: Mind, Matter, and the Life Sciences after Kant*
edited by Edgar Landgraf, Gabriel Trop, and Leif Weatherby

Vol. 24. *Staging West German Democracy: Governmental PR Films and the Democratic Imaginary, 1953–1963*
by Jan Uelzmann

Vol. 25. *The Lever as Instrument of Reason: Technological Constructions of Knowledge around 1800*
by Jocelyn Holland

Vol. 26. *The Fontane Workshop: Manufacturing Realism in the Industrial Age of Print*
by Petra McGillen

Vol. 27. *Gender, Collaboration, and Authorship in German Culture: Literary Joint Ventures, 1750–1850*
edited by Laura Deiulio and John B. Lyon

Vol. 28. *Kafka's Stereoscopes: The Political Function of a Literary Style*
by Isak Winkel Holm

Vol. 29. *Ambiguous Aggression in German Realism and Beyond: Flirtation, Passive Aggression, Domestic Violence*
by Barbara N. Nagel

Vol. 30. *Thomas Bernhard's Afterlives*
edited by Stephen Dowden, Gregor Thuswaldner, and Olaf Berwald

Vol. 31. *Modernism in Trieste: The Habsburg Mediterranean and the Literary Invention of Europe, 1870–1945*
by Salvatore Pappalardo

Modernism in Trieste

*The Habsburg Mediterranean and
the Literary Invention of Europe,
1870–1945*

Salvatore Pappalardo

BLOOMSBURY ACADEMIC
NEW YORK • LONDON • OXFORD • NEW DELHI • SYDNEY

BLOOMSBURY ACADEMIC
Bloomsbury Publishing Inc
1385 Broadway, New York, NY 10018, USA
50 Bedford Square, London, WC1B 3DP, UK
29 Earlsfort Terrace, Dublin 2, Ireland

BLOOMSBURY, BLOOMSBURY ACADEMIC and the Diana logo are trademarks of Bloomsbury Publishing Plc

First published in the United States of America 2021
This paperback edition published 2022

Volume Editors' Part of the Work © Salvatore Pappalardo, 2021

Cover design by Andrea Federle-Bucsi
Cover image © Shutterstock.com

All rights reserved. No part of this publication may be reproduced or transmitted in any form or by any means, electronic or mechanical, including photocopying, recording, or any information storage or retrieval system, without prior permission in writing from the publishers.

Bloomsbury Publishing Inc does not have any control over, or responsibility for, any third-party websites referred to or in this book. All internet addresses given in this book were correct at the time of going to press. The author and publisher regret any inconvenience caused if addresses have changed or sites have ceased to exist, but can accept no responsibility for any such changes.

Library of Congress Cataloging-in-Publication Data
Names: Pappalardo, Salvatore, 1978- author.
Title: Modernism in Trieste / by Salvatore Pappalardo.
Description: New York : Bloomsbury Academic, 2021. | Series: New directions in German studies ; vol. 31 | Includes bibliographical references and index.
Identifiers: LCCN 2020036729 (print) | LCCN 2020036728 (ebook) | ISBN 9781501369964 (hardback) | ISBN 9781501369971 (epub) | ISBN 9781501369988 (pdf)
Subjects: LCSH: Modernism (Literature)–Italy–Trieste. | Modernism (Literature)–Europe. | Italian literature–Appreciation. | National characteristics in literature.
Classification: LCC PN56.M54 P37 2021 (ebook) | LCC PN56.M54 (print) | DDC 809/.9112–dc23
LC record available at https://lccn.loc.gov/2020036729

ISBN:	HB:	978-1-5013-6996-4
	PB:	978-1-5013-6995-7
	ePDF:	978-1-5013-6998-8
	eBook:	978-1-5013-6997-1

Series: New Directions in German Studies

Typeset by Integra Software Services Pvt. Ltd.

To find out more about our authors and books visit www.bloomsbury.com and sign up for our newsletters.

*A
Elizabeth
Penelope e Veronica*

Contents

List of Illustrations   xi
Acknowledgments   xiii

Introduction: Trieste and the European Project—Ethics,
    Aesthetics, Politics   1
    Modernism and the Idea of Europe   7
    Habsburg Trieste, *urbs europeissima*   12
    Nonnational Affiliations in the Habsburg Empire   20
    Behind the Nation: Trieste and an Austrian
       Mediterranean Sea   26
    A Multilingual Habsburg Canon   38

1   The Adriatic Sea as a Phoenician Mediterranean, 1870–1925   47
    The Phoenicians in Greek and Roman Sources   50
    The Phoenicians between Orientalism and Classicism   57
    Phoenicianism in Trieste   60
    "Here I Am in Tergeste": The Fantasies of a Phoenician Freud   64
    A Semitic Hellenism: Theodor Däubler and the Poetics of
       Bilingualism   70
    A View of the Mediterranean Karst: Srečko Kosovel and the
       Ethics of Mediation   79

2   A Mediterranean Monarchy: Robert Musil and the Politics
     of Nonnational Loyalty, 1913–1943   91
    Vienna-Trieste, Summer 1913: *Die Adria-Ausstellung* and the
       Hohenlohe Decrees   94
    Musil's War Journalism 1916–1918: Italian Irredentism in
       the *Soldaten-Zeitung*   106
    Europe in Musil's Essays, 1912–1923   108
    Ulrich, the Man without Patriotic Qualities   114
    Trieste in Kakanien 1913: Leo Fischel and Count Leinsdorf   117
    Paul Arnheim, Ancient Phoenician and Modern European   128

3	Trojan Trieste: Italo Svevo and the Aesthetics of Austro-Italian Liminality, 1890–1923	141
	Svevo's Politics of Literary Style	149
	The New Europe in Svevo's Pacifist Essay, 1918–1922	154
	One Last Austrian Cigarette: Zeno, the Habsburg Phoenician, 1923	166
	Literature and the Language of Lies	172
4	Habsburg Hybrid: James Joyce and the Ethnolinguistics of Hiberno-Punic Mythography, 1904–1939	187
	What Is in a Name? Italo Svevo and Giacomo Joyce	188
	Joyce and the "United States of Europe of the Future"	190
	The Metamorphosis of Irish History	193
	Joyce's Mediterranean Classicism	201
	Europe Minor	204
	The Phoenician Wakes	216

Conclusion: The Danube Flows into the Mediterranean — 233

Bibliography — 242
Index — 258

Illustrations

0.1 Environs of Trieste (1:100,000), Karl Baedeker, *Baedeker's Austria-Hungary, with Excursions to Cetinse, Belgrade, and Bucharest* (Leipzig, London, and New York: K. Baedeker, 1911), 275   8

0.2 "Map of the Proposed United States of Greater Austria" by Aurel Popovici in 1906 with the distribution of ethnic groups of Austria-Hungary in 1910 based on map entitled "Distribution of Races in Austria-Hungary" from *Historical Atlas* by William Shepherd, 1911. Wikimedia Commons. Photograph: Andrei Nacu   21

2.1 Postcard with aerial view of the Austrian Adriatic Exhibition, 1913. Wikimedia Commons. Illustrator: Alois Kasimir (1852–1930)   96

2.2 Prater Rotunda with reconstruction of the Bell Tower and of the Praetorian Palace in Koper, Slovenia, for the Austrian Adriatic Exhibition, 1913. Wikimedia Commons. Photograph: Unknown   96

2.3 Three women in Dalmatian folk costume in front of a reconstruction of the Venetian House in Piran, Slovenia, for the Austrian Adriatic Exhibition, 1913. The Venetian House is a fifteenth-century building in the Venetian Gothic style, here part of the Bosnia-Hercegovina pavilion. Wikimedia Commons. Photograph: Unknown   97

2.4 Bertold Löffler (Austrian, 1874–1960). *Vorzeichnung für eine Postkarte der Adria-Ausstellung*, 1913. Tuschfeder, Kreide, Wasserfarben. Inventory number: 116235/1. © Wien Museum   100

2.5 Kurt Libesny (Austrian, 1892–1938). *Poster for the Austrian Adriatic Exposition*, 1913. Color crayon, tusche, and spatter lithograph. Sheet: 630 x 470 mm. (24 13/16 x 18 ½ in.). The Baltimore Museum of Art: Gift of Henry E. Treide, BMA 1956.85.50. Photography By: Mitro Hood   101

Acknowledgments

This book is the result of a long personal and professional journey that has taken me from the slopes of Mt. Aetna on my native island of Sicily to the small town in Germany between the Rhine and the Black Forest where I grew up, to Trieste, and then to Philadelphia and Baltimore in the United States. Over the course of these years, I have contracted many debts of gratitude. The seeds for this project were planted when I was studying at the *Scuola Superiore di Lingue Moderne per Interpreti e Traduttori* of the University of Trieste. I felt strangely at home in Trieste. Perhaps it was the city's combination of Germanic past and Italian present; or maybe it was the privilege of immersing myself in the study of translation and cultural mediation in the architectural gem that is the Slovenian *Narodni Dom*; or it could have been simply because Trieste is a city where the mountains dip their feet in the sea. From those years, I would like to thank Giuseppina Restivo, John McCourt, and Renzo S. Crivelli for their support and guidance. While Giuseppina encouraged me to continue my studies in the United States, John helped me navigate the path ahead. Thanks to his advice, I embarked upon the rewarding journey in the Program of Comparative Literature at Rutgers University. I would like to thank Elin Diamond and Alessandro Vettori for their leadership as directors of the Program. I am hugely indebted to my mentor Fatima Naqvi. I am grateful for the brilliance and wisdom with which Fatima taught me all things Austrian. She guided me with her exemplary scholarship and dedication as a teacher, with great generosity and warmth, unfaltering optimism, and an uplifting sense of humor. I was extremely fortunate to work with Paola Gambarota, Elizabeth Leake, and Jean-Michel Rabaté. Their encouragement and support over the years has been invaluable. At Rutgers, I was fortunate to have friends like Maria Kager, Roberto Nicosia, and Lara Santoro.

I would like to thank many friends and colleagues, from a variety of disciplines, both ancient and modern, for their input and encouragement. At Towson University, I am fortunate to have found such a welcoming community that includes Jennifer Ballengee, Ziad

Bentahar, David Bergman, Frances Botkin, Christopher Cain, Nicole Dombrowski-Risser, Erin Fehskens, Alhena Gadotti, George H. Hahn, Jacob Hovind, Adam Jabbur, John McLucas, Margherita Pampinella, Diego del Pozo, Jacqueline Shin, and Jonathan Vincent. Along the way, I have benefited from the feedback of many dear friends and talented scholars: Elisabeth Attlmayr, Andrea Appleton, Paul Saint-Amour, Emily S. K. Anderson, Aaron Butts, Roberto Maria Dainotto, Elisabetta d'Erme, Cristina Gragnani, Pieter Judson, Daša Ličen, Leonardo Lisi, François Massonnat, Katherine S. Nash, Carl Hendrik Niekerk, Nicoletta Pireddu, Saskia Elizabeth Ziolkowski, and Andrew Zitcer. Among them, I would like to thank in particular Vincenzo Alfano, exemplary scholar and companion of many laughs and adventures in Trieste and across Europe; and the generous friends I am fortunate to have in Samantha Boccaccio and Roberto Flospergher, for their continued hospitality and guidance along Miramare and the northern Adriatic littoral.

Much of this book was written during my sabbatical leave granted by Towson University. In addition, research for this book has been funded by a number of institutions. I had the generous support of a two-year Transliteratures Fellowship at Rutgers University. The Andrew W. Mellon Foundation supported preliminary investigations with a Graduate Fellowship in the Humanities for summer research and then with a Dissertation Completion Fellowship when this project was still at a predoctoral stage. Later, at Towson University, I received funding from the Towson Academy of Scholars and the Faculty Development and Research Committee. In the later stages of the project, my research was assisted by an ACLS Project Development Grant from the American Council of Learned Societies. To all, I am extremely grateful for their support over the years.

Many thanks go to the wonderful staff in libraries, archives, and museums who through their generous help and indefatigable commitment have helped me in my research. In the United States, I would like to thank our own librarians at the Albert S. Cook Library at Towson University, the staff at the Rare Book & Manuscript Library at the Columbia University Libraries in New York, the Princeton University Library, and the Baltimore Museum of Art. In Austria, my gratitude goes to the anonymous archivists at the Österreichische Staatsbibliothek in Vienna and the Wien Museum. In Italy, my thanks go the staff at the Museo del Risorgimento in Milan, the archivists at the Biblioteca dei civici musei di storia e arte di Trieste, and the Biblioteca Civica Attilio Hortis in Trieste.

This book would not have been possible without the support of my family. I would like to thank my parents, Consolazione and Gaetano, my brothers Giuseppe and Manuel, my sister-in-law Lucia, and my parents-in-law, Robbie and Jim. I carry in my heart their generosity of spirit and openhearted embrace. Words cannot adequately express my unending gratitude for my wife, Elizabeth, who has supported this project in so many ways. She has helped me sharpen and refine the ideas in this book, challenging my assumptions and widening my horizons. Together we have built a life of love, laughter, and learning. I am grateful for the patience and infectious enthusiasm of our daughters, Penelope and Veronica, young and daring citizens of the world, who constantly bring joy and amazement into our lives.

Baltimore
Summer 2020

Part of the introduction appeared as "Habsburg Loyalties as Intellectual Affinities: Non-National Allegiances in Robert Musil and Bernard Bolzano" in *Robert Musil's Intellectual Affinities*. Musiliana, Band 17, edited by Todd Cesaratto and Brett Martz (Bern, Oxford, New York: Peter Lang, 2017), 149–175, elements of which also appear in chapter 2. Parts of chapter 2 appeared as "The Betrayal of the *Urbs Fidelissima*: Habsburg Trieste in Robert Musil's *Der Mann ohne Eigenschaften*" in *The German Quarterly* 89, no. 2 (Spring 2016): 169–185. Portions of chapter 3 appeared as "One Last Austrian Cigarette: Italo Svevo and Habsburg Trieste" in *Prospero: Rivista di Letterature Straniere, Comparatistica e Studi Culturali* 16 (2011): 67–88. A section of chapter 4 was published as "Waking Europa: Joyce, Ferrero, and the Metamorphosis of Irish History" in *Journal of Modern Literature* 34, no. 2 (Winter 2011): 154–177. I would like to thank the editors of these journals and volumes for their permission to reprint material.

Introduction: Trieste and the European Project—Ethics, Aesthetics, Politics

The European spirit feeds on books.[1]
—Claudio Magris, *Danube*

On the morning of August 25, 2018, the city of Trieste awoke to a disconcerting scene. Overnight, the elegant Adriatic waterfront, right across from the majestic Habsburg architecture of *Piazza Unità d'Italia*, had been turned into a makeshift, open-air campsite. Wrapped in blankets, exhausted migrants were sleeping on benches, much to the chagrin of municipal authorities who tried to quickly remove the refugees from public sight. In the absence of an established relocation protocol, the incident highlighted how Trieste was unprepared to receive these asylum seekers despite the fact that the Adriatic city remains a strategic stopover, if not the arrival point, on what is known as the Balkan route of the refugee crisis. On their way to Western Europe, these refugees had walked for hundreds of miles through mountains and forests from Syria, Turkey, or Greece across Bulgaria, Serbia, and Croatia. Like others before and after them, they had undertaken a dangerous journey that frequently claims casualties along the way. Yet, the passage on land is considered safer than embarking on a journey at sea. Records from previous years had shown that approaching Europe via the Mediterranean was indeed an even more perilous venture. According to the United Nations High Commissioner for Refugees (UNHCR), between 2014 and 2017 more than 13,000 refugees and migrants were reported dead or missing at sea along the Central

---

[1] Claudio Magris, *Danube*, 265. "Lo spirito europeo si nutre di libri." *Danubio* (Milan: Garzanti, 1986), 312.

Mediterranean route that extends from northern Africa to southern Europe.[2] The victims along this dangerous corridor are part of heterogeneous groups of migrants: they include refugees and asylum seekers who escape from violence, warfare, and genocide in the Middle East and Sub-Saharan Africa as well as immigrants fleeing chronic poverty in search of improved social and economic opportunities. Ominously representative of this emergency is the capsizing of a vessel on April 19, 2015 off the coast of Libya, to date the deadliest recorded shipwreck in Mediterranean history, which claimed the lives of almost 800 refugees. The sheer volume of these refugees has overwhelmed the European Union and national governments in the region. The ethical response to this global emergency has been, alas, utterly inadequate. In this general unpreparedness, the complex logistics of timely rescue, efficient documentation, and proper transfer add to a more insidious negligence stemming from lingering anxieties about nationalist identity politics that this refugee crisis has triggered within the Europe Union.

Much is at stake here, not only the lives of tens of thousands of displaced people, but also the uncertain future of the EU's institutions and its guiding principles, as well as the larger questions of what it means to be, or who gets to be, European. Ironically, in 2012, just a few years before the migrant crisis started, the European Union had been awarded the Nobel Peace Prize in what sounded like a celebration of shared humanitarian values. The official motivation for the prize applauded a European ethos and its related ethics of pacifist egalitarianism, stating that the members of the union had "for over six decades contributed to the advancement of peace and reconciliation, democracy and human rights in Europe."[3] Controversial like many other decisions adopted by the Norwegian Nobel Committee, the award recognized the determination of European institutions to establish lasting peace on a historically war-torn continent by means of multilateral diplomatic partnerships, a shared legal system, and common monetary policy. The first international treaties, signed in the 1950s when the memories of Europe's internal war refugees were still fresh, constituted important milestones for the European Union of today and perhaps, in the most optimistic anticipations of some federalist enthusiasts, for a United States of Europe of the future. This time of European soul-searching seems like a fitting occasion to reflect upon

---

[2] The report can be found at www.unhcr.org/en-us/partners/donors/5aa78775c/unhcr-2018-central-mediterranean-route-situation-supplementary-appeal-january.html?query=Mediterranean, accessed on September 24, 2020. This data does not account for persons missing in 2018.

[3] See nobelprize.org/nobel_prizes/peace/laureates/2012/, accessed on September 24, 2020.

Trieste and the European Project—Ethics, Aesthetics, Politics   3

the project of European unity given that treaties and policies alone would not have been sufficient to create a unified Europe. The founding figures had to first embrace the *idea* of Europe. While the steps toward greater European integration are often seen as the result of economic and political agreements signed in the aftermath of the Second World War, the idea of a cultural and political union in Europe reaches us via an extensive textual journey and a longstanding intellectual tradition. What is often ignored is the contribution that modern literary fiction has offered to the debates surrounding the cultural and political unity of the continent.[4]

This book is about what I call the literary invention of Europe, an invention articulated by the political aesthetics of a modernist literary imagination that challenged the rise of xenophobic nationalism during the period that spans from 1870 to 1945. The focus of this study is the Mediterranean port city of Trieste, a border town at the crossroads of German, Italian, and Slavic cultures, where overlapping national claims, interlacing multicultural ties, and multiple loyalties converged to make the city a capital of a transnational literary modernism. Before and after the First World War many writers and intellectuals ascribed to Habsburg Trieste the role of cultural mediator and saw the city as an urban experiment for a future United States of Europe. They believed that the cultural heterogeneity of Trieste had produced an Austro-European identity, characterized by a manifold set of loyalties and emotional attachments to ethnic, cultural, and linguistic communities. Overlapping rather than juxtaposing, and intermingled rather than contiguous, these multiple allegiances were not mutually exclusive but could simultaneously coexist within single authors and their oeuvres. Habsburg intellectuals recognized in the survival of this nonnational mindset a potential antidote to the virulent excesses of nationalism, and a possible paradigm of identity for a future European community. This aspired configuration of a European Trieste was in many ways a

---

[4] Exceptions to this trend are Pascal Dethurens, *De l'Europe en littérature. Création littéraire et culture européenne au temps de la crise de l'esprit (1918–1939)* (Geneva: Droz, 2002), whose argument about Europe as a "literary creation" already gestures toward the notion of a fictional invention without, however, engaging in a deeper analysis of the literary and rhetorical strategies that such a creative endeavor would imply. See also Paul Michael Lützeler, *Plädoyers für Europa. Stellungnahmen deutschsprachiger Schriftsteller 1915–1949* (Frankfurt am Main: Fischer Verlag, 1987), *Die Schriftsteller und Europa: von der Romantik bis zur Gegenwart* (Munich: Piper, 1998), and his more recent *Kontinentalisierung: Das Europa der Schriftsteller* (Bielefeld: Aisthesis, 2007). While Lützeler collects an invaluable array of texts, he focuses on the larger German-speaking world without distinguishing between German, Swiss, and Austrian perspectives.

response to the deep internal lacerations in the social fabric that pitched the city's different communities against each other.

One does not need to be particularly prone to skepticism at best and cynicism at worst to recognize that the European project often derails its self-serving rhetoric of utopian politics into a history of failed ethics. So, when viewed from Habsburg Trieste, how does a modernist literary aesthetics, at times entangled in Europe's moral bankruptcies, offer alternative parameters for a discussion about the European project? One brief answer relies on the fact that in order to accommodate the multiplicity of cultural belongings, the Europe envisioned by the authors discussed in this book implicitly counters the equation between citizenship and nationality, leaving full participation in civic life open to its citizens' many differences. Far from projecting a current pluralist ethos onto a world of an allegedly unproblematic openness to cultural difference, this study is instead concerned with the cultural cosmopolitics of a literary program and the unresolved social divisions from which it emerged. If Habsburg Trieste represents the juncture of a local cosmopolitanism that attempts to bridge the chasm between a cultural specificity and an enlightened border-crossing transculturalism, the trajectory of this literary discourse appears fleeting and ultimately failing. Both in its theorization and practical application, cosmopolitanism presents itself as characterized by an ethics of mutual acceptance that affords equal dignity to different forms of diversity, efforts of reciprocal validation among individuals and groups, the active promotion of empathy for the Other, the individual's ability to navigate different social and cultural contexts, and the mastery of several languages seen as a vehicle for intercultural communication.[5] The risk of idealization of such an ethical program remains concrete if one were to ignore the fraught relationships between cosmopolitanism and the social coercions of established power structures when embraced by economic and political elites as part of their strategy of cultural

---

[5] In *Cosmopolitanism: Ethics in a World of Strangers* (New York: Norton & Norton, 2006), Kwame Anthony Appiah argues that cosmopolitanism is not the stance of uprooted individuals without any specific loyalties to particular groups. Instead, he speaks of a cosmopolitan patriotism or a rooted cosmopolitanism that begins with membership in local communities or ethnic groups. This group membership is then accompanied by the ethical responsibilities of care and inclusion that each individual has for other individuals belonging to different cultural and ethnic groups.

domination. My approach to Trieste considers the city in its literary dimension and tries to interrogate the very ambiguities of a rhetoric of European cosmopolitanism. The image of the Adriatic city as the locus of intercultural mediation remains both historical and mythological, real and at the same time the powerful product of a literary myth that registers the regret of missed opportunities reverberating in the nostalgia for a sentimentalized Habsburg Trieste.[6]

This does not mean, however, that *Modernism in Trieste* is solely and narrowly concerned with Triestine literature. This book adopts Trieste as the framework for an investigation of the narrative and rhetorical strategies of European literary modernism.[7] The biographies and aesthetic projects of Robert Musil, Italo Svevo, and James Joyce are deeply embedded in the multinational fabric of the Austro-Hungarian Empire; they create a highly politicized, fictional projection of a multicultural Austria, and by extension of a multicultural Europe, anchored in Habsburg Trieste. Writing in different languages and from three different perspectives—Austrian, Italian, and Irish respectively—Musil, Svevo, and Joyce offer a multifaceted portrayal of the city. They write in the aftermath of the First World War when, after more than five centuries of Austrian rule, the highly contested Trieste becomes Italian. Rather than engaging in a mournful imperial nostalgia, as the prevailing scholarly understanding would dictate, their fictional characters subscribe to a cultural and political Europeanism and refuse, through their flexible loyalties and shifting allegiances, to fully commit and subscribe to the nation.

This literary alternative to the national paradigm was articulated by a modernist classicism that rehabilitated the role of the Phoenicians,

---

[6] Jan Morris's *Trieste and the Meaning of Nowhere* (New York: Simon & Schuster, 2001) is a good example of an idealization of Trieste's Habsburg past that does not engage the problematic aspects of imperial domination. Pamela Ballinger eloquently describes the myth of cosmopolitan Trieste and its ties to imperial nostalgia in *History in Exile: Memory and Identity at the Borders of the Balkans* (Princeton, NJ: Princeton University Press, 2003).

[7] Significant contributions to the literary history of Trieste are Angelo Ara and Claudio Magris, *Trieste. Un'identità di frontiera* (Turin: Einaudi, 1982), Joseph Cary, *A Ghost in Trieste* (Chicago: University of Chicago Press, 1993), Katia Pizzi, *A City in Search of an Author: The Literary Identity of Trieste* (London: Sheffield Academic Press, 2001), Oliver Schneider, *Triest: Eine Diskursanalyse* (Würzburg: Königshausen & Neumann, 2003), Charles Klopp, ed., *Bele Antiche Stòrie: Writing, Borders, and the Instability of Identity. Trieste, 1719–2007* (New York: Bordighera, 2008), and Saskia Ziolkowski, "Trieste and the Migrations of Modernism: Fin-de-siècle Austria in the Italian Literary Landscape" (PhD Diss., Columbia University, 2009).

the Semitic seafarers of the ancient Mediterranean.[8] Around the turn of the century, a number of local antiquarians, archaeologists, and ancient historians were studying the presence of prehistoric settlements along the northern Adriatic shores and argued for a possible Phoenician origin of Trieste. While nationalist narratives in the nineteenth century identified the origin of their national culture in the Greco-Roman tradition, these intellectuals adopted a new approach to the often-maligned Phoenicians, electing the traditional rivals of the Greeks and Romans as an alternative cultural foundation for both Trieste and a new Europe. The articles published in the local magazine *Archeografo triestino* constitute the intellectual background against which developed a political reading that reinterpreted the Greek and Roman tale of the rape of the Phoenician maiden Europa, an important foundational myth for Europe. Medieval and Renaissance salvational theology had seen in the rape of Europa a prophecy of divine intervention in the world. The Zeus/Jupiter who had raped Europa in antiquity prefigured the Christian God who seized (from the Latin *rapere*) and thus saved the human soul. The rape therefore was read as a rapture, in which the divine took hold of the human. In contrast, by exploiting the political background of the myth and by reclaiming a new role for the Phoenicians, modernist authors associated with Trieste subvert nationalist mythologies of the early nineteenth century. Musil, Svevo, and Joyce are not the only writers with these concerns. The two Triestine poets, Theodor Däubler and Srečko Kosovel, who write in German and in Slovene respectively, engage in similar literary strategies. These writers adopt different approaches to the Phoenician question, each articulating culturally specific but interrelated narratives about the ancient sea power that contest the spurious epistemological hegemony of the nation. Kosovel, in particular, never writes about the Europa of antiquity but deploys a similar strategy by exploiting the Slavic counterpart of the Mediterranean abduction trope in the legend of Lepa Vida. By placing these authors in conversation with each other, this

---

[8] In *Classicism of the Twenties: Art, Music, and Literature* (Chicago: University of Chicago Press, 2014), Theodore Ziolkowski argues against the concurrent use of the labels "modern" and "classical" because modernism as a movement was far too loose to be employed in connection with the more highly organized classicism. My analysis is more aligned with Cathy Gere, who employs the category of "modernist classicism" in her *Knossos & the Prophets of Modernism* (Chicago: The University of Chicago Press, 2009) to explore the political imagination of the post–First World War world, when the Minoan civilization of Crete was imagined as a matriarchal and pacifist culture.

comparative study not only investigates modernist literary strategies but also envisions a Habsburg literary canon that conceptualizes, against nationalist readings of Central Europe, cultural integrity in an area characterized by linguistic multiplicity.

It is important to note that this reorientation toward the Mediterranean was a specifically Central European phenomenon and not, as one would suspect, a priority for Italian intellectuals. As Franco Cassano and Claudio Fogu have shown, the Mediterranean Sea was largely suppressed or disavowed by the agricultural elite that spearheaded the *Risorgimento* on the Italian peninsula.[9] Only after Italian unification did the Mediterranean enter the literary and cultural landscape of Italy and then only in the Decadentism of Pascoli and D'Annunzio's poetry, as a resurrection of the Roman *Mare Nostrum* in support of Italy's colonial empire. Ultimately, my approach to Trieste is one of disciplinary expansion. Since Trieste is located in Italy today, the related research is usually conducted in the domain of Italian Studies. While the cultural and literary history of the city has traditionally—and appropriately, to be sure—been placed within an Italian-speaking context, I would like to expand the focus, shifting our interpretative coordinates to an area that accounts for the role that Trieste also played in the German-speaking Austrian cultural imagination and in a European modernist context. In brief, this book reclaims Trieste for Austrian and Habsburg Studies and, more generally, calls for the incorporation of Austro-Italian affairs into the canon of literary studies concerning Central Europe.

Modernism and the Idea of Europe

This book looks at Trieste and Europe in a decidedly nonnational setting, challenging the widespread methodological approach that considers the nation or nation-states as the most appropriate context for modern history or modernist literary studies. Navigating literary currents and an ideological wave that opposed the rise of nationalism, *Modernism in Trieste* examines a Mediterranization of Europe, a Europe of multicultural regions rather than monolithic nations, anchored in a

---

[9] See Franco Cassano, *Southern Thought and Other Essays on the Mediterranean*, ed. Norma Bouchard and Valerio Ferme (New York: Fordham University Press, 2012), 125–131. See also Claudio Fogu, "We Have Made the Mediterranean; Now We Must Make Mediterraneans," in *Critically Mediterranean: Temporalities, Aesthetics, and Deployments of a Sea in Crisis*, ed. Yasser Elhariry and Edwige Tamalet Talbayev (New York: Palgrave MacMillan, 2018), 181–197. Fogu argues that the Mediterranean was largely ignored in narratives of Italian unification, as it "figured as an enemy, an obstacle, or a place of tragedy … and vacated from the image of the 'resurgent' body of the Risorgimental nation" (ibid., 186).

8   Modernism in Trieste

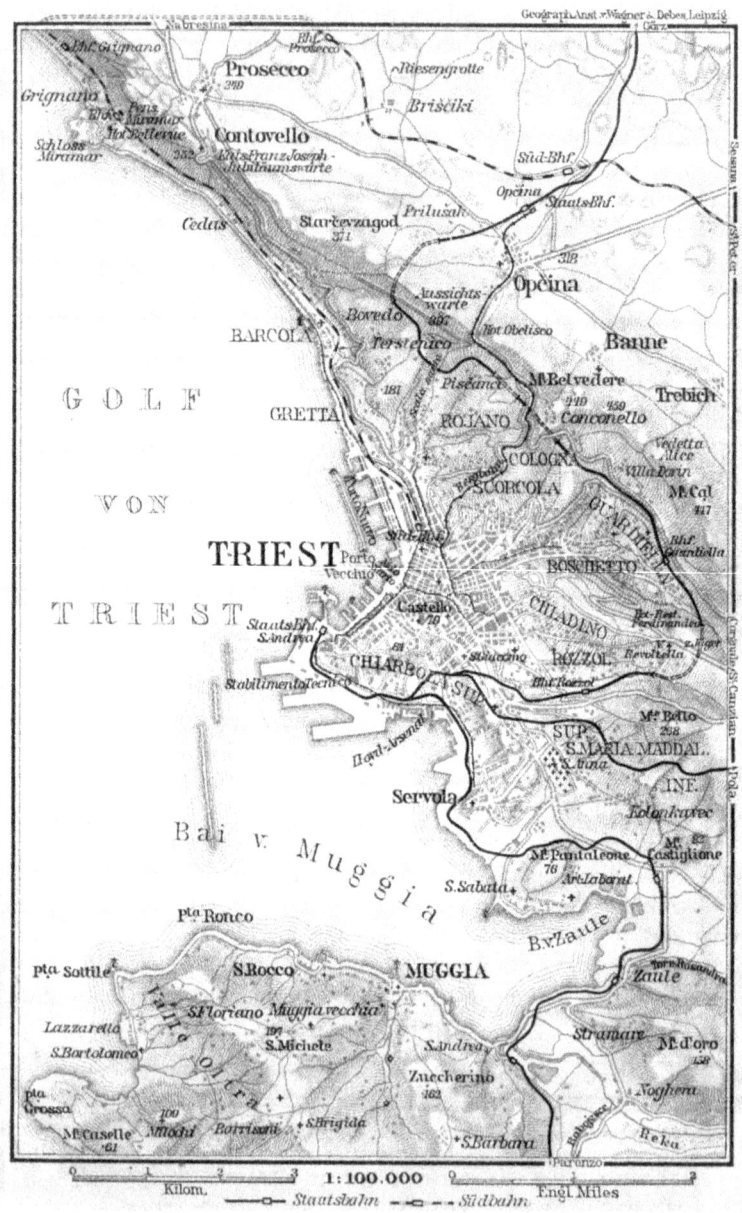

Figure 0.1 Environs of Trieste (1:100,000), Karl Baedeker, *Baedeker's Austria-Hungary, with Excursions to Cetinse, Belgrade, and Bucharest* (Leipzig, London, and New York: K. Baedeker, 1911), 275.

non-hegemonic, urban cosmopolitanism.[10] This book calls attention to the rhetorical and ideological connections between literary modernism and notions of a nonnational and anti-colonial Europe, integrating our critical understanding of textual and aesthetic strategies of political resistance in the face of nationalist rhetoric. While this present study emphasizes the centrality of Trieste as a capital of literary modernism, it is important to bear in mind that the Adriatic city occupied a double periphery: Trieste was located at the southernmost edge of the Habsburg territories, but is also tucked away in the northernmost corner of the Mediterranean Sea. My intention is to recalibrate the coordinates of a cultural and literary geography, relocating the city from its peripheral positions to a neuralgic center of transregional and transnational networks. Trieste, a city that is simultaneously continental and maritime, becomes the locus of a disciplinary confluence where Habsburg Studies and Mediterranean Studies intersect. The relationship between the city and the empire was mutually beneficial. The Adriatic city was the only major commercial outlet to the Mediterranean Sea in an otherwise landlocked empire, a status that was the result of precise economic policies that the Habsburgs promoted. Only after the Habsburgs took possession of the city did Trieste become part of a Mediterranean network. Vice versa, through Trieste the Austrian Empire was able to cultivate its aspirations to rise as a Mediterranean monarchy.

Like their counterparts in other European cities, intellectuals in Trieste pondered ideas of European unity at a time of intense modernist ferment. Modernism, in its aesthetic response to the socio-cultural and politico-philosophical challenges of modernity, oscillated between an enthusiastic acceptance of Western colonial supremacy and a critical engagement with European imperialist discourse. The generation of modernist artists and writers coming of age between the early 1880s and

---

[10] In "On Hercules' Threshold: Epistemic Pluralities and Oceanic Realignments in the Euro-Atlantic Space," in *Imperialism in the Wider Atlantic: Essays on the Aesthetics, Literature, and Politics of Transatlantic Cultures*," ed. Tania Gentic and Francisco LaRubia-Prado (Cham: Palgrave Macmillan, 2017), 19–46, Nicoletta Pireddu sees the Mediterranean as a locus where Europe can articulate, together with other cultural and political entities, an alternative to the binary constructions of a global logic that divides the world into Western and non-Western, North and South. She traces in the novels of Hédi Bouraoui the genealogy of a Phoenician Mediterranean, the Mediterranean of Hannibal, as a model of non-Eurocentric Europe and a starting point for new intercontinental connections. Her work is aimed at "undermining of the persistent dichotomy between the alleged universalism of the Eurocentric position and the localism ascribed to the discourse of the world's periphery, but also the equally ideological tendency to neglect Europe's own contribution to a non-authoritative transcultural discourse" (ibid., 22).

the late 1940s took a particular interest in the theorization of a European cultural and political identity. Questions of European cosmopolitanism emerged in part also thanks to new migratory movements toward the city. The rise of industrial capitalism at the end of the nineteenth century and the subsequent mass urbanization made modern cities the growing centers of cultural and artistic exchange that attracted a multitude of expatriate writers, transplanted artists, and deracinated intellectuals. It is this configuration of the modern cityscape that informs, since the transnational turn in modernist studies, our understanding of modernism as a cultural and literary phenomenon that is construed as both metropolitan and cosmopolitan, and equally polyglot and polycentric. The urban geographies of European modernism locate these centers of exchange in cultural capitals like Paris, London, and Berlin, but also Zurich, Dublin, and Petersburg. Literary modernism often combines an aesthetics of exile with the politics of home, by which poets and writers theorized about questions of physical and spiritual communities. Intellectuals as diverse as T. S. Eliot, Thomas Mann, Annette Kolb, Bertha von Suttner, Miguel de Unamuno, and Paul Valéry argued for European unity with the largely shared understanding that Europeans had a common past, rooted in a whitewashed Greco-Roman antiquity and a principled Christian universalism.

The European project to which these intellectuals subscribed has a long and rich intellectual history. It is a genealogy that extends from the Christian thinkers of medieval Europe to the political philosophers of the Enlightenment, a tradition that tended to presume that a European universalism is inherent in the cultural and literary heritage of the West. Ideas of Europe were often motivated by a Eurocentric chauvinism that postulated an alleged cultural and racial superiority over non-Europeans. Openly or implicitly racist, phallocratic, Orientalist, and anti-Semitic, these attitudes had been and continued to remain the basis for Western imperial and colonial endeavors that imposed a socio-economic asymmetry not only on a global scale but also within Europe itself, between a cultured and capitalist North and its internal Other, the backwater of a rural Mediterranean South.

At the juncture of a paradoxical double bind, Trieste was both an insider and an outsider to Europe, a judgement that depended on what aspect of the city an observer chose to emphasize. When viewed from Vienna, Trieste was an Austrian city and the poster child of the empire's European mission. At the same time, if one focused on the Mediterranean dimension of Trieste, the Adriatic city appeared as the gateway to the East and the South, residing within the purview of an Austrian colonial gaze and its Orientalist representations. From this northern perspective, Trieste's Mediterranean location was the site of a multicultural exoticism and could not pass as European by any stretch of the imagination.

Trieste embodied the necessary southern otherness against which a northern and western concept of Europe could be measured, a surrogate for the kind of Mediterranean that Cassano has described as "the negative counterweight of Europe."[11] Expanding on Cassano's notion of southern thought, Roberto Dainotto has forcefully argued that in this inner-European Orientalism, the south becomes the "indispensable *internal* Other," a subaltern, marginalized, and silenced minority within Europe.[12] He explains that in this history "it is no longer the confrontation with the exotic Other (the Persian, the Muslim, the American savage, and so on) that interests the theorists of Europe, but rather a dialectical confrontation of Europe with itself, with its own internal Other."[13] This internal Orientalism inherent in theories of Europe had traditionally excluded areas like Spain or Sicily, whose Arab Muslim domination during the Middle Ages disqualified them from the European Christian community. It is precisely from the margins of Europe, as Dainotto shows, that an alternative genealogy of Europe emerges in the writings of the Sicilian historian Michele Amari (1806–1889). Amari wrote against dominant theories of Europe that considered the South backward because supposedly incapable of the two highest achievements in the development of a civilization, namely the longing for freedom and the nation. Instead, he described in his *History of Muslims of Sicily* (*Storia dei musulmani di Sicilia*) the Arab-Berber conquest of Sicily as the origin of a European social democracy, thus locating in an Afro-Semitic genealogy an important source of European identity. Amari argued that the Sicilian Vespers anticipated the French Revolution, showing that Sicily was capable of that popular pursuit of liberty and civic consciousness that were considered the prerequisites of a modern European nation. Amari's message was that Sicily had nothing to learn from northern European nations like France because it had received the notions of liberty and equality from Islam long before any other European country. Therefore, Sicily did indeed meet the criterion to be eligible for the status of European civilization. Nevertheless, the Sicilian historian continued to judge Europeanness by the same standards imposed by the tradition of Kant and Montesquieu, whose very theories of Europe had excluded the South. As Dainotto puts it, "Amari was thus widening the confines of Europe to include his Sicily, but he was not widening a theory of Europe."[14] In the end, Amari does much to dislodge the Mediterranean from its dual status as marginal

---

[11] Cassano, *Southern Thought*, 132.
[12] Roberto Dainotto, *Europe (In Theory)* (Durham, NC: Duke University Press, 2007), 4.
[13] Ibid., 51.
[14] Ibid., 197.

province and premodern antechamber of Europe but fails to offer a new and significant way to think about Europe.

There are obvious parallels between Amari's Sicilian project and the Afro-Semitic origins of Europe theorized by the authors in this book. Nevertheless, contrary to Amari's Mediterranization of European identity, the reclamation of a Phoenician, nonnational paradigm indeed does fundamentally alter the theoretical parameters of Europe. More than a simple relocation of origins or an addition of previously excluded ethnic groups, the theory of Europe inherent in these texts signals a displacement of the traditional ontological and epistemological categories that have dominated the discourse of Europe. Against the nineteenth- and twentieth-century idea that the nation is the indicator of civilization and the teleological result of historical progress, this theory of Europe argues that the nation is incompatible with the European project. The Europe these writers envision via Trieste is one of culturally diverse regions that are fundamentally nonnational. This is a Europe not of nations, but of multicultural regions. As such, this kind of regionalism represents an attempt to preserve a local multiculturalism threatened by the homogenizing standards of a national discourse. Dainotto, once again, cautions against the slippery dialectics of nation and region in which regionalism borrows the rhetorical arsenal of the nation in order to take over its functions of social community building.[15] It is therefore important to distinguish this cosmopolitan vernacularism from other forms of regionalism that promote a revival of past traditions via bucolic narratives of authenticity and purity, or that mourn a traditional past by articulating a rhetorical opposition to the modern city.

Habsburg Trieste, *urbs europeissima*

In what way, then, does the cosmopolitan modernism that flourished in Paris, London, and Berlin differ from the Habsburg Europeanism that developed in Vienna, Prague, and Budapest? How does Trieste, in particular, articulate its own version of an urban and cosmopolitan Austro-Europeanism? *Fin-de-siècle* Trieste was indeed a city of irreconcilable differences but also of productive encounters, a microcosm of the Habsburg Empire: multinational in its composition, international in its commercial networks, transnational in its loyalties to communities beyond its borders.[16] By the turn of the century, for those invested in praising Austria's success, the Adriatic city had acquired a reputation

---

[15] Roberto M. Dainotto, *Place in Literature: Regions, Cultures, Communities* (Ithaca, NY: Cornell University Press, 2000).
[16] Alison Frank, "Continental and Maritime Empires in an Age of Global Commerce," *East European Politics and Societies* 25, no. 4 (2011): 779–784. doi:10.1177/ 2F0888325411399123.

as the most European city, *urbs europeissima*, as the historian Eduard Winkler has defined it.[17] In both Vienna and Trieste, a great number of intellectuals believed that the social, cultural, and political dynamics of the polyglot and multicultural monarchy offered a roadmap for a future European integration. German Austrian writers often conceived of the European project as an extension of the paternalistically benign empire that could harmonize the manifold cultures within its borders. According to this condescending view, the Austrian German-speaking elite was the *Kulturträger*, the civilizing force operating in Eastern Europe. Hugo von Hofmannsthal repeatedly argued in his political essays during the First World War and well into the 1920s that a new Europe required the spirit of old Austria that mediated among the different nationalities and between East and West.[18] In this established synonymity between Austria and Europe, Habsburg metropoles encapsulate a model of interethnic coexistence that appeared to be, with some necessary adjustments, worthy of imitation. Similar to Hofmannsthal, Stefan Zweig identified turn-of-the-century Vienna, in a quite generous assessment, as an absorbing and welcoming receptacle of all streams of European intellectual movements. Viennese culture was for Zweig a "synthesis of all Western culture" because "nowhere else was it easier to be European."[19] Their Italian Austrian counterparts in Habsburg Trieste perceived, as we will see below, the Adriatic city in analogous cosmopolitan terms.

Any literary history of Trieste would not be complete without considering its urban cartography of ethnic, religious, and linguistic multiplicity. For most of its modern history—from 1382 to 1918—Trieste was controlled by the authority of the Habsburg Empire. State-sponsored immigration waves transformed a small and insignificant fishing town into a prosperous miniature Europe on the Adriatic Sea, a seaport bustling with a motley crew of foreign merchants. In the last decades of the nineteenth century, the main social strata included a German-speaking

---

[17] Eduard Winkler, *Wahlrechtsreformen und Wahlen in Triest 1905–1909: eine Analyse der politischen Partizipation in einer multinationalen Stadtregion der Habsburgermonarchie* (Munich: Oldenburg Verlag, 2000), 338.

[18] See *David Luft, Hugo von Hofmannsthal and the Austrian Idea: Selected Essays and Addresses, 1906–1927* (West Lafayette, IN: Purdue University Press, 2011).

[19] Stefan Zweig, "seine Kultur eine Synthese aller abendländischen Kulturen ... Nirgends war es leichter Europäer zu sein." *Die Welt von Gestern. Erinnerungen eines Europäers* (Frankfurt am Main: Fischer Verlag, 2003), 40. Important sources for turn-of the-century Vienna are Carl E. Schorske, *Fin-de-siècle Vienna: Politics and Culture* (New York: Random House, 1979), Allan Janik and Stephen Toulmin, *Wittgenstein's Vienna* (London: Weidenfeld and Nicholson, 1973), and Jacques Le Rider, *Modernity and Crises of Identity: Culture and Society in fin-de-siècle Vienna* (Malden, MA: Polity Press, 1993).

class of imperial administrators, as well as army and navy officers; sizable Italian-speaking middle and upper classes of patricians and merchants, insurers, and bankers; and Slavic-speaking peasants, workers, and intellectuals, who moved from the rural hinterland into the city in search of economic opportunities. The languages spoken in Habsburg Trieste included most of the idioms spoken in the empire, such as Italian, German, Slovene, Serbo-Croatian, Czech, and Hungarian, along with languages spoken in the adjacent Ottoman Empire, namely Turkish, Armenian, and Greek. Ashkenazi Jewish immigrants introduced Yiddish. Strong commercial ties with the Mediterranean basin brought Spanish, Sicilian, and Maltese into the city. English and French, widespread international languages of trade, were spoken as well.[20] It is important to point out that language use was often a class marker rather than the expression of national consciousness. Incoming merchants spoke a variety of languages, while the locals were largely dialectophone, speaking the Triestine vernacular as their first language. Triestino, what James Joyce called "Viennese Italian," became a sort of *lingua franca* among the diverse populations that inhabited the city.[21] In a largely Catholic state, imperial policies also built a religiously diverse cityscape that included, in addition to Jewish communities, Lutheran and Calvinist groups, Anglicans and Waldensians, Greek and Serbian Orthodox churches, as well as an Armenian Uniate community.

A profound commercial pragmatism, together with this cultural and linguistic diversity, determined a widespread indifference to questions of national belonging in Trieste's political landscape during the nineteenth and early twentieth centuries. Triestine merchants were keenly aware of the fact that the city's history of economic prosperity depended on Austrian policies, so much that they declared an unwavering dynastic loyalty to the Habsburgs during the 1848 nationalist revolutions that swept through Europe. Such dynastic patriotism earned the city the honorific title of *urbs fidelissima*, "most faithful city," as well as the status of *reichsunmittelbare Stadt*, which marked a privileged feudal relationship with the Emperor. The Austro-Mediterranean commercial expansion continued in the following decades and allowed the city to weather the Great Depression in the aftermath of the Vienna Stock Exchange crash of 1873. The ensuing economic recession, however, caused frustration and anxiety in the merchant class, which was

---

[20] For studies of the multilingualism in the Habsburg Empire, see Rosita Rindler Schjerve, ed., *Diglossia and Power: Language Policies and Practice in the 19th Century Habsburg Empire* (Berlin: Walter de Gruyter, 2008) and Michaela Wolf, *Die vielsprachige Seele Kakaniens. Übersetzen und Dolmetschen in der Habsburgermonarchie 1848–1918* (Vienna: Böhlau Verlag, 2012).

[21] James Joyce, *Giacomo Joyce* (New York: Viking Press, 1968), 1.

open to contemplating more profitable alliances. A warm reception of Italy's proclamation of independence in 1861 demonstrated that the city was not impermeable to the Romantic rhetoric of national deliverance. The prospect of unification with the newly founded kingdom across the border, supported by an ethnic and cultural kinship, seemed to offer an enticing commercial alternative. The more shrewd supporters of an Italian takeover knew that the recourse to national mythologies alone would not amount to an efficient rhetorical strategy capable of convincing the pragmatic merchant class in Trieste. Their argument was based upon the assumption, or rather gross miscalculation, that the city's economic status could be upheld, if not improved, once Trieste joined Italy. As a result, the years leading up to the Great War saw the rise of a political movement that rivaled the traditional imperial loyalty of those faithful to the Austrian crown: a relatively new ethnolinguistic nationalism known as Irredentism that vociferously demanded that the city be annexed to Italy.[22] Political Irredentists, conducting a very efficacious activist campaign, were highly motivated but numerically a minority in the city. The two outlooks added to an increasingly complex network of paradoxically intertwining positions: an Italian cultural Irredentism advocated for larger cultural autonomy for ethnic Italians but did not necessarily support a schism with Austria. The Austro-Marxists of the Triestine Socialist party staunchly opposed separatism, arguing for a constitutional reform of the empire within a sort of European federation of Habsburg territories.[23] Angelo Vivante (1869–1915), the most

---

[22] The term Irredentism has its origin in the Italian expression "Italia irredenta," meaning "unredeemed Italy," and referred to the nationalist claims of territories inhabited by ethnic Italians in the Habsburg Empire. After Italy's unification in 1861, Italian-speaking territories like Istria and Dalmatia, as well as cities such as Trieste, Trento, and Gorizia, remained under Austrian rule and thus had to be saved from foreign occupation. The term, suggesting a Christological redemption, reveals how the rhetorical strategies of the Italian nationalist movement added a religious dimension to the political struggle.

[23] An entire tradition of Italian nationalist historiography on Trieste has vehemently underscored the Italian character of city, emphasizing and exaggerating the city's desire to join Italy. Consequently, even the absence of an explicit exaltation or celebration of Austria-Hungary was taken as a sign of the most fervent Irredentism. Angelo Ara, however, described this approach as heavily influenced by the Fascist appropriation of the Italian *Risorgimento*, arguing that between 1848 and 1918 the support or at least neutrality toward the Habsburg state was much more widespread than the Italian nationalist historiography has claimed in the past. Angelo Ara, *Fra nazione e impero. Trieste, gli Asburgo, la Mitteleuropa* (Milan: Garzanti, 2009). Mark Thompson argues that Trieste counted around 500 active Irredentists and no more than 4,500 sympathizers. Irredentists, according to Thompson, exaggerated their Austrian oppression and overstated their support in the city. Mark Thompson, *The White War: Life and Death on the Italian Front 1915–1919* (New York: Basic Books, 2009).

articulate of Triestine Socialists, argued in his 1912 *Adriatic Irredentism* (*Irredentismo adriatico*) that it was in Trieste's best interest to maintain its status as multicultural port within the Dual Monarchy. He dexterously exposed Italian separatism as a risky strategy to extort more economic concessions from Austria. The sober and unassuming tone of his well-documented analysis—Vivante provides numbers and statistics—also threatened to disarm the pompous grandiloquence of Irredentist rhetoric that framed social class tensions as national conflicts. Defending the right of German Austrians, Italians, and Slovenes to call Trieste their home, Vivante emphasized the city's urban cosmopolitanism and its historical commitment to nonnational politics. Trieste's time-honored dynastic loyalty to the House of Habsburg and its marginal status in the context of Italian history suggested as much, not to mention the city's established tradition of municipal and multicultural patriotism that presented itself as a viable alternative to both the Italian nation-state and the Austrian crown. The threat of Irredentist separatism, idle as it was for many of its boisterous proponents, nonetheless fueled nationalist aspirations.

National activists in the Adriatic city were encouraged by poets, writers, and intellectuals in Italy, where Trieste and Trento were considered the symbols of a painfully truncated national unification. Trieste became the object of an ardently feverish desire in the patriotic lyricism of Giosuè Carducci, in the histrionically militant Irredentism of Gabriele D'Annunzio, and in the aggressively bellicose Futurism of Filippo Tommaso Marinetti. Marinetti, in particular, held his first Futurist soirée in Trieste on January 12, 1909, describing the city with the rhetorically explosive epithet "our beautiful powder magazine."[24] Unlike these poets, however, writers and intellectuals in Trieste frequently envisioned an alternative model of Italian identity, an Austro-Italian character that diverged from the rambunctious intemperance of the nationalism that was being imported from across the border. Open to European intellectual and literary currents, Trieste developed what Sherry Simon has called a "culture of mediation" where translations represented a considerable part of the city's intellectual life.[25] The numerous translators were often erudite women, highly engaged journalists and prolific writers educated at the universities of

---

[24] The title of his speech was "Trieste, la nostra bella polveriera," reprinted in Filippo T. Marinetti, *Teoria e invenzione futurista* (Milan: Mondadori, 1983), 247. All translations from Italian, German, and Slovene are mine, unless otherwise indicated.

[25] Sherry Simon, *Cities in Translation: Intersections of Language and Memory* (New York: Routledge, 2012), 58.

Vienna, Graz, or Florence, and generally more independent and emancipated than women in Italy. In addition to Triestino, they were fluent in at least three languages, namely Italian, German, English, or French. Amalia Popper translated some of Joyce's short stories from *Dubliners* into Italian, Luisa Macina Gervasio translated Goethe, Clelia Trampus translated German Romantic poets, while Emma Conti Luzzatto translated Heine and Chamisso.[26] The remarkable quantity of translations between Italian and German in Trieste is indicative of how many intellectuals before the war conceived of the city as a bridge between Italy and the German-speaking world.

In the name of this Habsburg Italianness a group of intellectuals, among whom were Scipio Slataper (1888–1914), Giani Stuparich (1891–1961), and Giani's younger brother Carlo Stuparich (1894–1916), attributed to Trieste the role of intercultural mediator among the ethnic groups in the city.[27] Part of a narrow circle that included Elody Oblath (1889–1971), Anna Pulitzer (1889–1910), and Luisa (Gigetta) Carniel (1887–1969), these writers were the Triestine contributors to *La Voce*, the influential cultural review and literary magazine founded by Giuseppe Prezzolini and published in Florence between 1908 and 1916. In a series of articles published in 1909 known as the "Triestine Letters," Slataper described Trieste in terms of its "double soul," the conflict characterized by the city's commercial interests tied to its loyalty to Austria and Trieste's feeling of cultural kinship and aspirations to join Italy.[28] Slataper's collaboration with *La Voce* lasted until 1912. In these years, his opinions were still informed by the nonnational Adriatic multiculturalism of an earlier generation that feared that the rise of an exclusionary nationalism in the region would dismember the social and economic fabric of entire communities rather than unite them. Rejecting political Irredentism, Slataper's articles read like a solemn profession of this cosmopolitan credo. He believed that the historical task of Trieste was to be a crucible and promoter of the three main civilizations of the city. Trieste was "our little corner of Europe" where the most pressing

---

[26] For an extensive discussion of female writers in Trieste, see *Bianco, rosa e verde: scrittrici a Trieste fra '800 e '900*, ed. Roberto Curci and Gabriella Ziani (Trieste: Lint, 1993) and *Oltre le parole: scrittrici triestine del primo Novecento*, ed. Gabriella Musetti (Trieste: Vita Activa, 2016).
[27] Slataper is best known for his lyrical novel *Il mio Carso*, first published in 1912.
[28] Scipio Slataper, *La Voce*, March 25, 1909. The *Lettere triestine* are a series of five articles Slataper published in the magazine between February 11 and April 22 of 1909.

problems of the Western world converged, namely "Germanism and Slavism, the Balkan question, commercial hegemony, Austrian future—and Italian character."[29]

Slataper's acknowledged sources of inspiration are the aforementioned Angelo Vivante, as well as Niccolò Tommaseo (1802–1874) and Pacifico Valussi (1813–1893). Vivante, together with other Triestine Austro-Marxists like Giuseppina Martinuzzi (1844–1925), contended for greater cultural autonomy for both the Italian-speaking and Slavic populations in Trieste but argued against the annexation of the city to Italy. In their belief that Italians, Slovenes, and Croats were interdependent groups, they attempted to modernize the vision of Tommaseo and Valussi, who belonged to a previous generation of early-nineteenth-century intellectuals and who were proponents of a multilingual and multicultural patriotism. Tommaseo and Valussi witnessed the crisis of a liberal and emancipatory conception of nationhood, which was gradually replaced by an ethnic nationalism characterized by an aggressive monolingualism and a xenophobic monoculture. They argued that in polyglot and multicultural regions, inhabiting different social communities simultaneously was a matter of routine. Tommaseo and Valussi proposed what might be called a cosmopolitanism from below, one that is based upon the everyday interactions of the working and middle classes, made up of traders and merchants, peasants and burghers. They envisioned heterogeneous regions such as the northern Adriatic seaboard as modern laboratories of social mediation in which heterogeneous communities practice the acceptance of difference and try to resolve internal conflicts without nationalizing them. Together with other Dalmatian intellectuals of their generation, such as Stipan Ivičević (1801–1878) and Ivan August Kaznačić (1817–1883), Tommaseo and Valussi aimed at a federal reorganization of their region, fashioned on the Swiss model.

Slataper believed it necessary to introduce and explain to a cultured Italian readership largely unfamiliar with Triestine affairs the subtle elusiveness of a city that was a place of geographic, historical, and cultural transitions, where "everything is double or triple, starting with the flora and ending with ethnicity."[30] Slataper indeed saw himself as the product of the syncretic forces of the Habsburg Empire: in the same year, he writes an often-quoted letter to his future wife Gigetta, where he comments on his own multicultural background: "You know that I am Slav, German, and Italian," arguing that membership in one

---

[29] Scipio Slataper, *Scritti politici* (Milan: Mondadori, 1954), 168. The article, "L'avvenire nazionale e politico di Trieste," was originally published in *La Voce*, May 30 and June 6, 1912.
[30] Slataper, *Scritti politici*, 93.

culture does not disqualify an individual from participating in the life of other communities.[31] When the author tells her in his private correspondence "Trieste è la mia patria," Slataper employs the term that is usually reserved for the Italian homeland—an echo of the "Trieste nazione" rhetoric, a rhetoric that sees the city as a place of pacification.[32] Likewise, in the 1914 poem "Caffé Tergeste," the poet Umberto Saba (1883–1957) described the city as a place of conciliation between the Italian and the Slav.[33] Because of their self-appointed mission to promote intercultural exchange, Slataper and the brothers Stuparich started to plan the publication of a periodical eloquently entitled *Europa* that was aimed, unlike the more narrowly Italian national *La Voce*, at publishing articles about a wide range of European cultures. Working with enthusiasm, the group had already assigned specific areas of investigation to its members. Slataper was to tackle the Slavic question and the political situation in the Balkans, while others were to study Germany and Scandinavian countries. In the first of his "Triestine Letters" published in *La Voce*, Slataper had polemically denounced Trieste as a city without cultural traditions, preoccupied as it was by its distracting and all-consuming commercial activities.[34] Now their overall ambition with *Europa* was to transform Trieste, already a privileged observatory of continental cultural trends, into a vibrant intellectual center from which they planned to follow the debates of the time, such as the future of democracy, the role of religion in modern society, and the social and political breakthroughs of feminism. The ultimate goal of *Europa* was a modernization and internationalization of Italian literary culture as well as the development of future political cooperation among countries. The publication of the first issue was scheduled for 1914, but the outbreak of the First World War brought an abrupt conclusion not only to the logistics of the editorial project but also to its ideological underpinnings. Swayed by the rhetoric of heroic belligerence and national liberation, all three intellectuals abjured their pacifist

---

[31] Scipio Slataper, *Alle tre amiche: lettere*, ed. Giani Stuparich (Milan: Mondadori, 1958), 421.
[32] Ibid., 424.
[33] Umberto Saba, *Songbook. The Selected Poems of Umberto Saba*, trans. George Hochfield and Leonard Cathen (New Haven, CT: Yale University Press, 2008).
[34] Slataper, "Trieste non ha tradizioni di coltura," February 11, 1909. Slataper's provocation was intended to stimulate a discussion about the emergence of a new and distinctively Triestine art that would make the convergence of the city's multiple cultures a productive encounter. In *1910: The Emancipation of Dissonance* (Berkeley: University of California Press, 1996) Thomas Harrison sees in Slataper's ambition a wider artistic impulse in conversation with Expressionism.

credo and embraced the Irredentist interventionism of war volunteers, joining the Italian Army. Slataper and Carlo Stuparich both fell on the battlefield, along with an entire generation of young Triestine intellectuals that perished during the First World War.

Nonnational Affiliations in the Habsburg Empire

Giani Stuparich, who survived his participation in the war, evokes these youthful projects in his 1948 recollection *Trieste in my Memories* (*Trieste nei miei ricordi*), reaffirming decades later that Habsburg Trieste indeed constituted a model for European integration. "Never like in the years preceding the First World War were we so close to a mutual understanding among Europeans," he writes, "so close to the United States of Europe."[35] In the same decade, Stefan Zweig records a similar regret for the failure of a liberal humanism whose political commitment to a continental federalization appeared to the author one of many missed opportunities of an entire generation of European intellectuals and writers. Published in 1942, *The World of Yesterday: Memories of a European* (*Die Welt von Gestern. Erinnerungen eines Europäers*) remains a romanticized, albeit bitter, chronicle of the collapse of a moribund empire and a cosmopolitan pacifism that Zweig saw as a product of the Austrian spirit. Stuparich and Zweig's memoirs both aspire to combine the intimacy of an autobiographical account with a comprehensive cultural history that engages in a mournful memorialization of the empire. Today, their idealism certainly appears utopian, naïve, and shortsighted. Yet these nostalgic idealizations of Habsburg multiculturalism echo more pragmatic approaches of the prewar period, concrete projects elaborated by political activists who believed, perhaps correctly, that a constitutional reform of the Habsburg provinces into a multinational federation was the only sustainable strategy of survival for the empire. Austro-Marxist thinkers such as Otto Bauer and Karl Renner supported a social democratic federalization within the legal boundaries of the monarchy, in which national membership was no longer a matter of territorial belonging but a question of personal commitment. The legal scholar Aurel Popovici, who was part of a group of counselors of the heir to the imperial throne Archduke Franz Ferdinand, published a detailed proposal in 1906 that remapped the traditional Habsburg crown lands and envisioned a United States of Greater

---

[35] Giani Stuparich, *Trieste nei miei ricordi* (Milan: Garzanti, 1948), 55. Years later, Stuparich disavowed Irredentism and admitted his Socialist sympathies, arguing that he had hoped until the end that the old Habsburg Empire could be transformed into a confederation of nations in which Trieste did not have to give up its Italian character. Giani Stuparich, "La realtà di Trieste," *Il ponte* 10, no. 4 (1954): 549–556.

Trieste and the European Project—Ethics, Aesthetics, Politics 21

Figure 0.2 "Map of the Proposed United States of Greater Austria" by Aurel Popovici in 1906 with the distribution of ethnic groups of Austria-Hungary in 1910 based on map entitled "Distribution of Races in Austria-Hungary" from *Historical Atlas* by William Shepherd, 1911. Wikimedia Commons. Photograph: Andrei Nacu.

Austria that gave Trieste and its metropolitan hinterland ample administrative autonomy.[36] Similarly, before the First World War the philosopher and politician Tomáš Masaryk believed that the only viable political context for the Czechs and other small nations was a Habsburg federation. After the war, this Habsburg reformist tradition became for many writers and intellectuals the source of their opinions and projects about European integration. In addition to a democratization of the empire, the proposals registered an important paradigm shift. For Bauer and Renner, Popovici and Masaryk the thorny nationality question in the empire could only be solved if the Austrian crown ceased to regard the empire as a nonnational political body and accepted a constitutional validation of its national composition. Growing out of

---

[36] Aurel Popovici, *Die Vereinigten Staaten von Groß-Österreich: politische Studien zur Lösung der nationalen Fragen und staatsrechtlichen Krisen in Österreich-Ungarn* (Leipzig: Verlag von B. Elischer Nachfolger, 1906).

the nonnational empire, these projects of administrative unity and diplomatic cooperation, social peace and cultural exchange, underwent a process of political-philosophical translation and were now imagined in the context of a Europe of nations.

Precisely this emphasis on the growth of a national consciousness in the Habsburg territories has represented a conventional approach to the study of nineteenth- and twentieth-century Central Europe according to a methodology that elects the nation as an epistemological lens through which we read modern cultural, literary, and political histories. I contend, however, that in Habsburg Trieste nonnational commitments proved surprisingly resilient, despite the successful discursive strategies of a nationalist rhetoric that elected itself as the standard-bearer of modernity. Shifting the focus to the urban milieu of the Adriatic city, I develop this argument against the background of recent Habsburg historiography that reexamines the crucial presence of nonnational allegiances in the context of polyglot and multicultural areas. Scholars such as Pieter Judson, Jeremy King, and Tara Zahra have convincingly argued that national indifference represented an essential challenge to the rise of nationalism, showing how political activists in German-Czech Bohemia successfully framed social conflicts—access to resources, political enfranchisement, economic disparities, education, and taxation—in terms of national struggles.[37] Their studies have shown that relegating nonnational allegiances to a premodern era, specifically to the period preceding 1848, is misguided and methodologically flawed.

With a slightly different emphasis, Dominique Kirchner Reill has studied the trajectory from nonnational sentiments to what she defines as the "Adriatic Multi-Nationalism" of Dalmatia, Trieste, and Venice.[38] Following the intricate interplay of sub-national regions, emerging nation-states, and supra-national formations, Reill argues that in many intellectuals the desire for local autonomy of their multicultural regions along the Adriatic took precedence over the urge to form

---

[37] For nonnational sentiments in the Habsburg Empire, see Jeremy King, *Budweisers into Czechs and Germans: A Local History of Bohemian Politics, 1848–1948* (Princeton, NJ: Princeton University Press, 2002), Pieter Judson, *Guardians of the Nation: Activists on the Language Frontiers of Imperial Austria* (Cambridge, MA: Harvard University Press, 2006), and Tara Zahra, *Kidnapped Souls: National Indifference and the Battle for Children in the Bohemian Lands 1900–1948* (Ithaca, NY: Cornell University Press, 2008).

[38] Dominique Kirchner Reill, *Nationalists Who Feared the Nation: Adriatic Multi-Nationalism in Habsburg Dalmatia, Trieste, and Venice* (Stanford, CA: Stanford University Press, 2012).

nation-states. Dalmatian and Triestine intellectuals who envisioned cultural and political autonomy for their Italo-Slavic Adriatic multiculturalism described their affiliation in terms of a pluralist and polyglot "nation." Their reluctance to dismiss the nomenclature of nationhood bespeaks the difficulty of finding an adequate vocabulary to describe a multicultural regional patriotism in an age of nationalism. At any rate, as Reill perceptively argues, this Adriatic multinationalism "lays bare how much our understanding of nationalism has been shaped by its later developments rather than by its original possibilities."[39] In addition, Reill shows how the northern Adriatic region became home to a vision of a Mediterranean *de facto* cosmopolitanism. The waters of this Adriatic contact zone muddled these diverse nations not only in terms of commercial exchanges but also, more importantly, in the very private sphere of peoples' family connections and the hybrid dialects they spoke. Political projects of federalization in the region, both inside or outside of the Habsburg confines, went hand in hand with a cultural validation of local vernaculars. The abovementioned Dalmatian patriot and linguist Niccolò Tommaseo argued for the publication of dictionaries of every dialect, not just standard languages.

Judson and Reill's studies have shown that in the last decades of the Habsburg Empire the rise of nationalism did not abruptly supplant nonnational affiliations, but that these forms of identification coexisted with a widespread popular indifference to nationality as well as with a systematic fluidity of linguistic and cultural identities. As Judson puts it, "Phenomena such as bilingualism, apparent indifference to national identity, and nationally opportunist behaviors expressed the fundamental logic of local cultures in multilingual regions, a logic that neither nationalist activism nor so-called modernization processes were capable of destroying."[40] When large strata of the population started electing a nation of belonging, national affiliations were certainly informed by ideas of ethnic and linguistic communality, but also by social customs such as religious affiliations, intermarriage, friendships, or even more prosaic and contingent circumstances, such as the choice of a particular tavern one frequented. Judson has also shown how difficult it is to identify national attachments that often were in flux, changing according to temporary considerations and shifting opportunities of upward social mobility. Bilingual individuals and bicultural families often rejected even rudimentary forms of national identity, preferring to name themselves according to their region or religion.

---

[39] Reill, *Nationalists*, 12.
[40] Judson, *Guardians*, 3.

Even historians who recognize the nature of nations as rhetorical constructs and "imagined communities," to use Benedict Anderson's felicitous expression, continue to treat nations as real and natural entities, a misconception that is particularly misleading when it comes to the study of ethnically and linguistically heterogeneous areas, as is often the case with Habsburg territories. After the collapse of Austria-Hungary, American president Woodrow Wilson famously suggested a geopolitical reorganization of Europe in his Fourteen Points. A guiding principle of this remapping was the inviolable right of national self-determination, which was later adopted as an important doctrine in international law. Nonetheless, Wilson's legal and political framework of the nation was vague, insufficiently theorized, and ultimately inadequate as it envisioned national communities as abstract, uniform, and monolithic groups. The indeterminacy of his legal principle required diplomats and political scientists to examine the possibility of its practical application in postwar Central Europe. The questions that needed to be addressed were manifold. How should borders between these nations be drawn? How can the international community determine who belongs to what nation? Who has the right to vote if questions of nationality were to be solved by democratic election? In the process of geopolitical emancipation of the nations under former Habsburg rule, international observers were baffled by the quite unexpected hurdle they encountered. In interviews and surveys, they often quoted a frequent lack of national identification. Residues of this nonnational logic in the former territories of the empire still perplexed political analysts. Margaret Macmillan describes this process in her book on the political transformations in the wake of the First World War, in which she refers to Central Europe as "a protean world of shifting allegiances."[41] She reports the following reactions from Central European territories, where "a modern ethnic nationalism superimposed itself on an older, different world."[42] As late as 1920, when outside investigators were trying to determine the national makeup of former Habsburg territories, they received only evasive answers from rural Central Europeans who were "absolutely indifferent to all national questions."[43] Instead of classifying themselves as members of a given nation, these peasants frustrated the expectations of international observers. The

---

[41] Margaret Macmillan, *Paris 1919: Six Months that Changed the World* (New York, NY: Random House, 2002), 207.
[42] Ibid., 240.
[43] Ibid., 12.

identity markers that these farmers recognized and validated were religious affiliation and geographic origin. This territorial patriotism was bound to physical and social geography and, once again, did not exclude membership based on language. Their indifference to the nation eludes classic definitions of nationhood that we have considered as the dominant paradigm of modernity. It is worth remembering that in Central Europe the transition from flexible and multiple cultural allegiances to a dominant national paradigm was only accomplished later via forced expulsions, mass migrations, and policies of ethnic cleansing.[44]

To categorize national indifference and nonnational allegiances as marginal phenomena from exclusively rural areas or remnants of a feudal past is to misunderstand the ideological complexity of historical modernity.[45] Nationalists perceived the multicultural and polyglot composition of Habsburg metropoles like Vienna, Prague, Budapest, and Trieste as a threat to their vision of homogeneous and monolingual communities. The reason for such a perceived menace was that nonnational sentiments represented a formidable challenge to the national paradigm, even though the latter ultimately ended up successfully imposing itself as the dominant category of self-definition. National indifference has been classified into many categories, such as localism or regionalism, cosmopolitanism, intermarriage, Catholicism, or socialism. These phenomena have often been described in decidedly pejorative terms, as immoral, opportunistic, and retrograde behaviors that betray the general interests of a national group.[46] Likewise, bilingualism has been considered evidence of cultural backwardness, synonymous with a lack of national consciousness and duplicity, as well as detrimental to the cognitive development in children. Bereft of an unwavering commitment to the nation, speakers with an extensive

---

[44] In his autobiography *Mein Prag* (Vienna: Paul Zsolnay Verlag, 2008), Peter Demetz describes a revealing personal anecdote from the year 1938, two decades after the collapse of the empire, which illustrates his indecisiveness when he had to choose one nationality, Czech or German, over another.

[45] Frederic Jameson has argued that the feudal order and the capitalist revolution continued to coexist until the end of the Second World War. Modernism, then, must be understood as the result of an incomplete modernization, which displays the dialectic of two separate temporalities, "that of the new industrial big city and that of the peasant countryside." Frederic Jameson, *A Singular Modernity: Essay on the Ontology of the Present* (London: Verso, 2002), 142.

[46] Tara Zahra, *Kidnapped*, 98.

use, let alone native command, of another language raised the suspicion of being easily assimilated into a different national group. Pressured to assimilate, imperial subjects gradually embraced—some enthusiastically, some half-heartedly—a nation of their choosing. With the collapse of the Austro-Hungarian Empire, Habsburg loyalties became suddenly defunct but the affiliated nonnational sentiments continued to survive, occasionally reasserting themselves in a historical context that deemed their function progressively inadequate. Scholars of literary modernism, generally focused on the abstract master-narratives of the nation, have largely overlooked the national indifference of authors and their fictional characters, in which a lingering suspicion of the political fiction of the nation survived. The skeptical attitude toward the nation does not originate in a narrow and provincial regionalism, nor does the attention to nonnational allegiances stem from a naïve celebration of a multicultural, and at times elitist, cosmopolitanism or from an ill-concealed imperial nostalgia. It reflects the quotidian reality of multilingual speakers and their flexible commitments to different linguistic, cultural, and religious communities, an attitude dictated by shifting social and economic opportunities. The nationalization of private life and the public sphere that has inculcated a militant monolingualism in the new state formations and its cultural institutions has also encompassed, in the words of Rogers Brubaker, "the silencing or marginalization of alternative, nonnationalist political languages."[47] The successful establishment of the nation as an epistemological lens tends, at best, to relegate nonnational commitments to a realm of arcane ruins upon which we occasionally stumble on our path to understand modernity, or at worst, to blind us completely to their stubborn resilience.

Behind the Nation: Trieste and an Austrian Mediterranean Sea

The history of Trieste and its modern literature are usually written in terms of a teleological progress toward the emergence of the national

---

[47] Rogers Brubaker, *Nationalism Reframed: Nationhood and the National Question in the New Europe* (New York: Cambridge University Press, 1996), 20. I take the notion of a "militant monolingualism" in nation-state formations from Vicente Rafael, who has written about monolingualism in the context of Translation Studies. Rafael argues: "In the context of this militant monolingualism, we sense how the work of translation was geared to go in only one direction: toward the transformation of the foreign into an aspect of the domestic, and thus of the plurality of native tongues into the imperious singularity of a national tongue." Vicente Rafael, *Motherless Tongues: The Insurgency of Language amid Wars of Translation* (Durham, NC: Duke University Press, 2016), 110.

Trieste and the European Project—Ethics, Aesthetics, Politics 27

paradigm, dominated by the accounts of a supposedly prevalent Italian Irredentism and the dream of national deliverance from the stifling yoke of Austrian imperialism. Katia Pizzi describes this dominant narrative about Trieste's national longing, emphasizing the inferiority complex of many Triestine writers who, driven by an almost neurotic angst, grappled with what they perceived as the city's marginal and belated Italianness. Mainly focused on authors who write in Italian, Pizzi insightfully traces Trieste's literary engagement with a constant recreation of its history and tradition that she sees as largely national. She admits that Trieste's literary heritage is characterized by "a latent national diffidence," arguing, however, that such reservations remain largely unexpressed.[48] Similarly, Richard Robinson relies upon the "national emergence within imperial structures," reading Trieste's border as the delimitation among its "nations."[49] Robinson sees the city not in terms of an idiosyncrasy, but as the site of a paradigmatic European border in the context of shifting geopolitical maps. In his readings of Central European literature that include Roth's borderland *Heimat*, Joyce's political spaces, and Svevo's "border modernism," Robinson accounts for the complexities of boundaries that bind as much as they divide.[50] Borders are constitutive of many Triestine anxieties, but the city also resists the dichotomies of border dialectics that oppose the certainties of the self to an absolute other, the local here and a displaced somewhere else. Trieste is the locus where *place*, often the privileged trope of nativism and insularity, is always in the process of becoming *space*, connected to communities beyond its real or imagined borders. This is true for all of Trieste's identity constructions: for its association with other Mediterranean port cities; for its dynastic loyalty connected to the imperial capital Vienna; for both Italian and Slovenian Irredentism, which always looked outwards; and the deep connection with a larger European community.

These national narratives depict a scenario in which Trieste fulfills its historical destiny thanks to the disintegration of the Austro-Hungarian Empire and the establishment of a new geopolitical order. After more than five centuries of Austrian rule, the city finally enjoys its national emancipation and becomes Italian. The intoxicating enthusiasm for the newly acquired status then subsides almost immediately, given the rapid decline of Trieste's commercial wealth within the new context of

---

[48] Katia Pizzi, *A City*, 30.
[49] Richard Robinson, *Narratives of the European Border: A History of Nowhere* (New York: Palgrave Macmillan, 2007), 9.
[50] Ibid., 57.

28   Modernism in Trieste

an Italian economy that favors other port cities.⁵¹ The bitter disenchantment following frustrated expectations of financial prosperity radicalized Irredentism into an uncritical embrace of Fascist ideology with its aggressive antagonism toward the languages and cultures of ethnic minorities, especially the Slovenian and Croatian communities. Symptomatic of the growing nationalist violence after the First World War was a pogrom against the Slavs in the city, a devastation culminating in the arsonist attack on the *Slovenski Narodni Dom* ("The House of the Slovenian People"), the Slovenian cultural center, located in downtown Trieste. On July 13, 1920, Fascist squadrons set the imposing multi-story building on fire and organized a cordon to prevent the firefighters from reaching the flames. In the violence and looting, the Slovenian community lost records, books, and its archive.

In the realm of letters, this nationalist trajectory can be observed, for instance, in the literary career of Ida Finzi, alias Haydée (1867–1946). From her *Vita triestina avanti e durante la guerra* (1916) to the nationalist verses of *Rime di Trieste e d'una vita* (1935), Haydée espouses a view that vehemently rejects Trieste's cosmopolitan history, celebrating the city's liberation as the culmination of *Risorgimento* hopes and aspirations. The "maternal nationalism" in her poetic production accepts the Fascist relegation of women to the domestic sphere, capitalizing on a trope that sees Trieste as a stereotypical damsel in distress liberated by the virility of an assertive Italy.⁵² Haydée remains an influential figure for the Triestine intelligentsia after the First World War, mainly comprised of the women who did not participate in the battles that claimed the lives of an entire generation of men. Pia Rimini (1900–1945) followed Haydée's embrace of the Fascist construction of femininity as nurturing mother figures in her novel *Eva e il paracadute* (1931). Fortuna Morpurgo, alias Willy Dias (1872–1956), while rejecting Fascism as a political direction came to espouse in her literary production much of the romantic sentimentalism found in Haydée and D'Annunzio. Katia Pizzi has shown how the "matrilineal patriotic genealogy" of these writers went hand in hand with a solid rejection of

---

⁵¹ In her book *Making Trieste Italian, 1918–1954* (Rochester, NY: Boydell Press, 2005), Maura Hametz records the transition from Habsburg Trieste to Italian Trieste, showing how the multiple processes of Fascist Italianization were the result of brutal inculcation and forcible coercion, but also of voluntary assimilation. For the Italo-Slavic tensions of the postwar years, see Glenda Sluga, *The Problem of Trieste and the Italo-Yugoslav Border: Difference, Identity, and Sovereignty in Twentieth-Century Europe* (Albany: The State University of New York Press, 2001).
⁵² Pizzi, *A City*, 147.

the Habsburg past and a vitriolic anti-Slavic rhetoric.[53] Paradoxically, the Triestine women who embraced Irredentism first and Fascism later owed their educational opportunities to old Austrian imperial policies, which, far from embracing any full feminist emancipation, were nonetheless much more geared toward challenging traditional gender roles than any Italian pedagogical institution of the time would have deemed appropriate. These women were educated at the *Ginnasio Femminile* and the *Civico Liceo Femminile*, institutions that became centers of Italian nationalism founded by the very Habsburg administration its female students came to loathe.[54] The bourgeois intellectuals educated at these schools represented a relatively homogeneous front that embraced the self-appointed role of maternal guide to national liberation. A second wave of deep disappointment is evident in the writings of Triestine intellectuals in the 1940s and 1950s, especially in the texts by Elody Oblath (1889–1971) and Anita Pittoni (1901–1982), who now perceived the ideas of liberation, floated in the laboratory of ideas that was Trieste, as shattered illusions at best and broken promises at worst.[55]

The horrors of the Second World War in particular made the old Habsburg Empire look comparatively quaint in the eyes of these intellectuals. The bitter resentment for the broken promises of history gives rise to a misguided imperial nostalgia, the melancholic remembrance of a naïvely idealized era.[56] The memory of Habsburg Trieste becomes part of what Zweig reconstructed as his world of yesterday, a time of widespread optimism, financial security, and relative social harmony. Much of the literary and historiographic production after the fall of the Austro-Hungarian Empire engages in the mythologizing memorialization of Habsburg Trieste that celebrates the cosmopolitanism and tolerance of a multiethnic and polyglot commercial emporium open to cultural difference and religious diversity. This modern mythography of the Adriatic city tends to quietly dismiss the interethnic conflicts and cultural clashes; the ethnocentric, xenophobic, and chauvinist tribalism of the city's nationalisms; the open and institutionalized discriminations against the Slovenian-speaking community; the asymmetrical distribution of wealth; and the more or less widespread episodes of

---

[53] Katia Pizzi, "Gender, Confession and Ethnicity: Women Writers and Trieste," *Journal of Romance Studies* 7, no. 1 (Spring 2007), 73. doi:10.3828/jrs.7.1.71.
[54] The institutions were founded in 1872 and 1881 respectively.
[55] See for instance Anita Pittoni's "Amarezza di Trieste," published in *Il Giornale* on June 22, 1954. See this mention in Curci and Ziani, *Oltre le parole*, 389.
[56] For the generation of Triestine intellectuals after the First World War, see Renate Lunzer, *Irredenti redenti* (Trieste: Lint Editoriale, 2011).

anti-Semitic prejudice and violence.[57] In his seminal study of the Habsburg myth, Claudio Magris claimed that a Habsburg Europeanism constituted an integral component of a postwar imperial nostalgia that mourned the fallen monarchy, a view that has largely dominated cultural and literary historians who have studied the empire in general and Trieste in particular.[58] In the same vein, writing half a century after Magris, Marjorie Perloff sees this imperial nostalgia as one of the defining characteristics of what she calls Austro-Modernism after the First World War.[59] While this reading of Austrian postwar literature in many ways still retains its validity, this book proposes a literary history that also accounts for the intricate cultural politics that dominated the last decades of the Habsburg Empire and, specifically, the interlocking taxonomies of cultural belonging that irremediably complicate this Habsburg nostalgia.

Even in the effort to debunk the cosmopolitan myth of Trieste, an effort that guards us from the rhetorical pitfalls of a facile nostalgia, the critique of the mournful remembrance has accepted the nation as an all-inclusive paradigm, obfuscating in this way the rich articulation of a cultural syntax in which metropolitan, regional, national, and supranational identifications interact following a logic of subordination and interdependence. In other words, Habsburg modernist authors and their fictional characters did not simply identify with a nation, whether a *Kulturnation* or an ethnolinguistic community that insists on the specific territorial confines of a nation-state. In the cases in which such associations occurred, this acceptance was never unchallenged by shifting allegiances and contending models of identification

---

[57] For a history of Anti-Semitism in Trieste, see Maura Hametz, "Zionism, Emigration, and Anti-Semitism in Trieste: Central Europe's Gateway to Zion 1896–1943," *Jewish Social Studies* 13, no. 3 (2007): 103–134. https://muse.jhu.edu/article/230679.

[58] Heidi Schlipphacke identifies different modes or temporalities of nostalgic longing, from an anticipatory nostalgia, already present before the collapse of the empire, to a progressive kind of nostalgia, one that reaches back to the past in order to imagine new future coordinates. "The Temporalities of Habsburg Nostalgia," *Journal of Austrian Studies* 47, no. 2 (2014): 1–16. doi:10.1353/oas.2014.0023. For the specific Triestine brand of Habsburg nostalgia, Maura Hametz shows in the same volume how today the city's institutions deploy a contemporary discourse on imperial nostalgia as a vehicle for Trieste's economic rebirth in the region and its border-crossing cooperation within the geographic triangulation that connects Trieste to neighboring Slovenia and the adjacent Austrian region of Carinthia. "Presnitz in the Piazza: Habsburg Nostalgia in Trieste," *Journal of Austrian Studies* 47, no. 2 (2014): 131–154. doi:10.1353/oas.2014.0029.

[59] Marjorie Perloff, *Edge of Irony: Modernism in the Shadow of the Habsburg Empire* (Chicago: The University of Chicago Press, 2016).

Trieste and the European Project—Ethics, Aesthetics, Politics   31

that called into question the nation's claims to fulfil a historical-political destiny. Instead, this book claims that Trieste became in the course of its history a nexus of competing identity politics in which the nation offered but one among the many possibilities of attachment. In doing so, I follow Katherine Arens who argues that Austrian literary studies, broadly conceived, "calls for interpretative paradigms outside the mental strictures imposed by the maps of the (post)colonial national imperia and nation-states theorized as the cores of nineteenth- and twentieth-century Europe."[60] Her recent study appropriately "aims at thinking beyond the nation-state, at recovering another kind of historical identity narrative," one that "provides a narrative about Europe that has always been central to one-time Habsburg regions' identity discourses, often in lieu of the national narratives that remain the provenance of the many regions' subcultures that have since sought to establish nation-states guaranteeing them cultural-political hegemony."[61] For many Austrian authors understood, Arens maintains, the "Austrian mind" as "the birth pangs of a multicultural Europe, as represented in a political entity that resisted ethnic nationalism."[62] Habsburg Trieste indeed challenged the rise of nationalism, perceiving itself as genuinely "hinternational," to say it with the Bohemian poet Johannes Urzidil, and cultivating, among other affiliations, a pride in municipal independence and a dynastic loyalty tied to the House of Habsburg.[63] A number of nonnational affiliations survived the end of

---

[60] Katherine Arens, *Vienna's Dream of Europe: Culture and Identity beyond the Nation-State* (London, New York: Bloomsbury Academic, 2015), 8. In the same vein, Katherine Sorrels states: "The focus on situational identity and on non-national networks, loyalties, and sentiment frees the region from methodological nationalism and recovers parts of its history therefore obscured. It moves beyond the stigma of primordial and incurable ethnic and nationalist hatred that the region has for so long carried." *Cosmopolitan Outsiders: Imperial Inclusion, National Exclusion, and the Pan-European Idea, 1900–1930* (New York: Palgrave Macmillan, 2016), 7.
[61] Arens, *Vienna's Dream*, 15–16.
[62] Arens's book studies the German-speaking tradition of the Habsburg Empire but acknowledges the polycentric nature of this Austrian political imagination. Arens continues: "Vienna and its smaller sister cities in the empire modeled various kinds of emerging public networks and spaces functioning between center and periphery to join regional and ethnic causes to a 'national cause,' and they created in their inhabitants a profound sense that they had the shared civic and ethical duty to engage in public discussion and public enlightenment." Arens, *Vienna's Dream*, 293–294.
[63] The Bohemian poet Johannes Urzidil (1896–1970) coined the portmanteau "hinternational," a term that combines the emotional attachment to a particular place with a positionality behind and beyond the nation. *Prager Triptychon* (Munich: Wilhelm Heyne, 1960).

the empire and while socially and politically not always viable after the war, they prominently figure in postwar literature, where they dwell shrewdly disguised, hide in plain sight, or defiantly challenge nationalist readings of the modernist novel. The political nationalism of the Italian Irredentists in Trieste, for instance, clashed with the dynastic allegiance to the Austrian crown of a cosmopolitan merchant class, with the reformist thrust of a monarchic federalism, and with a traditional regional patriotism of multicultural territories in the empire. Modernism in Trieste, in brief, developed a literary invention of Europe that is decidedly nonnational. As this book will illustrate, the distance from national identifications in Trieste originated from at least three sources: first, a municipal version of a Habsburg *Landespatriotismus*, the attachment to local multicultural communities; second, a Jewish indifference to the nation; and third, an open network of local identities characteristic of the Mediterranean region.

The origins of this Habsburg Europeanism can be traced back to forms of *Landespatriotismus*, an early modern regional patriotism, divorced from national identity and characterized by a loyalty to the local traditions of linguistically and culturally heterogeneous territories or cities in the empire. In both rural and urban areas, multilingualism, ethnic and religious intermarriage, as well as opportunity for upward social mobility determined a general indifference to national identity. Traditionally, historians and literary scholars agree that after the 1848–1849 revolutions in Europe the emergence of a more virulent ethnic and linguistic nationalism largely replaced these forms of regional allegiance. Any resurfacing of this Habsburg regionalism in early twentieth-century literature and culture is generally considered the survival of vestigial remnants of an allegedly pre-national logic. This book shows, however, that these nonnational loyalties did not belong to a pre-national mindset, holding the status of anachronistic bystanders.[64] They were, rather, a vital part of a complex ideological network that constituted the experience of modernity.

At the beginning of the twentieth century, Jews in Trieste had become a relatively small but important and wealthy community, whose generous donations paid for the construction in 1912 of the largest synagogue in Europe at the time. This community produced Jewish writers who,

---

[64] Arens's book offers "cases of post-nationalism from the nationalist era of Europe, as they were staged in a region with a pre-national political heritage." *Vienna's Dream*, 295. In line with a common understanding of modernity and nationhood, Arens treats nonnational loyalties as pre-national phenomena. My attempt at decoupling modernity and modernism from the nation counters the idea that nonnational allegiances are divorced and alien to the feeling of being modern.

according to Katia Pizzi, "constitute the modernist essence of Triestine literature."[65] Habsburg Jews, and in particular the Jewish community in Trieste, were characterized by an anti-national tendency stemming from their emotional attachments to multiple communities. Their cultural and political allegiances were numerous: at once invested in the Irredentist cause of the Italians, Triestine Jews were also fervent Zionists and faithful to the supranational Habsburg state that had offered legal support for their integration and emancipation.[66] Joseph Roth, in particular, describes a cultural-political attitude that is valid for both rural Eastern Jews and Jewish communities in larger Habsburg cities. In his 1927 essay, *The Wandering Jews* (*Juden auf Wanderschaft*), Roth claims that nationality is a Western concept, utterly alien to Eastern Jewry: "National self-determination is an intellectual luxury for a group that has nothing more serious to worry about. If there is one nation that is justified in seeing the 'national question' as essential to its survival, then surely it is the Jews, who are forced to become a 'nation' by the nationalism of others."[67] Roth emphasizes how the bilingualism and multiple cultural identities of the European Jewry were forced to squeeze into the monolithic dimensions of ethnolinguistic nationalism. Habsburg subjects from rural areas had to succumb precisely to this nationalism of others. I contend that metropolitan centers were not immune to what Roth ascribes to rural areas. In parallel fashion, imperial Trieste also succumbed to the nationalism of others, the Irredentism imported from Italy. In fact, what Roth describes in terms of language and national affiliation also applies to Trieste: "Only in the East do people live who are unconcerned with their 'nationality,' in the Western European sense. They speak several languages, are themselves the product of several generations of mixed marriages, and fatherland for them is whichever country happens to conscript them."[68] For Roth, the family chronicle of

---

[65] Pizzi, *A City*, 34.
[66] In his book on Joseph Roth and the Eastern Jewish tradition, Claudio Magris argues that it was relatively easy for Austrian Jews to identify with the supranational Habsburg state, founded on nonnational principles. *Lontano da dove. Joseph Roth e la tradizione ebraico-orientale* (Turin: Einaudi, 1977).
[67] Joseph Roth, *The Wandering Jews* (New York, London: W. W. Norton & Company, 2001), 51–52.
[68] Ibid., 15. This statement seems to be contradicted by an episode in Roth's *The Radetzkymarch*. In the novel, Franz Joseph visits the military garrison in Galicia, where he notices the subtle but piqued insubordination of one of his colonels, a Triestine officer who keeps his coat collar high and open in a vain and coquettish demeanor. In the rigid protocols of imperial etiquette, the deliberate violation of the military dress code appears to the Emperor as sheer monstrosity. The blatant disobedience of the high-ranking military staff is particularly distressing because of the colonel's origin, Habsburg Trieste, formerly known for its traditional imperial loyalty.

his novel *The Radetzkymarch*—a narrative hybrid suspended between allegorical fable and realist historical novel—records the epochal transition from what he sees as an agricultural world of dynastic patriotism and authentic human relationships to the artificial bonds established by capitalist nationalism.

Roth occasionally argued that his roots lay in Mediterranean Europe. This attention to the Mediterranean is particularly important in the context of the Adriatic city. As a Mediterranean port city, Trieste was part of a network of both regional and global sea routes, maritime connections mapped onto fluid borders. Fernand Braudel reminds us that the Mediterranean basin is a space of migrating cultures, confluences, and interactions that traverse and transcend borders, an area organically connected to its European, African, and Asian hinterlands. As such, German, Baltic, Slavic, Levantine, Arabic, and African histories and cultures remain an integral part of a Mediterranean that challenges the idea of impermeable borders.[69] In the same vein, Predrag Matvejević has claimed that the inhabitants of the Mediterranean usually belong more to a city than to a state or a nation, an assessment that is certainly true for the sense of belonging in a generation of *fin-de-siècle* Triestine intellectuals who saw the city as an integral part of a larger Mediterranean culture.[70] The most evident expression of this nonnational and Mediterranean Trieste is the circulation of a Phoenician myth of origin, an alternative genealogy of the city's origin that competes with the other two powerful and alluring aetiological myths, namely Trieste's Roman derivation, presented by the Irredentists as evidence of the Italian character of the city, and the foundation of the Habsburg port, emphasized by the Austro-loyalists.[71]

---

[69] Fernand Braudel, *The Mediterranean and the Mediterranean World in the Age of Phillip II*, vol. 1 (Berkeley: University of California Press, 1995).

[70] Predrag Matvejević writes, "Mediterraneans feel closer to their cities than to their states or nations; indeed cities are their states and nations and more." *Mediterranean: A Cultural Landscape* (Berkeley: University of California Press, 1999), 16. The title of the book in the original Croatian is *Mediteranski brevijar* (1987) and defines the text as a sort of breviary.

[71] In defining the relationship between Mediterranean Studies and questions of modernity, Ian Chambers shrewdly comments on the regulatory actions taken by the establishment of hard borders. He writes, "Cultural routes and commercial journeys, as well as pre-national modalities of identification, have subsequently been absorbed and regulated, if not buried in oblivion, in the more rigid demarcations imposed by modern colonial wars, nationalisms, and the freezing of frontiers." *Mediterranean Crossings: The Politics of an Interrupted Modernity* (Durham, NC: Duke University Press, 2008), 36.

The reasons behind the claims of a Phoenician origin of Trieste and the northern Adriatic seaboard are multiple. At the turn of the century, Trieste was trying to redefine its role within the two major spheres of socio-cultural and political influence, a reflection triggered by the economic crisis of 1873 and the city's loss of the free-port status in 1891. Irredentists took advantage of these commercial predicaments, arguing that Trieste's loyalty to Austria should be reconsidered and that the city's rightful place was Italy, which gained independence in 1861 just across the border. In the context of what Slataper defined Trieste's "double soul," the contradicting allegiances to both Austria and Italy, the cosmopolitics of a Phoenician origin represented an alternative to this stifling dichotomy. The invented tradition of these Habsburg Phoenicians suggested a third way, an Austro-Italian cultural particularism exclusive to the Adriatic city. The ancient mercantile culture of the Phoenicians therefore offered a prestigious genealogy of Trieste's commercial vocation, establishing an ideal continuity between the successful trading activities of the ancient sea power and the city's economic ambitions in the modern Mediterranean. By locating their Mediterranean origin in a Phoenician lineage, these writers also tried to resolve a crucial impasse: despite nationalist arguments, Trieste was a bustling port city not because of its links to Italy, whose history is geographically linked to the Mediterranean Sea, but because of the Austrian imperial policies that made Trieste the epicenter of the political imagination of a Mediterranean Habsburg monarchy. In addition, while nationalist narratives in the nineteenth and early twentieth centuries identified the origin of their national culture in the Greco-Roman tradition, the Phoenicians were perceived as a nonnational and cosmopolitan culture. Equidistant from the philhellenism of German Weimar classicism and the *Romanitas* of the Italian *Risorgimento*, wholeheartedly embraced by the Irredentists, the declarations of a Phoenician character allowed these authors to subvert modern nationalist mythologies that glorified ancient Greek and Roman cultures as the cradle of European civilization. In other words, these authors elected the Phoenicians as an alternative cultural foundation for a new Europe, a Europe whose origin was neither Greco-Roman nor Judeo-Christian, and whose mission was neither national nor imperial-colonial. Against the visceral territoriality of *Blut und Boden*, the emphasis on blood and soil of modern nationalisms, these intellectuals aligned themselves with an ancient sea power which they understood to be a nomadic and diasporic culture whose scattered urban centers were bound together by a network of trading routes and commercial enterprises, and thus one that was not attached to a land where roots could grow.[72] Preferring the rudder to the plough, the Phoenicians were, more than uprooted in this somewhat simplistic and distorted reconstruction, not rooted at all, characterized by an identity that was aquatic, simultaneously porous and absorbent, shifting and constantly redefining itself through its multiplicity of local town traditions. Despite their coastal settlements on land, the Phoenicians were perceived as a pan-Mediterranean culture conducting a lifestyle of constant displacement that made them, in modern parlance, a supranational people.[73] It is perhaps no surprise, then, that Western nationalisms did not harbor any great interest in the Phoenicians, a culture that could potentially capsize projects of national belonging, while the cosmopolitan modernism of a Mediterranean city like Trieste embraced their legacy.

In order to fully appreciate the political nature of this modernist strategy, it is useful to bear in mind how Italian Fascism and German Nazism developed a sustained rhetoric of anti-Phoenician propaganda. The appropriation of the Greek and Roman worlds served the construction of a self-aggrandizing heritage, a noble line of tradition that could be claimed with scientific authority. The historiography of classical antiquity under these regimes was characterized by a vision that divided ancient populations into racial groups, classifications in which Phoenicians and Carthaginians functioned as the Semitic antagonists of Greeks and Romans. The public iconographies of both regimes are rife with examples of such appropriations, from Mussolini's busts imitating Roman sculptures, to Hitler's ambitious plans of architectural grandiosity for Berlin, magnificent capital of the Third Reich, to Leni Riefenstahl's film *Olympia*.

The political instrumentalization of the Roman world was a central strategy in the Fascist movement in Italy. In 1919, Mussolini had

---

[72] Andrew Wallace-Hadrill insightfully argues, "The Phoenicians, east and west, may thus be thought of as victims of a double *damnatio memoriae*, the vanquished enemies of Greece and Rome, and the forerunners of the colonized Middle East and North Africa." "Afterword" in *The Punic Mediterranean: Identities and Identification from Phoenician Settlement to Roman Rule*, ed. Josephine Crawley Quinn and Nicholas C. Vella (Cambridge: Cambridge University Press, 2014), 300.

[73] Peter van Dommelen clarifies how Phoenicians were not co-opted by nationalist narratives: "The role of nation states might at first sight seem of limited relevance to the construction of Punic identities, as the Punic world does not coincide with any one country. As it extends across much of the western Mediterranean, the Punic world could indeed be seen as supra-national in modern terms." Peter van Dommelen, "Punic identities and modern perceptions in the western Mediterranean," in *Punic Mediterranean*, 48.

founded the "Fasci Italiani di Combattimento," selecting the Roman iconography of the *fascio littorio*, a bundle of wooden rods holding an axe representing law and government, as a sign of unity and power in the tumult of the Italian postwar period. Once in power, the regime recontextualized the *Risorgimento* mission to elevate Italy to the splendor of Rome: Mussolini chose the epithet *dux*, fashioning himself in the image of a victorious Roman leader, and introduced the compulsory study of Latin and Roman history in schools. Fascist historiography and archeology molded the Romans in their own image, envisioning the ancient world as constituted by racially homogenous proto-national civilizations who were conscious, proud, and protective of their cultural distinctiveness. According to this view, the Romans imposed standardization and uniformity upon the populations they conquered, abhorring local identities and all forms of syncretism. An openly hostile rhetoric to the Phoenicians and Carthaginians, Semitic ancestors of modern Jews, increased after the adoption of the Racial Laws in 1938.[74] According to the regime-sponsored journal *La Difesa della Razza*, the conflict between Aryans and Semites could be traced back to Rome's earliest legends described in Vergil's *Aeneid*. The passion between pious Aeneas and the Phoenician Dido, predestined to fail, paved the way for an everlasting conflict.

Similarly, Hitler considered Roman history to be a guide in the tumult of modernity, an idea already outlined in *Mein Kampf*. Hitler's amateurish interpretation of antiquity saw the ancient world as a battlefield between Aryan races, in this particular context represented by Greeks and Romans, and Oriental forces, bent on the destruction of civilization.[75] The Nazis saw the Persian and Punic Wars as exemplary of the dichotomy between Indo-Germanic Aryans and Oriental Semites,

---

[74] Joshua Arthurs shows how Fascist historians, although admitting that the ancients had not developed a scientific theory of biological racism, recast figures such as Cato the Elder as a genuine racist by personal inclination or texts like Livy's *Ab Urbe Condita* as a racial history of Rome that culminated in the clash of civilization with Carthage. Likewise, archeology in Libya "minimized the presence of Greek and Carthaginian remains. The ubiquitous traces of Roman rule testified to its 'vigorous' desire to 'leave its imprint' on the land, while the lack of Carthaginian structures demonstrated that culture's 'mercantilist' priorities." *Excavating Modernity: The Roman Past in Fascist Italy* (Ithaca, NY: Cornell University Press, 2013), 130.

[75] In *Greeks, Romans, Germans: How the Nazis Usurped Europe's Classical Past* (Oakland: University of California Press, 2016), Johann Chapoutot shows how German National Socialism interpreted ancient history in terms of racial conflict. He argues that Hitler saw himself as an heir of the Roman struggle to defeat its Semitic enemies, lumping together Phoenician Carthage and Jerusalem.

Africans, and Semitic Jews.[76] Reinterpreted through the prism of Nazi racialist thought, Punic Carthage was the Semitic nemesis of Rome, the ultimate symbol of hegemonic power and colonial expansion. Carthaginian hostility was placed in a tradition of Semitic challenges to imperial authority, similar to Jerusalem's defiance against Roman rule. The regime also distorted the philhellenism of Weimar classicism, politicizing the positions of Goethe, Schiller, Novalis, and the brothers Schlegel who, in the wake of Winckelmann's 1764 *History of the Art of Antiquity* (*Geschichte der Kunst des Altertums*), postulated a profound affinity between the Greek and German *Geist*. Both for the Fascists and the Nazis, the Phoenicians and Carthage became shorthand for any kind of enemy, synonyms for aliens who needed to be obliterated.

A Multilingual Habsburg Canon

Reading modernist literature requires a stereoscopic vision, a lens that allows us to bring into focus the tensions between the nation and the nonnational, recognize alternative identity narratives, and record almost forgotten paradigms of cultural belonging. Literary Trieste offers a privileged perspective into the complex relationships between aesthetics and politics, historical modernity and literary modernism, exposing the signals of an early crisis of nationhood as a paradigm of self-definition in an age of triumphant nationalism. The fiction written in and around the Adriatic city represents an invitation to read Central European literature anew. The shared Habsburg literary culture of the authors discussed in this book extends well beyond the chronological demarcation of the first postwar period. We usually see in the First World War a moment of rupture with past cultural and political affiliations, but I would like to emphasize the continuity between the antebellum and the postwar literature associated with Trieste, in which competing forms of allegiance were not suddenly abandoned but became *topoi* of a modernist sensibility that extends over the First World War, the conventionally agreed-upon watershed moment. The timespan of the texts I treat in the following pages only partially overlaps with the periodization that distinguishes early, high, and late European modernism.

The multilingual Habsburg literary canon that this book presents here with the works written by Däubler, Kosovel, Musil, Svevo, and Joyce provides the proper context for a comparative study of the interconnecting trajectories of cultural-political narratives as well as linguistic,

---

[76] Chapoutot argues that Cato the Elder's famous phrase *Delenda est Carthago* possessed as much racial as historical meaning. Rome was able to destroy a Phoenician civilization with both African and Asian roots, which could have smothered a nascent Western civilization in the cradle if Hannibal had managed to sack Rome. Chapoutot, *Greeks, Romans*, 295.

rhetorical, and stylistic devices of a literary Europeanism. The authors that constitute this Habsburg culture each articulate a specific iteration of the literary invention of Europe, a heterogeneous collection of tropes, rhetorical strategies, and textual correspondences that together trace either the parallel developments or the intersections of shared aesthetic projects and political commitments.[77] The stratagems of this cosmopolitan modernism gravitating around Trieste operate within a contact zone and fall into manifold categories: Däubler's poetics of bilingualism, Kosovel's ethics of mediation, Musil's politics of the non-national, Svevo's aesthetics of liminality, and Joyce's ethnolinguistics of myth. Expressed both in their critical writings and literary fiction, these approaches to Europe are governed by the duality of modernist temporalities in which an alternative Phoenician past is summoned to imagine an ever-pending post-national futurity, invested in divining the social and cultural coordinates of a forthcoming body politic.

The modernist classicism that reclaims the Phoenicians as the protagonists of a Habsburg Mediterranean is crucial to their literary invention of Europe. The Phoenicians are sporadically mentioned in Anglo-American modernism—one thinks of the poetry of Hilda Doolittle or Ezra Pound—as enigmatic figures that hail from a proximate but decidedly Eastern Orient. In T. S. Eliot's *The Waste Land*, the fabricated tarot card of the drowned Phoenician Sailor anticipates the mysterious and premature death of Phlebas the Phoenician, with whom the reader is asked to sympathize.[78] In contrast, in this expansive Habsburg literary canon, the ancient maritime population is central to a political imagination that tells the story of a future Europe. The protagonists of this story are the three main characters of Europa, Hannibal, and Zeno. Although all three figures are originally Phoenician, they are adopted to comment on specific Habsburg phenomena. These Habsburg Phoenicians, then, construct a literary invention of Europe that engages in a range of discursive threads. Emanating from Trieste, they intersect with ideas about race and Jewish identity; embody the literary strategies

---

[77] This modernist invention of Europe presents affinities with what Rebecca Walkowitz defines as a cosmopolitan style (i.e., a set of aesthetic strategies of literary modernism relevant to projects of antiracism and decolonization). She has shown how modernists adapted their narrative strategies for a number of political enterprises, describing cosmopolitanism in terms of "multiple or flexible *attachments* to more than one nation or community, resisting conceptions of allegiance that presuppose consistency and uncritical enthusiasm; and a vernacular or popular tradition that values the risks of social deviance and the resources of consumer culture and urban mobility." *Cosmopolitan Style: Modernism beyond the Nation* (New York: Columbia University Press, 2006), 9.

[78] T. S. Eliot, *The Complete Plays and Poems, 1909–1950* (New York: Harcourt Brace, 1950), 38–47.

that denounce the colonial dynamics of Austrian representations of non-German populations in the Empire; record the nonnational, multicultural, and polyglot patriotism of a dwindling Austrian way of life; and deploy strategies of resistance in the face of nationalist marginalization.

The chapters in this book offer different perspectives, revealing the fundamentally prismatic quality of Trieste, a city that refracted and put into sharper relief whatever literary, cultural, or political agendas were projected onto it. Constantly designated to encapsulate the quintessential core of their identities and beliefs, different groups claimed ownership over Trieste, namely nationalists and cosmopolitans, Austrians, Italian, Slovenes, different religious groups, as well as any combination of them. Taken together, however, these chapters tell us something about Trieste as a whole. What holds together the fragments of this ideological mosaic is that all groups had to contend with the Habsburg legacy of the nonnational. In other words, the modern literary history of Trieste calls into question the supremacy of national metanarratives, making previously unreadable nonnational accounts finally legible.

Trieste's comparative cosmopolitanisms posit a literary hermeneutics that disrupts and tests the limits of our national literary histories, suggesting that the nation may not always be the most suitable framework to read and understand literature.[79] The authors described in this book appear as obstinate and uncooperative misfits in national histories. With its invitation to consider Trieste in the realm of Austrian Studies, the chapter on Musil sets the tone for disciplinary relocations and the flexibility of established categories, welcoming Trieste to an additional and complementary home. The Svevo chapter, then, does much to unhinge Trieste from an Italian national tradition, leaving the author in a deterritorialized limbo of sorts. Joyce, who simultaneously inhabits different literary spaces, is in many ways also a Triestine writer, whose Habsburg Italianness determined many of his beliefs about how to be Irish. As much as Trieste has been the home for anyone who claims it as such, the city also constantly works to dislodge domesticated borders, pointing to many a methodological inadequacy when we confine authors behind bolted gates.

It may be tempting to read *Modernism in Trieste* as a book that presents the literary modernisms growing out of the Habsburg Empire as the threshold between an old and a new Europe, as the record of a transition from nonnational to militantly one-dimensional national allegiances. The resilience of a nonnational sense of belonging in an age of rampant nationalism, however, suggests a different story. The

---

[79] Dainotto, *Place*, 8.

chapters that follow will show how these authors rethink the parameters of modernity, the allegedly uncontested hegemony of the nation, and the idea of Europe. This book does not trace the story of a linear evolution, of an inescapable progression toward a superseding modern but rather relays the fraught ontology of modernity in its arena of contested identity politics. By envisioning a nonnational Europe, the aesthetic projects of these authors show how the nation was already undergoing an intrinsic and structural crisis at the time of its consolidation. In other words, for these authors the category of the modern posed an existential challenge to the normativity of the nation. Their aesthetic projects disanchor Europe from its national moorings and, by making the Phoenician Mediterranean constitutive of a polycentric and polycratic community, allow for Europe's own repressed and disavowed Afro-Semitic alterity to emerge. Their literary texts forcefully beg to reconsider and redefine what Europe is or may become, calling into question the validity of a longstanding intellectual tradition that excluded the Mediterranean South from a northern-based and racially white European identity. This Mediterranean Europe of local cosmopolitanisms is fundamentally incompatible with and stubbornly impervious to the philosophy of the nation advanced by Herder and Fichte in which a native language was the distinctive attribute of a monolingual nationhood. For the authors discussed in this book, Trieste remained an outlier against the background of nineteenth-century ideas of the nation that often overlapped with dreams of social and political emancipation in postimperial Europe. They expose the exclusionary nature of the nation as an utterly inadequate model not only for the local situation of Trieste but also for Europe in general. The ethos of this future intercultural and multilingual community is not merely postcolonial but also fundamentally anti-colonial in its rejection of imperial drives. If the nation is indeed the imagined community that Benedict Anderson described, the national paradigm in Europe, squeezed between what we have considered a pre-national past and the futuristic Habermasian post-national geography, would be a relatively brief historical parenthesis in a world that is fundamentally nonnational. It may be premature to think of a Europe that is not organized around national principles, but the very nature of fiction alerts us to alternative possibilities and offers to provide insights from approaches that, however unsuccessful, are worth exploring. The literary modernism of Musil, Svevo, and Joyce thus unsettles the affiliation between modernity and the nation with its urgency to envision different horizons and to reimagine the parameters of future community building. With the cyclical resurgence of an acute refugee crisis in the Mediterranean and the rise of xenophobic nationalism, their texts remain a powerful reminder of the possibilities that a united Europe beyond the nation-state could afford.

Europe's alternative Phoenician genealogy is a common thread that runs through the following chapters. Chapter 1, "The Adriatic Sea as a Phoenician Mediterranean, 1870–1925," first delineates a profile of the Phoenicians, of whom relatively little is known if not from Greek and Roman sources who mention them with unmistakable bias. It then proceeds to recover the writings of local antiquarians, archaeologists, and ancient historians who, in the second half of the nineteenth century, started publishing in the volumes of the magazine *Archeografo triestino* their studies about the Phoenician presence on the northern Adriatic shores. The evidence of Phoenician presence in the Bay of Trieste and contacts with the Istrian peninsula were mixed with folk etymologies and local legends that claimed that the city was founded by a Phoenician hero. The work of these local historians did not remain unnoticed. Sigmund Freud came in contact with these debates during a brief research leave in Trieste, where he was studying marine biology. The possibility of a Phoenician origin of Trieste, and hence a Semitic genealogy of the most important Habsburg port, very much resonated with Freud, who had been cultivating a strong identification with the Punic general Hannibal since his childhood. The chapter also emphasizes how this Triestine antiquarianism constituted the intellectual background against which a modernist classicism destigmatized the role of the Phoenicians in the Western tradition. Emblematic for this reassessment is the lyrical Expressionism of Däubler, who saw himself as the German poet of the Mediterranean. His retelling of the rape of the Phoenician maiden Europa in his poem *Paean and Dithyramb* exploits the ancient political genesis of the tale, crafting the abduction into a foundational myth for what he considered a syncretic European civilization. Similarly, Kosovel projects his collection of avant-garde poetry *The Golden Boat* onto the Mediterranean. Via the Slavic legend of the "beautiful Vida," the Slovene-speaking Triestine poet turns to the trope of an abducted maiden in the Mediterranean in order to lament the destruction of Europe.

Chapter 2, "A Mediterranean Monarchy: Robert Musil and the Politics of Nonnational Loyalty, 1913–1943," begins by tracing the late Habsburg infatuation with the Adriatic Sea. We tend to think of the Habsburg Empire as a continental state in Central Europe, where images of stony Alpine landscapes and thick forests join the iconography of the Danube flowing through the traditional Crown Lands. Yet, in the course of the second half of the nineteenth century, the Austrian Littoral (*Österreichisches Küstenland*) started to vigorously enter the popular cultural imagination. This was in part due to an easy but strategically insignificant victory in the naval battle of Lissa/Vis against Italy in 1866. The Austrian loss of Venice after Lissa reinforced the function of Trieste as the Habsburg gateway to the Mediterranean. Austria's

Imperial Navy, whose language of command was Italian until 1848, was never a strong player on the international stage. Although—and perhaps because—dreams of a powerful fleet never fully materialized, the fantasy of a Habsburg Mediterranean became a central rhetorical strategy in the Empire's self-representation. The 1913 Adriatic Exhibition, held in the Vienna Prater, celebrated the colonial holdings of the Dual Monarchy, staking a powerful claim to the Adriatic as a sphere of Austrian influence. It is within this Austro-Mediterranean context that this chapter reconstructs Musil's fashioning of Trieste as a quintessential Habsburg metropolis. Musil's connection to Trieste ran deep in his life and work, to the extent that he once was even mistaken for a Triestine author.[80] Yet, it was in the course of his work as editor for the warfront newspaper *Die Soldaten-Zeitung* that Musil came to understand that the political vicissitudes of the Adriatic city were a privileged temperature gauge for the Empire at large. He incorporated these insights into his novel *The Man without Qualities*, where the crisis of the traditional dynastic loyalty of Trieste marks the beginning of the end for the Dual Monarchy. Musil's narrator presents a kaleidoscopic gallery of major figures and minor characters who are often distrustful of national affiliations. One of them, the industrialist Arnheim, is highly skilled at the art of manipulation and embodies many a Phoenician wickedness. With Arnheim's "Phoenician skull" the narrator seizes the opportunity to comment on the structural racism of pseudoscientific disciplines like phrenology and modern imperial discourses that saw Phoenician mercantilism as a forerunner of modern European capitalism.

Similar considerations of capitalist enterprise within a unified European economy animate the writings of Italo Svevo. Chapter 3, "Trojan Trieste: Italo Svevo and the Aesthetics of Austro-Italian Liminality, 1890–1923," considers Svevo's essay "On the Theory of Peace" in relation to German-speaking theorists such as Walther Schücking and Alfred Hermann Fried. The essay survives as an unpublished fragment that nonetheless offers insights into a political position that for Svevo

---

[80] In a 1907 review of *The Confusions of Young Törleß*, the reviewer Hermann Rehlander makes an extremely curious but no less intriguing blunder. He describes Musil as "ein geschulter Seelenforscher, der sich aus den Büchern der Irrenärzte und der Philosophen über die Verschlingungen des ungelenken Geschlechtslebens aufgeklärt hat." Surprisingly, he also indicates Trieste as Musil's hometown, calling him "ein Triester Jüngling." Given the fragmentary reconstructions of Musil's biography relative to these years, one can only speculate about the reasons that prompted the reviewer's blunder of positing a Triestine Musil. Robert Musil, *Klagenfurter Ausgabe: kommentierte Edition sämtlicher Werke, Briefe und nachgelassener Schriften; mit den Transkriptionen und Faksimiles aller Handschriften*, eds. Walter Fanta, Klaus Amann, and Karl Corino (Klagenfurt: Drava, 2009), KA/Kommentare und Apparate/Kontexte/Zeitgenössische Rezensionen.

became increasingly difficult to assert in public in the aftermath of the First World War. In the text, he suggests that a durable peace in Europe can only be achieved with the creation of a borderless continental trading space where people and goods are free to circulate. Farsighted in his pronouncements, Svevo anticipates in the text the creation of the European Single Market. He echoes Nietzsche when he argues that this movement will continue to shape an ethnically and culturally hybrid European population. Writing like a true Habsburg intellectual, Svevo makes the case against national affiliations in Europe. Svevo never published his essay, as he started to work on the drafting of *Zeno's Conscience*. My interpretation of Svevo's novel proposes that the origin of the protagonist's name is not the Greek philosopher Zeno of Elea, as commonly assumed, but the Phoenician Zeno of Citium, founder of Stoic cosmopolitanism. Like Musil's Arnheim, Svevo's Zeno engages in duplicitous financial transactions, but both characters ultimately owe much of their role as Phoenician protagonists of a modern Europe to Freud's Hannibal fantasy. My reading shows Svevo's distance from Triestine Irredentism and portrays the author as an Austrian Jew writing in an imperfect Italian. The author stages in *Zeno's Conscience* a Trojan Trieste in which the narrator undermines Italian cultural nationalism and the city's prewar longing for unification with Italy. I argue that a writer with multiple cultural allegiances such as Svevo does much to unsettle well-trodden terrains of the Italian literary tradition. The chapter places him in an interstitial position on an ideal map of European literature: Italian modernism after all starts, among other less surprising places, in Austria.[81]

Chapter 4, "Habsburg Hybrid: James Joyce and the Ethnolinguistics of Hiberno-Punic Mythography, 1904–1939," argues that Austrian Trieste exerted such a profound and abiding influence on Joyce that this multilingual literary canon is an entirely appropriate and complementary home for the Irish author. In his 1907 lecture, "Ireland: Island of Saints and Sages," while speaking about Irish history and culture, Joyce also engages with the debates about cultural and national allegiances in Habsburg Trieste. The lecture starts for Joyce an ongoing thought process that becomes a thematic thread running through his works and leading up to *Ulysses*, where the protagonist Bloom, of Austro-Hungarian descent and modeled after Svevo, resorts to a Habsburg *Landespatriotismus* when prompted to define the "nation."

---

[81] It is hard to disagree with Mario Lavagetto who provocatively stated, "If somebody wanted or had to tell the story of Italian literature of the twentieth century, they could begin their story with Austria, more precisely with Trieste." *La gallina di Saba* (Turin: Einaudi, 1974), 237. My translation.

Embedded in a traditional Austrian political philosophy, Bloom's famous response should therefore not be mistaken as the vague and flustered reaction of a naïve character. *Finnegans Wake*, written and published long after Joyce left Trieste, is the book that in many ways is inextricably linked to the author's sojourn in the Habsburg metropole. The text's literary language echoes the multilingualism of Trieste and furthermore posits a splintered cross-cultural epistemology through which the reader is invited to read human history from different perspectives. While *Ulysses* is unmistakably already a tale of two cities, the *Wake* achieves this ethnolinguistic fragmentation via its constantly shifting poetic topographies, mapped onto a world in which it is impossible to distinguish whether Joyce writes about Dublin or Trieste, or whether a particular character is Irish, Phoenician, or both. Irish nationhood is seen in its fleeting and temporary contingency, the product of historical transience. Joyce, like Däubler before him, rewrites the rape of Europa but places the abduction in the context of a fictional prehistory of Ireland, validating the conjectures of many Celtic Revivalists who believed in a Phoenician origin of the Irish. This Phoenician ancestry constitutes the narrative architecture that organizes the disjointed development of the myriad labyrinthine storylines and subplots, while gesturing toward a transference of the origins of Ireland, not British and Atlantic anymore, but instead European and Mediterranean.

Finally, in the conclusion of the book, "The Danube Flows into the Mediterranean," I extend the trajectory of these chapters to briefly discuss the legacy of these works in Claudio Magris and Jacques Derrida. Their literary and philosophical continuations reflect, respectively, upon the legacy of Austrian literature and the significance of the Europa myth, the ancient story that continues to shape the way we think about the ethics, aesthetics, and politics of Europe.

One The Adriatic Sea as a Phoenician Mediterranean, 1870–1925

In 1915, the journalist Amy Bernardi published a tourist guidebook of the northern Adriatic littoral, describing the regions of Istria and Dalmatia as idyllic holiday destinations for Italian travelers. Presenting them as contested border areas, Bernardi emphasized the exclusively Italian character of these Adriatic regions.

> Thus all of Istria, less colorful than Dalmatia, but equally threatened by the Slavs of the mountains and the interior, sees its Italianness flourish against the background of the sea. It flourishes growing from the deep roots of imperial Rome and Latin Christianity that here happily followed the sporadic colonizations and incursions of Greeks and Phoenicians. It flourishes manifesting itself in its entirety, as could logically be expected, in Venetian forms and figures because of that unbridled political expansion that between the thirteenth and eighteenth century made the Adriatic a truly Venetian gulf.[1]

In an extended floral metaphor, Bernardi attributes the blossoming of Istria to its deep roots grounded in the Roman Empire and Latin Christianity. Similar to the neighboring Dalmatia, the shoreline of Istria overlooks *Mare Nostrum* and remains threatened by bands of undifferentiated Slavs ominously approaching from the mountains and the

---

[1] "Tutta dunque l'Istria, meno colorita della Dalmazia, ugualmente minacciata dagli Slavi del monte e dell'interno, vede la sua italianità, così, fiorire sul mare. Fiorire dalle radici profonde della romanità imperiale e della cristianità latina succedute ivi felicemente alle sporadiche colonizzazioni e incursioni elleniche e fenicie: fiorire manifestandosi nella sua interezza, com'era logico, in forme e figure veneziane, per quella irrompente forza di espansione politica che fra il decimoterzo secolo e il decimottavo, fece dell'Adriatico, davvero, un golfo veneziano." Amy Bernardi, *L'Istria e la Dalmazia* (Bergamo: Istituto Italiano d'Arti Grafiche, 1915), 65.

hinterland. In asserting ownership over the Mediterranean and describing the region as a solidly Roman province, Bernardi echoes common nationalist arguments that sought to legitimize Italy's claims over the northern Adriatic region and Trieste by means of a classicist historicism that postulated a continuity between antiquity and the modern world.

Bernardi's nationalist cultural geography draws from a textual archive of nineteenth-century literature and historiography. After all, her descriptions were strongly supported by the venerable literary tradition of the Italian *Risorgimento*, which exalted Italy's Roman heritage while postulating a national identity in opposition to a rhetorically constructed Phoenician or Carthaginian alterity. The lyrics of Goffredo Mameli's 1847 "Il Canto degli Italiani," a military march that still serves as the national anthem of Italy, illustrate this tendency to define Italianness against Phoenician antagonists. In the text, a personified Italy finally awakes from a millenarian slumber and proudly girds her head with the helmet of Scipio Africanus, the Roman general who defeated Hannibal in the Battle of Zama. Scipio's success crucially contributed to Roman triumph during the Second Punic War. The military victory was often seen as a defining moment in the history of Rome, now capable of expanding its rule in the Mediterranean Sea.[2] In his famed 1877 poem "Saluto italico," Giosuè Carducci, considered by many of his contemporaries the national poet of Italy, urged his verses of "ancient Italic fashion" to soar to the Gulf of Trieste and greet its Roman ruins, to salute the divine smile of the Adriatic Sea, and to flutter as far as the Istrian city of Pola, proudly displaying its temples to Rome and Caesar.[3] Carducci's ode to the Italian character of Trieste and the Adriatic Sea closes with a final tribute to Joachim Winckelmann, the scholar and art historian of Greco-Roman antiquity who died in Trieste. In the poem, the marmoreal and bellicose glance of Winckelmann's statue stares down a vaguely defined invading foreigner. One can see the ideological construct that would later lead Bernardi to disparage the sporadic Greek and Phoenician colonizations, settlements that in her view did not justify any heritage claims. Her point about other prehistoric communities should not be read as a simple side note; it challenges a widespread, resilient alternative myth of origins that identified the Phoenicians as the earliest identity-shaping settlers in the region.

---

[2] The lines encapsulating the anti-Carthaginian sentiment are: "Fratelli d'Italia / l'Italia si è desta / Dell'elmo di Scipio si è cinta la testa." Goffredo Mameli and Michele Novaro, *Inno di Mameli (Il canto degli italiani)* (Milan: Ricordi, 1948).

[3] In "Saluto Italico" Carducci writes, "Oh al bel mar di Trieste, a i poggi, a gli animi/volate co'l nuovo anno, antichi versi italici ... salutate il divin riso dell'Adria/fin dove Pola i templi ostenta a Roma e a Cesare." Giosuè Carducci, *Tutte le poesie* (Rome: Newton & Compton, 1998), 483.

Various local histories and legends suggested a Phoenician origin for the northern Adriatic seaboard and the city of Trieste despite the survival of ample archeological and architectonic evidence attesting to their Roman character.[4] Today, it is commonly held that the Illyrians, a motley crew of extinct Indo-European tribes, were among the first populations to occupy the northeastern Adriatic region, founding the urban center of Tergeste, the earliest settlement of Trieste. The toponym Tergeste seems to derive from the union of the Venetic root *terg*, meaning "market," with the common suffix *-este* indicating a "place." It is not entirely clear whether these ancient Veneti were in fact Illyrians, an association that has been made in the past. Whatever the case, this Venetic marketplace was absorbed into the Roman orbit in the second century BCE, when Rome conquered the Istrian peninsula subjugating the local populations. Subsequently, the Latin transliteration of the term Tergeste reinterpreted the morphological boundaries of the noun as *ter gesta*, with the meaning of "thrice founded" or "conquered three times," attesting to the difficult process of Romanization of the area.

The Roman origin story was challenged by other accounts of the city's foundation. Next to the Illyrian/Venetic hypothesis, a number of myths and legends compose a wide spectrum of possible origin stories, the most prominent of which imagine early Trieste as a Phoenician settlement. According to Pliny the Elder, the Argonauts returned from their mission to recover the Golden Fleece navigating on the Danube and its tributaries and then entered the Adriatic Sea via the River Timavus, not far from Trieste. The ancient Greek geographer Marcianus of Heraclea added to this story line an intriguing plot twist, namely that one of the Argonauts, the demigod Tergesto decided to settle down, becoming the founder and namesake of the city. In other accounts, Tergesto or Tergesteo is either a Phoenician seafarer struck by the beauty of the Karst landscape, or else a Trojan hero, who settled down in the northern Adriatic after fleeing the fall of Troy.

These legends started to gain currency among the proponents of what one could call the Phoenicianism of nineteenth-century Trieste, intellectuals who were invested in rewriting the origin of the city. An incorrect but widely circulated folk etymology even went so far as to identify the Phoenician term *Tarshish* as the origin of the toponym Tergeste, explaining the linguistic origin of the root as Semitic rather than Latin. I am less interested in the accuracy of these linguistic and ethnographic claims than in the cultural politics governing this pseudo-etymology and the push to destigmatize the Phoenicians in the context of a city pondering its Mediterranean

---

[4] The survival of Roman architecture in Trieste—remains of a temple to Jupiter and Minerva, a theater, and a fairly well preserved Roman Arch—testifies to the long Roman presence in the city.

identity. It is hard to assess whether or not the origin of northern Adriatic settlements was indeed Phoenician. The arguments, however, reveal a great deal about the scholars and antiquarians who made them.

The Phoenicians in Greek and Roman Sources

The Phoenicians do not occupy the same position of cultural prestige that Greek and Roman civilizations enjoy in modern receptions of the ancient Mediterranean, a circumstance that makes their rehabilitation in Habsburg Trieste particularly noteworthy. The Phoenicians were a Western Semitic maritime tribe, related to the ancient Hebrews, skilled in seafaring and famous for their commercial activities in the Mediterranean, where they established, over the course of centuries, a highly organized network of interconnected trading posts and colonies. Already flourishing in the third millennium BCE, the Phoenician homeland was located along the Levantine littoral, a coastal region that is now part of Lebanon, Syria, and Israel. When discussing the Phoenicians, it is useful to keep in mind the particularities of modern historical nomenclature that usually distinguishes between the Canaanite period, the history of Phoenicia proper, and the Punic age that designates the history of the Phoenicians in the western Mediterranean and their most prominent colony Carthage from the sixth century BCE onwards. The end of Phoenician history in the eastern Mediterranean is usually made to coincide with Alexander the Great's conquest of the coastal cities in the Levant in 332 BCE.[5] The Phoenicians referred to themselves as the Canaanites, which is also the terminology modern historians prefer when they discuss their civilization before the collapse of the Bronze Age in the eastern Mediterranean around 1200 BCE. After the social and political reorganization of the region, this population of merchants is known as the Phoenicians, a term that probably derives from the ancient Greek word *phoínikes*, which roughly translates to "the people of the reddish-purple cloth," a reference to their prosperous textile industry that manufactured a widely valued purple dye that they exported. Between the ninth and sixth centuries BCE, the Phoenicians expanded westward, establishing trading posts and colonies in the central and western Mediterranean, in northern Africa, and on the Atlantic coast. Their emporia stretched from major cities in the Levant—Tyre, Sidon, Byblos, and Ugarit—to Kition on Cyprus; Motya, Panormus, and Lilybaeum on Sicily; Nora and Karalis on Sardinia; Melita on Malta;

---

[5] Here I follow the terminology and the periodization suggested by Maria Eugenia Aubet, *The Phoenicians and the West: Politics, Colonies, and Trade* (Cambridge: Cambridge University Press, 2001). Another important and comprehensive guide to Phoenician history and civilization is Sabatino Moscati, ed. *The Phoenicians* (London: I. B. Tauris Publishers, 1999).

and to Gadir (modern-day Cádiz) on the Atlantic coast of the Iberian Peninsula. The most powerful Phoenician colony in the west was obviously Carthage, a major economic and political center that enjoyed greater independence from the Phoenician motherland and that became, together with its allies in northern Africa, Rome's archenemy during the Punic Wars (264–146 BCE).

It is important to note that the Phoenicians did not necessarily perceive themselves as belonging to a coherent or an internally unified and recognizable culture that seamlessly encompassed the inhabitants of these cities. Citing a lack of clear evidence for a general Phoenician patriotism, Josephine Quinn has forcefully argued that the Levantine Phoenicians did not share a common history and group identity in the modern sense, and that the notion of a shared Phoenician heritage only developed in the context of Carthaginian imperial ambitions, as a way of uniting the cities of the Phoenician diaspora in the western Mediterranean.[6] The concept of a Phoenician identity was constructed as a constitutive alterity, a complementary otherness, by Greeks and Romans who defined themselves in opposition to external groups.[7] Even Tyrians and Sidonians used the term to designate a colonial relationship between trading outposts and Levantine mother cities rather than to describe an ethnic identity, thus imposing the category of "Phoenician" unto others rather than making a claim for their own purposes.[8] Phoenicians often cultivated a metropolitan identity, embracing their local urban culture and their commercial activities at sea, defining themselves as Tyrians

---

[6] Josephine Quinn argues in her book *In Search of the Phoenicians* (Princeton, NJ: Princeton University Press, 2018) that the notion of a Phoenician identity was an invention of nineteenth- and twentieth-century Lebanese and Irish nationalists who were looking for a genealogical antecedent that could justify their claims to a modern nation.

[7] Quinn shows how the Roman imperial elites encouraged the notion of Phoenician identity: "Designating Phoenicia as a political region allowed its Roman rulers to administer their imperial territory in an explicitly local framework." Ibid., 147–148.

[8] Ibid., 143. While David Abulafia does not seem to share Quinn's conviction that the Phoenicians as such did not exist in the Levant, he echoes her point about Carthaginian identity politics. Abulafia writes about the infamous child sacrifice practice in Carthage, stating: "Child sacrifice was a way of affirming their identity as servants of Baal, Melqart and the Phoenician pantheon and as Tyrians hundreds of years after their forefathers had migrated from Lebanon to North Africa, Sicily, and Sardinia. So, while the artistic output of the Phoenicians—and particularly of the Carthaginians—may appear lacking in originality, these were people with an overpowering sense of their identity." David Abulafia, *The Great Sea: A Human History of the Mediterranean* (Oxford: Oxford University Press, 2011), 82.

or Sidonians rather than Phoenicians. Maria Eugenia Aubet attributes the lack of a unified Phoenician culture to the physical geography of the Levantine shoreline.[9] The cities along the coastal plain were divided by river valleys and mountainous territories that favored the separate development of individual city-states. In addition, the steep elevations of Mount Lebanon to the west discouraged the growth of extensive agricultural settlements, while the natural harbors on the coast encouraged the inhabitants to look toward the Mediterranean Sea.[10]

In the ancient world, the Phoenicians were known for a number of important accomplishments and contributions. In *The Histories*, Herodotus credits the Phoenicians with the invention of the modern alphabet, which the mythological Cadmus reportedly brought to the Greeks, who then adopted and adapted it for their use. The Phoenician origin of the Greek alphabet became an accepted model, shared also by Pliny the Elder. Whether accurate or not, Herodotus's theory of dissemination points to the Phoenician development of a phonetic writing system in the course of the second millennium BCE in which each letter corresponded to a sound, an important innovation that diverged from the cuneiform writing of the Sumerians and from Egyptian pictographic hieroglyphs. For their writing, the Phoenicians imported considerable amounts of papyrus from Egypt to the port of Byblos, which the Greeks considered an important center of this innovative writing technology. Thanks to the Phoenicians, alphabetic writing spread across a number of ancient Mediterranean cultures.

Skillful and experienced seafarers, the Phoenicians were famous for their masterful shipbuilding, their expertise in navigation techniques, and the construction of ports. They were adept at stellar navigation, a method based on the observation of the position of celestial bodies in the night sky. Their recognized status as a Mediterranean thalassocracy, a technologically advanced sea power knowledgeable in navigation and astronomy, was so widespread that in the ancient world Polaris, the North Star, was known as the Phoenician Star. The ability to orient themselves and plot maritime itineraries following astronomical charts allowed them to navigate far from coastal shores, on open sea, and in the Atlantic Ocean, an achievement that neither Greeks nor Romans, let alone the river-navigating Egyptians could claim. Herodotus famously reported that a Phoenician crew, sponsored by the Egyptian pharaoh Necho II, circumnavigated the African continent in the sixth century BCE. A century later, the Carthaginian Hanno set sail to

---

[9] Aubet, *Phoenicians and the West*, 17.
[10] Quinn calls this outward projection to the sea a "shore-to-ship perspective." Quinn, *Phoenicians*, 66.

explore the western coast of Africa. Accounts of the navigational skills of the Phoenicians also include remarkable tales of northbound sea voyages. Himilco, another Carthaginian explorer, noted in his periplus that he reached as far north as the Irish Sea. Similarly, searching for valuable sources of amber and tin, the Phoenician sailor Pytheas of the Greek colony of Massalia (modern Marseilles) sailed northwards in the fourth century BCE, supposedly circling around the British islands and Ireland. Ancient sources believed in the alleged Phoenician circumnavigation of Africa and Great Britain, which seems to be at least plausible given their nautical capabilities and the quality of their vessels. More importantly, however, we will see how the suggestions of a Phoenician arrival on Ireland's shores will provide a flimsy yet stubborn narrative in seventeenth- and eighteenth-century Irish Orientalist antiquarianism, an important but not exclusive source of Joyce's reception of Phoenicio-Gaelic lore.

Phoenician ships were usually built with the famed wood that grew in the extensive Cedar forests of Mount Lebanon, a mountain range in the ancient Levant. Cedar timber became an important export in the commercial activities of the Phoenicians because of its multiple applications in the ancient Mediterranean. Resistant to decay and insects, Lebanese cedar was a common construction material for temples. In the Bible, King David commissioned the building of his palace with cedars of Lebanon (2 Samuel 5:11), while King Solomon used the prized timber for the Temple in Jerusalem (1 Kings 5:20). The Egyptians, regular trading partners of the Phoenicians, used cedar wood oil and resin in embalming and mummification processes. A literary reference to these Phoenician cedars can be found in the *Epic of Gilgamesh*, when the heroes Gilgamesh and Enkidu embark upon a journey to slay Humbaba, the guardian of the Forest of Cedars, in order to plunder the prized wood. The episode appears as some sort of mythological retelling of a colonial venture, suggesting a political rivalry between eastern Semitic Akkadians and western Semitic Phoenicians.

Central to Phoenician commerce in the ancient Mediterranean was the production of a highly prized purple dye, a resistant cloth colorant extracted from the marine gastropod *Murex brandaris*. The production process of this rare dye was extremely laborious, but the results were a strong and durable tincture that did not fade as easily as other colors. This Phoenician invention became a luxury item in antiquity, appreciated by Greeks and Romans alike. Robes of Tyrian purple, in particular, became a status symbol in imperial Rome and gradually an indication of regality. In addition to signaling wealth and political power, this royal purple was later incorporated in the chromatic symbolism of religious garments and Catholic liturgical colors.

It has become a commonplace to draw attention to the irony that the inventors of alphabetic writing did not leave much written testimony of their rich literature. Of the purportedly extensive tradition of literary works, historical records, technical manuals, and religious and philosophical treaties, only few Phoenician texts survive, as their palace archives and collections of official documents were almost completely lost or destroyed in antiquity. What we know of the Phoenicians therefore stems from secondhand reports, from opinions mediated via indirect accounts and often tinged by a deeply rooted prejudice. The Judeo-Christian tradition saw the biblical Canaanites as rivals of the neighboring tribes of Israel. A fundamental conflict arose when the tribes of Israel converted to monotheism, while the Canaanites refused to abandon the traditions of their polytheist pantheon. Greco-Phoenician and Roman-Punic relations were often characterized by fierce antagonism. The Phoenicians were important competitors of Greek trade. Between the sixth and third centuries BCE, the Phoenicians and Greeks were engaged in a series of wars waged in Sicily, which resulted in Carthaginian hegemony in the west of the island and Greek control in the east. During the Punic Wars, Carthage challenged the expansionist ambitions of Rome in the Mediterranean. When, in the course of the Second Punic War, the formidable Carthaginian general Hannibal collected a number of spectacular military victories on the Italian peninsula, endangering the very existence of Rome, the Romans came to view Carthage as its proverbial archenemy. The tangible threat of Roman annihilation assumed the contours of a traumatic experience, haunting the Roman cultural imagination for centuries to come.[11] As a result of these rivalries, a profoundly engrained prejudice against the Phoenicians spans centuries of Greek and Roman historiography, mythography, and literature.

In the course of their respective linguistic histories, both ancient Greek and Latin developed idiomatic expressions, i.e., fixed and crystallized phrases, to indicate Phoenician wretchedness. These almost proverbial clichés indicate how engrained this anti-Punic sentiment became over time. In *The Republic*, Plato reiterates the opinion that the Phoenicians are materialistic and greedy, determined to accumulate wealth, as opposed to the Greeks who pursue knowledge with their

---

[11] The figure of Hannibal came to be regarded as the quintessential antihero who triggered an existential anxiety in Roman historians and authors. Loyalty to Rome implied an open hatred for Carthage. In *Comedy and the Rise of Rome* (Oxford: Oxford University Press, 2004) Matthew Leigh identifies a "Roman trauma" (45) in the wake of the Second Punic War, asking in the context of Plautus's comedy whether "the fear of slaves in arms or the pain of the Hannibalic disaster [could] ever entirely be repressed" (56).

philosophical investigations. Plato also uses the idiomatic expression "Phoenician tale" by which he meant an artfully crafted and persuasive lie, characterized by a deceptive verisimilitude. Likewise, Posidonius of Rhodes called the origin story of the city of Gadir a "Phoenician lie."[12] The Romans used an idiomatic expression that similarly emphasized Phoenician deception and dishonesty. In his damning description of the Carthaginians and Hannibal, the Roman historian Livy emphasizes their *Punica fides*, an ironic expression in which "Punic trustworthiness" indicated proverbial disloyalty and treachery. During the early imperial period of Rome, the phrase *Punica fides* was synonymous with the highest degree of dishonesty.

The prejudicial sentiments intrinsic in these linguistic expressions were fueled by a history of ambivalence toward the Phoenicians, frequently admired and begrudged for their wealth and technological advances and often viewed with suspicion. Archaic Greek sources already considered the Phoenicians uncultured barbarians, untrustworthy and avaricious merchants, ready to deceive their trading partners whenever the opportunity arose. This prejudice emerges as early as the eighth century BCE. In Homer's *Odyssey*, the Phoenicians are described as skilled artisans and sailors, adept at the subtle art of fabricating falsehoods, and as ruthless and deceitful traders.[13] Centuries later, Plutarch describes the Carthaginians as unrefined and capricious, submissive toward their overlords, but fiercely despotic toward their subalterns. Appian echoes Plutarch's unflattering portrayal, depicting the Phoenicians as fickle, and emphasizing their great arrogance and brutality. An entire tradition of Roman intellectuals and historians, from Cato to Livy and Juvenal to Horace, also emphasizes Phoenician dishonor. This reputation was earned, in the opinion of these commentators. Phoenicians, they believed, did not keep their word and broke diplomatic treaties.[14] The chauvinism of Roman political propaganda

---

[12] For the Greek expression of the "Phoenician tale," see Benjamin Isaac, *The Invention of Racism in Classical Antiquity* (Princeton, NJ: Princeton University Press, 2014), 326; and Quinn, *Phoenicians*, 53–54.

[13] The representation of Phoenicians in Homer is complex and ambiguous, since they are also depicted in a favorable light. In *The Raft of Odysseus: The Ethnographic Imagination of Homer's Odyssey* (Oxford: Oxford University Press, 2001) Carol Dougherty argues, among others, that the Phaeacians are Homer's literary representation of the Phoenicians. The idealized Phaeacians, mysterious seafarers who take Odysseus back to Ithaca on self-steering ships, "work together with the demonized Phoenicians to articulate the range of possible modes of exchange available in the world of the *Odyssey*" (120).

[14] Isaac traces a history of the expression including Cicero and Sallust, who employs the expression "Punica fides" in a "clearly proverbial sense." Isaac, *Invention of Racism*, 329.

during and after the Punic Wars stressed with great hyperbole what was seen as a Phoenician natural inclination for conceit, effeminacy, and merciless cruelty, exemplified by the Carthaginian practice of human and child sacrifice. One other negative stereotype for the Carthaginians can be found in Plautus' comedy *Poenulus* (*The Little Phoenician*) where, between the title character's effeminate mannerisms and innuendos of incest, the author's ridicule is also aimed at the Carthaginian facility with foreign languages, a multilingualism perceived as suspicious and thus subject to chauvinist vilification. The Roman playwright, however, also stages sympathetic Carthaginian characters, occasionally taking aim at the widespread Phoenician stereotypes he himself employs. In an exceptionally rare occurrence for Roman literature, his protagonist Hanno delivers a speech in the Punic dialect.[15]

A similar challenge to this Roman prejudice can be found in what perhaps remains the most articulate literary illustration of the hostility between Rome and Carthage, namely Vergil's *Aeneid*. By addressing the anti-Punic bias of the imperial period, the Roman poet provides an eloquent picture of the fate of the Phoenicians in classical lore. The scandal of Aeneas's tryst with the powerful Carthaginian queen Dido, ruler of a city that will become the archenemy of Rome, is condensed in an episode of Book 4. A bejeweled Aeneas sportingly dons a mantle of Tyrian purple, while overseeing, like a diligent proprietor, the assiduous construction of the Punic capital. Vergil's rhetorical objective here clearly is to provoke shock and amazement in his Roman audience: Aeneas the righteous, acting under the emasculating influence of a barbarian seductress, becomes an effeminate and uxorious philo-Carthaginian who intends to settle down with foreigner and foe. Vergil writes a fictional prequel to the political enmity between Rome and Carthage when the inconsolable Dido curses future relations between the two cities before committing suicide on an improvised funeral pyre. On his journey in the underworld, in Book 6 of the poem, Aeneas encounters the ghost of the indignant Dido. Apologetically, the Trojan hero tries to explain his reasons to her, but Dido does not deign him worthy of a glance or a response. The once commanding and confident queen, leader of her people, is now reduced to a spectral apparition, to a ghost with eyes cast down who does not speak. One cannot help but see in the muted Dido a powerful symbol of the Phoenicians, a silenced minority whose ghostly presence haunts the classical tradition.

---

[15] Quinn suggests that the presence of the transliterated Punic text suggests a certain Roman familiarity with the language of the Carthaginians. Quinn, *Phoenicians*, 168.

The Phoenicians between Orientalism and Classicism

Throughout the long history of European classicism, the Phoenicians remained a silenced and marginalized culture. In its different disciplines, classicism expressed a profound and explicit veneration for Greek and Roman antiquity, simultaneously cradle and golden age of Western civilization that stretched from the Homeric epics to classical tragedy, Periclean Athens, and imperial Rome. Greek and Roman institutions, art, architecture, and literature were considered a repository of guiding values and principles in aesthetic, artistic, and political realms. From the classicism of the Italian Renaissance to the French dramatist tradition of Corneille and Racine, and from the English Augustan Age of Pope and Swift to the Weimar classicism of Goethe and Schiller, the admired values encapsulated by antiquity included equilibrium and moderation, discipline and restraint, order and proportion. These classicisms often ignored the Phoenicians or, in the case of any mention, inherited from ancient sources a series of prejudices and stereotypes that indexed them as an Oriental Other. Bereft of the philosophical acumen of the Greeks and the military strength of the Romans, the Phoenicians allegedly also lacked artistic genius and moral principles in their business dealings and political institutions.[16] The establishment of classical studies as an academic discipline in the nineteenth century uncritically reflected these negative attitudes, vehemently denying that Phoenicians, or Egyptians for that matter, had exerted any influence whatsoever on the Greco-Roman world.[17] Greek and Roman blood and soil were imagined as uncontaminated.[18] No cultural or religious syncretism, let alone intermarriage or miscegenation, could taint the image of Greek and Roman antiquity in which these Levantine Semites were foreign barbarians. Their colonization of the Mediterranean was downplayed as the sporadic establishment of trading posts that never became permanent settlements. Notions of ethnic purity and territorial integrity

---

[16] An exception to this trend is Aristotle's favorable judgement of the Carthaginian constitution, discussed in *The Politics*.

[17] Martin Bernal claims that the classicisms of the nineteenth century that admire Greeks and Romans operated at the explicit exclusion of other ancient Mediterranean cultures such as black Egyptians and Semitic Phoenicians. The rise of classicism was accompanied by racism and anti-Semitism. Martin Bernal, *Black Athena: The Afroasiatic Roots of Classical Civilization*. Vol. 1. (New Brunswick, NJ: Rutgers University Press, 1987), 337–399.

[18] As the historian J. B. Bury put it, "The Phoenicians, doubtless, had marts here and there on coast and island; but there is no reason to think that Canaanites ever made homes for themselves on Greek soil or introduced Semitic blood into the population of Greece." J. B. Bury, *A History of Greece to the Death of Alexander the Great* (London: Macmillan, 1914), 77.

were projected onto the ancient world at the expense of the Phoenicians, navigators who also happened to be intimately related to modern Jews. The image of the Phoenicians that emerged was the result of the rhetorical triangulations of Classicism, Orientalism, and anti-Semitism. Consequently, the Phoenicians seem to have carried very little weight in the invention of national traditions. Theodor Mommsen, for instance, in his widely read *History of Rome* saw Phoenician Carthage as a proto-capitalist administration that, contrary to Western civilizations, lacked the ability to self-govern and the drive for national state building.[19] Nineteenth- and twentieth-century nationalist discourses that identified in ancient Greece and Rome the alleged predecessors of their glory and models for their imperial and colonial enterprises were thus openly hostile to the Phoenicians and Carthaginians.[20]

After centuries of obscurity, scholars across Europe began to learn more about the Phoenicians during the eighteenth and nineteenth centuries. What in part piqued this unprecedented interest was the deciphering of the Phoenician alphabet. Scholars in the seventeenth century had already been aware of the linguistic affinities between Hebrew and Phoenician, later subsumed along with Arabic, Aramaic, and Ethiopic, in the Semitic language family. This assumption was confirmed by the French archeologist Jean-Jacques Barthélemy, who decrypted the Phoenician alphabet in 1758 from a bilingual inscription in Ancient Greek and Punic found in Malta a century earlier. The first manual of the Phoenician language, along with a collection of inscriptions, was then published by the German scholar Wilhelm Gesenius in 1837.

Nevertheless, the beliefs about Phoenician inferiority persisted. In 1860, Ernest Renan, the prominent intellectual and one of the founders of Phoenician Studies in France, embarked upon an archeological mission to Lebanon, where he discovered more Phoenician inscriptions, which he published in 1864 in *Phoenician Expedition* (*Mission de Phénicie*). Trained as a philologist, Renan's arguments about the Phoenicians started with consideration about Semitic linguistics. According to Renan, the syntactical poverty of Semitic languages and lack of explicit conjunctions was indicative of a general lack of mental discipline, which made the minds of the Phoenicians incapable of formulating scientific inquiries, mathematical abstractions, or metaphysical philosophy. In

---

[19] Theodor Mommsen, *Römische Geschichte*. Bd. 1 (Berlin: Weidmann, 1861), 479–491.
[20] A short-lived English attitude toward the Phoenician is a notable exception to this general trend. George Rawlinson, like many other Victorians, cultivated a positive image of the Phoenicians as dutiful merchants and good seafarers, an image that played into the dreams of imperial grandeur spearheaded by the British Navy. *History of Phoenicia* (London: Longman, 1889).

his famous speech, "What Is a Nation," Renan posited that Greeks and Romans were the forerunners of modern nations but not the intellectually challenged Phoenicians. The simplicity of the Semitic mind was more inclined to develop religious spirituality, according to Renan, which explained the rise of Jewish monotheism. The 1859 archeological excavations of Carthage, conducted by Charles E. Beulé, intensified the interest in the Phoenicians, decades before modernist classicism received its decisive impulse with Heinrich Schliemann's excavation of Troy in 1871 and Arthur Evans's work in Mycenae and Minoan Crete in the early 1900s.

Gustave Flaubert, already influenced by the writings of Renan, became fascinated with the excavations of Carthage and decided to visit the site, as research for his successful and influential novel *Salammbô*, published in 1862, three years after the dig began. Published during the heyday of French realism, Flaubert's historical novel is set in Carthage, shortly after the end of the First Punic War. Two strands of prejudice come together in the novel: inherited prejudices from Greek and Roman sources along with contemporary political discourses about the French nation seen as the heir of Rome. Flaubert displays an impressive knowledge of Phoenician and Carthaginian history and archeology but ultimately deploys a rhetorical arsenal of Orientalist stereotypes that depicts the Phoenicians as barbarians.[21] Famous are the scenes of the initial revolting feast at the palace of Hamilcar, a feast that served the exotic Punic cuisine; the episode of the child sacrifice to Moloch, a scene that causes even the rebellious mercenaries at war with Carthage to watch aghast, in utter horror of Carthaginian barbarism; or the graphic sadism in the episode of the public torture of Mâtho, black leader of the mercenary uprising. The voluptuous Salammbô, fictional sister of a young Hannibal, is explicitly described as the embodiment of Carthage itself, a feminized and sexualized, exotic Other. Her rise and fall parallels the fate of the entire city. Flaubert implicitly compares this state of affairs with French bourgeois society and the French nation. He constructs dichotomies that oppose French honor to the diplomatic and political opportunism in the shifting alliances with the mercenaries, French monolingualism to the multicultural and polyglot motley crew of wildly assorted soldiers for hire, and French bourgeois sobriety to Carthage's wild and opulent decadence, unbridled passions, and trivial superstitions. The anti-Phoenician slant of *Salammbô* was very successful in Europe. Giovanni Pastrone's 1914 silent film *Cabiria*, a widely acclaimed film set during the Second Punic War, was indebted

---

[21] For the relationship between Classicism and Orientalism in perceptions of the Phoenicians, see van Dommelen, "Punic identities."

to Flaubert's novel. Gabriele D'Annunzio wrote the screenplay for the movie, as well as some of the intertitles. The movie trafficked in the same stereotypes about Phoenicians that had circulated for centuries. In the meantime, however, a contrary movement had arisen not long before in Trieste, one that sought to redeem the beleaguered Phoenicians, offering them a more respectable place in the history of antiquity.

Phoenicianism in Trieste

Generally open to intellectual currents in Europe, Trieste became in the course of the second half of the nineteenth century particularly receptive to the innovations represented by this continued scholarly interest in the Phoenicians. At the time a growing number of intellectuals engaged in a more sustained study of local history, focusing mainly on Roman antiquity in Trieste and the Istrian peninsula. These researchers were often engaged and dedicated dilettantes who were highly cultured but lacked any formal education in diachronic linguistics, archeology, or ancient history. The most important figure was undoubtedly Domenico Rossetti (1774–1842), a lawyer by training and founder in 1810 of the *Società di Minerva*, a very influential local historical society that was an intellectual trendsetter in the city, shaping public debates and informing general opinions.[22] Starting in 1829, the *Minerva* started publishing the *Archeografo triestino*, a journal that made research about prehistoric Trieste, Friuli, and Istria available to a wider audience. As the name of the journal implies, the publications were aimed at "writing the origins" of Trieste and its surroundings. A friend and close collaborator of Rossetti was Pietro Kandler (1804–1872), also a lawyer and self-made layman historian and archeologist of sorts who published mainly on the Istrian peninsula. He was rather successful in his site visits around the region and ended up briefly cooperating with Theodor Mommsen. Neither Rossetti nor Kandler conceived of their work as a means to fuel any Italian nationalist agenda, but they supported the development of Italian culture within Habsburg Austria. For all their enthusiasm for Adriatic antiquity, they insisted that the ancient material cultures they observed were vestiges of the Roman presence in the region, even at a time when more rigorous archeologists recognized that many prehistoric sites were in fact older fortified structures that

---

[22] Daša Ličen offers an excellent overview of the organization's historical evolution, showing how "the society played a solid public role" and how "it should also be understood as an opinion-making organization with broader importance on the urban scene in Trieste" (36–37). See Daša Ličen, "The Vagaries of Identification in the *Società di Minerva* in Trieste (1810–1916)," *Traditiones* 46, no. 1–2 (2017), 35–54. doi: 10.3986/Traditio2017460403.

predated the arrival of the Romans.[23] Outside the Greco-Roman world, their knowledge and assumptions about the prehistoric Mediterranean were shaky at best. Kandler, in particular, believed that ancient populations as diverse as Celts, Gauls, Veneti, Liburnians, and Phoenicians were all descendants of the same ethnolinguistic family.[24] Still, both were open to accepting evidence suggesting a more heterogeneous composition of the ancient Adriatic region. Today both are recognized for their attention to the regional specificity of the earliest Adriatic settlements. This is especially true in light of later developments and a nationalist centralization in Adriatic archeology during the Fascist regime that sponsored the exclusive study of Roman architecture at the expense of local prehistory.

Renan and Flaubert's writings about the Phoenicians spread in Europe in the mid-1860s, and the development of a distinctly pronounced Triestine Phoenicianism followed suit, beginning some years later, in 1870. It is important to note that the person who sparked this Phoenicio-centrism was not an amateur, but a scholar of Semitic languages. Wilhelm Eisenstädter (1844–1902) was a professor who had recently moved from Vienna to Trieste. His main works included his doctoral thesis *Saadja's Arabischer Midrash zu den zehn Geboten*, published in Vienna in 1868. In 1870, he published, with the Italianized form of his name, Guglielmo Eisenstädter, *Le scomparse dieci tribù d'Israele* in Italian. In the same year, he also published in the daily newspaper *L'Osservatore triestino* (*The Trieste Observer*) an article that was destined to exert an important influence on the Triestine intellectual elite. Eisenstädter was the first to suggest a Phoenician etymology of the toponym Tergeste, arguing that the word was a corruption of the Phoenician term *Tarshish*, which he interpreted to mean "delight of the traveler."[25] The ramifications of this glottological assumption were manifold. It supported his argument that ancient Phoenician navigators not only reached the northern Adriatic habitually but that they also appreciated the harbor of Trieste as a safe haven, where they could easily dock their vessels, disembark to gather provisions, and eventually establish a thriving community. The hypothesis offered scholarly validation to popular legends that told the story of the Phoenician founder Tergesteo, who

---

[23] Ara and Magris are quite generous in their assessment of the work of Rossetti and Kandler, praising their antiquarianism as characterized by constant philological and archeological scruple. Ara and Magris, *Trieste*, 23.

[24] Pietro Kandler, letter of January 10, 1870. See *Il Carteggio Pietro Kandler–Tomaso Luciani (1843–1871)*, ed. Giovanni Radossi (Rovigno: Centro di Ricerche Storiche, 2014), 312.

[25] Guglielmo Eisenstädter, "L'antichissima Trieste ed i fenici," *L'Osservatore triestino* 82 (April, 12, 1870), 653–654.

had settled on the shores of the Bay of Trieste. This etymological proposition was quite radical as it suggested new and different roots for Trieste, cutting at the core of the ideological framework of many of Eisenstädter's colleagues. Part of an attempt to identify the elusive location of the biblical city of Tarshish, Eisenstädter's bold Phoenicianism amounted to an unapologetically revisionist reinterpretation of Trieste as Phoenician and not Roman, as Semitic and not Latin. The context of these claims helps to put this Triestine Phoenicianism in perspective. Eisenstädter suggested this in a widely read newspaper, and not in a scholarly journal, which helped to popularize his linguistic hypothesis. In addition, *L'Osservatore triestino* was unabashedly pro-Austrian and was often considered the unofficial mouthpiece of the imperial government in Trieste. This is not to suggest that the article was already part of a sustained political campaign to promote the image of a Habsburg Mediterranean. A Phoenician origin, however, certainly aligned with the Austrian effort to cut the rhetorical supply chain of those Triestines who insisted on a Roman, and by proxy Italian, foundation of the city.

From the standpoint of diachronic linguistics, Eisenstädter's etymology appears rather questionable, but his suggestion gained traction among antiquarians while it was, for the time being, debated in academic circles. The biggest endorsement came from Pietro Kandler, who publicly praised Eisenstädter as an insightful Orientalist. While popular with Italian intellectuals, the reception of Eisenstädter's etymology was less favorable among Slovenian scholars in Trieste. In his history of Trieste and its surroundings, Josip Godina-Verdéljski emphasized the long and established presence of Slavic-speaking populations in the area, expressing his outright rejection of Eisenstädter's ethnolinguistic hypothesis.[26] He first dismisses Kandler's well-known belief in a Thracian origin as a hilarious blunder, calling Eisenstädter's Phoenician lineage equally comical. Godina-Verdéljski exposes Kandler's contradictory statements, wondering how his acceptance of a Thracian derivation squares with Eisenstädter's postulation of a Phoenician origin of the term Tergeste.

Despite such criticisms, over the next two decades many intellectuals either accepted this Phoenician origin for Trieste and its environs or, when not completely convinced of its validity, at least regarded it as a plausible hypothesis that perhaps simply needed further substantiation. The pages of the *Archeografo triestino* registered a robust and prolonged

---

[26] Josip Godina-Verdéljski, *Opis in zgodovina Tersta in njegove okolice z uverstitvijo kratkega geografičnega in zgodovinskega pregléda starih in sadanjih slavjanov* (Trieste, 1872), 279. I would like to thank Daša Ličen for her generous assistance with nineteenth-century Slovene.

exchange about Phoenician settlements in the region. Figures such as Bernardo Benussi, Emilio Frauer, and Pietro Tomasin published articles about ancient history, paleography, and etymology related to the matter. Among the many interlocutors in this discussion, the prominent archeologist Pietro Pervanoglù (1833–1894) often attempted to demonstrate a pervasive prehistoric Phoenician presence in the northern Adriatic, a presence that so far had neither been theorized nor corroborated by archeological evidence with such insistence. Pervanoglù was born in Trieste of Greek parents and lived in Greece where he taught archeology at the university. In 1867, he returned to Trieste, where he became a collaborator of the *Archeografo*. In the course of the 1870s and 1880s, Pervanoglù made a number of significant assertions that reconceptualized the Adriatic Sea as a Phoenician Mediterranean, arguing among other things that the Semitic seafarers introduced Bronze Age culture in the northern Adriatic seaboard. Pervanoglù disputed the notion that the Phoenicians colonized the Adriatic only sporadically, endeavoring to demonstrate that they navigated as far north as the Adriatic to fish shellfish for the production of their famed purple dye. This assessment was validated by the presence, in Roman times, of a purple dye factory on the Istrian coast. According to Pervanoglù, every identifiable navigational pattern in the prehistoric Mediterranean could be traced back to the Phoenicians, who colonized the Mediterranean basin in its entirety before Greeks and Romans developed their civilizations.[27] Familiar place names such as *Adria* and *Italia* were, in his opinion, of Phoenician etymology. Weaving together a mythological historicism, a misplaced confidence in ancient historians, and etymologies of dubious validity, Pervanoglù attempted to prove that the Illyrians, original inhabitants of Istria and Dalmatia, were in fact of Phoenician descent. He then followed Eisenstädter's opinion when he claimed, combining assumptions derived from the fields of paleoethnology and ethnolinguistics, that the ancient settlement of Tergeste was undoubtedly Phoenician. These outlandish theories were as methodologically flawed as they were successful. The Phoenician origin of Trieste did not take hold in academic studies, but it cast a long shadow in popular cultural histories of the city, where it occupies a prominent position among folk tales and legends.

The debates about the Phoenician origin of Trieste did not escape a young and promising medical student of anatomy, physiology, and

---

[27] Pietro Pervanoglù, "Corcira nelle attinenze con la colonizzazione delle coste del Mare Adriatico," *Archeografo triestino* 11, no. 3–4 (1885): 344–359. https://www.google.com/books/edition/L_Archeografo_triestino/Zw8vAAAAYAAJ?hl=en&gbpv=0.

applied zoology who spent a month in the Adriatic city in the summer of 1876. He had just won a competitive scholarship from the University of Vienna, thanks to which he was able to embark upon his first major research project. This nineteen-year-old student received a research grant to study male reproductive organs in eels at the Institute of Marine Zoology in Trieste. He lived three blocks from the harbor, and every morning he went to purchase eels from the fishermen who brought in their catch from the previous night. His name was Sigmund Freud.

"Here I Am in Tergeste": The Fantasies of a Phoenician Freud

By the time Freud arrived in Trieste, Eisenstädter's bold hypothesis had already gained in popularity, engaging the city in a vigorous public debate. The validation of a Phoenician origin of Trieste, which attributed to a Semitic people a foundational role in Austrian history, suggested to the young Freud a different way of thinking about his own Jewishness.[28] Like many of his contemporaries, Freud conflated Semitic populations, growing up in a time in which talk of the Phoenicians was often code for all things Jewish. Freud quickly grew fascinated with Trieste. How could he not? This was his first major sojourn away from home. The city was a Habsburg metropole, familiar enough for the Viennese youth, but it was also a Mediterranean port, on whose streets and quays beautiful women were promenading. Besides, the city was apparently founded by a Phoenician sailor, showing to the world what ancient Levantines could accomplish. This appealed to the teenage Freud, eagerly on the lookout for Semitic role models since his childhood. Biographies of Freud generally overlook his brief stay in Trieste and attribute to his experience the status of juvenile impressions that would not bear much weight in the later development of his work. Yet, Freud's research mission in the Adriatic city was, for all its brevity, both intensely formative and highly influential. If Rome evoked for Freud childhood memories and the difficult relationship with his father, and Athens offered access to the mythical world of ancient Greece, then Trieste provided Freud with a more nuanced appreciation of classical antiquity, one that encompassed a Semitic genealogy. This would become crucial for his own personal psychoanalytic excavations later, when he returned to his youthful

---

[28] In "Freud in Trieste: Journey to an Ambiguous City," *Psychoanalysis and History* 12, no. 2 (2010): 129–151. doi:10.3366/pah.2010.0002, Laura Gandolfi suggests that the "view of the Adriatic Sea and the proximity to the same waters that washed the shores of Greece, Egypt and, what is today, Israel, was a time of fundamental importance for the young Freud, and would become a frequent metaphor in his future work" (138).

Phoenician fantasy, his identification with Hannibal, in order to posit a self-confident Semitism in *The Interpretation of Dreams*.

In his letters from Trieste, one can already discern Freud's early deliberations on the intersection of art and science, history, and archeology that will exert a significant influence on the progression of his ideas.[29] His research program investigating the elusive reproductive organs of eels laid the groundwork for his future understanding of psychobiological sexuality.[30] Freud's theory of the uncanny also feeds upon an experience in the city, when he was wandering in the unfamiliar streets of Trieste. On a stifling summer afternoon, Freud lost himself and kept returning, as much as he tried to break free from his circular route, to the same street in an unnamed brothel district.[31] In addition, evidently struck by the ancient character of the city, Freud's impressions about Trieste and its surroundings were already informed by his budding interest in archeology. He reports his visit to the city's archeological sites on the very day of his arrival, adding that the Triestine women walking among the ancient ruins looked like "Italian goddesses" to him.[32] In a letter written to Eduard Silberstein on March, 28, 1876, Freud writes, "Here I am in Tergeste," using the ancient name of the city to emphasize his immersion in Triestine antiquity. He then employs its modern name when referring to his daily occupation of dissecting eels in the laboratory and observing women in the streets to whom he refers in terms of urban fauna: "Know then, that Trieste is a very beautiful city and that the beasts are very beautiful beasts."[33] Freud develops a fondness for the Adriatic Sea and the Bay of Trieste, the contours of which he reproduces in a drawing sketch within the letter.

His correspondence shows that Freud perceived the larger metropolitan area of Trieste, including the nearby municipality of Muggia, to

---

[29] Freud visits Trieste in March and April 1876 for a first research trip, and then returns to the Adriatic city from September 2 to October 1 of the same year. For the importance of Freud's research stay in Trieste, see Laurence Simmons, *Freud's Italian Journey* (Amsterdam: Rodopi, 2006).

[30] Ursula Reidel-Schrewe, "Freud's Debut in the Sciences," in *Reading Freud's Reading*, ed. S. L. Gilman, J. Birmele, J. Geller, and V. D. Greenberg (New York: New York University Press, 1993), 1–22.

[31] Freud's account of this uneasiness resurfaces in his essay on "The Uncanny." See Paul Ferris, *Dr. Freud: A Life* (Washington, DC: Counterpoint, 1997), 37 and Laurence Simmons, *Italian Journey*, 67–73.

[32] The letter is dated April 23, 1876. Because of an epistolary game in which Freud and Silberstein impersonate characters from Cervantes, some of these letters are written in Spanish. When this is the case, I quote from the English translation. *The Letters of Sigmund Freud to Eduard Silberstein, 1871–1881*, trans. Arnold J. Pomerans and ed. Walter Boehlich (Cambridge, MA: Harvard University Press, 1990), 153.

[33] Freud, *Letters to Silberstein*, 141.

be solidly and historically Jewish. In another letter to Silberstein, dated April 23, 1876, Freud wonders about the antiquity of the Jewish ghetto in Muggia, a town in the outskirts of Trieste, expecting to recognize Semitic features in the local women of the town. Freud's expectations are evidently frustrated by the physiognomy of these women but they are an indication of his understanding of the Trieste area as Italian and Semitic in origin.[34] Although Freud does not further elaborate on his knowledge about the history of Trieste, his letters leave no doubt that he is familiar with the current philological and archeological debates surrounding the origins of the city and its nearby area. Commenting on the beauty of the Adriatic Sea and the Trieste port, he wonders where the name came from and concludes, "I will leave it up to philologists, archeologists, and metaphysicians ... to decide whether Trieste takes its name from the harbor or the harbor from Trieste."[35] Freud alludes quite explicitly to the debate of philologists and archeologists who are investigating the origin of Trieste's name, deferring to their expertise in the matter. Freud then continues that he prefers to tell Silberstein about his Triestine experience in person rather than in writing, given the poor quality of paper available in Trieste.[36]

The choice to discuss Trieste in person rather than in his letters may explain the conspicuous absence of references to Johann Joachim Winckelmann, who was assassinated in Trieste in 1768 and then buried in the city. Winckelmann's sudden and mysterious death had sent shock waves throughout Europe, and many intellectuals conjectured about the circumstances of his killing. Half a century after Winckelmann's death, the chief antiquarian in Trieste, Domenico Rossetti, paid homage to the founder of ancient art history in several different ways. He reconstructed Winckelmann's last moments in a biography, *Johann Winckelmann's letzte Lebenswoche*, in 1818 and commissioned the erection of Winckelmann's cenotaph in 1833. His cenotaph became one of the most important tourist attractions in Trieste and was included in the 1873 Baedeker travel guide of Austria, Freud's constant traveling

---

[34] "In Muggia sind wie gesagt die Frauen schöner, meist blond merkwürdigerweise, was weder mit italienischer Abkunft noch mit jüdischer stimmt, Slaven sind die Leute nicht, sie kennen die Sprache nicht." Sigmund Freud, *Jugendbriefe an Eduard Silberstein 1871–1881* (Frankfurt am Main: Fischer Verlag, 1989), 177.

[35] "Denn schön ist die Adria in der Tat. Triest liegt—bekanntlich im Inneren eines kleinen Busens, vernünftiger ausgedrückt—Triest besitzt eben einen sogenannten Hafen, welcher der Hafen von Triest heißt, wobei ich die Entscheidung, ob Triest so heißt vom Hafen oder der Hafen von Triest, den Philologen, Archäologen und Metaphysikern (schönes Gesindel) überlasse." Ibid., 159.

[36] Freud adds that it would be "stupid" to write, preferring to tell Silberstein more when they have the opportunity to speak again. Ibid., 157.

companion. We have no evidence that Freud visited Winckelmann's funerary monument in Trieste and the contiguous Museum of Antiquities, but it is difficult to believe that Freud did not visit Winckelmann's cenotaph,[37] especially because the ancient art historian had been on Freud's mind shortly before he left Vienna for Trieste. In a postscript to a letter to Silberstein from June, 13, 1875, nine months before he arrived in the Adriatic city, Freud briefly mentions Jean Paul Richter's novel *Siebenkäs*, where the figure of Winckelmann is mentioned in conjunction with the Carthaginian general Hannibal.

Richter's association between the two figures will later reappear in Freud's *Interpretation of Dreams*, where he ponders whether his impatience to reach Rome resembles the attitude of Winckelmann or Hannibal.[38] The two figures represent for Freud the two different poles of his love–hate relationship with Rome. Winckelmann, driven by a quest to discover the archaic Greek origins of German culture, became the founder of modern archeology and art history, disciplines that promoted a Greco-Roman view of the Mediterranean. The Carthaginian general, on the other hand, was the main foe of the Romans and was often depicted as the personification of treachery and appalling cruelty, proverbial Phoenician qualities. In this dualism, Freud's preference lies with Hannibal. As part of his attempt to work through his obsession with the eternal city, Freud realizes that he had stopped at Lake Trasimene, where a famous battle between the Romans and Carthaginians took place, and that he had followed Hannibal's same path on the Italian peninsula. He draws a parallel between his hesitation to reach Rome and the reluctance of Hannibal, who fell short of conquering the city when the opportunity arose. Since his school days, Freud has sympathized with the Carthaginians rather than the Romans in the lessons about the Punic Wars, revealing: "To my youthful mind Hannibal and Rome symbolized the conflict between the tenacity of Jewry and the organization of the Catholic Church."[39] The young Freud turns Hannibal from antagonist of Rome into the protagonist of a private fantasy.

While the audacious and cunning Hannibal provides Freud with a model of Jewish heroism, Trieste's Phoenician origin was for the founder of psychoanalysis another instance where the "tenacity of Jewry" emerged vigorously. It would certainly be rewarding to discuss how the city came to represent for Freud a formative rite of passage, marking his transition into young adulthood and into his career as a researcher. More pertinent to my argument is how Trieste became for

---

[37] Gandolfi, "Freud in Trieste," 148.
[38] Schorske calls this obsession Freud's "Rome neurosis." *Fin-de-siècle Vienna*, 190.
[39] Sigmund Freud, *The Interpretation of Dreams* (New York: Avon Books, 1965), 229.

Freud the virtual crossroads where Winckelmann and Hannibal had in essence met, where the real Winckelmann had died and where the story of an intrepid Phoenician founder bolstered Freud's identification with Hannibal. The link between Phoenicians and Hebrews was usually made to disparage modern Jews, but Freud could reverse the argument, listing the Phoenician deeds represented by Hannibal and the foundation story of Trieste among important achievements in Jewish history.

Freud's conflation of Jews and Phoenicians hinges upon the ethnic and cultural-linguistic affinity between the two groups. This kinship was, by the time Freud published *The Interpretation of Dreams* in 1899, an established trope of anti-Semitic discourse in Germany and Austria. In the same year, Houston Stewart Chamberlain published his notorious *Die Grundlagen des neunzehnten Jahrhunderts* where he reiterated classical prejudices about Phoenician mercantilism, contrasting it to Greek science and philosophy. More than a simple reiteration of stereotypes, Chamberlain's argumentation drew a parallel between ancient Phoenicians and modern Jews. While both groups are portrayed as highly undesirable racial mixtures, Phoenicians operate as a sort of displaced Semitic group that chronologically preceded the rise of Jewish communities proper. Since they never embraced monotheism, Phoenicians were characterized by a "spiritual sterility" that never allowed them to produce any higher metaphysical thought. They are essentially Jews who, however, never "recognized any prophets."[40] Phoenicians are thus considered proto-Jews, that is, Jews before and behind the Jews, Semites who not only temporally preceded the Jews but also, in nineteenth-century racial hierarchies, were spiritually and morally inferior to them.

With Hannibal, Freud contributes to move the Phoenicians from this moral backdrop into the ethical foreground of Western history. Much about Hannibal could be admired: He was the resolutely defiant underdog who challenged with cunning and perseverance a mightier and better organized enemy, a spirit of rebellion that had to be emulated in the face of discrimination and injustice. Moreover, the Carthaginian general leads Freud to recover a crucial childhood memory. Freud remembers that when he was about ten or twelve years old, his father told him the story of how in his youth a Christian came up to him and knocked off his cap into the mud. To young Sigmund's question on how his father reacted, the parent replied that he simply picked up the cap. The father's avoidance of conflict strikes Freud as utterly unheroic behavior. He then adds: "I contrasted this situation with another which fitted my feelings better: the scene in which Hannibal's father, Hamilcar

---

[40] Houston Stewart Chamberlain, *Die Grundlagen des neunzehnten Jahrhunderts* (Munich: Bruckmann, 1915), 159–163.

Barca, made his boy swear before the household altar to take vengeance on the Romans. Ever since that time Hannibal had had a place in my phantasies."[41] His father's passive response made a deep impression on the young Freud. His identification with the Carthaginian general became a touchstone in his life, one that was both Oedipal and political.[42] It was a fantasy with which he tried to come to terms with the perceived inadequacy of his father's submissive attitude and meek acceptance of bullying. Freud could see himself surpassing his father in heroism since Hannibal became more famous and feared than his father Hamilcar. It was also a more general reflection of Freud's response to the sociopolitical challenges represented by the growing anti-Semitism and aristocratic authoritarianism in Catholic Austria.[43] Freud's Hannibal complex is a Semitic fantasy that allowed him to metamorphose Phoenicians into Jews, providing him with an alternative model of Jewish masculinity. Against the stereotype of widespread male gender constructions that imagined diasporic Jews as passive victims of a socially sanctioned marginalization, Freud sees in Hannibal a boldly assertive and unapologetically aggressive alpha male, the embodiment of what Max Nordau in 1898 had called a "muscular Judaism." Before Nordau imagined a mentally and physically fit Zionist Jew, Freud wished for a strong and assertive Jewishness when confronted with his father's account of anti-Semitic discrimination and physical violence.

In Trieste, Freud's identification with Hannibal found a fertile terrain for its development from intimate coping strategy into a sign of Jewish pride to be publicly asserted in his later work. This recuperation of the Phoenicians was an important feature of the Austrian zeitgeist emanating from Trieste. Freud's Hannibal signals a crucial reorientation both in the sense of a reclaiming of an Orientalist trope in order to assert a Mediterranization of Europe and in the sense of a reversal of direction of the flow of ideas, this time not from Vienna to Trieste, but from the Adriatic city back to the imperial capital. In the following chapters, we will see how Freud's Hannibal is the harbinger of a Mediterranean modernity, one casting a long shadow that touches Vienna with Robert Musil and, via a circular route, makes its way back to Trieste, where the most Freudian of Triestine authors, Italo Svevo, features a Phoenician hero in his novel.

---

[41] Freud, *Interpretation*, 229–230.
[42] Peter Gay, *Freud: A Life for our Time* (New York: Norton, 1988), 12. In the same vein, Schorske elucidates Freud's dichotomy of Winckelmann and Hannibal in terms of an oedipal triangle and a symbolic patricide. Schorske, *Fin-de-siècle*, 192.
[43] William McGrath, "Freud as Hannibal: The Politics of the Brother Band," *Central European History* 7, no. 1 (1974): 31–57.

A Semitic Hellenism: Theodor Däubler and the Poetics of Bilingualism

Theodor Däubler (1876–1934), the most prominent German-speaking poet of Trieste, was born in the same year in which Freud was conducting his marine biology research in the Adriatic city. After his childhood spent in Trieste, Däubler started traveling the world as a cabin boy on a Mediterranean cruiser. A restless eccentric with no formal education and a penchant for a bohemian lifestyle, Däubler spent in his adult life long sojourns in Germany, Italy, and Greece, while maintaining a strong devotion to his native city. In a fashion often characteristic of turn-of-the-century Triestine intellectuals, Däubler felt no particular affinity for any strictly defined national identification. His double attachment to German and Italian literary traditions is representative of Trieste's culture of mediation but also of the fluidity of commitments, irreducible cultural tensions, and conflicting aspirations of other Triestine writers like Slataper or the brothers Stuparich, with all of whom he entertained a friendship. Däubler was close to Slataper's ideas of cultural Irredentism, advocating for larger local autonomy and the opening of the Italian university in the city. He flirted with Italian Futurism, attractive because of its Nietzscheism, but ultimately rejected its nationalist political program. Over time, his attachment to Trieste became nostalgic and emotional, prompted by the fear that the city of his childhood memories and source of his poetic inspiration could vanish after the First World War. Däubler considered himself a German poet of the Mediterranean, whose classical past he understood as a history of overlapping networks of communication and transcultural exchange.[44] His enthusiastic philhellenism was therefore subsumed in a more inclusive Mediterranean dimension of antiquity, resulting in a modernist classicism in which a Phoenician substratum was crucially constitutive of the spirit of archaic and classical Greeks.[45] In many ways, this view of a hybridizing classical world was an extension and adaptation of his own Italo-German biculturalism. Däubler ultimately structures his literary invention of Europe within a framework of linguistic and cultural syncretism. In his self-proclaimed role as interpreter of a Habsburg

---

[44] Däubler insists on the Mediterranean dimension of his work in his letters and autobiography. See Theodor Däubler, *Wir wollen nicht verweilen. Autobiographische Fragmente* (Leipzig: Insel Verlag, 1915), 75. His writings are also collected in *Dichtungen und Schriften*, ed. Friedhelm Kemp (Munich: Kösel, 1956).

[45] See Thomas Keller, "Fremdheit ohne Alterität. Die Nordlicht-Mythologie Theodor Däublers," in *Interkulturelle Lebensläufe*, ed. Bernd Thum and Thomas Keller (Tübingen: Stauffenburg, 1998), 191–234, and Thomas Rietzschel, *Theodor Däubler. Eine Collage seiner Biographie* (Leipzig: Phillip Reclam, 1988).

Mediterranean, he elevates his poetics of bilingualism to a defining aesthetic principle of Trieste's modernism.

Däubler's private correspondence illustrates the multiple allegiances and loyalties of many former Habsburg subjects who had to express a national choice after the Great War. In a letter written shortly before the outbreak of war, Däubler describes national commitments in terms of a fiasco: "As a Viennese once said: the nation has failed with Däubler."[46] His commitments instead oscillated between a heartfelt loyalty to Italian letters and a concurrent sense of belonging to German language and culture. While he often declared that Mediterranean Trieste was his *Heimat*, Däubler also kept his distance from a metropolitan patriotism when he felt that this attachment to Trieste's urban identity was manipulated into an exclusivist position.[47] During the First World War, he saw himself as an intellectual above the fray, refusing to subscribe to the nationalist partisanship of the war. Therefore, shortly after Italy joins the hostilities, with emotions running high in Trieste, he proudly declares in a letter dated June 2, 1915 that he "will not be seduced by the pedantic local patriotism" of Irredentists, contemplating a Slavification of Trieste, or a Latinization of Bolzano for that matter, as irrelevant. In a tone that may have come across as brusque, Däubler clarifies that neither Germany nor Italy, but the Spirit remains his fatherland. This does not prevent him from rooting for a German and Austrian victory, not because of a misguided political chauvinism, he explains, but because their armies fight for his language.[48] The entanglement of loyalties and commitments does not become less complex after the war. In a letter from Berlin, dated February 24, 1920, he writes to Arthur Moeller van den Bruck, "I often think of Trieste, thinking of its good-natured, open, and enthusiastic people who taught me to strive for freedom and to love Italy. I am an Italian now ... But I am not an Italian poet, just a faithful child, a 'triestino irredento!'" At the same time, he declares, "I also love my fate as a German poet ... Please greet Trieste with its sea

---

[46] Däubler in a letter dated March 1, 1914 comments on his ideological distance from the nation, "Wie ein Wiener sagte: bei Däubler hat die Nation versagt" (474). Quoted in Marina Bressan, "Theodor Däubler: A Mediator between Florentine Futurism and German Modernism" *International Yearbook of Futurism Studies* 4 (2014): 450–476.

[47] Däubler, *Fragmente*, 22–23.

[48] "Vom kleinlichen Lokalpatriotismus lass ich mich keineswegs verleiten, es ist schliesslich nur schmerzlich, aber vor den Sternen gleichgültig, ob Triest slavisiert wird, oder Bozen latinisiert wird. Mein Vaterland ist der Geist. Meine Heimat ist das Mittelmeer. Meine Aufgabe die deutsche Sprache ... Ich hoffe auf Deutschlands Sieg, ja auch Österreichs Sieg, denn die kämpfen für meine Sprache. Warum darf ich nicht mitkämpfen? Aber mein Vaterland bleibt der Geist. Nicht Deutschland, nicht Italien!" Bressan, "Mediator," 475.

and its hills for me, deliver greetings from its son, who lives far from his homeland."[49] Däubler describes himself with irony as a liberated Triestine. His insistence that Trieste is his *Heimat* echoes Scipio Slataper's aforementioned letter to Gigetta Carniel, in which Slataper calls Trieste his *patria*, intending a multicultural patriotism. Like many other Triestines, Däubler did not see these German and Italian loyalties as contradictory, but complementary instead, simultaneously defining separate and related aspects of his life. A case in point is his choice in the spring of 1919, when Däubler was obligated to make a decision about his political nationality. As a citizen of Trieste, he still possessed an Austrian passport, but refused to become a German citizen. When his Austrian passport expired, he opted for Italian citizenship. For all his emphasis on his identity as a German author, he preferred to become an Italian citizen. This multiplicity of loyalties reveals a profound affinity, as we will see later, with Italo Svevo.

Däubler is best known for his monumental epic poem *Northern Lights* (*Das Nordlicht*), first published in 1910 and then revised in 1921. Written during his extensive travels in Italy, mainly in Venice, Naples, Rome, and Florence, but with a newfound enthusiasm for the German language, the text recounts a cosmic origin story characterized by the author's signature coinage of bold neologisms and the use of an idiosyncratic phraseology.[50] In the mystical cosmogony of the text's primordial universe, the aurora borealis represents the striving of a female-coded Earth for a sort of stellar apotheosis in which she can conjoin the Sun, a masculine life principle. In the preface, the author explains his poetic choices, justifying the unconventional use of grammatical gender with his dual language background: "It was now very clear to me: all life derives from the Sun. My bilingualism—I am a Triestine—came to assistance. In Italian, you say: il sole (masculine), la luna (feminine). I compared the two and decided in my youthful private mythology

---

[49] "Ich denke ständig an Triest, an sein gutes, offenes und begeistertes Volk, das mich lehrte nach Freiheit zu streben und Italien zu lieben. Jetzt bin ich Italiener … Ich bin aber kein italienischer Dichter, nur ein treues Kind, ein 'triestino irredento!' Ich liebe Italien, vor allem Triest, und alle in Deutschland wissen es schon. Sie haben es während des Krieges verstanden. Aber jetzt habe ich auch mein Schicksal als deutscher Dichter lieb … Grüßen Sie mir bitte Triest mit seinem Meer und seinen Hügeln von mir, von seinem Sohn, der weit von der Heimat lebt!" Bressan, "Mediator," 471.

[50] One has to agree with Raymond Furness, who describes Däubler's style as characterized by "grotesque neologisms and frequently bizarre rhymes." *Zarathustra's Children: A Study of a Lost Generation of German Writers* (Rochester, NY: Camden House, 2000), 160.

to use the Italian grammatical gender for the celestial bodies."[51] German, the language in which the poet is writing, appears insufficient in conveying Däubler's gendered cosmology. While German assigns the masculine gender to the nouns "sun" and "moon," and the feminine gender to the term "earth," the poet believes that the light of the sun is rather paternal in character, the earth decidedly maternal, and that lunar rays are gender neutral, even though emanating a strong feminine aura.[52] Däubler's mythographic poetry defies German grammatical conventions through the adoption of an alternative gender attribution, taking advantage of the grammatical possibilities afforded by Italian, the poet's other language.

Däubler's cosmic dichotomy between masculine and feminine celestial bodies is inextricably linked to the linguistic peculiarities of his Triestine bilingualism. Trieste, then, becomes the geopoetic vantage point from which he articulates his modern adaptation of the myth of Europa, in which the polarity between man and woman is transferred to the Greek god Zeus and the Phoenician maiden Europa. Däubler's 1924 *Paean and Dithyramb (Päan und Dithyrambos)* is a celebration of ancient Greek culture, which, in markedly Nietzschean fashion, is a synthesis of Dionysian and Apollonian principles. In the text, Däubler retells the classical myth of the rape of Europa in a sequence of seven sonnets. His modernist mythography retraces the young maiden's destiny from her premonitory dream, the arrival of Zeus in the guise of a bull, to her abduction, and the origin of the Taurus constellation. The sexual encounter is described in terms of an astronomical duality that opposes the sun to the moon. Europa glances with a lunar gaze ("Europas Mondblick"), while Zeus ceremoniously displays a solar ancestry ("Sonnenkunft").[53] Däubler's retelling of the rape of the maiden explores the multiple layers of the ancient tale. As an aetiological myth, it claims to explain the origin of the name of the continent, as Europe is named after the abducted girl. The bull's ascendance to the sky gives rise to the constellation of Taurus, in a narrative development that bestows a

---

[51] "Ganz klar stand es vor mir: alles Leben kommt von der Sonne. Meine Zweisprachigkeit—ich bin Triestiner—kam mir da zustatten. Im Italienischen heißt es: il sole (männlich), la luna (weiblich); ich verglich und entschied mich in meiner kindlichen Privatmythologie für die italienische Einsetzung der Geschlechter bei den Gestirnen." Theodor Däubler, *Das Nordlicht* (Leipzig: Insel Verlag, 1921), 7.

[52] "Das Sonnenlicht war väterlich, die Erde mütterlich, der Mond unentschieden, aber mit stärkerem weiblichen Einschlag." Ibid., 8.

[53] Theodor Däubler, *Päan und Dithyrambos. Eine Phantasmagorie* (Leipzig: Insel Verlag, 1924), 26.

cosmogonic dimension to the myth. The narrator's emphasis on Zeus's courtship makes the tale a myth that explores the psychological aspects of desire and sexuality.

With the emphasis on Europa's foreignness, an alterity that encompasses a different ethnic origin and a marked racial difference, Däubler exploits the political dynamics underlying the myth. Europa's Afro-Semitic origin becomes evident when she is described as Zeus's "dark bride," who is "slender as a palm."[54] The reference to the palm is revealing, as it was a symbol of Carthage, the Phoenician colony in northern Africa. In the classical sources of the rape of Europe, the myth carries a prominent political message. In the version of the Sicilian Greek poet Moschus, the rape encapsulates the cultural tension and trading rivalries between Greeks and Phoenicians. The quest for commercial supremacy is contained in the poem's famous ekphrasis, where Moschus describes a finely wrought golden basket that Europa holds in her premonitory dream. In Ovid's *Metamorphoses*, the rape stages the political rivalries between Rome and Carthage. Since Europa is a Phoenician princess, the abduction at the hands of a Greek or Roman god makes the scene an ethnic rape, a violent assertion of cultural dominance.

It was relatively easy for Freud to interpret the figure of Hannibal as the protagonist of a bold Phoenician tradition that contributed to the writing of Western history. To make Europa, the victim of an infamous rape, the assertive protagonist of Phoenician lore required a rhetorical operation of greater magnitude. Däubler adopts the ancient versions of the story but profoundly alters the interpersonal dynamics of the Phoenician girl and the Greek god, turning Zeus' politicized rape into an ardent courtship encompassing the medieval genre conventions of the troubadour *Minne*. Däubler's Europa exercises judgment and expresses a romantic preference. In addition, with its lively and colorful descriptions, Däubler's abduction of Europa owes much to the tradition of visual representations of the myth in Italian Renaissance painting, in particular to the art of Paolo Veronese and Tiepolo. Via Zeus' courtly and seductive wooing, and Europa's willingness to leave with him, Däubler places his retelling of the myth in the tradition of Veronese, where Europa is radiant and seemingly departing of her own free will, rather than Titian, in whose painting the sexual violence is unmistakable.

Däubler makes this pictorial inspiration evident when he discusses Veronese's use of color in his *The New Point of View* (*Der neue Standpunkt*). For Däubler, it is clear that in Veronese's Europa motif, the painter breaks from his previous masterful shading of sky blue and mother-of-pearl

---

[54] "Des Königs Phönix palmenschlanke Tochter ... dunkle Braut." Ibid., 24.

grey with a "triumphantly opposing symphony of colors," a chromatic harmony Tiepolo imitates in his own rendering of the Europa myth.[55] In Däubler's art criticism, which is often as hyperbolic and eccentric as his poetic language, colors are described as "European" without any further explanation. Tiepolo's compositions allegedly include "European colors" like "yellow-red" and "flesh-color," irradiated by a "half-pale Europe-light."[56] The naked body of Europa's pink flesh is described as "purple-drunk."[57] Purple evidently belongs to the maiden Europa and not, in Däubler's frankly bizarre ethno-chromatic classifications, to Europe. It is, rather, an Afro-Semitic color that presents itself in a number of hues and shades. The color purple is an unequivocal reminder of Europa's perceived ethno-cultural background since it is associated with the Phoenicians, inventors of the renowned purple dye. Däubler's association of Europa with the color purple suggests that in 1915 he already thinks of Europa as a Phoenician. In addition, purple is a color associated with the African continent: "Africa remains the world of shadows and of its wonderful purple blueness."[58] As will become clear below, what this color scheme suggests is that for Däubler the origins of Europa, and hence the continent named after her, are Semitic in origin. The chromatic richness of Däubler's version of the myth is therefore not simply a function of the author's Expressionist poetics but, as his art criticism pointedly suggests, a textual strategy aimed at reinforcing the political implications of the narration. Disguised as a bull, Zeus leaps into the water and traces a purple arch, painting the seascape with a familiar hue to accompany and reassure Europa on their journey to Crete.[59] Purple is, once again, Europa's Phoenician identity marker. Love conquers all differences, ethnic and otherwise, in this clumsily celebrated interracial couple. The emphasis on the love of the couple aims to translate the decidedly troubling aesthetics of sexual violence

---

[55] "Beim Raub der Europa wirds am anschaulichsten, wie sich Veronese mit einer Farbensymphonie triumphatorisch seiner eignen Komposition entgegenstellt. Von dem in Fleischfarben nüsternden Maul des Stieres geht er farbenverschwenderisch aus, um sein Europäertum überall goldig, blond oder brünett, im Bild hervorblitzen, heraustaumeln zu lassen. Tiepolo verstand ihn, griff nach dem Motiv des Raubes der Europa und türmte einen Aufbau aus Farben seinen Kompositionen der vier Weltteile im Würzburger Schloß entgegen." Theodor Däubler, *Der neue Standpunkt* (Dresden: Hellerauer Verlag, 1916), 117.
[56] "In ihren Farben, den europäischen, dämmern gelbrote Überraschungen aus Brokat und Wolkenbombast. Fleischfarbene Kleider, Tiere, halbblasses Europalicht flimmert aus allen Ecken und Schlitzen." Ibid., 117.
[57] "trunkenviolett." Ibid., 117.
[58] "Afrika bleibt noch lange die Welt der Schatten und ihrer wunderbaren lila Blauheiten." Ibid., 118.
[59] "Sein Satz erschwingt die See auf Purpurbogen." Däubler, *Pään*, 25.

into an ethics of intercultural exchange. With this mystifying metamorphosis of the rape, Däubler wishes to rewrite a tale of male chauvinist aggression into a romance of blissful concord, turning the story of old Greek and Phoenician rivalries into the foundational myth of a modern multicultural Europe, where traditional enemies finally unite. Däubler's Europa myth, and the political Europe it implies, is characterized by a pacifying cosmopolitanism that, however, fails to critically engage its colonial and imperial subtext.[60]

For Däubler, the Europa myth is the story of a Semitic Hellenism in which the Phoenician origin of Europa achieves a higher synthesis in the encounter with the Greek Zeus. The author envisioned this union of Phoenicians and Greeks in a reflection upon the ancient Mediterranean, where he argues that the Expressionist quest for the "New Man" coincided with the emergence of the Phoenician in the ancient world: "And then came the Phoenician, a *homo novus*, captured by the epiphany of the sea … The Hellene did not fly over the sea, he was the first to plough, till, and calculate the sea. Homer was his poet. The people of the sea are Greek."[61] For Däubler, archaic Greek navigation, the one Homer described in *The Odyssey*, conceals a Phoenician prehistory. Homer's narrative strategy already encapsulates a dynamic of cultural syncretism that governs much of the later literature and that culminates in the Europa legend. Däubler returns to the story material in the autobiographical poem "Homecoming to Hellas" ("Heimkehr nach Hellas"), written in 1926 while travelling in Egypt. Däubler imagines setting foot in Crete immediately after Europa disembarks on the island, dismounting a garlanded bull. The Greek island of Crete is described as the Phoenician mainland. Its mountain peaks are covered with snow, appropriately colored purple, while majestic cedars and cypresses tower overhead. Europa brings her Phoenician blood as a gift to the Greeks, in the form of a flood from Syria, streaming into

---

[60] Theodore Ziolkowski argues that in comparison to more explicitly politicized retellings of the Europa legend, "the theme of Europa is invoked here not for substantive reasons—no erotic play or sexual tension, no political implications—but for sheer melody." *Minos and the Moderns: Cretan Myth in Twentieth-Century Literature and Art* (New York: Oxford University Press, 2008), 42. The critic is not incorrect in saying that Däubler's poem does not explicitly engage in contemporary politics. My point is that Däubler is addressing cultural and geopolitical tensions between Greeks and Phoenicians inherent in the ancient myth.

[61] "Einmal aber kam der Phönizier, ein homo novus. Den erfaßte das Meererlebnis … Der Hellene flog nicht über See, er beackerte, bestellte, überrechnete als erster das Meer. Homer war sein Dichter. Der Meermensch ist Grieche." Theodor Däubler, *Lucidarium in Arte Musicae: Des Ricciotto Canudo aus Gioja del colle* (Leipzig: Insel Verlag, 1917), 13–14.

"our blood."⁶² For Däubler, the epitome of this ancient Mediterranean cosmopolitanism was the archeological site of Baalbek, located in Phoenicia, which hosts the largest surviving Roman temple complex from antiquity, dedicated to the Heliopolitan triad that included the syncretic deities of Baal-Jupiter, Astarte-Aphrodite, and their son Adon-Mercury. Däubler's modernist classicism operates under the assumption that all ancient populations were inextricably intertwined. Visiting the site that was the seat of an important regional cult in Phoenician, Greek, and Roman times, he admires the architecture of "Hellenistic-Asiatic origin."⁶³ He describes the temple to Aphrodite as "rotund forms whose rhythmic impetus came from the East, arrived on Carthaginian soil, and from there was incorporated into the Etruscan-Roman."⁶⁴ Defying notions of purity and neatly differentiated categories, the Mediterranean is where Africa, Asia, and Europe run together.

Däubler's understanding of ancient Mediterranean cultures is informed by Nietzsche's belief that the Phoenicians exerted a crucial influence on the Greeks. In a time in which the presence of Phoenician settlements in Greek territories was not at all a settled matter, Nietzsche believed that the Phoenicians were responsible for many fundamental aspects of the ancient Greek world. He gave them credit for the organization of civic life in the polis, the adoption of the alphabet, and the worship of certain gods. The Greeks, in brief, were indebted to the culturally superior and more technologically advanced Phoenicians, who they sought to emulate.⁶⁵ In parallel fashion, Däubler's retelling of the Europa story is prompted by Nietzsche, who had predicted the potential for multiple modern appropriations of Europa's polyvalent myth. In *Beyond Good and Evil*, Nietzsche addresses the Phoenician maiden directly:

---

[62] "Des Mondes silberne Vollkommenheit erglänzt / Auf Kretas froh beschäumten Klippenmeer / In lila Schnee entzückt mich der geliebte Ida / Bei Zeder und Zypressen in versunkner Bucht / Betrete ich, auf Marmor, urgeweihte Stätte / Europa ist gelandet: auf bekränztem Stier / Hat Flut aus Syrien unserm Blute sie beschert." "Heimkehr nach Hellas." In Thomas Rietzschel, *Däubler*, 259–260.

[63] "Es gibt in Kleinasien und hier nämlich viel Großbauten aus der Imperatorenzeit, die noch viel deutlicher rein hellenistisch-asiatischen Ursprungs sind." Theodor Däubler, *Der Fischzug* (Hellerau: Hegner, 1930), 110.

[64] "Gewiß handelt es sich um eine Schwunghaftigkeit, die aus dem Osten kommt, dessen Rhythmik sich zuerst auf Asiens, dann auf karthagischem Boden hat dem Etruskisch-Römischen einfügen lassen." Ibid.

[65] For Nietzsche the Phoenicians also embodied problematic aspects. In his critique of Christianity, he wrote, "There is a cruelty and religious Phoenicianism in this faith," identifying the Phoenician practice of animal and human sacrifice as the origin for their general willingness to sanction sacrificial victims and social scapegoats. *Beyond Good and Evil*, III, 46.

O Europa! O Europa! We know the horned beast that always most attracted you, that ever anew attracts and endangers you! Your ancient tale could once again become a "story" – once again a huge foolishness could master you and carry you away! And underneath no god is concealed, no! only an "idea," a modern "idea"![66]

Nietzsche reads Europa as a young woman with agency who asserts her sexual desire when she seeks out the company of the bull displaying phallic horns. For Nietzsche, the Phoenicians were intermediaries (*Vermittler*) from which the Greeks learned about the Egyptians and Assyrians. By crossing the boundaries of traditional divides, Europa also becomes an agent of intercultural mediation between Phoenicians and Greeks. This role of translators among civilizations is what connects Nietzsche's reading of Phoenician Europa with his theorization of the "good European," a modern conciliator through which the philosopher advocates for the rise of a cultural, political, and economic Europeanism that should supersede territorial nationalism. Nietzsche believed that Jews are the harbinger of a modern pan-Europeanism because they carry forward the structural syncretism and ethnic hybridity of the ancient Mediterranean world embodied by their Semitic cousins. In the same text, Nietzsche mockingly defines nationalism as an atavistic, almost pathological attack of what he calls "fatherlandishness and soil addiction," and hopes for a return to reason, embodied by his notion of "good Europeanism."[67] In *Human, All too Human*, Nietzsche observes in the section "The European and the Destruction of Nations" that "good Europeanism" means working on the merging of nations. According to Nietzsche, a mixed European population will emerge thanks to increased trade and industry, the cosmopolitan life of intellectuals, and the nomadic practices of those who do not own land. The Germans, because of their age-old, proven trait of being the nations' interpreter and mediator will be able to help in this process.[68] Although the connection is never made explicit, both Germans and Phoenicians are for Nietzsche the quintessential European mediators.

---

[66] Ibid., VII, 239.
[67] Nietzsche speaks of "dumpfe zögernde Rassen ... welche in unserm geschwinden Europa halbe Jahrhunderte nöthig hätten, um solche atavistischen Anfälle von Vaterländerei und Schollenkleberei zu überwinden und wieder zur Vernunft, will sagen zum 'guten Europäerthum' zurückzukehren." *Jenseits von Gut und Böse*, VIII, 241.
[68] "wobei die Deutschen durch ihre alte bewährte Eigenschaft, Dolmetscher und Vermittler der Völker zu sein, mitzuhelfen vermögen." *Menschliches, allzu Menschliches*, VIII, 475.

The myth's pacification of Greeks and Phoenicians reflects Däubler's own wish of conciliation between Germans and Italians. For Däubler, Trieste's Europeanness is due to the Phoenician origin of the classical Mediterranean. In a passage of Däubler's autobiographical fragments, he describes his origins, his heritage as a Triestino, in terms of Europa's "purple roots": "And underneath us, in a flash, begin to kindle with every jump purple roots into the darkness, and we swirled them forth, darting in flight back into the dark: and we tore open the night, so that she had to bleed!"[69] The striking purple color of these roots suggests that Däubler may have seen himself, in Nietzschean fashion, as a German poet with deep Phoenician roots. Together with many other Expressionists, he is indebted to Nietzsche's cultural critique of bourgeois society. Däubler's temperament and inclination was, however, alien to Nietzsche's elitist and occasional anti-democratic leanings. What the Triestine poet shares with Nietzsche is the idea that the "good European" is the harbinger of a crisis of nineteenth-century nationalism and that Greek life is a Phoenician imitation. For Däubler, the Europa myth epitomizes the Greco-Phoenician encounter, a Mediterranean syncretism of cultures that he considered constitutive of both Trieste and European civilization in general. Europa brings an advanced Phoenician culture to Greece, which absorbs it and then in turn becomes the cultural, philosophical, and scientific foundation of Europe. In other words: It is through the Greeks that Europa becomes Europe.

A View of the Mediterranean Karst: Srečko Kosovel and the Ethics of Mediation

He looked askance at me as I tried to explain to him
that Croatian Istrians were not of Roman descent.[70]
—Boris Pahor, *Necropolis*

When Amy Bernardi was raising the specter of vaguely defined Slavic hordes descending from the mountains and threatening the racial purity of Roman Trieste, she had the Slovenian and Croat communities of the Karst plateau in mind. In line with Italian Irredentist efforts of social and political marginalization, her description relegated the Slavs of the Triestine hinterlands to the rhetorical fringes of civilization. Had

---

[69] "Und unter uns entglühten uns im Nu, bei jedem Sprunge, Purpurwurzeln ins Dunkel, und wir wirbelten sie wieder hervor und stiessen uns, dahinfliegend, abermals selber zurück in die Finsternis: Und wir rissen die Nacht auf, dass sie bluten musste!" Däubler, *Fragmente*, 36.
[70] Boris Pahor, *Necropolis*, translated by Michael Biggins (Champaign, IL: Dalkey Archive Press, 2010), 146.

he ever been asked about it, Srečko Kosovel (1904–1926), like his fellow Slovene Triestine writer Boris Pahor (1913–), would have probably shown little patience for Bernardi's exaltation of the Roman legacy in the Adriatic region and her characterization of the rural Slavs as barbarians. At the same time, his positions would have been closer to Josip Godina-Verdéljski, in whose opinion the mere suggestion of a Phoenician origin of the city sounded equally ridiculous. Kosovel never directly mentioned any Phoenicians or Carthaginians in his writings. Yet, the Mediterranean inspiration of his modernist poetry and his socialist-inflected literary pan-Europeanism squarely places Kosovel in the context of the authors discussed in this book.[71] Kosovel was born in Sežana, a small village on the Littoral Karst, in the outskirts of Trieste and some fifty miles from the Slovenian capital Ljubljana. Trieste had been flourishing as a significant center of Slovenian culture since the middle of the nineteenth century, and had firmly established institutions and a Slovenian political party at the time Srečko Kosovel was writing.[72] Although he grew up in Ljubljana, Kosovel can rightfully be considered part of the rich group of modern Slovene-speaking intellectuals from Trieste.[73] These include poets like Igo Gruden (1893–1948), the novelists Vladimir Bartol (1903–1967) and Alojz Rebula (1924–2018), the avant-garde painters Avgust Černigoj (1898–1985) and Milko Bambič (1905–1991), as well as a successive generation of writers such as Boris Pahor (1913–) and Zora Tavčar (1928–).

Like other Triestines of his generation, Kosovel was part of a literary culture whose regional multicultural patriotism made him suspicious of monolithic conceptions of the nation. Kosovel's literary invention of Europe, then, moves from a denunciation of the rhetorical ostracism of Slovenes in Italian discourses of Triestine identity to the affirmation of an inclusive ethics of mediation. Kosovel resists the social and

---

[71] For Kosovel's ties to Trieste, Ljubljana, and the Karst see Ana Jelnikar, *Universalist Hopes in India and Europe: The Worlds of Rabindranath Tagore and Srečko Kosovel*. (New Delhi: Oxford University Press, 2016), 189.

[72] The 1910 Austrian census reported that the population of Trieste identified as 62 percent Italian and 25–30 percent Slovene. These numbers, largely accepted by later Slovenian historiography, are significant because they place the number of Slovenes in Trieste at 60,000. Ljubljana at the time counted 52,000 inhabitants. The fact that Trieste had a larger Slovene population than the future capital of the nation should give a sense of how important the Adriatic city was for Slovenes at large. For these numbers, see Sluga, *Difference*, 30.

[73] For an account of Italians and Slovenes in Trieste, see Marina Cattaruzza, "Slovenes and Italians in Trieste, 1850–1914," in *Ethnic Identity in Urban Europe. Comparative Studies on Governments and Non-dominant Ethnic Groups in Europe, 1850–1940*. vol. 8, ed. Max Engman, F. W. Carter, A. C. Hepburn, and C. G. Podey (New York: New York University Press, 1991), 189–217.

historical pressure to assimilate to the culture of the Italian-speaking majority and claims, from a position of marginality, the right to be simultaneously Triestine, Slovenian, and European. More than simply contesting the dichotomies of center and periphery, Kosovel's ethical claim from the margins—ethnic, geographic, and linguistic—dissolves the fallacious bond that equates moral integrity with the ethnic homogeneity of the national body politic. For Kosovel, the danger that Triestine Irredentism posed extended beyond its local coordinates because it posited a nationalism that thrived on the equivalence between citizenship and nationality. Belonging to a minority "nationality" within the modern and violently homogenizing nation-state meant to be excluded from the social and civic privileges of the hegemonic nation. Kosovel came to understand that national belonging, despite its claims to construct social solidarity, necessarily implies a dynamic system of exclusions and hierarchies that regulates the distinction between insiders and outsiders, natives and foreigners, between participants in the majority and members of an internal minority. What he found unacceptable in the postwar divisions of the region was the national claim of exclusivity over individuals, i.e., the notion that subjects could not simultaneously belong to multiple cultural and linguistic communities.[74] The minority status did not necessarily have to be determined by the identification with an alternative ethnic group but could be defined by other kinds of affiliations such as social class, language use, or religious faith. Kosovel was vehemently opposed to the Italian Irredentism that turned into anti-Slavic Fascist violence in Trieste, but he also kept his distance from Slovenian and other emerging Slavic nationalisms that trafficked in a similar dialectics of belonging and exclusion.[75] Kosovel's ethics of mediation rejects the structural closure of national belonging in favor of a humanist openness to heterogeneous affiliations. This attitude fed into his socialist internationalism, introduced to Kosovel by the fellow Triestine Slovene Vladimir Martelanc (1905–1944). Socialism provided the closest ideological repository for his ideas, even though his humanist ideals never fully overlapped with the political agendas of the time. The aim of Kosovel's construction of Europe was to expose the divisions in society that capitalist-imperialist propaganda had sown with its appeals to nationalism, and to divorce the idea of the *narod*, an idea similar to the German concept of *Volk*, from the exclusive representative claims of the nation.

---

[74] Jelnikar, *The Worlds*, 218–221.
[75] David Brooks describes Kosovel's attitude in terms of a "political anti- and inter-nationalism." *The Golden Boat: Selected Poems of Srečko Kosovel*, trans. Bert Pribac, David Brooks, and Teja Brooks Pribac (Norfolk: Salt Publishing, 2008), 10.

An eclectic poet, Kosovel was influenced by a number of European avant-garde movements including German Expressionism, Russian Constructivism, French Dadaism and Surrealism, and Italian Futurism. Kosovel's collection of poems *The Golden Boat* (*Zlati Čoln*), which was completed by the end of 1925 but published posthumously in 1954, describes the spectacular physical geography of the Trieste Bay. Kosovel dramatically juxtaposes the stony landscape of the Karst Plateau with the maritime backdrop of the Adriatic Sea. His work shows evident points of contact with both Slataper's aesthetics of the rural Karst and Däubler's poetics of the Mediterranean, but their affinities are not limited to this shared literary geography.[76] They describe the same Karst region with a similar neo-Romantic melancholy, although there is no evidence to suggest that they read each other's work. Kosovel's poetry emerges from a broader literary culture that envisioned Trieste's multicultural patriotism as a potential paradigm for a reformed Europe. His verses are part of a modernist literature of mediation that, however, coexisted with one of segregation and exclusion, exile and displacement. His denunciations are a reminder of how, through cultivated divisions and erected barricades, Triestine authors often failed to translate into practice such visions of European exchange. Authors across linguistic and ethnic divides often purposefully ignored or were simply unaware of each other's work, leading parallel lives that never intersected. Even in the years leading up to the First World War, intellectuals who may have thought of Trieste as a cosmopolitan city effectively lived within their own cultural bubble. Many Italian-speaking modernists were largely ignorant of Slavic languages.[77] The rapid rise of Fascism in Trieste transformed the city in the aftermath of the war, when the cultural and political climate became increasingly parochial and intolerant. The goal of the Fascists in Trieste was to promote Italian cultural supremacy and to completely eliminate the ethnic and cultural Slovenian presence in the city.

In 1920, a squad of Fascists attacked the *Slovenski Narodni Dom*, the Slovenian cultural center in downtown Trieste that included a theater,

---

[76] Marija Dović argues that Kosovel "can rightfully be considered one of the great Mediterranean modernists" (240). "From Autarky to 'Barbarian' Cosmopolitanism: The Early Avant-Garde Movements in Slovenia and Croatia," in *Mediterranean Modernism. Intercultural Exchange and Aesthetic Development*, ed. Adam J. Goldwyn and Renée M. Silverman (New York: Palgrave Macmillan, 2016), 233–250.

[77] See Katia Pizzi, "A Modernist City Resisting Translation? Trieste between Slovenia and Italy," in *Speaking Memory: How Translation Shapes City Life*, ed. Sherry Simon (Montreal: McGill-Queen's University Press, 2016), 45–57.

a bank, and the Balkan Hotel. The building also housed the headquarters of *Edinost* ("Unity"), a cultural society that became the Slovene nationalist party. Soon thereafter, teaching in Slovenian was outlawed in the city, and by 1927 even speaking the language was prohibited. The anti-Slavic pogroms struck Kosovel. In the poem "Italian Culture" ("Italijanska Kultura"), Kosovel denounces the rise of Fascist violence: "The Slovenian National House in Trieste, 1920. / The Workers House in Trieste, 1920. / Wheat fields in Istria on fire. / Fascist threat during the elections ... Edinost is burning, burning / our nation choking, choking."[78] The poem includes very few verbs, suggesting an initial inaction and helplessness that gives way to a strategy of resistance. He contrasts Italian Fascist violence with "[a] humanistic Slovenism," the development of a cultural emancipation and self-determination that, in Gandhian fashion, seeks affirmation without oppression.[79] Kosovel's Slovenian spiritual nation did not easily fit into larger Yugo-Slav projects in the sense that his critique of the nation did not limit itself to Italian Fascism, but extended to Slavic nationalisms. He recognized in the Kingdom of Serbs, Croatians, and Slovenes a similar kind of nationalist tendency that he observed in other countries.[80]

The collection begins with poems set in a windy and inhospitable Karst, where the *burja* blows with inexorable strength. The other protagonist is the Adriatic and the maritime city of Trieste that, more than the landlocked Ljubljana, remains central in *The Golden Boat*. Kosovel sees Italian and Slovenian nationalisms as a pathology that cuts Adriatic multiculturalism to the core. In "Near Midnight" he writes that "The heart—Trieste—is ill."[81] Death reaps its victims in a ghastly harvest, here in the form of insignificant flies that die in a cup. The nocturnal setting evokes recollections of the city, while the poetic voice directly addresses "Beautiful Vida," detecting sorrow in her memory.[82] The traditional story of the fair Vida is a medieval legend in which the

---

[78] Kosovel, *Golden Boat*, 137.
[79] Ibid.
[80] Peter Scherber describes this seeming paradox in terms of astonishment. "It is at first sight astonishing to see [Kosovel] primarily in opposition with his own Slovene compatriots and Yugoslav politicians, and hardly ever as a critic of the Italian occupiers of his own home territory, the Karst, and the Slovene coastal region" (157). "Regionalism versus Europeanism as Leading Concepts in the Works of Srečko Kosovel," *Slovene Studies* 13, no. 2 (1991): 155–165. doi:10.7152/ssj.v13i2.14296. Along the same lines, Jelnikar points out that Kosovel is "remarkably free of resentment toward the Italian oppressors, and he certainly disavows the path of victimhood." Jelnikar, *The Worlds*, 210–211.
[81] Kosovel, *Golden Boat*, 93.
[82] Ibid.

comely woman is lured by a Saracen into boarding his ship. Once on board, Vida realizes that she has been abducted as the ship fares to a distant land, either Moorish Spain or Turkey, where she either is forced to marry her abductor or become a wet-nurse for a foreign queen. In other versions, she abandons her husband and child voluntarily, seduced by a life of luxury and riches, but regrets her decision when the ship is at open sea. The myth has been retold by many authors, from the acclaimed Slovene national poet France Prešeren (1800–1849) to Ivan Cankar (1876–1918) and the aforementioned Boris Pahor. For Kosovel, the myth was equally important. In 1920, Kosovel founded with other friends the literary magazine *Lepa Vida*. In his poetry, the tale becomes a parable of Slovenian life.

The legend of Lepa Vida is a Balkanic adaptation of the Europa myth, an Adriatic offshoot of the ancient Greek/Phoenician archetype. According to the Slovenian ethnologist Ivan Grafenauer, the Lepa Vida motif originated in the Eastern Mediterranean, within a tradition that reaches back as far as Herodotus.[83] Grafenauer sees the ancient Greek historian's account of the kidnapping of Io as the first historical source for the Lepa Vida motif. In *The Histories*, Herodotus tells the story of how Phoenician merchants or pirates abducted Greek women, among whom figured the very Io herself. In revenge, Greeks, and more specifically Cretans, abducted the Phoenician princess Europa, a story that then made its way into ancient Greek mythological lore. In Grafenauer's reconstruction, the abduction theme later assumed a larger Mediterranean dimension as it spread with a number of variants and contaminations that appear in Sicilian, Calabrian, and Albanian legends. During the ninth and eleventh centuries, a variation on the motif of an abducted maiden at sea spread in the Balkanic area when Arab Muslim raiders roamed the southern Mediterranean shores and the Adriatic coastline. There are obvious commonalities between the rape of Europa and the kidnapping of Vida. Both stories are Mediterranean myths that contain an abduction motif and involve anxieties about miscegenation as the result of a cross-cultural or interracial encounter. The relationship between the two cycles is less typological than it is genetic: it is not one of parallel development, but one of historical continuity and local dissemination.

Kosovel reimagines the Slovenian folktale of the fair Vida, but rather than simply making Trieste the setting of the legend, one can easily read Kosovel's personification of Trieste as the mournful Vida. Against the backdrop of an indifferent "roaring of the sea," Trieste, allured by the promise of a better life by both Italian and Slovene nationalisms,

---

[83] Ivan Grafenauer, *Lepa Vida. Študija o izvoru, razvoju in razkroju narodne balade o Lepi Vidi* (Ljubljana: Akademija znanosti in umetnosti), 1943.

realizes her plight only after her abduction into a world of violence. In the poem, the identification of Vida with the beauty of Trieste is made explicit by Kosovel's use of the same adjective for both ("Lepa Vida" and "Zato je Trst lep").[84] The bitterness of her memories, an exile far away from home, overlaps with the poet's own banishment. The Adriatic becomes the locus of a continental demise in "Ecstasy of Death" ("Ekstaza smirti") where "the golden towers of Western Europe" are "drowning in the burning, red sea."[85] In his biography of Kosovel, Boris Pahor ties "Ecstasy of Death" to the burning of the *Narodni Dom*, reading the verse "Just born, and already you burn in the fire of evening"[86] as an echo of the arsonist attack, which for Kosovel signaled the ultimate shattering of Europe.[87] The poem also contains a transfiguration of the fair Vida, who reappears in the guise of a beautiful woman tragically seduced by gold:

> The death of Europe will be beautiful, beautiful,
> Like a luxuriant queen dressed in gold
> She will lie in a coffin of dark centuries,
> And die silently, as if she were
> Closing, ancient, her golden eyes.
> —All is ecstasy, the ecstasy of death.—[88]

The dying queen of Europe is a hybridization of the Slovenian folk heroine Vida and the Europa of classical mythology, a poetic imbrication of similar interlacing motifs. Kosovel's gold-clad queen evokes the description of Däubler's Europa myth where the Phoenician princess has a premonitory dream in which she receives a heavenly dowry in the form of a shower of gold that rains from the sky. The dream is prophetic, as it announces the arrival of her "golden prince" Zeus.[89] Däubler, as mentioned above, is inspired by Moschus, in whose poem Zeus's promise to Europa is sealed by her dream of the golden basket.

In the collection, the golden boat functions as the vessel of an extended metaphor that allows the narrating voice to fare through a series of images that describe the capsizing of the European project. At the helm of this boat is an unnamed narrator, who describes himself

---

[84] "That is why Trieste is beautiful." Kosovel, *Golden Boat*, 93.
[85] Ibid., 53.
[86] Ibid.
[87] Boris Pahor, *Srečko Kosovel: pričevalec zaznamovanega stoletja* (Ljubljana: Znanstvena založba Filozofske fakultete, 2008), 11.
[88] Kosovel, *Golden Boat*, 53.
[89] "Wo kommt ihr goldener Prinz?" Däubler, *Päan*, 24.

as an observing "golden sailor."[90] He is later replaced by an imperialist "syphilitic captain," who asks Slavic barbarians to undress only to realize that they are unaffected by the disease.[91] Despite the undressing, no spoils are to be collected. Gold gradually loses its enticing splendor, until its negative connotation assumes a scatological dimension. In the poem "Kons. 5," gold becomes equal to manure.[92] Widespread disease grips the sea. A sail, moving up and down a mast with a "sickly stupor" and flying over "the grey of sulphuric waters," is stuck on an immobile vessel.[93] It hovers like the dejected banner of Europe's pathological decadence.

Contrary to other diagnoses of Europe's dissolution—one thinks of Oswald Spengler's apocalyptic cultural pessimism—for Kosovel, the decadence of Europe is the result of the profound and self-destructive crisis of imperial capitalism. While his poetry is often moved by a critique of the aggressively belligerent nationalisms in Europe, he subscribes to an idea of Europe that is synonymous with an anti-colonial humanism. In a letter to Dragan Šanda on September 13, 1923, Kosovel describes himself in terms of both a Slovenian cultural identity and a European sense of belonging: "My life is mine: *Slovene, modern, European*, and eternal."[94] As a Triestine modernist, Kosovel writes from a dual perspective that is both marginal and liminal, a perspective that allows him to proclaim and at the same time call into question his Slovene and European identities. Simultaneously an insider and an outsider to both the larger Slovenian and European communities, he is able to critically distance himself from the very identity constructs that he so ardently defends in his writings. While deeply concerned with the rights of a small and emerging nation such as Slovenia, Kosovel sees the Slovenian *narod* as a combi-*nation* of an Adriatic regionalism with a cosmopolitan Europeanism. This Europeanism imbued with ethical responsibilities for others conceives of the *narod* as inclusionary and multicultural. In another letter to Šanda, dated September 15, 1925, he writes, "A nation only becomes a nation when it becomes aware of its humanity."[95] With this conditional provision inherent in its very existence, Kosovel's "nation" is characterized by a structural paradox as it always subsists on the brink of its negation, namely the nonnational.

---

[90] Kosovel, *Golden Boat*, 52
[91] Ibid., 139.
[92] Ibid., 76.
[93] Ibid., 64.
[94] "Moje življenje je moje, *slovensko, sodobno, evropsko* in *večno*" (emphasis in the original). Srečko Kosovel, *Zbrano Delo*. Vol. 3.1 (Ljubljana: Državna Založba Slovenije), 321.
[95] Kosovel, *Zbrano Delo* 3.1: 323–4, quoted in Jelnikar, *The Worlds*, 210.

A nation can call itself such only if its claim to life contains the intrinsic recognition of the rights of others. The implication is that if a national cultural group contravenes this stipulation, it loses its right to call itself a nation. This lack of ethical commitments prompted his harsh condemnation of the League of Nations, which he described as a society of oppressors spreading deceptive falsehoods.[96] To Kosovel, one of the main betrayals of the League was its lack of protection for minorities within modern nation-states. The treatment of Slovenes in Italy and Austria, or smaller Slavic groups like Sorbs and Kashubs spread over new borders, made Kosovel suspicious of the nation's ability to guarantee the survival of marginal groups. Kosovel's regional patriotism, a resounding echo of the Habsburg *Landespatriotismus*, offers an alternative paradigm of belonging when one's nation fails to keep its humanist promise. This is why Kosovel's multicultural regionalism and Europeanism are not in opposition to each other, but on the contrary feed one another. Kosovel hoped for a new beginning, noting, "our ideal is a new European person."[97] He envisioned this new European of the future to be free to develop their own cultural distinctiveness in a world of leveling nationalisms. Quixotic as this future world may have been, we should not think of it as utopian in the sense of a non-place that exists outside of history. Kosovel's hope for a future Europe emerges from very specific historical and geographic coordinates.

At any rate, Kosovel's case is emblematic of a widespread literary Europeanism in Trieste, where intellectuals envisioned their projects for a future Europe in tightly sealed parallel compartments, and rarely involved sustained exchanges across perceived cultural divides. Katia Pizzi has discussed this lack of internal conversations in terms of a "missed transculturalism" in the region. She has perceptively suggested that both Slataper and Kosovel's attempts at "achieving a common European identity" were in fact an effort to evoke "an abstract entity called Europe [which] may have acted as a neutral ground, able, by virtue of its remoteness, to diffuse the powerfully divisive forces at play closer to home."[98] Therefore, while Italophone and Slovene-speaking Triestines imagined transcultural identifications in the larger context of the European world of letters, their cultural and political

---

[96] "The League of Nations is a lie."
[97] "Naš ideal je evropski človek, različen po svojih obrazih, a samo eden v svojem velikem stremljenju: ljubiti vse ljudi in v tej ljubezni delati. Ali je narod separatističen, če hoče živeti? Če se hoče razvijati sam v svoji smeri, če hoče izkristalizirati svoje telo v svojem duhu. Bodimu eno po duhu in ljubezni, a ohranimo svoje lastne obraze." *Zbrano Delo* Vol 3.1, 658–659.
[98] Katia Pizzi, "Triestine Literature between Slovenia and Italy: A Case of Missed Transculturalism?" *Primerjalna književnost* 36, no. 1 (2013), 149.

ideals did not seem to apply easily to their own city. Against the background of the multiple and fractured literatures of Trieste, the city remained the center from which these authors always looked elsewhere and projected their writing beyond the narrow horizon of a literary provincialism. Slataper, for instance, saw the Slavs of the Karst as the new barbarians who would reform Europe, but we have no evidence that he knew of Kosovel's work. Svevo, another glaring example, never mentions the Slovenian population of Trieste in his writing. Nevertheless, a comparative approach to this splintered capital of literary modernism shows how Trieste is not only a city of painfully missed opportunities. In their efforts to reimagine Europe, Slataper, Däubler, and Kosovel follow parallel paths that do not intersect, but that was not true of every intellectual of the time. The writers we will discuss in more detail in the following chapters, namely Musil, Svevo, and Joyce, engage in a more robustly interconnected literary invention of Europe. Like Slataper, Däubler, and Kosovel, they imagined the rise of a new transcultural subject, a diverse *Homo Europaeus* that resisted and challenged the constrictive and exclusionary identity paradigm via a nonnational regional patriotism. But unlike them, Musil, Svevo, and Joyce also attempt to weaken the perceived internal borders in Trieste in the name of a European cross-culturalism. They knew about each other's work: Musil read Svevo with great pleasure, Joyce helped steer Svevo's literary career, and Svevo influenced Joyce in important ways. The division between these two groups of writers is not always clear-cut. Däubler's rewriting of the rape of Europa presents affinities with Joyce's adaptation of the myth, even though their similarities may have ended here. While in Paris in 1903, before Joyce moved to Trieste, the two became involved in a bar fight, conducted first in French and then in Latin, over literary matters. Joyce remained curious about Däubler's work until at least 1919, when he borrowed the Triestine's work from Philip Jarnach, but we have no further evidence of a more sustained exchange.

In the following chapters, we will see how the Habsburg Mediterranean and its rhetorical appropriation of the Phoenicians became a powerful trope in the construction of this literary Europe. One of the questions that interest us is what the rehabilitation of the Phoenicians suggests about a particular strand of European modernist classicism that developed after the First World War. A return to the classical tradition was certainly a response to an urgent need for order and reason in the tumultuous years following the war, when the crisis in social, cultural, and political realms was particularly acute. Like in other cultural movements that revisited Greek and Roman antiquity, modernists continued to see the classical world as an exemplary model of equilibrium and harmony. Unlike their classicist predecessors, however, modernists tended to express less optimism about the expressive possibilities of imitation, believing that the heights of the classical world could not be fully replicated. The modernist engagement with the classics is thus less deferential, and often characterized by irony, parody, and satire. Another crucial difference rests with the political uses that European modernism makes of the classical world: nationalists engaged in the pervasive invention of tradition, choosing the Greek and Roman world as the original model of their national and imperial ambitions. The modern classicists that resurrected the Phoenicians had constructed just as utopian a view of the classical world as the self-proclaimed heirs of Greek and Roman antiquity. But they emphasized pacifist cosmopolitanism rather than belligerent nationalism, hybridity rather than racial purity, movement and border crossing rather than fixed territorialities. In aligning with the Phoenicians, the writers we discuss in the following chapters attempt to renew the modernist classicism in which they participate. Thanks to its imagined Phoenician identity, in which literary modernism meets the Mediterranean, Trieste emerges as the privileged locus of an alternative modernity.

Two A Mediterranean Monarchy: Robert Musil and the Politics of Nonnational Loyalty, 1913–1943

In general, Trieste grants,
Both from the mountain upon which it rests and from the sea,
An extraordinarily beautiful view.
The sea in all its glory, the innumerable masts of the ships,
The bustle of people of all clothing and language,
Everything appears appealing and new.
It offers a particularly strange sight to view large sea ships in the canals
In the middle of the city square, whose masts tower over the surrounding houses.[1]
                          (Franz Grillparzer, Diary entry, 1819)

In Opicina I sat on a hill for two hours in the morning.
In Trieste I spent hours gazing upon the open wide sea.[2]
      (Adalbert Stifter, Letter to Johann Ritter von Fritsch, 1857)

Grillparzer and Stifter's contemplative travelogue descriptions of Trieste's calm Mediterranean waters, its towering ship masts, and its

---

[1] "Überhaupt gewährt Triest, sowohl vom Berge herab, an dem es liegt, als von der Seeseite betrachtet, einen außerordentlich schönen Anblick. Das Meer in seiner Herrlichkeit, die zahllosen Masten der Schiffe, das Gewimmel von Menschen aller Kleidung und Sprache, alles ist ansprechend und neu. Einen besonders fremden Anblick gewährt es, mitten auf dem Platze der Stadt bedeutende Meerschiffe in den Kanälen liegen zu sehen, deren Masten die umliegenden Häuser weit überragen." *Tagebücher und Reiseberichte*, ed. Klaus Geissler (Berlin: Verlag der Nation, 1980), 249.

[2] "In Opschina bin ich zwei Stunden Morgens auf einem Hügel gesessen. In Triest habe ich Stunden verbracht, um in das freie weite Meer zu sehen." *Adalbert Stifters Sämmtliche Werke*, ed. August Sauer, vol. 19, *Briefwechsel* (Prague: Gesellschaft zur Förderung deutscher Wissenschaft, Kunst und Literatur in Böhmen, 1901–1927), 28–29.

bustling crowds of polyglot merchants testify to the profound attraction that the Adriatic city held for Austrian authors. Both writers regard the Habsburg Empire's domestic coastline with a combination of intense curiosity and profound awe. Grillparzer's keen spirit of observation renders a crisp portrayal of the industrious seaport with its manifold stimuli and assiduous activity. Refreshingly beautiful, albeit overwhelmingly barbaric, is the impression he collects from the colorful scene at this busy gateway to southern and eastern Europe. Stifter's letter, conversely, records a life-changing experience. He had never seen the sea before, and after years of longing, he enjoys the panoramic view of a maritime spectacle for the first time. For both authors, the view of the Adriatic catalyzes a Mediterranean metamorphosis that leaves them renewed, transformed, and enriched. During his 1909 Dalmatian journey, Hermann Bahr, like Grillparzer and Stifter before him, became infatuated with the same view from the Opicina promontory, nestled between the majesty of the Alps and the splendor of the sea. Bahr's observation of having arrived at a vaguely defined "nowhere" captures an Austrian colonial gaze that reframes Trieste as a place outside of historical reality.[3] In the nineteenth and early twentieth centuries, such travel arrangements were anything but unusual. It was common, in fact, for intellectuals, affluent travelers, and Austrian families of privilege to spend their holidays in Trieste and its environs. The captivating geography of the Austrian Littoral included other vacation resorts such as Sistiana and Duino, whose rocky seascapes would soon comprise the geopoetic scenery of Rainer Maria Rilke's elegies.

Connecting the Austrian inland to maritime trading routes, Trieste also stimulated audacious political fantasies. While Stifter was resting on the Opicina promontory overlooking the Gulf of Trieste, he could probably discern an active construction site in the distance. Two years before, the Archduke Ferdinand Maximilian, the younger brother of Emperor Franz Joseph, had commissioned the construction of the Miramare Castle in the outskirts of Trieste, which was already underway when Stifter arrived. The Viennese architect Carl Junker designed the castle along with a luscious botanical garden where the archduke could cultivate his beloved tropical vegetation. Finished in 1860, the castle eventually became the archduke's primary residence before he pursued his ill-fated political aspirations in Mexico. As a nexus of inspiring

---

[3] Hermann Bahr, *Dalmatinische Reise* (Berlin: Fischer, 1909). Nonetheless, the travel impressions of Trieste become an opportunity to criticize the imperial administration's unwillingness to open an Italian university in the city. According to Bahr, the Austrian crown unwittingly fosters the city's Irredentists, who are denied the possibility of developing their Italian cultural institutions within the confines of the Habsburg state.

dramatic landscapes and neo-medieval architecture, imperial assertiveness, and floral exoticism, the Miramare Castle assumes the features of a powerful symbol for Habsburg Trieste itself. The Adriatic city represented the Crown's bold ambitions for maritime trade on a global scale and embodied at the same time an exotic yet internal Otherness.[4] Despite this double status, the position that Trieste—the monarchy's major commercial seaport and multicultural emporium—occupied in the Austrian literary imagination still constitutes an aspect that has not been sufficiently studied.

It is precisely in this Austrian tradition of the "Italian Journey" that Robert Musil identifies Trieste's political turmoil before the First World War as one of the symptoms of the empire's imminent demise. The author fictionalizes the Triestine question in his sardonic political parody *The Man without Qualities* (*Der Mann ohne Eigenschaften*), writing in a distinctly Austrian context, separate from the longstanding German tradition that extends from Winckelmann and Goethe's *Italienische Reise* to Thomas Mann's novels.[5] While German treatments of voyages to Italy usually belong to the genre of travel literature, Musil becomes the

---

[4] Scholars have debated whether the analytical frameworks developed by postcolonial studies can be applied to the Habsburg Empire. Proponents of this applicability argue that the Austrian colonies were not located overseas as in the French or British empires, but that they were territorially contiguous, and contained within the borders of the empire. Historians have shown, on the other hand, how the economic asymmetry that defines the colonial relationship between prosperous metropolitan centers and exploited peripheries does not easily apply to the Habsburg Empire. Local economies often prospered along with the capital Vienna. Literary historians, however, are more interested in a discursive colonialism and find a postcolonial approach to aesthetic questions and literary representations of Austria's own Orientalism a useful critical platform. Studies have shown that the cultural perceptions of a diverse and non-German environment follow a colonial logic of representation. For postcolonial approaches, see Wolfgang Müller-Funk, Peter Plener, and Clemens Ruthner, ed. *Kakanien Revisited: Das Eigene und das Fremde (in) der österreichisch-ungarischen Monarchie* (Tübingen: Francke, 2001) and Johannes Feichtinger, Ursula Prutsch, and Moritz Csáky, ed. *Habsburg Postcolonial: Machtstrukturen und kollektives Gedächtnis* (Innsbruck: Studienverlag, 2003). Robert Lemon discusses the rhetorical strategies of late Habsburg Orientalism, focusing on Musil's *Törless* along with Hofmannsthal and Kafka. Robert Lemon, *Imperial Messages: Orientalism as Self-Critique in the Habsburg Fin de Siècle* (Rochester, NY: Camden House, 2011).

[5] More recent approaches explore the theoretical and philosophical aspects of Musil's works. See, for instance, Patrizia McBride, *The Void of Ethics: Robert Musil and the Experience of Modernity* (Evanston, IL: Northwestern University Press, 2006), Mark Freed, *Robert Musil and the NonModern* (New York: Continuum, 2011), and Stijn De Cauwer, *A Diagnosis of Modern Life: Robert Musil's Der Mann ohne Eigenschaften as a Critical-Utopian Project* (Brussels: Peter Lang, 2014). In contrast, I emphasize the social and political satire of the novel.

interpreter of a Habsburg tradition that places Italian landscapes within the domestic sphere of a multicultural and multinational empire. He does so, writing against the grain of an Austrian Orientalism that placed Trieste outside of history and modernity. The mapping of Trieste in Musil's literary geography remains a topic that has not yet received the attention it deserves. This conspicuous absence is indeed surprising if one considers that Habsburg Trieste was economically, politically, and strategically too important a city to occupy only a marginal role in a monumental novel with the ambitious objective of offering a panorama of the social milieu of prewar Austria and its capital Vienna. This chapter contends that Musil's literary invention of Europe hinges upon Trieste, a city that for the author encapsulated all the promises and failures, tensions and contradictions of the Habsburg world. For Musil, the acute conflict between the traditional imperial order and the rise of Italian Irredentism in the Adriatic city signaled an internal and structural crisis of the nation at the very height of its affirmation. So, rather than seeing Trieste as yet another example of a failed model of interethnic cohabitation, Musil was more interested in the potential that a nonnational sense of belonging carried in the larger ideological landscape of European modernity. Musil understood Trieste's Europeanism as the expression of a Habsburg transculturalism, through which a state patriotism of multilingual regions allowed its citizens to simultaneously inhabit different communities. The cultural topography of Trieste thus offered Musil the epistemological coordinates of an unfinished futurity, a Europe to come governed by a politics of nonnational loyalty.

Vienna-Trieste, Summer 1913: *Die Adria-Ausstellung* and the Hohenlohe Decrees

Musil's monumental novel begins on a sunny day in August 1913 in Vienna, the imperial metropolis of the fictional country Kakanien. The narrator makes the implicit promise to offer with the imagined setting an unadorned experience of the extradiegetic world. With stark scientific precision, or at least so it seems, the novel narrates the real Vienna, a European capital with its chaotic traffic congestions and anonymous casualties of modern life. But the supposed pledge is hardly honored. The barometric low hanging over the Atlantic is explained with reassuring but misleading pseudoscientific jargon, aimed at fooling the unsuspecting reader. Unless Musil's narrator refers to an exceptional weather pattern for the day in which the novel starts, meteorological reports in all likelihood looked very different that day. The summer of 1913 in Vienna was indeed chilly, cloudy, and unusually rainy. So much that these unseasonable weather conditions almost ruined the inaugural ceremony of the most anticipated public event in Vienna that year, determining a much lower turnout of anticipated visitors over the course of the extended summer.

What Musil's narrator does not mention is that from May 3 to October 5, 1913, the *Österreichische Flottenverein*, the Austrian Navy League organized in the Vienna Prater, under the patronage of the heir presumptive Archduke Franz Ferdinand, the *Österreichische Adria-Ausstellung*, an exhibition celebrating Austria's colonial holdings located along the Adriatic seaboard and its hinterlands. For Franz Ferdinand this ambitious endeavor, which was destined to remain the last major international exhibition in the Austro-Hungarian Empire, was an opportunity to advance his economic and political agenda for the future of the Dual Monarchy, which he hoped to transform into a strong and internationally respected sea power.[6] The Adriatic Exhibition overlapped with other important occasions of public interest, since 1913 also marked the 65th jubilee of the Emperor's ascent to the throne while, in the meantime, the Balkan Wars were fought not far from Vienna. Against the backdrop of increasingly worrying warfare on the Ottoman frontier, the *Adria-Ausstellung* was conceived as an effort to promote an Austrian peace in the region.[7] Modeled on the successful world fairs of the previous century—the ones held in London, Paris, Chicago, and Vienna itself—the large theme park contained exhibitions that displayed the most recent developments in naval architecture, forestry and fishery, botany, and marine zoology, while featuring presentations of local folklore and ethnology pertaining to the Balkan peninsula. At the same time, the empire could boast the strength of its commercial and military navies as well as promote Austrian tourism to seaside resorts and spa towns in Istria, Dalmatia, and Bosnia-Hercegovina. Emperor Franz Joseph presided over the pompous inaugural ceremony, officially conducted by the patron of the Exhibition, Franz Ferdinand. Also present were Minister President Karl von Stürgkh, along with the highest court dignitaries, representatives of the ministerial and diplomatic corps, various other international guests of honor, and imperial government delegations from the Adriatic territories. From Trieste came the *Landesstatthalter*, Prinz Konrad zu Hohenlohe-Schillingsfürst, as well as Alfonso Valerio, mayor of the city. The event conjoined public education and political propaganda, attracting, despite the rainy weather in the summer months of that year, an overall number of over two million visitors with peaks of 80,000 guests on a single Sunday. The

---

[6] Milan Vego, *Austro-Hungarian Naval Policy, 1904–1914* (New York: Routledge, 1996), 182.
[7] The official catalog of the Adriatic Exhibition defined the event "ein Friedenswerk." *Österreichische Adria-Ausstellung Wien 1913. Offizieller Catalog mit einem Plan* (Vienna: Elbemühl, 1913), x.

Figure 2.1 Postcard with aerial view of the Austrian Adriatic Exhibition, 1913. Wikimedia Commons. Illustrator: Alois Kasimir (1852–1930).

Figure 2.2 Prater Rotunda with reconstruction of the Bell Tower and of the Praetorian Palace in Koper, Slovenia, for the Austrian Adriatic Exhibition, 1913. Wikimedia Commons. Photograph: Unknown.

Exhibition was installed in the park area around the Rotunda building, which had been erected for the 1873 Vienna World Fair. Visitors entered the Exhibition near the west access of the Rotunda through an entrance that was a replica of the city gate in Dalmatian Zadar/Zara. The guests immediately reached a large artificial lake, excavated specifically

Figure 2.3 Three women in Dalmatian folk costume in front of a reconstruction of the Venetian House in Piran, Slovenia, for the Austrian Adriatic Exhibition, 1913. The Venetian House is a fifteenth-century building in the Venetian Gothic style, here part of the Bosnia-Hercegovina pavilion. Wikimedia Commons. Photograph: Unknown.

for the Exhibit, imitating a harbor in the Adriatic Sea. The waterfront extended into what the organizers named the *Canale grande*, an eleven-meter-wide artificial channel that in turn led to a large *Café-Insel* and a full-size reproduction of the Trieste-built Austrian Lloyd steamship "Wien," which housed a sizable restaurant. The entire surface area of the water amounted to almost 12,000 square meters (approximately 3 acres). The *Canale* could be crossed by three Venice-inspired bridges offering access to exhibition halls on both sides of the banks. The exhibition halls were replicas of famous buildings in the Austrian Adriatic surrounded by a built scenery of towns and villages, churches, and a small mosque. Among the artistic and architectural reproductions one could count the Praetorian Palace in Koper/Capodistria, the Rector's Palace of Dubrovnik/Ragusa, the Municipal Building of Split/Spalato, the colonnades and narrow passageways of Opatija/Abbazia, the St. George Church in Lovran/Lovrano, and the splendid mosaics of the Euphrasian Basilica in Poreč/Parenzo. Male and female actors, dressed in traditional folk costumes, walked through the streets and alleys to enhance the appearance of ethnic and cultural authenticity.

All installations had to be as genuine and realistic as possible: for the aquaria of the Natural Museum on display, the organizers shipped to Vienna the equivalent of sixty cubic meters (more than 2,000 cubic feet) of seawater from the Bay of Trieste. On proud display was an entire section devoted to Trieste, the shiny crown jewel of the Habsburg Mediterranean. The port city told a remarkable success story. Steadfast in resolve and true to her dynastic commitment, Trieste was commercially irreplaceable and politically invaluable. Trieste was the tangible demonstration of Austrian administrative achievements and the metaphorical springboard from which to dive into future endeavors in the Adriatic and beyond. The Trieste exhibit showed panoramic views of the city and the port area, as well as pompously boasting the latest work of civil engineering such as the San Vito road tunnel, opened to the public in 1911. On display were also the geological attractions of the region with a reconstruction of a Karst grotto that led to a panorama of the Miramare Castle. Creating the powerful illusion of an adventurous and culturally edifying maritime journey, the exhibit offered the spectacle of an exotic yet domesticated Mediterranean atmosphere. A red and white lighthouse, visible from afar, clearly indicated that the goal of the *Adria-Ausstellung* was a celebration of an already well-established Austrian imperial power in the Adriatic. But the exhibition was also much more than a simple glorification of past annexations and territorial gains. The vividly painted dioramas and the movie theater showing cinematographic renderings of pleasant sea voyages offered visitors the unmistakable notion that the whole project was in large part the affirmation of a renewed and modernized colonial fantasy that made visible the many new economic opportunities and chances of exploitation that the Habsburg Mediterranean offered. The message was often embraced by the press, which did not fail to extol the virtues of the Adriatic Exhibition. Commentators saw in the ambitions of new colonial explorations the source of renewed imperial strength.

To make the public realize the full extent of Austria's civilizing mission, the organizers needed a clear visual illustration for its Viennese audience, one that tapped into classical representations of colonial might and maritime conquest. The promotional material for the Exhibition, which included photographs, postcards, commemorative stamps, and posters, often featured modern adaptations of the myth of Europa. One such attempt to capture Austria's colonial imagination is the sketch for a postcard designed by Bertold Löffler (1874–1960), the painter and illustrator associated with the Vienna Secession. Löffler's postcard clearly imitates Renaissance paintings of the Europa motif, with the helpless girl transported on the open sea, her hair blowing in the wind. One could gloss Löffler's postcard with a passage from Musil's novel, in which Ulrich, deconstructing the Platonic dualism between body and soul, tries to convince his new lover Bonadea of the mystical transport inherent in boxing: "Muscles and nerves leap and fence with the 'I'; but this 'I'—the whole body, the soul, the will, the central and entire person as legally distinguished from all others—is swept along by his muscles and nerves like Europa riding the Bull."[8] Both Ulrich and Löffler conceive of Europa as a helpless maiden holding steadfast to keep her equilibrium while she is carried away. But Löffler's Adriatic Europa is not riding a bull, as she is perched upon a dark octopus about to envelop her with an outstretched tentacle. The substitution contributes to an even more ominous scene. The sinister embrace of the octopus occurs in the context of a conspicuous contrast of colors. The warm ochre robe and the red slippers of the maiden stand out against the white background, the black octopus, and the icy blue of the sea. Löffler's draft may have been deemed too revealing of the insidious nature of Austria's colonial endeavors. The sketch did not make the cut. A different tone was needed. The Adriatic Exhibition, after all, was

---

[8] Robert Musil, *The Man without Qualities* (New York: Vintage, 1996), 24. In the German original the passage is as follows: "die Muskeln und Nerven springen und fechten mit dem Ich; dieses aber, das Körperganze, die Seele, der Wille, diese ganze, zivilrechtlich gegen die Umwelt abgegrenzte Haupt- und Gesamtperson wird von ihnen nur so obenauf mitgenommen, wie Europa, die auf dem Stier sitzt." Robert Musil, *Der Mann ohne Eigenschaften* (Hamburg: Rowohlt, 2006), 28–29.

Figure 2.4 Bertold Löffler (Austrian, 1874–1960). *Vorzeichnung für eine Postkarte der Adria-Ausstellung*, 1913. Tuschfeder, Kreide, Wasserfarben. Inventory number: 116235/1. © Wien Museum

Robert Musil and the Politics of Nonnational Loyalty, 1913–1943 101

Figure 2.5 Kurt Libesny (Austrian, 1892–1938). *Poster for the Austrian Adriatic Exposition*, 1913. Color crayon, tusche, and spatter lithograph. Sheet: 630 x 470 mm. (24 13/16 x 18 ½ in.). The Baltimore Museum of Art: Gift of Henry E. Treide, BMA 1956.85.50. Photography By: Mitro Hood.

intended as a celebration, filled with the optimism of those who look forward to a bright future.

The official poster for the Adriatic Exhibition struck that very note. It was conceived by the painter and graphic designer Kurt Libesny (1892–1938), who is known for his propaganda billboards during the First World War and commercial Art Deco advertising placards in the 1920s. His 1913 Art Nouveau poster for the Exhibition fully captures the complex rhetorical strategies of the Habsburg colonial propaganda. Framed by two captions of descriptive labels about the Exhibition, the central image of the poster features an armor-clad knight on horseback who holds in his right hand the reins of a battle-ready stallion in full barding. On the knight's right forearm hangs a shield with the insignia of the Austrian double-headed eagle. His helmet, held by its strap, drops behind on his shoulders. A caparison-like blanket casually drapes his upper leg above the knee, arranged in such a way as to suggest a rescue mission. The horse is clad with a criniere to guard its neck, while a decorated chanfron equipped with a sharp spike on the forehead protects the animal's face and signals the cavalier's readiness to charge. The posture of the knight is belligerent: the reins are pulled so that the head of the horse is arched, suggesting a forward movement. A peytral to safeguard the chest of the horse completes the sophisticated and detailed equestrian paraphernalia. With his left arm, the knight holds a mermaid whose fishtail lies over the horse's back. While the Austrian knight maintains a stern look forward, the body language of the mermaid is more relaxed and unmistakably sexualized. She smiles lasciviously, her head hanging back, while her breasts are exposed. Both the knight and the mermaid wear head decorations in the form of a flower headband, which suggests a ritualistic union between the two such as an imminent wedding ceremony. What evokes this matrimony is also the color scheme. While Löffler's visual vocabulary emphasized color contrast, Libesny opts for greater chromatic harmony. The two figures and the horse are colored in shades of black, white, and grey with the exception of some flowers in their headbands, several dots on her fishtail, and a long necklace on her chest that are in deep red. The couple is riding against the background of a large sunset of a reddish orange color that gradually fades into a light yellow hue closer to the horizon and then recedes into an ochre-colored sea.

Libesny revives and offers a visual representation of the old Habsburg motto *Bella gerant alii, tu felix Austria nube* ("Let the others wage war, you happy Austria, marry!") that encapsulated the expansionist strategy of the old imperial elite. The sexual politics here are less concerned with inter-dynastic marriages than they are with the sanctioning of colonial expansion via the trope of institutional marriage. The viewer can see in the background a jagged shoreline with coastal settlements, suggestive of either small villages or a larger city, and numerous sailboats faring back and forth. The iconography of the medieval knight saving the damsel in distress is juxtaposed with Austria's imagined and promulgated role in the Adriatic, a saving and civilizing force. The knight signals the *pax austriaca* in the coastal territories of the Adriatic Sea, a hard-fought peace that will be defended, once again, with arms if necessary. The peaceful but battle-ready knight embodies the counterintuitive Latin adage *Si vis pacem para bellum*, "If you want peace, prepare for war," so dear to Musil's character, General Stumm von Bordwehr.

The mermaid is a personification of the Adria. The Austrian knight-errant comes to the rescue of the water nymph, but her relocation on the horse leaves her without any agency whatsoever. Her piscatorial extremity restricts mobility and is an unsurmountable handicap outside her native aquatic environment. Libesny presents the colonial relationship underlying the Austrian possession of Adria in obvious sexualized overtones. Not only is she carried: she is also carried away from her home. Precisely this staged ambiguity between her evident helplessness and projected willingness to be rescued, a common colonial trope we have seen in Däubler's reception of classical mythology, is highly reminiscent of the iconography of the rape of Europa, the maiden carried away by the supposedly saving grace of the divine bull. In Libesny's poster, the aesthetics of sexual violence conveys a politics of colonial domination. Like in other colonial narratives, the story must project an implicit positive response onto the victim in order to be complete with a socially constructive and morally edifying message. It is not enough to assert Austria's imperial presence in the Adria: the Adria must willingly accept the civilizing mission of her culturally and technologically superior rescuer. In this modern transmutation of a classical trope, the Habsburg Adria is the new Europa.

While Trieste's commercial emporium and its picturesque backgrounds of the littoral Karst were all favorite topics of discussion during the Exhibition in Vienna, the talk of the town in Trieste during the month of August in 1913 was of a different nature. The Austrian *Statthalter*, the abovementioned Prinz Hohenlohe, was a special guest at the inauguration of the Exhibition at the beginning of May. Already in that occasion, he had angered Italian Irredentists by declaring in his opening remarks that Trieste should be considered a *Nationalitätenstadt* that did not belong to any nationality, given its role as commercial port of the empire. On August 21, 1913, Hohenlohe decided to relieve all Italian-born municipal clerks of duty. His decrees immediately stirred up much controversy. Street demonstrations, public protests, and incendiary newspaper articles gave voice to a general discontent. In the past, the Austrian monarchy had allowed the employment of *Reichsitaliener* within the ranks of the Habsburg municipal bureaucracy. This concession, made when neither the Habsburg administration nor the Italians in Trieste were concerned about nationalism in the Adriatic city, was part of an effort to grant Trieste ample local autonomy. Now, the official rationale of the new legislation was to limit foreign interference in state affairs, but behind the decrees stood a growing fear that the questionable allegiances of these Italian clerks fueled the Irredentist movement in the city. The decision stirred up much protest among Italian nationalists, who saw Hohenlohe's decrees as a maneuver to undermine their power in the city. What angered Italian Irredentists even more was the enthusiastic reception of the Hohenlohe decrees by the Slovenian community in Trieste, who welcomed the announcement as a new opportunity to enhance their presence in the public administration. Hohenlohe's intention was not necessarily to favor a pro-Slovenian agenda, but the circumstances were such that the Irredentists interpreted the ordinance in this way.[9] The Slovenian community in the city was grappling with the end of the Second Balkan War, which had ended two weeks earlier, pondering the immediate consequences of the Bulgarian aggression of its former ally Serbia. Many Slovenian intellectuals in Trieste considered the city as an essential center of their cultural and political life, continuing to envision a gradual Slovenian nation-building process within the framework of the Austrian state, often preferring this Austro-Slav solution to any projects of a future Yugo-Slav confederation.[10] The Austrian loyalty of the Slovenians also angered the separatist Italians, who suspected a conspiratorial coalition between the Slavic community and the imperial administration aimed at weakening Italian influence in the city. Against this background of competing interests, the Hohenlohe decrees looked like a major imperial interference in local matters, adding fuel to the mounting tension between Italian-speaking and Slovene-speaking Triestines. The whole

---

[9] According to Elio Apih, Hohenlohe did not necessarily intend to strengthen the position of Slovenes in the city, but to reduce the number of Italian Irredentists in key positions of the public administration, not disdaining an alliance with members of the socialist internationalism in the city. Elio Apih, *Trieste* (Bari: Laterza, 2015), 80–81.

[10] Bulgaria would now be excluded from such a state project. The political body that would host the southern Slavs saw the light after the First World War as the Kingdom of Serbs, Croats, and Slovenes. It was colloquially called Yugoslavia, land of the south Slavs.

affair caused an awkward diplomatic crisis between the Kingdom of Italy and the Austro-Hungarian Monarchy, now members of the Triple Alliance. The Italian government in Rome sent an official grievance to the Austrian authorities, who chose to ignore the complaint. The Italian press ran indignant articles accusing the Austrians, despite their official alliance in foreign policy matters, of an ill-concealed Italophobia in the context of domestic affairs.

During his extended medical leave in 1913, Musil stayed in Italy from August to December and had the opportunity to observe the vociferous resurgence of Irredentism in Trieste.[11] On his journey to Rome, Musil stopped in Trento, the other hotly contested Habsburg Italian city, just two days after the protests in Trieste began, observing firsthand a question that would come to be of the utmost importance to Italy's decision to join the war in 1915. Robert and his wife Martha (née Heinemann) were travelling in Italy at that time and must have closely followed the news coming from Trieste and Rome. We have no evidence that Musil witnessed in person the local controversy that would soon turn into a diplomatic incident, but traveling through the empire's Italian-speaking territories and residing in Rome offered him the possibility to follow the Triestine question closely. The author came to understand that Trieste's traditional dynastic patriotism was now facing a formidable competitor, namely the belligerent nationalism of Italian separatists that the Hohenlohe decrees exacerbated. In the mid-1920s, Musil fictionalized the experiences from his trips to Italy— in particular those to the northern Adriatic seaboard. The incest episode between Anders and Agathe in the "Journey to Paradise"[12] was set "somewhere in Istria or on the eastern border of Italy or on the Tyrrhenian Sea."[13] Musil's Italian journey, however, provided other lasting impressions. My contention is that the events of August 1913 in Trieste had a crucial impact on Musil's understanding of the nationalist conflicts in the empire. With the benefit of hindsight, Musil later realized that the dwindling *Kaisertreue* of the once loyal Habsburg Trieste marked the beginning of the end for the monarchy. Evidence of this attention comes from Martha Musil's letter to the author dated December 6, 1915. She writes, telling him news about the political scene at home, "The Stürgkh Ministry has been partially reorganized:

---

[11] Musil was diagnosed with general neurasthenia and given a generous six-month leave from his librarian post at the Technical College in Vienna.
[12] "Reise ins Paradies."
[13] "[i]rgendwo in Istrien oder am Ostsaum von Italien oder am Tyrrhenischen Meer." Musil, *MoE*, 1652.

Hohenlohe has now become Minister of the Interior; I have forgotten about the two others who have changed."[14] The now former *Statthalter* of Trieste seems to be a familiar figure to the couple; he is the only politician whose name she spontaneously remembers. Two years after the fact, the memories of his controversial ordinances seem to be still fresh. It is likely that Musil followed the issue in the Austrian press as well. As we will see below, Count Leinsdorf's outrage in *The Man without Qualities* echoes the language of the conservative journal *Österreichische Rundschau*, published by the royal and imperial press (*K. u. k. Hof-Buchdruckerei*). In the September edition of that year, the journal published an article by M. von Leja, "Die Austrofizierung der Triester Stadtbeamten," in which the new legislation is praised: "Thanks to the issued decrees, the behavior hostile to Austria in Trieste has now been stopped permanently. In a few years, one will be able to fully appreciate the great merit that Prince Hohenlohe has acquired in dealing with our first port city."[15] In a quite ominous and prophetic tone, the article continues, "The conditions in Trieste illustrate on a small scale that a policy based on peace at all cost can never achieve a satisfactory result."[16] Austria-Hungary is inching closer to the war.

Musil's War Journalism 1916–1918: Italian Irredentism in the *Soldaten-Zeitung*

In his military service during the First World War, Musil came to realize the tactical significance of Trieste's geographic position for the Dual Monarchy. After being stationed in the Dolomites as an infantry lieutenant just north of Trieste on the Italian front, he then occupied a strategic position in the imperial state propaganda machine, authoring and editing newspaper articles for what was initially called the *Tiroler Soldaten-Zeitung* (June 1916 to April 1917) and for *Heimat* (1918). Musil joined the editorial staff of the *Tiroler Soldaten-Zeitung* in June 1916, officially assumed the position of managing editor in October of the

---

[14] "Das Ministerium Stürgkh ist teilweise neu zusammengestellt: Hohenlohe ist jetzt Minister des Inneren geworden; die beiden anderen, die gewechselt haben, habe ich vergessen" (*KA/Lesetexte/Vorkriegs- und Kriegskorrespondenz 1895–1918*).

[15] "Durch die jetzt herausgegebenen Erlässe wird nun dem österreichisch-feindlichen Gebaren in Triest endgültig ein Riegel vorgeschoben. In einigen Jahren wird man erst in der Lage sein voll zu würdigen, welch großes Verdienst sich Fürst Hohenlohe dadurch um unsere erste Hafenstadt erworben hat." M. von Leja, "Die Austrofizierung der Triester Stadtbeamten," *Österreischische Rundschau* 36 (1913), 387.

[16] "Die Verhältnisse in Triest geben derart im kleinen ein Beispiel, daß eine auf Frieden um jeden Preis fußende Politik nie einen befriedigenden Erfolg erzielen kann." von Leja, "Austrofizierung," 388.

same year, and proceeded with a complete reorientation of the newspaper.[17] The renamed *Soldaten-Zeitung* abandoned its regional scope and aimed at addressing a readership beyond the Tyrol. The military newspaper's mission was to provide the civilian population with reports from the war front. Circulating also in Vienna, the publication emphasized the necessity of the empire's unity, promoting the old Austrian *Gesamtstaatspatriotismus*, a state patriotism that operated outside the logic of modern ethnolinguistic nationalism. To this end, the newspaper adopted an official position that did not simply counter the constitutional legitimacy of burgeoning nationalist aspirations. More radically, the newspaper articles negated the sociopolitical validity of the national paradigm. The question of Italian Irredentism featured prominently in Musil's new editorial direction. The annexation of the culturally Italian but politically Austrian cities of Trento and Trieste was an important part of Italian interventionist rhetoric since the two cities were for Italian nationalists the painful reminder of an incomplete process of unification. Musil contrasted the arguments of the Irredentists with a manifold rhetorical strategy that combined sober critique with flowery propaganda, mordant sarcasm with bitter irony. Musil anchored his main argument against Irredentists in the traditional nonnational, dynastic devotion of the Adriatic city, the *urbs fidelissima* that had sworn allegiance to the Emperor during the 1848 revolution in Europe. The reiterated stance in the articles of the *Soldaten-Zeitung* was that contrary to the claims of the Irredentists, the majority of the Italian-Austrian population continued to remain true to the Austrian monarchy. The high treason of separatists could be explained with a generational conflict in which mischievous and adventuresome youngsters rebelled against the unambiguous pro-Austrian will of the people. In the last editorial of the *Soldaten-Zeitung*, entitled "Legacy," Musil summarized his overall experience at the newspaper, describing his handling of Italian nationalism as "a sober and ruthless treatment of the Irredentism question."[18] His service in the Austrian military familiarized Musil with different regionally inflected, nonnational formulas of belonging such as Bohemian regional patriotism or Adriatic multiculturalism that developed on a parallel track with Czech nationalism, Italian Irredentism, and Hungarian claims to independence. Musil's experience at the

---

[17] Mariaelisa Dimino, Elmar Locher, and Massimo Salgaro, ed. *Oberleutnant Robert Musil als Redakteur der Tiroler Soldaten-Zeitung* (Paderborn: Wilhelm Fink, 2019).

[18] Musil describes "eine nüchtern rücksichtslose Behandlung der Irredentafragen." "Vermächtnis," *Soldaten-Zeitung* 44 (April 15, 1917), 4. The essay articulates Musil's "retrospective programmatic stance." Roman Urbaner, "Schriftführer Musil. Der Jahrhundertschriftsteller als Chefredakteur der *Soldaten-Zeitung*," *Quart Heft für Kultur Tirol* 5 (2005), 60.

war front was certainly formative, serving the author as a rhetorical training ground. Whether he fully embraced the war propaganda or dexterously impersonated through an ideological ventriloquism opinions that were not his own, these writings represent an experimental site of oratorical finesse whose benefits the author would reap in his later essayistic and novelistic enterprises.

Europe in Musil's Essays, 1912–1923

Placing Musil's war propaganda texts in conversation with later essays shows that he was not simply parroting official directives of the imperial war effort machine when it came to questions of national belonging. His essays before the outbreak of the conflict confirm that he was indeed skeptical of national identities, suggesting that the author agreed with the nonnational positions of the state propaganda during the war, while not necessarily with its foreign policy strategies. The nonnational vocation of the Austrian military derived from the practice of bringing together officers from the most diverse ethnic and linguistic backgrounds. Their loyalty to the House of Habsburg, represented by the black and yellow flag, transcended claims to a national origin. Musil's critical writings before and after the war show his abiding interest in the interethnic dynamics underlying the multicultural state, and his analysis of the tensions between nonnational allegiances and nationalism in Austria. In "Politics in Austria" (1912), the author sees, with his usual tongue-in-cheek perspective, Habsburg multiculturalism as a possible model for a global breakdown of national barriers: "Austria could be a world experiment" given the "cultural symbiosis of different peoples" that can be observed in the ethnically heterogeneous regions of the empire.[19] Musil later returns to the notion of the ethnic and cultural symbiosis fostered within a great number of Habsburg territories. In "Buridan's Austrian" (1919), Musil retrospectively claims: "In theory, giving our mingling of peoples, we ought to have been the most exemplary state in the world: this is so clear that it is not at all evident why, in practice, we have emerged as a European scandal, right behind Turkey."[20] The model of cultural exchange and ethnic hybridity,

---

[19] Robert Musil, *Precision and Soul. Essays and Addresses*, edited and translated by Burton Pike and David S. Luft (Chicago: The University of Chicago Press, 1990), 19. "Österreich könnte ein Weltexperiment sein" thanks to its "kulturelle[n] Symbiose verschiedener Völker." Musil, "Politik in Österreich" in *Gesammelte Werke* (Hamburg: Rowohlt, 1978), 2:993.

[20] Musil, *Precision*, 100. "Wir hätten theoretisch mit unserer Völkerdurchdringung der vorbildlichste Staat der Welt sein müssen; mit solcher Sicherheit, daß sich eigentlich gar nicht sagen läßt, warum wir praktisch nicht darüber hinausgekommen sind, ein europäisches Ärgernis zu sein, gleich hinter der Türkei." Musil, "Buridans Österreicher" in *Gesammelte Werke*, 8:1031.

says the author, becomes defunct in the wake of a global war that was waged in the name of national deliverance.

After a brief flirtation with pan-German nationalism, Musil comes to approach the concept of the nation as the result of a successfully crafted political fiction two years later in his 1921 essay "'Nation' as Ideal and as Reality," in which he states: "Frankly speaking, however it has been formulated, 'nation' is a fantasy."[21] Musil's word choice can be misleading, as is often the case in his essays. Instead of indicating with the German term "Ideal" a lofty ideal to which one can and should aspire, Musil employs the term ironically to indicate a delusion. The essay remains significant for Musil's deep understanding of the dynamics of nationalism. Musil observes that nationalism subordinates an individual's primary identifications such as class, geographic origin, sex, gender, language, and religious affiliation to its claim of absolute supremacy. Accordingly, an individual is primarily defined by his or her nationality. Before one can recognize oneself as a woman or a man, a Jew or a Protestant, a teacher or a carpenter, gay or straight, one must first be German, Italian, or French. Nationalism subsumes these primary identifications and may exclude any of these categories from its definition of who belongs to a given nation and who is "naturally" excluded from it.[22] Deconstructing the logic of national belonging and exclusion, Musil argues that the main bond between human beings is their profession, which ultimately shapes their contribution to society: a German peasant has more in common with a French farmer than with a compatriot of a different social extraction.

The fictional nature of the nation as *Einbildung* does not indicate, however, that it could or should be easily dismissed. The author recognizes the powerful allure that the nation exerts upon multiple strata of postwar society, and its remarkable capacity to mobilize the masses. Even so, he deconstructs racialist assumptions of ethnic purity, so dear

---

[21] Musil, *Precision*, 112. "Gerade gesprochen, ist die Nation eine Einbildung in allen Fassungen, die man ihr gab." "Die Nation als Ideal und Wirklichkeit" in *Gesammelte Werke*, 8:1071. Musil's essay is one of the earliest texts of the twentieth century to express a negative critique of racism. Markus Zisselsberger has argued that Musil's view of the nation as social-political imaginary anticipates Benedict Anderson's idea of the nation as an "imagined community." "Cultural Nationalism in the Twilight of History: Robert Musil's Austrian ImagiNation," *Modern Austrian Literature* 37, no. 1–2 (2004): 21–45.

[22] In *The Man without Qualities*, the narrator echoes this idea, arguing that the inhabitants of any country possess an entire set of at least nine social and psychological characters, "einen Berufs-, einen National-, einen Staats-, einen Klassen-, einen geographischen, einen Geschlechts-, einen bewußten, einen unbewußten und vielleicht noch einen privaten Charackter." Musil, *MoE*, 34.

to European nationalisms, by stating that nations are "Rassengemische," echoing Nietzsche's postulation of a mixed European race and the resulting abandonment of the national paradigm.[23] Ultimately, the most pressing political goal for a future Europe should be solving the crisis of the nation-state, finding a way out of "the dead end of imperial nationalism."[24] Steering away from this path was no easy feat. Although Nietzsche represented one of the most important influences on the Austrian writer, Musil had to grapple with the fact that he was writing at a time in which membership in the nation was slowly becoming the dominant sense of belonging and the nation-state was replacing other forms of political organization. This progression, so central to modernity, was felt most acutely in the transition from the old empire to the new countries in Central Europe.

Musil is perhaps the most attentive witness and astute interpreter of these radical transformations. As an individualist, incapable of committing to the agenda of a given political party, Musil judged political movements and parties independently from their overarching ideology, looking at how they approached, solved, or negated concrete problems. This, however, never meant that Musil was disinterested in politics. He spoke about politics from the margins of literature, far from party intellectuals and the political establishment.[25] His critical essays, often characterized by an unorthodox usage of political vocabulary, are textual experiments in which Musil refused to fully commit to any ideological dogmas. They describe ideas in flux, a checkered trajectory of conflicting positions encompassing a brief flirtation with proto-fascist rhetoric, an occasional proximity to socialist ideas, and a final deconstruction of nationalist notions of ethno-racial purity. Fluctuations notwithstanding, Musil generally professed a strong commitment to democratic

---

[23] Musil, *Gesammelte Werke*, 8:1063. Musil's debt to Nietzsche is well known. Nietzsche had a profound impact on the young Musil, an impact that the author will later define in terms of a self-discovery. In a letter dated August 12, 1938, Musil counts Nietzsche's *Jenseits von Gut und Böse* und *Genealogie der Moral* among the "Bücher, ... die ich in meiner Jugend dazu mißbraucht habe, mich selbst zu erkennen" Musil, *Briefe*, ed. Adolf Frisé (Hamburg: Rowohlt, 1981), 1:837.

[24] "Sackgasse des Imperial-Nationalismus" Musil, *Gesammelte Werke*, 8:1075.

[25] Klaus Amann has shown how Musil used to be misunderstood as an apolitical writer because of his unorthodox and idiosyncratic use of common political terminology. A case in point is his usage of the term *unpolitisch*, literally meaning "apolitical." Musil employs the term as synonymous with "autonomous" and "independent" which is indicative of Musil's freedom from the pragmatic constraints, claims, and obligations of politics seen as a social institution. See Klaus Amann, *Robert Musil, Literatur und Politik: mit einer Neuedition ausgewählter politischer Schriften aus dem Nachlass* (Hamburg: Rowohlt), 2007.

values. His reaction to the general war euphoria of the first months of the First World War was not immune to the nationalist rhetoric of the time. Musil publishes the essay "Europeanism, War, Germanness" in *Die Neue Rundschau* in September 1914. The conflagration of the war shattered Musil's belief in Nietzsche's "ideal of the European persona" that transcended state and nations, a Europeanism replaced now by the secular mysticism of a brotherly, pan-German union.[26] Musil, however, soon abandons this nationalist rhetoric. By the early 1920s, his ideological experimentalism is already settled on an idea of transcultural Europe that acknowledges the unintended consequences of the old Habsburg social and civic life. Rather than indulging in a misplaced imperial nostalgia, Musil recovers Nietzsche's "good Europeanism" and comes to value the social dynamics of hybridization that the Danube Monarchy had fostered. This lack of wistful longing shows that Musil did not mourn Austria-Hungary in the ways in which many of his contemporaries remembered it, but as a platform of ideological possibilities that could be recuperated and explored later. His 1919 term *Völkerdurchdringung*, translated by Burton Pike and David Luft as "mingling of peoples," possesses a wider semantic range that includes concepts of interpenetration, permeability, and transfusion. Musil recognizes in the ethnically and linguistically mixed Habsburg imperial subjects the crystallization of a transcultural identity—fluid, open-ended, and capable of incorporating cultural alterity—which remains an alternative possibility to the monolithic impositions of national belonging.

Richard Coudenhove-Kalergi, founder of the jingoist Pan-Europa movement, had applauded Musil for his support of a United States of Europe, but his praise was more self-serving than accurate. Musil was not celebrating Europe's imperial legacy, fueled by a belligerent nationalism, but envisioned a post-imperial democratic foundation that allowed for a multidimensional collection of identities that could be inhabited simultaneously and that did not exclude each other. Differently from many contemporary thinkers who associated European identity with the essence of a superior Western subject, Musil conceives of the European by virtue of the external and contingent socio-historic conditions, which render anyone potentially capable of barbarism or high-minded philosophical investigations. But what happens to this multicultural subject that emerges from the material reality and the historic conditions of the empire once said empire no longer exists?

---

[26] "wir haben nicht gewusst, wie schön und brüderlich der Krieg ist, teils mit unserer Absicht, denn es schwebte uns ein Ideal des europäischen Menschen vor, das über Staat und Volk hinausging." Musil, *Gesammelte Werke*, 8:1020.

Already by the end of the war, Musil starts to rethink his positions in an untitled essay fragment, dated 1918.[27] Here, Musil envisions only two viable options for the geopolitical balance in Europe: "either an armed peace or the dissolution of the state in a European or world community."[28] Musil persevered in this opinion for many years. In a letter to the chief editor of the *Prager Presse*, dated April 1921, he insists on the creation of a European community, pointing out the need for a revision of the Versailles Treaty. In the letter, Musil continues to see the Paris Peace Treaty as an intolerable injustice inflicted upon the Germans. The new reconfiguration of Europe should avoid the punitive logic of economic retaliation. Instead of a constitution of states divided by bestial rivalries, this form of European unification should occur in a fashion that is, in Musil's words, *überstaatlich* and possibly *unstaatlich*.[29] Musil believed in a future that would mark the gradual disappearance of nation-states, an evolution that would imply that the state apparatus would be deprived of its coercive power of appellation, i.e., the nation's calling upon the individual, determining to what nation a given person belongs. In this Europe of the future, the social and political organization of civic life should wield limited power over individual choices and primary identity markers.

In 1922, Musil publishes "Helpless Europe," in which he attempts a broad historical diagnosis of the postwar period. The author takes a position against essentialist conceptions of identity, arguing that the subject lacks any predetermined and innate qualities. Here Musil conceives of identity as the product of sociohistorically determined circumstances, which make human beings capable both "of cannibalism as well as the Critique of Pure Reason."[30] In his outright rejection of racial theories, Musil extends his critique of nationalism to European

---

[27] The text is conventionally referred to as "Das Ende des Krieges." For the purpose of identification, Adolf Frisé, the editor of Musil's collected works, assigns to Musil's untitled essays a conventional title and puts it in square brackets.

[28] "Es gibt zwei Möglichkeiten: Machtfrieden oder Auflösung des Staats in einer europäischen oder Weltgemeinsamkeit." Musil, *Gesammelte Werke*, 8:1341.

[29] "Uns Deutschen ist ein unerträgliches Unrecht zugefügt worden. Es ist unvermeidlich, dass wir nach einer Neugestaltung Europas streben. Es ist unvermeidlich, daß wir eine Revision der Frieden fordern. Aber sie soll keine restitutio in integrum sein, sondern sie muß aus der Machtpolitik und Revanchekette hinausführen. Statt einer Konstitution Europas in rivalisierenden Bestialstaaten muß eine Form der Vereinigung der in sich geeinten Völker untereinander gefunden werden, überstaatlich und möglichst unstaatlich." Musil, *Briefe* 1:227. Musil's sense of belonging to a broader sphere of German-speaking culture should not be mistaken for political pan-Germanist nationalism.

[30] "Dieses Wesen ist ebensoleicht fähig der Menschenfresserei wie der Kritik der reinen Vernunft." Musil, *Gesammelte Werke*, 8:1081.

chauvinism. He takes a jab at the Spenglerism of Hermann Hesse's 1919 essay on *The Brothers Karamazov* where Hesse denounced the alleged Slavification of the European spirit, a process that he thought responsible for the decline of Europe. Motivated by a postwar resentment, Hesse fears a dangerous regression to a matriarchal order that, in his view, destabilizes the essential patriarchy of Europe. He equates Russia with a primordial Asia, establishing a dichotomy between an enlightened West, opposed to an occult and mysterious East.[31] Hesse's literary demonization of Dostoevsky is not the only aspect that troubles Musil. Hesse deploys a typical Orientalist trope that refuses to attribute to a constructed eastern alterity the privilege of historical development and hence the ability for social and political progress. To Musil, the most pernicious aspect of Hesse and Spengler's cultural analysis was the scientific pretense of their dogmatic positions. In addition, as an anti-Enlightenment thinker, Spengler was promoting a nationalist ideology that contested the values of liberal democracies. At this point in Musil's intellectual maturation, the Austrian author could not be farther removed from Spengler, Hesse's exclusionary essentialism, and the general postwar rhetoric of identifying a scapegoat for the First World War.[32] Musil's main argument is that the European is not annihilated by an external threat, but by causes that are intrinsic to Europe's cultural morphology. Europe stagnantly dwells in a helpless state not only because of the rise of nationalist ideologies, but especially since the intellectual elite shares the same idealist philosophy. According to Musil, Hesse is attempting to save a lofty European ideal, but does not realize that he himself—through his Western European chauvinism—is the cause for its crisis. Musil returns to criticize Spengler a year later, in a fragmentary draft for the essay "The German as Symptom," where he notes that the European mind is not doomed to decadence, but, on the contrary, is in transition toward a new but still unknown configuration.[33]

---

[31] "Die Brüder Karamasow oder Der Untergang Europas," in Hermann Hesse, *Gesammelte Werke*, vol. 12 (Frankfurt am Main: Suhrkamp, 1970), 320–337.
[32] In March of the year before, Musil had mocked Spengler's cultural pessimism in the essay "Geist und Erfahrung" with the witty subtitle "Anmerkungen für Leser, welche dem Untergang des Abendlandes entronnen sind." Musil, *Gesammelte Werke*, 8:1042.
[33] "Der heutige Zustand des europäischen Geistes ist meiner Ansicht nach kein Verfall, sondern ein noch nicht vollzogener Übergang, keine Überreife, sondern Unreife." Musil, *Gesammelte Werke*, 8:1367.

Ulrich, the Man without Patriotic Qualities

This sense of an open-ended future permeates Musil's encyclopedic and unfinished novel. Just as Musil saw his essays as textual experiments in a larger analysis of Austrian prewar society, so does he conceive of *The Man without Qualities* as a fictional exploration of the ideological complexity of modernity. In the novel, much of the author's earlier philosophical reflections about the mode of negative subjectivity take on a political spin.[34] Musil believed that a defining question of modern Austrian society was the clash between traditional Habsburg nonnational allegiances and the affirmation of the national paradigm. He could not exempt his protagonist from addressing this conflict. In the essay written for a school assignment, a young and undisciplined Ulrich offers a mordant and radical critique of patriotism. The topic of the school essay is *Vaterlandsliebe* in Austria, a writing assignment whose pedagogical objective combined a grammar exercise and the patriotic indoctrination of the student body. As such, the assignment was intended to comply with state-sanctioned educational guidelines that establish straightforward and unproblematic learning goals. The unsuspecting teacher who assigned the essay was certainly not envisioning a challenge to the very heart of such a delicate matter. Yet, upon its completion and circulation among teachers and members of the school administration, the essay ignites a heated controversy, ultimately provoking a multistep chain reaction. Showing an early tendency toward skepticism and freethinking, teenage Ulrich offers an interpretation of the love of fatherland that is inadvertently inflammatory, dismaying parents and educators alike. Ulrich's main argument can be condensed in the solemn declaration: "anyone who really loved his country must never regard it as the best country in the world."[35] Carried away by what seems to him a profound thought, the young student continues, with an additional insight that

---

[34] In an oft-quoted diary entry, Musil writes: "Der Dichter eilt der polit.[ischen] Entwicklung voraus. Was Dichtung ist, ist etwas später Politik." Musil, *Tagebücher*, 1:582. Literature anticipates, almost prophetically, changes in the political arena. Philip Payne suggests that Musil, equating ethics and aesthetics, "sees his writing as a force for change. The impetus behind his novel is to persuade his readers of the need for renewal of civilization and to prompt them to think about the direction that might be followed." *Robert Musil's "The Man without Qualities": A Critical Study*. (Cambridge: Cambridge University Press, 1988), 34.

[35] Musil, *MwQ*, 13. "Ulrich schrieb in seinem Aufsatze über die Vaterlandsliebe, daß ein ernster Vaterlandsfreund sein Vaterland niemals das beste finden dürfe." Musil, *MoE*, 18–19.

carries wide-ranging implications, that "God Himself probably preferred to speak of His world in the subjunctive of possibility (hic dixerit quispiam—'here someone might object that ...'), for God creates the world and thinks while He is at it that it could just as well be done differently."[36] Ulrich distances himself from the patriotic and patriarchic values of the empire, a position for which he is suspected of calumny against the fatherland and blasphemy against God. The reactions to the essay range from harsh disapproval to profound embarrassment. The father is angered by what he perceives to be an invective against the *father*land, which indirectly calls into question his authority as head of the family. This school paper initiates the intergenerational conflict between the conservative father and Ulrich, who will grow up to constantly question traditional values. The ensuing scandal calls for speedy disciplinary consequences. Ulrich is not officially asked to resign—an official expulsion would have been damaging to the reputation of the family—but he is immediately transferred to a Belgian private school. The paternal punishment for Ulrich's insubordination could not be more ironic. Quite contrary to his father's intention, the son, instead of correcting and redeeming himself, continues to nurture his antipatriotic sentiments in Belgium. The narrator relates with unconcealed gusto how Ulrich's disdain for common ideals attains international scope in his pampered exile.[37] His alleged moral perdition is described with a sarcasm that mocks the rhetoric of nationalism, exposing it as childishly absurd.

With the divine subjunctive of possibility, an early version of the *Möglichkeitssinn*, the sense of possibility assumes the features of a radical theological and cosmological skepticism. Ulrich's statement borders on utter heresy, as he subverts the creation myth in *Genesis*. According to the biblical tradition, God reacts to the creation of the world with recurrent satisfaction: "God saw all that He had made, and it was very good" (Gen. 1:13). To Ulrich, the order of the world is not supported by philosophical necessity but by a fundamental contingency whose origin has a divine stamp of approval. God could create things in one manner, or in a radically different fashion. This rewriting of the biblical

---

[36] Musil, *MwQ*, 13–14. "Ja mit einem Blitz, der ihn besonders schön dünkte, obgleich er mehr von seinem Glanz geblendet wurde, als daß er sah, was darin vorging, hatte er diesem verdächtigen Satz noch den zweiten hinzugefügt, daß wahrscheinlich auch Gott von seiner Welt am liebsten im Conjunctivus potentialis spreche (hic dixerit quispiam = hier könnte einer einwenden ...) denn Gott macht die Welt und denkt dabei, es könnte ebensogut anders sein." Musil, *MoE*, 18–19.
[37] Musil, *MwQ*, 14. "Dort lernte Ulrich, seine Mißachtung der Ideale anderer international zu erweitern." Musil, *MoE*, 19.

creation myth does not merely amount to a sacrilegious profanation in the Judeo-Christian tradition. It also calls into question the established order in the universe. The fickle and capricious nature of God's will carries implications in the realm of political theory. What is called into question is the political doctrine of royalty by divine right, a challenge that obviously undermines the very legitimacy of the monarchy as an institution and, by extension, the emperor's entitlement to the throne. Young Ulrich's challenge of the emperor's right to rule is a touchy subject, especially after the *Ausgleich* of 1867 between Austria and Hungary, which downgraded in one half of the Habsburg territories the Austrian emperor to Hungarian king. In Ulrich's destabilizing logic it is not surprising that later, in one of his attempts to become a great man, he admires and chooses as his inspiration Napoleon, "who had tried to turn Europe upside down," a political profanity in the Austria built upon Metternich's Restoration.[38] The circumstance that Ulrich develops these ideas in his Belgian exile adds insult to the injury. One cannot help but notice that Ulrich wishes to resume, in his boyish fantasy of conquest and splendor, the heroic deeds of Napoleon in Belgium, exactly where his military campaign came to an abrupt halt. The disillusionment that comes with adulthood and years of academic training, however, will shatter all such dreams of glory.

Ulrich's sweeping critique does not spare any form of Habsburg loyalty, from dynastic allegiance to state patriotism and ethnic nationalism. He manages to simultaneously subvert three pillars of society, undermining patriarchal authority, the legitimacy of the imperial government, and a foundational theological principle. In his attack against the triptych of fathers made up of his *pater familias*, the imperial *Kaiservater*, and God the Father, he challenges the validity of institutions such as family, state, and church.[39] Ulrich's theological reflections need to be read in the context of the political relationship between Catholic Austria and the Church. The Concordat between the Habsburg monarchy and the Holy See of 1855 granted the Roman Catholic Church ample powers over matters of education, placing elementary school under the supervision of bishops. Strong liberal objection put pressure on Emperor Franz Joseph to repeal the highly controversial agreement, which was declared lapsed in 1870. In 1874, elementary school education returned

---

[38] Musil, *MwQ*, 31. "der Europa auf den Kopf zu stellen versuchte." Musil, *MoE*, 35.
[39] A key of interpretation of Ulrich's school essay is offered by a diary entry of the late 1930s. Musil writes: "Vater, Landesvater, Gottvater: es war die Tonleiter des alten Österreich in der Kindheit meines Vaters … Und während die Kinder aufwuchsen, wandelte sich das alte Österreich; Gottvater tat der Autorität des Landesvaters Abbruch." Musil, *Tagebücher*, 1:963.

under state direction, while the government continued to compensate priests for religious instruction in schools. While the novel does not give precise dates about Ulrich's school years, at the time of Ulrich's essay the Concordat must have been a topic of heated debates between conservatives and liberals, whether it was still enforced or had already been rescinded. In Ulrich's school essay a Nietzschean critique of nationalism—the philosopher's mocking denunciation of a atavistic fatherlandishness—is easily recognizable. Musil's profound understanding of the transcultural dynamics of Habsburg loyalties allowed him to gauge how these nonnational philosophies developed in the particular social and historical context of Austria, where a long tradition of manifold alternatives to the nation competed with German and European conceptualization of nationhood.[40] Still powerful and relevant, but critically challenged, nonnational modes and approaches to social and political life begin to fold under the pressure of new national formulas.

Trieste in Kakanien 1913: Leo Fischel and Count Leinsdorf

Historically, the place where these nonnational loyalties had been politically most relevant was Austrian Trieste. Musil therefore portrays the Adriatic city as the ultimate repository of an allegedly premodern Habsburg *Landespatriotismus*, a regional multicultural patriotism that configured and organized social life differently from the increasingly successful ethnic nationalism. Musil depicts this indifference to national identity in two other characters. Through the figures of the aristocrat Count Leinsdorf and the Jewish banker Leo Fischel, the author illustrates respectively the city's dwindling dynastic allegiance and the supranational mentality of its mercantile bourgeoisie. The positions of these two profoundly discrepant characters—Leinsdorf is the expression of an old feudal aristocracy, while Fischel is the product of a dynamic capitalist mentality—register an almost paradoxical convergence in their emotional attachment to Trieste.[41] By depicting the

---

[40] According to Stefan Jonsson, Musil recognized in the intercultural dynamics of empire elements for a future community building, elaborating a notion of transculturation that anticipates concepts developed by postcolonial theory, such as hybridity, border culture, and *métissage*. Musil posits a transcultural subject without a nation, attached to a multiplicity of cultures, histories, and identities that enable the individual to transcend them. *Subject without Nation: Robert Musil and the History of Modern Identity* (Durham, NC: Duke University Press, 2000), 264–265.

[41] Fischel and Leinsdorf are not the only secondary characters through which the narrator explores sociopolitical questions. In his book *Politik und Literatur in Musils Mann ohne Eigenschaften. Am Beispiel des Dichters Feuermaul* (Königstein: Hain, 1981), Josef Strutz argues that especially marginal characters in the novel are paradigmatic for Musil's intellectual subtlety and political thought.

Adriatic city as the last, crumbling bastion of nonnational allegiances, Musil models Trieste's political upheavals into a synecdoche for the empire's fate, making the city a microcosm of the Habsburg monarchy. The city's paradigmatic character within the larger Habsburg context becomes explicit in what I call the "Trieste chapter" of the novel. The author's drafts reveal how much importance he attributed to the 1913 nationalist demonstrations in Trieste for the narrative progression toward the destructive *telos* of the First World War. In a programmatic annotation for chapter 20 of Book 2, Musil writes, "Make the Trieste story more relevant to the war."[42] In the episode, Count Leinsdorf bitterly complains about the growing Italian Irredentism in the city. Fischel, in contrast, identifies with the dynamic merchant middle class of Habsburg Trieste, where his father worked as a lawyer. His distance from nationalist concerns results from the combination of economic calculations and the liberal-humanist tradition of Enlightenment cosmopolitanism.[43]

When Ulrich pays a courtesy visit to Count Leinsdorf, he finds the aristocrat agitated, even taken by surprise, by the recent events that have shaken the empire. Leinsdorf complains about vociferous pro-German demonstrators rioting outside his palace windows, the increasingly pressing demands of Czech nationalists, and, more alarmingly, the dwindling loyalty of Italians in Habsburg Trieste. Upon Ulrich's arrival, Leinsdorf argues for a more resolute intervention in the protests of Trieste's municipal employees, sharply criticizing the government's politics of peace at all cost.[44] The controversial appointment of local administrators happens despite the fact that Kakanien is blessed with the "the best bureaucracy in Europe,"[45] as the mocking narrative voice states elsewhere. Leinsdorf's call for decisive action is also exquisitely ironic since the Parallel Campaign committee he brought to life is as

---

[42] "Der Triestiner Geschichte mehr Kriegsbedeutung geben." Robert Musil, *Klagenfurter Ausgabe*: Transkriptionen/Mappe VII/1.

[43] Musil's association of the Triestine Jewish community, from which Fischel originates, with the Enlightenment makes historical sense. Lois Dubin has argued that the Triestine Jewish community was unusually receptive to Enlightenment ideals, combining an openness to modern emancipating currents with a lifestyle rooted in the traditions of the past: "For the Jews of Trieste, tradition, Josephinian civil toleration, Enlightenment, and Haskalah all fit well together." *The Port Jews of Habsburg Trieste: Absolutist Politics and Enlightenment Culture* (Stanford, CA: Stanford University Press, 1999), 214.

[44] Musil, *MwQ*, 912. "Was sagen Sie denn zu der Geschichte mit den Triestiner Gemeindeangestellten? Ich finde, daß es für die Regierung hoch an der Zeit war, sich zu einer entschlossenen Haltung aufzuraffen." Musil, *MoE*, 840.

[45] Musil, *MwQ* 29. "der besten Bürokratie Europas." Musil, *MoE*, 33.

Robert Musil and the Politics of Nonnational Loyalty, 1913–1943 119

hesitant and ineffective as the administration he disparages. The count continues, explaining to Ulrich:

> For years the Austrian city of Trieste has been hiring only Italians, subjects of the King of Italy, in its civil service, to make a point that their allegiance is to Italy, not to us. I was there once on His Majesty's birthday: not a single flag in all Trieste except on the administration building, the tax office, the prison, and the roofs of a few barracks! But if you should have any business in some municipal office in Trieste on the King of Italy's birthday, you wouldn't find a clerk anywhere without a flower in his buttonhole![46]

Musil offers a fictional adaptation of the bitter controversy caused by Hohenlohe's controversial decrees. Framing the protests into a pedantic matter of regal birthday celebrations may appear as a comic twist to the contentious dispute in Trieste. To Leinsdorf, though, the local protest reveals an unacceptable betrayal of dynastic allegiance.[47] For someone who identifies with the nonnational constitution of the empire, these nationalist demands appear as radical and outlandish notions that lie beyond his comprehension. The question is one of political epistemology. Profoundly indebted to a nonnational mentality, Count Leinsdorf quite simply does not understand nationalism and vehemently resists this new and alien ideology.[48] As if the abhorrent question of dynastic betrayal were not enough, domestic and international affairs are

---

[46] Musil, *MwQ*, 913. "Das tut die österreichische Stadt Triest nun schon seit Jahren, daß sie nur Reichsitaliener in ihre Dienste nimmt, um damit zu betonen, daß sie sich nicht zu uns, sondern zu Italien gehörig fühlt. Ich bin einmal an Kaisers Geburtstag dort gewesen: nicht eine einzige Fahne hab ich in ganz Triest gesehen, außer auf der Statthalterei, dem Steuerbehörde, dem Gefängnis und den paar Kaserndächern! Wenn sie dagegen am Geburtstag des Königs von Italien etwas in einem Triester Büro zu tun haben, so werden sie keinen Beamten finden, der nicht eine Blume in seinem Knopfloch hat." Musil, *MoE*, 840.
[47] This dynastic patriotism and lack of nationalist identification is what makes Leinsdorf a *homo austriacus*. In *The Ambivalence of Identity: the Austrian Experience of Nation-Building in a Modern Society* (West Lafayette, IN: Purdue University Press, 2001), Peter Thaler discusses how Austrian monarchists "displayed only limited interest in questions of nationalism" because "their loyalties were attached to a very different concept of allegiance" (72). Thaler describes the *homo austriacus* in terms of a polyglot aristocrat or high-level imperial official, who worked as a supranational mediator between nationalities and who remained deeply immersed in the traditions of the Habsburg Empire.
[48] See John Malcolm Spencer, *In the Shadow of Empire: Austrian Experiences of Modernity in the Writings of Musil, Roth, and Bachmann* (Rochester, NY: Camden House, 2008), 87–92.

affected by these protests, too. For the Count, the possession of Trieste constitutes a great diplomatic advantage in a geopolitically unpredictable future. Explaining Austria's world mission to a perpetually skeptical Ulrich, Leinsdorf argues:

> It would amount to a world mission for the Empire, and it's not a question of whether they want to or not. You see, many people at the beginning have had to be made to do what's best for them. But think, too, what it would mean if we ended up allied with a grateful Jewish State instead of with the Germans or Prussia! Seeing that our Trieste happens to be the Hamburg of the Mediterranean, as it were, apart from the fact that it would make us diplomatically invincible to have not only the Pope on our side but the Jews as well![49]

Leinsdorf's expression "our Trieste ... the Hamburg of the Mediterranean" reaffirms the rhetoric of imperial possession one can observe in the description of the city as "our first port city" in the imperial propaganda. The imagery of colonial ownership suggested by the possessive adjective frames a more personal relationship that is first and foremost legal in nature, and yet almost emotional. At the very inception of the chapter, the narrator alludes to this connection when Leinsdorf is introduced with his official title of "Imperial Liege-Count"—in German "reichsunmittelbare[r] Graf."[50] As in the legal status granted to Trieste in recognition of its dynastic loyalty in 1848, the "imperial immediacy" of the Habsburg *Reichsunmittelbarkeit* meant that the city answered directly to the authority of the central government, without having to resort to any intermediate level of administration. Count Leinsdorf and "our Trieste" enjoy the same juridical and constitutional status. Leinsdorf takes Trieste's succumbing to the nationalist allure as a personal affront as it erodes the legal basis upon which his own privilege rests.

The government's inability to de-escalate the social and political tension bespeaks the inability of Austrian rule to properly address the Triestine question. Protesters in Trieste are obviously aware that in Vienna,

---

[49] Musil, *MwQ*, 918. "Die Monarchie hätte da geradezu eine Weltmission zu erfüllen, da kommt es nicht darauf an, ob der andere zunächst will! Wissen Sie, man hat schon manchen zuerst zwingen müssen. Aber bedenken Sie auch, was es heißt, wenn wir später mit einem dankbaren jüdischen Staat verbündet wären, statt mit den Reichsdeutschen und Preußen! Wo unser Triest sozusagen das Hamburg des Mittelländischen Meeres ist, abgesehen davon, daß man diplomatisch unüberwindlich wird, wenn man außer dem Papst auch noch die Juden für sich hat!" Musil, MoE, 845.
[50] Musil, *MwQ* 912 and *MoE* 839.

the empire is parading the city as one of its most prized possessions in the Adriatic Exhibition. The approach adopted by the Austrian government is a noninterventionist policy, in the hope that this will prevent more aggressive forms of protest. Despite the foreseeable ineffectiveness of this policy, Leinsdorf praises the implementation of a laissez-faire attitude as particularly magnanimous and easy-handed, in opposition to the more repressive and interventionist Prussian neighbor: "If our government forces the city to discharge its foreign staff, we will immediately be accused of Germanizing. That is the reproach that every government fears. Even his Majesty doesn't like it. After all, we're not Prussians!"[51] Musil's sarcasm surfaces again here. After having argued for a more assertive intervention in Trieste, Leinsdorf contradicts his previous statement, recognizing the advantages of more accommodating policies. Even the remote possibility of being compared to or associated with Prussia causes the Count profound dismay. The Emperor himself does not like to hear what the government and the aristocracy apparently perceive as deeply insulting slander. In accordance with the general spirit of the *Parallelaktion*, opposition to the Prussian neighbor—and its aggressive nationalism—is what defines Austria.[52]

Leinsdorf's ignorance about the rising tensions in Trieste emerges when he reveals that he is largely unaware of the Slovenian presence in the city, misconstruing the social and political dynamics between the Italian-speaking upper class and the rural Slovene-speaking peasantry and urban lower-middle class. Even Ulrich has a vague notion about the cultural and ethnic composition of the Adriatic city but seems to remember that Trieste was founded in Slavic territory. When

---

[51] Musil, *MwQ* 913. "Wenn die Regierung die Gemeinde zwingt, ihre ausländischen Angestellten zu entlassen, dann heisst es gleich, daß wir germanisieren. Und diesen Vorwurf fürchtet eben jede Regierung. Auch Seine Majestät hört ihn nicht gern. Wir sind ja keine Preußen!" Musil, *MoE*, 840.

[52] It might be surprising to see the liberal Musil sympathizing with an ultraconservative imperialist like Leinsdorf. Spencer, however, convincingly explains this unlikely association through the friendship between Ulrich and the Count. The critic places Ulrich's growing sympathy for the old aristocrat in the context of the supranational empire: "Nationalism, like dynasticism before it, will eventually become outmoded. The supranational thinking of old aristocrats like Leinsdorf will need to be reactivated at a later, post-national stage of modernity." Spencer, *Shadow*, 93. The reason for such partial rehabilitation of the empire is Musil's conviction that what needs to be saved from the old regime is its nonnational structure. As Spencer points out, for Musil "dynastic conservatism has some unintentionally progressive results: by an involuntary irony, Kakanien, the land of the past, points forward to a post-national, multicultural future." Spencer, *Shadow*, 98. Spencer puts it succinctly when he shows that "Musil finds nationally constructed identities to be simplistic, narrow, or even false." Spencer, *Shadow*, 105.

Ulrich reminds the oblivious Count of the Slovenes in the city, the aristocrat manages to fit this added circumstance into his impermeable nonnational worldview. The real danger for the Count is the public perception that the Austrian state might wish to Germanize Trieste, which would cause Triestines of different languages to bond together in an anti-government coalition. With great confidence, the Count envisions an extremely unlikely scenario in which "the Slovenes immediately side with the Italians."[53] Leinsdorf simply does not understand.

Traditional readings of Leo Fischel identify him as a member of the Jewish community of Kakanien's capital Vienna.[54] The novel, however, suggests a more complex family background for Fischel, presenting the character as the son of a lawyer from Trieste. The figure of the Triestine lawyer had engaged Musil's mind since the mid-1920s, when he composed the early drafts for Clarisse's fascination with Moosbrugger. A lawyer from Trieste occupies one of the cells in the asylum for the criminally insane that Clarisse visits. Musil's perception of Trieste shines through the brief psychological profile of the inmate. He sits in his cell with a reluctant but tenacious demeanor as if ready to resume his role as defense lawyer in court or like a political martyr awaiting his execution. Doctors and wardens treat him with deference and greet him in Italian.[55] In the characterization of this composite character remains recognizable the figure of Wilhelm Oberdank / Guglielmo Oberdan, the radical Irredentist who was executed after having planned to assassinate Franz Joseph in 1882 during the Emperor's visit to Trieste to celebrate the 500th anniversary of the city's submission to Austrian power. This episode never made it into the final version of the novel, but Musil recycled the Triestine lawyer to make him the father of Fischel. Retaining the Triestine father for Fischel helped Musil ground the character's deep preoccupation with international commerce in the mercantile mentality of the Adriatic city's middle class.

---

[53] Musil, *MwQ*, 913.
[54] Critics have generally considered Fischel's positions as the fictional projection of Musil's own convictions and thoughts, arguing that the author's sympathies lie with Fischel's nonnational thinking. Musil, like Fischel, "finds nationally constructed identities to be simplistic, narrow, or even false." Spencer, *Shadow*, 105. Musil, however, also sees Fischel as the embodiment of a less humanitarian capitalist supranationality. See Bernd Blaschke, *Der homo oeconomicus und sein Kredit bei Musil, Joyce, Svevo, Unamuno und Céline* (Munich: Wilhelm Fink, 2004).
[55] "Er trug Straßenkleidung bloß ohne Kragen, hatte schwarzes Haar und einen schwarzen Vollbart und sah aus, als ob er sogleich zu einer Verteidigung aufs Gericht gehen könnte, oder vielleicht auch wie ein politischer Märtyrer vor der Hinrichtung. Er war aus Triest ... Addio Avvocato! Sagte schnell der Arzt, und die Wärter schlossen mit einem merklichen gesellschaftlichen Respekt den Kranken ein." Musil, *MoE*, 1692.

The reader learns of Fischel's Triestine background in chapter 102 of Book 1, where the narrator describes the generational and ideological conflict between Fischel and his daughter Gerda, who is receptive to the allure of pan-German nationalism. Gerda's anti-Semitic friends, including her boyfriend, the militant right-wing extremist Hans Sepp, gather in Fischel's house in recurrent meetings that mockingly parallel Diotima's soirée salon. The discussions about the racial purity of the German nation increasingly irritate the accommodating Fischel and eventually lead to a heated clash between father and daughter. While dismissing meaningless appeals to a common humanity, Gerda describes her nation as a tangible, physical reality. From his thwarted attempt to present a cogent counterargument to his daughter's nationalist tirade, we learn that Fischel's father had been a lawyer in Habsburg Trieste.[56] He unsuccessfully tries to present the culture of Trieste as an alternative to Gerda's celebration of the nation. The text does not indicate that young Fischel grew up in the Adriatic city but suggests, nonetheless, that he was reared in a family whose members were at some point either part of Trieste's class of lawyers, bankers, and administrative clerks, or an integral part of the city's prosperous Jewish community. To refute Gerda's nationalist invective, Fischel also attempts to resort to biblical ideas of community that contradict the national paradigm, but both the Triestine origin of his Jewish family and liberal internationalism are muted in the discussion. There is merely a vague hint of a response to Gerda that remains suffocated and does not develop into a full thought. Gerda's brusque interruption and defense of the "Christian-Germanic commune" reveals a larger state of affairs.[57] The rhetoric of nationalism disrupts, silences, and disarms the voice of nonnational values. Fischel's rhetorical ineffectiveness emerges at the end of the discussion when he, unable to counter his daughter, disengages from the verbal confrontation and sends her to her room. When ordered to stay in her quarters until she regains some *Vernunft* she leaves with "an air of stubborn martyrdom."[58] In order to counter the religious inspiration of his daughter's nationalist doctrine, Fischel resorts to the Enlightenment values of reason, tolerance, and cosmopolitanism. This strategy

---

[56] Musil, *MwQ*, 521–522. "Ich kann mir unter Menschheit nichts vorstellen, Papa" erwiderte Gerda, wenn er ihr Vorhaltungen machte, "das hat heute keinen Inhalt mehr; aber meine Nation, das ist körperlich!" "Deine Nation!" begann dann Leo Fischel und wollte etwas von den großen Propheten sagen und von seinem eigenen Vater, der Rechtsanwalt in Triest gewesen war. "Ich weiß" unterbrach ihn Gerda. "Aber meine Nation ist die geistige; von der spreche ich." Musil, *MoE*, 479.
[57] Musil, *MwQ*, 522. "germanische Christbürgergemeinschaft." Musil, *MoE*, 479.
[58] Musil, *MwQ*, 522. "stillen Märtyrereigensinn." Musil, *MoE*, 479.

assumes the contours of a feeble gesture, symbolic not only of Fischel's oratory defeat, but also indicative of the liberal failure to oppose the rise of xenophobic protofascism. The subtlety of Musil's critique lies in the fact that this ideological dispute occurs within the domestic walls of a German-Jewish household made up of a Jewish father, an increasingly anti-Semitic mother, and a protofascist daughter.

The Fischel family becomes in the course of the narration the besieged "battleground of two contending philosophies of life."[59] Unlike the rude awakening to the harsh reality of his wife Klementine's growing anti-Semitism, which I will discuss below, Leo's oblivious aloofness leads to an almost apathetic resignation. Part of his passivity is the misguided hope that these social and political phenomena will slowly disappear. His faith in reason and progress, ideals of tolerance and human dignity are assailed and slowly displaced by preposterous racial theories and crude street slogans. In the same way that Count Leinsdorf flatly denies the existence of nationalism, Fischel's blind faith in humanist notions of equality convinces him that reason and understanding will eventually prevail in society.[60] This conviction leads him initially to ignore the rise of racial theories, underestimate the fact that they are also gaining ground in his own household, and eventually erode the solidity and happiness of his marriage. In a later conversation, Fischel has to acknowledge the presence of racism during a committee meeting of the *Parallelaktion*. Indignant, he reproaches General Stumm von Bordwehr, who is culpable of recognizing and thus dignifying the value of racial pride: "People must be judged not by their race, but on their merit."[61] Fischel's criticism of the misguided principles of scientific racism moves beyond their dismissal as dehumanizing bigotry. For him, social privilege assigned according to racial categories also contradicts the principles of meritocracy, which he sees as rationalist

---

[59] Musil, *MwQ*, 219. "Kampfplatz zweier Weltanschauungen." Musil, *MoE*, 204.
[60] Musil, *MwQ*, 219. "Dieser Glaube an die unerschütterlichen Richtlinien der Vernunft und des Fortschritts hatte es ihm lange Zeit ermöglicht, über die Ausstellungen seiner Frau mit einem Achselzucken oder einer schneidenden Antwort hinwegzugehn. Aber da es das Unglück gewollt hatte, daß sich im Verlauf dieser Ehe die Zeitstimmung von den alten, Leo Fischel günstigen Grundsätzen des Liberalismus, den großen Richtbildern der Freigeistigkeit, der Menschenwürde und des Freihandels abwandte, und Vernunft und Fortschritt in der abendländischen Welt durch Rassentheorien und Straßenschlagworte verdrängt wurden, so blieb er auch nicht unberührt davon. Er hatte diese Entwicklung anfangs schlechtweg geleugnet, genau so wie Graf Leinsdorf gewisse 'unliebsame Erscheinungen öffentlicher Natur' zu leugnen pflegte; er wartete darauf, daß sie von selbst verschwinden würden." Musil, *MoE*, 204.
[61] Musil, *MwQ*, 1103. "Man muss die Menschen nicht nach der Rasse unterscheiden, sondern nach Verdienst." Musil, *MoE*, 1015–16.

efficiency applied to the positions individuals occupy in society. Societal organization works more efficiently and profitably if key positions are held by meritorious individuals, not by people elected on account of birthright or ethnic background. His initial reluctance to participate in the *Parallelaktion* is largely the result of this outlook.

The Jewish banker is not alone in his willful ignorance. The narrator emphasizes that Fischel and Leinsdorf are, in this respect, like-minded characters. The Count is equally myopic in believing that the changes in the political climate are transitory. Leinsdorf dismisses the rise of nationalism and racism with an apotropaic euphemism that describes these opinions as "unpleasant political manifestations."[62] He knows that nationalism is not harmless, since he seems to agree with Fischel's assessment that opposes good business practices and nationalist fervor in a socioeconomic dichotomy. Not surprisingly, Leinsdorf uses Fischel's bank for his dealings on international stock markets. To be sure, there is a profound discrepancy between the banker and the aristocrat in terms of their ideological background. Fischel subscribes to a capitalist mentality that operates on a global scale, a mindset concerned with international business transactions that reach beyond limited national markets. Leinsdorf's opinions, on the other hand, are informed by an Austro-German ethnocentrism and an unwavering dynastic loyalty. While Fischel and Leinsdorf do not present a united front, their positions converge nonetheless in their critical distance from nationalism and in their views on Trieste. They have in common the same nostalgia for a liberal Trieste that was unresponsive to the allure of nationality. Fischel and Leinsdorf also share the same political shortsightedness that prevents them from recognizing the evident fact that these times of national indifference are slowly coming to a bitter end.

Fischel was first introduced in chapter 35 of Book 1 as an old acquaintance of the protagonist Ulrich. The banker is unenthusiastically surprised by Count Leinsdorf's invitation to the meetings of the *Parallelaktion*. The Austrian elite gets wind of Prussia's intention to celebrate the thirtieth year of Kaiser Wilhelm II's reign in 1918. Motivated to outshine the Prussians, the Austrians devise the plan to celebrate the seventieth jubilee of the Emperor Franz Joseph, which occurs in the same year. The request to participate in the preparations for the emperor's jubilee was contained in a circular missive to which Fischel had not responded, "because his sound business sense disinclined him from having anything to do with patriotic movements

---

[62] Musil, *MoE*, 204.

originating in high circles."[63] His disinclination stems from an inability to understand nationalist rhetoric, since Fischel "could form no concept at all of true patriotism or the true Austria."[64] His distrust of the nationalist direction of the *Parallelaktion* needs to be read in the context of Fischel's larger system of beliefs, built upon a practical, cosmopolitan credo, obstinately resistant to and naïvely dismissive of nationalist segregations. For him, nationalism, with its rhetoric of violence, racism, and anti-Semitic bouts, is a peripheral and negligible trend in a society governed by reason and progress.

Fischel's positivist faith in progressive social change combines with an optimism derived from the social and economic opportunities afforded by Jewish assimilation.[65] The Fischels' interfaith marriage seemed a hallmark of such integration. Leo's marriage to his Catholic wife Klementine occurred at a time in which anti-Semitism indeed appeared as a marginal and vulgar societal phenomenon. Discounting the crass prejudices of the common folk, Klementine sees her marriage to the Jew as the magnanimous gesture of an educated mind.[66] Over the years, this capricious motivation slowly succumbs to social pressure. Her disillusionment and gradual alienation from her husband grow when she realizes that the so-called progress has not relegated anti-Semitism to the margins of society. Discrimination against members of the Jewish community has entered mainstream mores, affecting their family livelihood directly. Leo's career has reached a plateau: he has a managerial role with the pro forma title of director and has been awaiting in vain a full promotion to director of the Lloyds Bank.[67] It is significant that Musil makes Fischel the managing director of the Lloyd Bank, a British banking institution founded in the eighteenth century. The name of the bank, in fact, inspired the designation of the *Österreichischer Lloyd*, a navigation company founded in 1836 from the merger of several insurance companies in Trieste. Thanks to generous government subventions, the company expanded and grew to become the biggest navigation firm in the empire. After the *Österreichischer Lloyd* was declared property of the Habsburg monarchy, it became

---

[63] Musil, *MwQ*, 139. "weil sein gesunder Geschäftssinn vaterländischen Aktionen, die von hohen Kreisen ausgingen, abhold war." Musil, *MoE*, 133.
[64] Musil, *MwQ*, 142. "stellte sich unter wahrer Vaterlandsliebe und wahrem Österreich überhaupt nichts vor." Musil, *MoE*, 135.
[65] Musil, *MwQ*, 141. "Direktor Leo Fischel von der Lloyd-Bank glaubte, wie es alle Bankdirektoren vor dem Kriege taten, an den Fortschritt." Musil, *MoE*, 135.
[66] Musil, *MwQ*, 218. "Wie es damals war, empfand sie nahezu etwas besonders Gebildetes dabei, sich über das naive antisemitische Vorurteil des gewöhnlichen Volkes hinwegzusetzen." Musil, *MoE*, 203.
[67] Musil, *MwQ*, 217. "Bankprokurist mit dem Titel Direktor." Musil, *MoE*, 202.

the symbol of the empire's global maritime commerce. Its commercial routes extended to the Suez Canal, later including, among other destinations, lines to Constantinople, Bombay, Singapore, and Hong Kong.

From Musil's posthumous chapter drafts, one can appreciate Fischel's future embracing of a more callous "philosophy of money."[68] In the plans for future chapters, Fischel separates from his wife, starts a relationship with Ulrich's former lover Leona, and quits his job as managing bank director. He is active in the import and export trade, and works for a "Trans-European Goods and Currency Exchange Company."[69] For all the changes Musil had in mind for Fischel, the character does not abandon his pragmatic nonnational, anti-war stance. In a conversation with Ulrich, Fischel condescendingly lectures his younger friend: "Believe me; the world would be more reasonable if left to the free play of supply and demand, instead of arming it with armor-plated ships, bayonets, diplomats ignorant of the economy and so-called national ideas."[70] As we will see in the next chapter, the Triestine author Italo Svevo, who was still in business with the Austrian navy during the war, would not have put it in much different terms.

The novel presents the interpersonal relationships involving Fischel as a case study of both unstated and more explicit forms of anti-Semitism. The planned character development of this figure, contained in the later drafts of the unfinished novel, was supposed to entail a surprising reversal of roles. Fischel's transformation into a profiteering wartime speculator was probably intended to guard readers against the straightforward equation of a nonnational mentality with an unproblematic cosmopolitanism. Fischel's later characterization continues to eschew anti-Semitic stereotypes and reads like a subtle authorial commentary on the financial hegemony of transnational capitalism and the neocolonial dynamics of modern globalized economies that the world war brought to the fore. In a development indicative of Musil's multifaceted relationship with his characters, the author takes a swipe at the unbridled appetites of capitalism but remains sympathetic to Fischel's continued nonnational politics and pacifist pragmatism that function as regulatory principles capable of restraining the predatory practices of capitalism.

---

[68] Musil, *MwQ*, 1683. "Philosophie des Geldes." Musil, *MoE*, 1389.
[69] Musil, *MwQ*, 1683. "Transeuropäische Waren- u[nd] Geldverkehrsgesellschaft." Musil, *MoE* 1389.
[70] This is my translation. "Glauben Sie mir, die Welt wäre viel vernünftiger, wenn man sie einfach dem freien Spiel von Angebot u.[nd] Nachfrage überließe, statt sie mit Panzerschiffen, Bajonetten, wirtschaftsfremden Diplomaten u.[nd] sogenannten nationalen Ideen auszurüsten." Musil, *MoE*, 1496.

Paul Arnheim, Ancient Phoenician and Modern European

Diotima, the gracious hostess of the Parallel Campaign meetings, is an enthusiastic supporter of the organization's ostensible guiding principles. She sees the planned festivities of the seventieth jubilee of the Emperor as a grand celebration of European pacifism and envisions 1918 as a "World-Austrian Year, in which Europe could recognize Austria as its true spiritual home."[71] Musil constructs Diotima as a failed prophetess of Austro-Europeanism, representative of what he came to understand as the general shortsightedness of Austrian intellectuals before the war. She subscribes to a vague essentialist idealism that Musil started to sharply critique in his essays of the 1920s. Painting an idealized picture of the multicultural and polyglot empire as a spiritual microcosm of Europe, her character exemplifies what Musil saw as an almost cultivated naïveté among Austrian intellectuals like Hugo von Hofmannsthal, Bertha von Suttner, Franz Werfel, and Stefan Zweig and who saw in a future United States of Europe the ideal continuation of the Habsburg Empire. What she presents as a European utopia organized around a peaceful comity of nations, both internal to Austria and within the larger continental context, in reality conceals an affirmation of the doctrine of the European balance of powers inherited from the Congress of Vienna. Her vision of international relations under Austrian hegemony is closer to the geopolitical diplomacy of the clumsy General Stumm von Bordwehr while in terms of the domestic situation she prefers to sweep under the rug the growing ethnic tensions and economic asymmetries among the gradually nationalized groups that inhabit the empire. Blind to the pragmatic opportunism of other members of the social gatherings who push their own cultural, political, and economic agendas, her infatuation with the Prussian businessman and polymath Paul Arnheim makes her the vehicle for Musil's larger critique of ineffective pacifist posturing, a judgement that invests other characters like Friedel Feuermaul.

Diotima's entanglement in the platonic love story with Arnheim is based on a perceived like-mindedness through which she projects her own Habsburg Europeanism unto him. She sees him as the unmistakable and quintessential European:

> Finally, she said that Arnheim was a European, a thinker known throughout Europe, that the conduct of affairs of state in Europe was not sufficiently European, not spiritual enough, and that

---

[71] Musil, *MwQ*, 248. "weltösterreichisches Jahr, wo der europäische Geist in Österreich seine wahre Heimat erblicken könnte." Musil, *MoE*, 231.

the world would find no peace until it was as permeated by a universally Austrian spirit as the ancient Austrian culture that embraced all the peoples, with their different languages, within the borders of the monarchy.[72]

Diotima holds the completely unjustified conviction that Arnheim is in perfect accord with her worldview. In her use of the term "European" as synonymous with "spiritual," she conceives of Europe as the old adhesive force of the Habsburg Empire that transcends cultural singularities. She does not realize that nationalists in the empire perceive this Habsburg embrace as a smothering grip. Arnheim's elitist and cosmopolitan Europeanism, conversely, is informed by the political and economic pragmatism of a magnate more at ease with an approach bordering on cynical *Realpolitik*. A German fluent in five languages, intelligent, well-read, and active in the armament industry, Arnheim is living as "a man conscious of living with the eyes of all Europe upon him."[73] Musil modeled Arnheim on Walther Rathenau, the Jewish industrialist and diplomat who served as Foreign Minister in the Weimar Republic and who was assassinated in 1922 while in office. He met Rathenau in person and developed a personal rivalry, probably also motivated by Musil's jealousy of successful authors of his generation (Musil was also envious of Thomas Mann's literary success).[74] Musil disliked Rathenau's 1913 *Zur Mechanik des Geistes*, a book that the Austrian writer reviewed in April 1914, expressing his fundamental disagreement with Rathenau's main argument. In the book, Rathenau opposed *Seele* (soul) to *Geist* (spirit), maintaining that the latter exerted an exaggerated and negative influence on Western civilization. According to Musil, such essentialist thinking lacked both theoretical depth and academic rigor.

In Diotima's eyes, Arnheim's polyglot education and his demeanor of a well-rounded humanist with a scientific background are the characteristics that make him a true European. In Musil's fictional universe,

---

[72] Musil, *MwQ*, 215. "Schließlich sagte sie, Arnheim sei ein Europäer, ein in ganz Europa bekannter Geist, die Leitung der Staatsgeschäfte in Europa geschehe zu wenig europäisch und viel zu ungeistig, und die Welt werde nicht Frieden finden, ehe ein weltösterreichischer Geist sie so durchwehe, wie die alte österreichische Kultur sich um die verschiedensprachigen Stämme auf dem Boden der Monarchie schlinge." Musil, *MoE*, 201.

[73] Musil, *MwQ*, 416. "ein vor ganz Europa lebender Mensch." Musil, *MoE*, 383.

[74] When Rathenau and Musil met, the politician put his arm over the writer's shoulder. Musil, susceptible by temperament, interpreted this show of amicable affection as a condescending gesture. This event appears in the novel when Arnheim offers Ulrich a position as junior partner in his business and puts his arm around him (*MoE* 643/*MwQ* 701–702).

however, a true European could only be someone of Phoenician descent, as the ancient myth of Europa clearly indicated. Diotima realizes this, not without dismay. During one of the meetings, she admiringly observes Arnheim from a distance: "She noted that he did not look in the least Jewish but was a noble-looking, reserved man of the classic-Phoenician type."[75] Clearly uncomfortable with the circumstance that the man she so admires is of Jewish lineage (he is Jewish on his father's side, while Jewish descent is matrilineal), she convinces herself that Arnheim does not present any physical characteristics that could be described as Jewish. Implicit in her reasoning that Arnheim is of nobler stock is a hierarchy of Semitic groups in which ancient Phoenicians are more acceptable than modern Jews. Diotima's anti-Semitism finds resonance in Ulrich's characterization of Arnheim, who he describes with the imperious poise of a "hard Phoenician skull."[76] Diotima and Ulrich's portrayal of Arnheim as a Phoenician echoes Musil's diary entry of January 11, 1914, the day the author met Rathenau in Berlin:

> Something Negroid in his skull. Phoenician. Forehead and anterior cranial vault form a spherical segment. Then the skull— behind a little decrease, a pile, moves up backwards. The chin line, furthest back from the skull, is almost less than 45 degrees to the horizontal line, which is emphasized by the small goatee (functioning more as a chin than as facial hair). Small, bold, aquiline nose. Curved lips apart. I don't know what Hannibal looked like, but I had to think of him.[77]

Musil's classification of Rathenau's cranium as Afro-Semitic in his diary entry shows how at this point he still believed in the racialist assumptions of phrenology, the pseudoscientific discipline that attributed to skull measurements indices of the moral character of so-called human races. Craniometrics distinguished between dolichocephalic structures, the allegedly longer heads of Aryan and Nordic races, and brachycephalic heads, supposedly smaller crania, of Asiatic and Semitic

---

[75] Musil, *MwQ*, 112. "Sie bemerkte, daß er nicht im geringsten jüdisch aussah, sondern ein vornehm bedachter Mann von phönikisch-antikem Typus war." Musil, *MoE*, 109.
[76] Musil, *MwQ*, 190. "phönikisch harte Herrenkaufmannsschädel." Musil, *MoE*, 178.
[77] My translation. "Etwas Negroides im Schädel. Phönikisches. Stirn und vorderes Schädeldach bilden ein Kugelsegment, dann steigt der Schädel—hinter einer kleinen Senkung, einem Stoß—rückwärts empor. Die Linie Kinnspitze— weitestens Hinten des Schädels steht beinahe unter 45° zur Horizontalen, was durch einen kleinen Spitzbart (der kaum als Bart sondern als Kinn wirkt) noch verstärkt wird. Kleine kühne gebogene Nase. Auseinandergebogene Lippen. Ich weiß nicht wie Hannibal aussah, aber ich dachte an ihn." Musil, *Tagebücher* 1:295.

populations. By the time Musil was working on the novel, he had abandoned his belief in such stereotypes. He now dismissed with lucidity the pseudoscientific premise of racial theory as a mental pathology that affected much of German nationalist idealism, but infused his characters with these convictions.[78]

Musil's association of Rathenau with Hannibal echoes Freud's identification with the Carthaginian general in the inscription of an alternative genealogy of the modern European. He takes up Freud's dialectics of autonomy and dependency in which Phoenicians were code for Jews, but could also transcend them and be regarded as a self-sufficient group. As Ulrich Boss has suggested, Arnheim's Phoenician character responds, as does Freud's strategy, to a need to both affirm and at the same time suppress his Jewishness.[79] In Musil's Arnheim, this double discursive thread, however, is not limited to questions of a more or less pronounced Jewish character. For the author, the common stereotypes about Phoenician deceptiveness and Carthaginian ruthlessness are located in the folds of a multilayered anti-Semitism; in the portrayal of Arnheim, they also intersect with questions of race. The association underlying the trope of "Negroid Phoenicians" enjoyed a somewhat widespread currency. In 1929, a year before Musil published the first volume of the novel, the German Orientalist Georg Rosen attributed the presence of black Africans in Ashkenazi Judaism to the Phoenician slave trade. Differently from Diotima's vision that Phoenicians and Jews are related but separate groups, Rosen's analysis conflated the two populations into a single syncretic Phoenician-Jewish group of traders who shared the same ethno-cultural traits and spoke, with Hebrew and Phoenician, two dialects of the same Canaanite language.[80] For Rosen,

---

[78] For Musil's discussion of the nationalist popular literature with its widely distributed pamphlets and improvised social criticism, see Musil, *Gesammelte Werke*, 8:1064.

[79] Ulrich Boss has shown how both Freud and Musil imagine the Phoenicians within a context of anti-Semitic and racial discourses that both distinguish and conflate Jews and Phoenicians. Boss argues that Arnheim is generally seen as an insider thanks to his Prussian acculturation and hyper-assimilation into bourgeois culture. Yet, as Diotima and Ulrich's thoughts reveal, he remains in the eyes of early twentieth-century racial theory recognizable as a Jew, albeit of a slightly different type. See his "Eine bemerkenswerte Einzelheit. Arnheims phönikischer Schädel im Kontext antisemitischer Rassendiskurse," *Musil-Forum. Studien zur Literatur der klassischen Moderne* 31 (2009/2010), 64–83. doi:10.1515/9783110271218.64; and his larger analysis of the intersection of racial thought and constructions of masculinity, *Männlichkeit als Eigenschaft: Geschlechtskonstellationen in Robert Musils Der Mann ohne Eigenschaften* (Berlin: De Gruyter, 2013).

[80] See Georg Rosen, *Juden und Phönizier. Das antike Judentum als Missionsreligion und die Entstehung der jüdischen Diaspora* (Tübingen: Mohr, 1929).

the contention that ancient Phoenician merchants played an important role in the Mediterranean slave trade made the racialization of Phoenicians a viable argument. Common as this association was, Rathenau himself conflated black Africans with Semitic Phoenicians. In *Zur Kritik der Zeit*, Rathenau singled out both groups, describing them as commercially superior and economically more efficient: "If we follow the idea that the world shows an interest in goods where they can be produced in the most perfect manner and with the least amount of labor, then Phoenicians and Central Africans are superior to us in their commercial insight."[81] Rathenau here echoes the widespread assumption that Phoenician mercantilism can be read as the prehistory of industrial capitalism.

Implicitly written in Arnheim is a history of social ascendance. Despite his noticeably small Phoenician-Negroid skull, the narrator seems to argue, Arnheim is capable of transcending his ancestral Afro-Semitic origins and embracing colonial self-representations of condescending Western philanthropy. Part of Arnheim's public image as champion of European imperial culture is his young black servant, modeled on the historical Angelo Soliman (1721–1796), the West African first enslaved as a child, who was raised and educated in Europe, and then brought to Vienna. Soliman's academic education was an Enlightenment-era experiment with the objective of assessing the intellectual capacities of Africans who were exposed to the same Western learning of the European academy.[82] Musil adapts the historical Soliman, who became a friend to the Emperor Joseph II, to the modern Vienna of the novel. The narrator describes Soliman with a whole array of physical stereotypes such as exaggerated lips and simian features, as well as tropes with the typical mix of infantilization and precocious

---

[81] "In dem Sinne, daß die Welt ein Interesse daran hat, jede Ware dort machen zu lassen, wo sie mit dem geringsten Aufwand an Arbeit in vollkommenster Ausführung erzeugt werden kann, sind Phöniker und Zentralafrikaner uns an wirtschaftlicher Erkenntnis überlegen." Walther Rathenau, *Gesammelte Schriften in fünf Bänden*. Vol 1. *Zur Kritik der Zeit* (Berlin: Fischer, 1918), 273.

[82] Musil laid out the foundational thinking for the Soliman character in the 1923 essay "Der deutsche Mensch als Symptom": "Ich glaube nicht an den Unterschied des deutschen Menschen vom Neger ... Die Begriffe Rasse, Nation, Volk, Kultur enthalten Fragen und nicht Antworten, sie sind nicht soziologische Elemente, sondern komplexe Ergebnisse." Musil, *Gesammelte Werke*, 8:1364. In addition, Musil seems to have the historical Soliman in mind when he writes: "Ich will behaupten, daß ein Menschenfresser, als Säugling in europäische Umgebung eingepflanzt, wahrscheinlich ein guter Europäer würde, und der zarte Rainer Maria Rilke ein guter Menschenfresser geworden wäre, wenn ihn ein uns ungünstiges Geschick als kleines Kind unter Südseeleute geworfen hätte." Musil, *Gesammelte Werke*, 8:1372.

sexualization. With Soliman's education, Arnheim asserts a colonial chauvinism while at the same time legitimizing his social position in Vienna as a member of the European imperial elite. Hyper-assimilated, Arnheim is the prototype of the new European, "the New Man, destined to take over the helm of history from the old powers."[83] He strives for a totality that for Musil is not attainable in the modern world.[84] As a Nietzschean leader of the masses, Arnheim is simultaneously Jew and Gentile, a Prussian involved in an Austrian patriotic project, both an industrial capitalist and a dynamic humanist intellectual, who is familiar with new scientific discoveries and has a heightened business acumen. He is a specimen of a novel *Homo Europaeus* who now replaces the Europe of feudal economies and traditional social hierarchies, to which Count Leinsdorf belongs.[85] But Arnheim is destined to fail in his "spiritualization of the economy," his quest to conjoin the "realm of the soul" with the world of capitalist profit maximization.[86] When he tries to realize his totalizing utopia, declaring his passion and love to Diotima, an inner voice holds him back. He hesitates, vacillating in his resolve, and fails to seize the moment in the fateful hour of decision. Galin Tihanov places Arnheim's faltering in the context of Musil's critique of German conservative ideology of the 1920s and 1930s in which an unwavering resoluteness in decisive moments was a sign of effective political leadership.[87] Here Musil's character embodies yet another Phoenician stereotype. Arnheim's wavering evokes Hannibal's hesitation at the gates of Rome. During Hannibal's Italian campaign, the Carthaginian general scored a spectacular victory at Cannae, which in theory could have afforded him the opportunity to march on Rome. The Romans' greatest

---

[83] Musil, *MwQ*, 357. "der neue Typus Mensch, der berufen ist, die alten Mächte in der Lenkung der Geschicke abzulösen." Musil, *MoE*, 330.
[84] In an essay fragment, written shortly after Musil met Rathenau, the author gives a concise definition of the new European who challenges obsolete paradigms of subjectivity: "Der Europäer war einst Christ oder Jude, heute ist er Neufriesianer, Wirtschaftsgeograph oder Farbchemiker auch mit der Seele." Musil, *Gesammelte Werke*, 8:1338. For Musil, this new European tends to choose as identity markers not traditional religious affiliations, but scientific disciplines such as Fries's philosophy of mathematics or the chemistry of textile dyes that inform their outlook on life. The construction of Arnheim seems to echo Musil's words in "Der deutsche Mensch als Symptom:" "Es zeigt sich, dass die Frage des europäischen Menschen: was bin ich? eigentlich heißt: wo bin ich? Es handelt sich nicht um die Phase eines gesetzlichen Prozesses und nicht um ein Schicksal, sondern einfach um eine Situation." Musil, *Gesammelte Werke*, 8:1375.
[85] "europäische Menschheit." Musil, *MoE*, 488.
[86] "Vergeistigung der Wirtschaft" and "Reich der Seele." Musil, *MoE*, 509.
[87] Galin Tihanov, "Robert Musil in the Garden of Conservatism," in *A Companion to the Works of Robert Musil*, ed. Philipp Payne, Graham Bartram, and Galin Tihanov (Rochester, NY: Camden House, 2007), 117–148.

fear was that he would now descend upon the city to plunder and raze it to the ground. For reasons one can only speculate about, Hannibal did not storm Rome. He faltered, so the story goes, in the very moment of decision, a hesitation that ultimately cost him the final victory. German historiography of these years exploited the trope of the undecided Hannibal *ad portas* as evidence of a lack of resoluteness, typical of fickle Semitic leaders.[88] Arnheim's parallel with Hannibal seems to be complete: he retraces the footsteps of the proud and skillful leader when he asserts his economic and political dominance, while also repeating the general's behavioral patterns in the moment of decisive failure.

Musil is much more interested in manipulating and ultimately subverting this historiography of Semitic ineptitude. While Fischel remains for Musil a case study of the gradual exacerbation of prejudice, Arnheim is the figure through which the author amplifies both the taxonomies of Jewishness and the lexicon of anti-Semitism in the novel. The character's cranial skeleton allows Musil to perform a vivisection of Austria's cultural anatomy. Yet, Arnheim, with his Phoenician skull, is not an Orientalist object of study to catalog under the rubric of historical curiosities. The novel makes him, rather, the subject of European history. As the plot inches closer to the eventual outbreak of the war, Musil confronts directly the rhetorical position of Kurt Libesny's poster for the Adriatic Exhibition. It is useful to remember how the poster presented Austria as the civilizing conqueror of Adriatic barbarity, seducing rather than explicitly raping the personified Adria. The composition of the poster was choreographed to recall the mythical abduction of Europa, a rhetorical move by which the Adriatic implicitly became a Phoenician sea to be dominated. In the characterization of Arnheim, the Phoenician strikes back, rejecting the relegation to passive spectator. Musil reverses the Orientalist stereotype of the poster's imagery but does not spin a comforting counter-narrative, at least not here. In the drafts for the end of the novel, Musil envisioned for Arnheim, as he did for Fischel, a reversal of sorts. The author's scant notes reveal an attempt at a rehabilitation of the industrialist who abandons the

---

[88] Once again, late nineteenth- and early twentieth-century interpretations echoed ancient concerns when they could neatly fit an anti-Semitic agenda. Rome indeed panicked after the overwhelming slaughter of troops at Cannae as it now fully realized how utterly inadequate Roman military strategy was at this point. In the moment, their fear of a Carthaginian invasion is understandable. However, Hannibal probably did not hesitate at the gates of Rome. It is doubtful that a talented military strategist like Hannibal ever had any intention to beleaguer the city, given that he did not have any siege machinery and equipment at his disposal.

armament industry in order to retire to pacifist and neutral Switzerland.[89] Whether or not Musil wished to ultimately emphasize the pacifist Phoenician at the expense of the warmongering Carthaginian in his character, now Arnheim's resolute machinations are the marker of a historical agency that will set in motion events with disastrous consequences. Modern European history unfolds along an axis of Phoenician protagonists. With Hannibalic patience and farsightedness, he devises a complex scheme of profit and expansion in what, through the Phoenician characterization of the Adriatic, the empire sees as its own Habsburg Mediterranean.

The first step is to persuade the members of the Parallel Campaign that he participates in the meetings as a pacifist intellectual, eager to pair the celebration of the Emperor with the organization of an international peace conference. Arnheim is able to take advantage of the Committee's inability to move forward with concrete actions. The many committee members represent numerous political positions and ideological directions that ultimately paralyze the plans of the Parallel Campaign. In addition to chronic procrastination, an overwhelmingly dysfunctional bureaucracy, and sheer incompetence, the assorted and often conflicting motivations of the committee members prevent anything from being accomplished. Dynastic loyalty, ethnolinguistic nationalism, imperial chauvinism, monarchic and democratic federalism, along with a pacifist Europeanism make up the wide range of politically charged motivations that contribute to the stagnation in the committee's decision-making process. As the subcommittees of the Parallel Action multiply, Arnheim voices his concern about the campaign's executive functions to Diotima: "No democracy of committees but only strong individual personalities, with experience in both reality and realms of ideas, would be able to direct such a campaign!"[90] In these self-promoting claims, Arnheim lets his political inclinations slip in casual conversation, revealing his suspicion of democratic decision-making and his support of authoritarian political leadership. Rather than borrowing from Rathenau's Weimar Republic ideals, Arnheim speaks with Musil's own abandoned vocabulary. In a subsequent gathering, Arnheim maintains, "We Germans ... are an ill-fated nation. Not only do we live in the

---

[89] Musil, *MoE*, 1933.
[90] Musil, *MwQ*, 113. "Nicht leicht ... werde auf diese Weise etwas Großes zustandekommen; nicht eine Demokratie von Ausschüssen, sondern nur einzelne starke Menschen, mit Erfahrung sowohl in der Wirklichkeit wie im Gebiet der Ideen, würden die Aktion lenken können!" Musil, *MoE*, 109.

heart of Europe, we even suffer the pains of this heart."[91] This sentence echoes Musil's pan-Germanist ideas expressed in "Europeanism, War, Germanness" where the author defined the German and Austrian people as the *Volk* "in the heart of Europe and with the heart of Europe."[92] Musil places in Arnheim's mouth words that he associates with his own nationalist and militarist rhetoric that he abjured after the war.

Before Ulrich fully realizes Arnheim's intentions, he views the industrialist's claims of seeking a harmonious balance between the world of letters and the field of economics with great suspicion. The Prussian entrepreneur supports the Austrian imperial status quo, trying to exploit the Parallel Campaign in order to gain control over the Habsburg oil fields in Ukrainian Galicia. His plan is eventually exposed by Ulrich, who is able to unmask Arnheim's intrigue and true motivation for his scheming presence at the Campaign meetings. Ulrich has an epiphany, thanks to which he recognizes the mutually beneficial relationship between Arnheim's planned colonial exploitation of the Galician oil fields and the military collusions of General Stumm von Bordwehr. In the interlocking interests of the strategic quid pro quo, Arnheim is granted drilling rights for the oil in exchange for a favorable selling price to the Austrian military navy. Because the peripheral region of Galicia is deployment territory and a buffer region bordering Russia, the military would provide armed protection in case of war. But that's not all. Arnheim produces ammunition and is trying to reach an arms deal to supply the Austrian army, so the military would protect Arnheim's oil fields with the cannons and bullets he is selling them in the first place.[93] Stumm von Bordwehr and Tuzzi, representatives of the armed forces and imperial diplomacy respectively, obviously understand the larger geopolitical tensions that the arms deal would produce

---

[91] Musil, *MwQ*, 641. "Wir Deutschen ... sind ein unseliges Volk; wir wohnen nicht nur im Herzen Europas, sondern wir leiden auch als dieses Herz." Musil, *MoE*, 587.

[92] My translation. "das Volk im Herzen Europas und mit dem Herzen Europas." Musil, *Gesammelte Werke*, 8:1021. Musil published this essay in September 1914 in *Die Neue Rundschau*.

[93] Ulrich bursts out at Stumm von Bordwehr: "'Natürlich hast du mit den Öllagern zu tun!' stellte Ulrich in plötzlicher Erleuchtung fest. "Das ist doch eine Frage, die eure Marinesektion angeht wegen der Schiffsfeuerung, und wenn Arnheim die Bohrfelder erwerben will, muß er euch das Zugeständnis machen, euch billig zu liefern. Andrerseits ist Galizien Aufmarschgebiet und Glacis gegen Rußland, also müsst ihr vorkehren, daß die Ölförderung, die er dort in Schwung bringen will, im Kriegsfall besonders geschützt wird. Also wird euch wieder seine Panzer-Blechfabrik bei den Kanonen entgegenkommen, die ihr haben wollt: Daß ich das nicht vorhergesehen habe! Ihr seid doch geradezu für einander geboren!'" Musil, *MoE*, 774.

in Europe. Arnheim's access to the oil fields and the government contract to supply the army will also require the installation of oil bases for the navy on the Adriatic, which, Tuzzi admits, "will upset the Italians" and which is Arnheim's "real objective."[94] Diotima's husband argues that these tensions will increase pacifist propaganda, but Arnheim knows well that his economic scheme will provoke a domino effect on the international stage and that his interests coincide with more than a military provocation. It is a potential *casus belli* for a war from which he would profit. With the assistance of a predatory capitalism, Austria's scheme of colonial exploitation in the Adriatic Sea comes full circle. Musil's fictional reconstruction of the world of 1913 could not miss the imperial ambitions that the Habsburg Empire cultivated in the Adriatic. In the novel, the Adriatic Sea is where the empire drowns and where ultimately the fate of Europe is decided.

The boasted plans of economic development in the Adriatic Sea, so central to the Vienna *Adria-Ausstellung*, in the novel assume a more markedly military function. The ostentatiously belligerent posture of the Austrian knight in Kurt Libesny's official poster for the Adriatic Exhibition had signalled precisely this martial dimension. The Exhibition presented to its audience an ostensible message of peace, but Musil argues in the novel that in fact a more aggressive military hawkishness animated the Austrian presence at sea. The same is true for the Parallel Campaign. To the question of whether Austria was unknowingly preparing for the war, Musil responds that for the political establishment in the novel the Parallel Campaign has been nothing but the protracted and gradual unfolding of a military plan for an aggressive imperialist war, at the beginning shrewdly camouflaged as a pacifist endeavor.

Conceived as a hybrid form of cultural criticism at the intersection of philosophical essayism and historical fiction, *The Man without Qualities* attempts a sober diagnosis of the societal symptoms leading up to the First World War, recording with seismographic precision the almost imperceptible tectonic shifts from an old Europe to a new social and political order. Despite lacking the benefit of greater historical distance, Musil recognized and exposed the profound ambiguity inherent in projects of European unity, placing Stefan Zweig's world of yesterday and post–First World War Europe on an ideological continuum. Many of Musil's contemporaries considered the conflagration of the war, with its absurd carnage and great geopolitical upheaval, a sudden rupture

---

[94] Musil, *MwQ*, 1092. "Denn wenn der Arnheim die galizischen Ölfelder und einen Liefervertrag mit dem Militärärar hat, müssen wir die Grenze natürlich schützen. Wir müssen auch an der Adria Ölstützpunkte für die Marine errichten und Italien beunruhigen … Das ist es, was der Arnheim will!" Musil, *MoE*, 1005–06.

with no apparent connection with the social, cultural, and political values of European intellectuals. Musil, on the contrary, came to understand that the conditions for the war matured in that very elite, within those liberal circles that advocated for continental cooperation but in which an aggressive nationalism and an unapologetic jingoism were intrinsic to political projects of a united Europe.

The shattering of these plans of European cooperation was felt more acutely in Habsburg Trieste. In the background of Musil's initial description of Vienna, the preamble of the *finis Austriae*, lurks the ominous shadow of the August 1913 protests. The Irredentist demonstrations suggested that nationalism had at last supplanted the sociopolitical identities encompassing dynastic loyalty and a multicultural patriotism that resisted and challenged national modes of identification. Musil's portrayal of this indifference to nationalism never translates into an ideological mythography that uncritically celebrates the multiculturalism of the city's cosmopolitan bourgeoisie. Rather than orchestrating an empty commemoration of these nonnational ideologies, Musil dramatizes with a mordant satire an antebellum society with all its paralyzing contradictions and multiple political directions. His fictional reconstruction requires an understanding of the political allegiances and cultural loyalties that were not aligned with national thinking. Musil's depiction of the declining *Landespatriotismus* in the municipal context of Habsburg Trieste offers insights into the author's awareness of the ideological complexities of his time, marked by a wide spectrum of allegiances in which nationalism represented only one of many possible options. The author recognized in the city's multiculturalism the vital presence of an old Habsburg identity characterized by multiple loyalties and emotional attachments to ethnic, cultural, and linguistic communities. The survival of this nonnational mindset represented, far from an obsolete remnant of a feudal past, a valid, albeit unsuccessful, alternative to the monolithic and exclusionary logic of national identifications. In the novel, this nonnational sense of belonging holds the promise to function as a potential antidote to the virulent excesses of nationalism but ultimately succumbs to the efficacious rhetorical stratagems of Italian Irredentism. Musil's vision for a transcultural Europe lies in the recuperation of this nonnational politics that, divested from its dynastic and imperial shell, will allow future Europeans the individual freedom to navigate their primary identifications of class, region, sex, gender, language, and religion without being absorbed by the claims of a totalizing national consciousness.

Just as these demonstrations had signaled a momentous turn of events for the Dual Monarchy, the concomitant Adriatic Exhibition in Vienna made the new strategic priorities of the Empire unequivocal. Musil recognized in the two contrasting projects for the Adriatic city the internal lacerations that would ultimately tear apart the fabric of the empire. This, however, was not the only paradox. The colonial dynamics of representation that framed Trieste in the *Adria-Ausstellung* were characterized by a glaring ambiguity. The Exhibit boastingly flaunted the Adriatic city as a maritime extension of Vienna, as the place from which to launch the grand mission of expansion into an Austrian Sea. Yet, Trieste was also very much part of the Adria that needed conquering. In brief, Trieste was excluded from the center but also paradoxically part of it. Trieste, then, does not merely provide the hermeneutical coordinates for Musil's historiographic fiction. The author's narrative exploration of the Adriatic city crucially contributes to our understanding of the empire's growing aspiration to become a Mediterranean monarchy, a European sea power capable of playing a key role on global markets. Simultaneously domestic and foreign, Trieste was central to strategies of economic policies and audacious imperial fantasies projected onto a Habsburg Mediterranean. Although the dreams of this Austrian thalassocracy were shattered by the end of the war, Trieste maintained its prominent status in the empire's cultural and political imagination until the very end.

Three Trojan Trieste: Italo Svevo and the Aesthetics of Austro-Italian Liminality, 1890–1923

The Italians prefer Senilità.
That is not the case with the French, and I don't believe it is the case with Valery Larbaud.
If you were to ask me, I would choose, without hesitation, my latest novel, Zeno.[1]

Letter from Italo Svevo to Heinrich Horvàt
28 July 1928

The previous chapter argued that Musil viewed the passionately disputed Trieste with its divided loyalties and multiple identities as indicative of the more general fate of the Dual Monarchy. His attention to Trieste was probably one of the reasons for his fondness for Italo Svevo. Svevo was not only Trieste's most representative contemporaneous author, but also a novelist who, in the last chapters of *Zeno's Conscience* (*La Coscienza di Zeno*), depicted humorously the very war battles in which Musil had actively participated.[2] Similar to Musil, Svevo

---

[1] "Die Italiener ziehen alle *Senilità* vor. Das ist aber nicht der Fall mit den Franzosen und ich glaube auch nicht mit Valery Larbaud. Wenn sie mich fragen, so würde ich mich ohne Zaudern für meinen Jüngsten entscheiden, *Zeno*." (original in German). Italo Svevo, *Epistolario* (Milan: Dall'Oglio, 1966), 884.

[2] In a diary entry from January 6, 1930, Musil notes that he and his wife Martha are reading Svevo's novel with great pleasure. "Sowohl Martha wie ich haben in den letzten Tagen mit großem Vergnügen *Zeno Cosini* von Italo Svevo gelesen." Musil, *Tagebücher, Aphorismen, Essays und Reden*, ed. Adolf Frisé (Hamburg: Rowohlt, 1955), 309. For a comparative reading of Musil and Svevo, see Saskia Ziolkowski, "Svevo's Uomo senza Qualità: Musil and Modernism in Italy," in *Gender and Modernity in Central Europe*, ed. Agatha Schwartz (Ottawa: University of Ottawa Press, 2010).

had been an initial outsider to the realm of letters, pursuing a career far from literary ambitions. And like Musil, Svevo intended to contribute with his critical writings to debates about the nonnational future of Europe. But while Musil's outside perspective does much to illuminate Trieste's profound connections with the Habsburg Empire, Svevo's literary strategies are more directly imbricated in the internal lacerations of the Adriatic city. Italian intellectual circles in the city saw reading and writing literary fiction as a means of enculturation into a single national tradition. Svevo aspired to belong to an Italian literary culture but also viewed the narrow parameters of Trieste's gated literary community as claustrophobic. Against a restrictive national normativity, Svevo articulates an aesthetics of Austro-Italian liminality that challenges the merit of such exclusionary loyalties. He conceives of a literary invention of Europe as the locus of a more authentic strategy of self-representation, a space that adequately accommodates his implicitly hyphenated identity. The European posture Svevo assumes is both one of open cosmopolitan stance and one of surreptitious and subversive stratagems in his works. His novels tackle the widespread politics of literary style according to which adherence to linguistic purity is interpreted as a sign of the morality and health of the nation. Svevo's Europeanism, made up of cleverly disguised nonnational allegiances and blatant linguistic contaminations, stages a Trojan Trieste that quietly dismantles the literary and cultural strategies of Italian nation building from within. As this chapter will show, this project of subversion wears the sardonic smirk of Zeno, Svevo's Habsburg Phoenician protagonist. Through this maverick, Svevo mockingly challenges the legitimacy of acceptable Italian prose, subverts genre conventions of the nineteenth-century novel, and frustrates many of the expectations of his Italian readers. Zeno's Phoenician background radically undermines one the most solid columns of the Irredentists' rhetorical edifice, one that took pride in its Roman foundation.

When the Triestine businessman of German and Hungarian ancestry Aron Hector Schmitz, called Ettore at home, published *A Life* (*Una vita*) in 1892, he decided to pursue his literary career as a novelist with the *nom de plume* Italo Svevo, meaning the "Italian Swabian." The adoption paid homage to author's multilingual background and dual cultural citizenship and affirmed in no uncertain terms that Habsburg Trieste was indeed a metropolis of mediation between German and Italian civilizations. Although this mission of cultural conciliation was certainly not a groundbreaking idea in the city, as we have seen in previous chapters, assuming a culturally composite pseudonym nevertheless took the features of a bold and ostentatious public performance for Svevo. It was a courageous gesture, in the early 1890s and again in 1923, when he published in Mussolini's Italy *Zeno's Conscience*, for Svevo to adopt and insist on the choice of a pseudonym that suggested a multiplicity of allegiances among his immediate friends and acquaintances, many of whom were enthusiastic Irredentists first and Fascists later. Schmitz settles on the name Italo Svevo after having published newspaper articles with two other pen names, "Erode," after the biblical Jewish king Herod, and Ettore Samigli.[3] While Svevo's use of Herod was probably inspired by the protagonist of Friedrich Hebbel's 1850 drama *Herodes und Mariamne*, the pseudonym "Samigli" is one of those cunning artifices that Svevo enjoys constructing. The name is ostensibly Italian, but it conceals a German Jewish origin. Samigli reads like a transliteration from the Hebrew equivalent of Schmitz and its Yiddish forms *Shlemil* and *Shlemazl*. Again, Svevo had in mind a German model, namely Adelbert von Chamisso's *Peter Schlemils wundersame Geschichte*. In Yiddish, shlemil designates a clumsy, inept, and unlucky person, much like Svevo's protagonists in his novels.

Svevo's new literary identity was destined to be perceived as defiantly European and cosmopolitan in the author's social milieu, especially because Svevo himself had been publishing, for pragmatic opportunism rather than genuine political convictions, in *L'Indipendente*, a local newspaper that was the unapologetic mouthpiece of the city's Irredentists. Svevo saw publishing in the newspaper as an entryway into the literary and cultural industry of Trieste, as it was the only avenue for young Triestine authors to become known. Svevo's role at the newspaper was to summarize articles from the international press, especially foreign politics in German and English. In a private memorandum, dated December 19, 1889, Svevo admits his profound discontent about his public behavior, lamenting the circumstances that force him to fake interest in matters for which he does not care much.[4] Despite the consternation and embarrassment that his pseudonym caused in Italian nationalist circles to which the author was connected via friends and family, Svevo decided to preserve it throughout his career. Mild-mannered and conflict-averse by temperament, Svevo justified his adoption with his usual humorous remarks, with which he made light of potentially controversial topics. Svevo explained away

---

[3] Marina Beer suggests that Heinrich Heine's poem "Yehuda Ben Halevy," whose protagonist bears the middle name Shmuel, may have also played a role in Svevo's use of his earlier pseudonym. "Alcune note su Ettore Schmitz e i suoi nomi: per una ricerca sulle fonti di Italo Svevo" in *Contributi sveviani* (Trieste: Lint, 1979), 11–30.

[4] Biographer John Gatt-Rutter sees Svevo's collaboration with *L'Indipendente* as "clearly an act, lacking conviction" (95) even though he conjectures that perhaps Svevo's disaffection was not with the Irredentist cause itself, but with the people in charge of the newspaper. *Italo Svevo: A Double Life* (Oxford: Clarendon, 1988), 95–115. For Svevo's thoughts about *L'Indipendente*, see Livia Veneziani, *Vita di mio marito* (Trieste: Edizioni dello Zibaldone, 1950).

the pseudonym, claiming that it was meant as a joke about his German-inflected Italian prose, for which his friends mockingly called him the "Ostrogoth."[5] Svevo's initial lack of success as a novelist both in Trieste and in Italy can be in part ascribed to the bicultural, Austro-Italian pseudonym and the perception that his writing was not patriotic enough.[6]

Patriotism or the alleged lack thereof was not exactly the issue at stake here. Svevo's patriotism was unwavering, and rather than unpatriotic, Svevo's pseudonym emerges from a different brand of patriotism, a Triestine urban *Landespatriotismus* whose double nonnational allegiance characteristically eschewed any references to modern nations or the ruling dynasties of Germany, Austria, and Italy. The hostile reception of Svevo's literary persona is evidence of the fierce competition between nonnational sentiments and national identification. The name makes a reference to another Italian Swabian, namely the Holy Roman Emperor Frederick II von Hohenstaufen, German ruler of the medieval Kingdom of Sicily. Adopting a political strategy of multicultural coexistence, Frederick was invested in presenting his kingdom as a linguistically, culturally, and religiously diverse Mediterranean monarchy, in what was outwardly projected as effective interfaith diplomacy and relative social concord. Frederick II's imperial court encouraged the development of the first literary tradition in the vernacular, the Sicilian School so much admired by Dante. The implicit parallel that Svevo draws between the medieval Kingdom of Sicily and Habsburg Trieste is evident, as both are associated with a culture that was both vernacular and transnational at the same time. Svevo's urban cosmopolitanism echoes the multicultural identity politics of the early Slataper with one crucial difference: Svevo never acknowledges in his texts the Slavic component of Trieste.

The open display of Svevo's composite European identity is part of a general strategy with which the author created a highly choreographed image, carefully constructed with prudent discretion in order

---

[5] Gatt-Rutter, *Double*, 113.
[6] Gatt-Rutter argues, "Svevo's writing was too negative and unpatriotic to be acceptable in Trieste. The silence about Svevo in Trieste was politically motivated and conspiratorial." Gatt-Rutter, *Double*, 231. Despite this difficult relationship, Svevo is often depicted as a champion of the Irredentist cause who loathed Austria. Even Kwame Anthony Appiah, who elects Svevo as an example of modern identity crises, mistakes Svevo's refusal to serve in the Habsburg army as a feeling of "no real alignment with Austria" (85) and does not see the author's unwillingness to put on a military uniform. See Appiah, *The Lies that Bind: Rethinking Identity, Creed, Country, Color, Class, Culture* (New York: Norton & Norton, 2018), 71–86.

to avoid embarrassing missteps. While the cultural syncretism in Italo Svevo has been interpreted as an act of inclusion, it has been read as a strategy that aims at concealing, if not indeed completely obliterating, the author's Jewish background from his public persona.[7] Raised in an observant household, Svevo grew up to become a secular and atheist Jew, for whom Jewishness was a matter of cultural belonging rather than religious faith. He rarely mentions explicitly Jewish matters in his public writings, with the exception of the previous pseudonym Herod and the early article entitled "Shylock" in which he argued that Shakespeare's *The Merchant of Venice* could not be accused of anti-Semitism. Throughout his life, Svevo tried to maintain a guarded distance from any kind of political controversy. Emphasizing his double allegiance to German and Italian literary cultures must have felt less divisive than revealing his Jewish origins, cautiously concealed from public scrutiny. Yet, the literary alias duplicates the structure of traditional European Jewish last names that often indicated a family's place of origin. The Swabian component of his pseudonym is a reference to Svevo's paternal grandfather, a Danube Swabian, a German-speaking colonist who settled in the Banat region of Hungarian Transylvania in the course of the eighteenth century. The pseudonym *svevo* therefore is really a toponym and, as such, very much rings like a Jewish surname that indicates a place of origin.[8] However hidden from sight, Svevo's Jewish transculturalism performs an adhesive function between the German and Italian, and indeed becomes the necessary premise for his multiple cultural allegiances.[9] The pseudonym appears like a

---

[7] The early critic Giacomo Debenedetti famously argued that Svevo was not a great writer because he had sacrificed his Jewishness to literary fame. In his 1929 essay "Svevo e Schmitz" Debenedetti claimed that Svevo, influenced by Otto Weininger's anti-Semitic and misogynist *Geschlecht und Charakter* (1903), was an example of Jewish self-hatred and that the author's difficult reception could be ascribed to his attempt to hide his Jewish origins. Debenedetti's article was first published in *Il Convegno* and is now reprinted in *Saggi Critici* (Milan: Mondadori, 1955), 49–94. Svevo scholars tend to reject this reading. We know that Svevo read Weininger, but included in *Zeno's Conscience* a parody of Weininger's sexism and anti-Semitism.

[8] His wife's last name "Veneziani," is a case in point, as it indicates Venice as the city of the family's origin, or the abovementioned "Eisenstädter," meaning from the city of Eisenstadt.

[9] Giuliana Minghelli in her *In the Shadow of the Mammoth: Italo Svevo and the Emergence of Italian Modernism* (Toronto: University of Toronto Press, 2002) shrewdly argues that Svevo's Jewishness is not completely absent from the pseudonym, claiming that "behind its orderly façade lurks the now hidden, yet defiant, code name 'Erode' to remind us of a subterranean contamination within the asserted hybrid of Italian and German identities" (7).

palimpsest from which the trace of his Jewish origin—in thoroughly ambiguous fashion, so typical of Svevo—either resists the author's attempt to erase it or is intentionally left for us to unearth.[10]

Such a palimpsestic reading of Svevo, one that investigates the traces of erased discourses, the infiltrations and contaminations of buried multilayered strata of meaning, is an entirely fitting methodology in the approach to an author known for his deliberately orchestrated ambiguity, his chronic reticence to completely reveal himself to the public. Only in his fiction did the ever vigilant Svevo feel more comfortable opening up, and even then only via a programmatic obfuscation, through a textual labyrinth of systematic sidetracking and diversion in which the author plays hide-and-seek with his readers. It is indeed a critical commonplace to describe Svevo in terms of what one might call an aesthetic of concealment according to which the author disguises himself in a series of rhetorical camouflages. An illustrative example is the author's *Profilo autobiografico*, Svevo's autobiographical note, drafted in 1928 by his old friend and lifelong nationalist Giulio Cesari and then revised by a self-censoring Svevo. The text, purportedly shedding light on the biography of a now famous author, is intentionally elusive and downright misleading, marked by glaring omissions and awkwardly staged postures. The profile emphasizes Svevo's qualifications as a lifelong and dedicated nationalist, glossing over his flaunted hybridity with evident discomfiture. His Jewish family background is never mentioned, while his foreign-born and Austro-loyal father is described as fully assimilated into Italian culture.[11] The text

---

[10] Svevo's complex relationship with his Jewishness has attracted the attention of many critics. Brian Moloney has explored the Jewish dimension of Svevo's oeuvre in "Svevo as a Jewish Writer," *Italian Studies* 28 (1973): 52–65. Elizabeth Schächter has investigated Svevo's Jewish upbringing in a religiously practicing household, the active role his parents took in the Jewish community, and what she describes as the emotional trauma of his conversion. See "The Enigma of Svevo's Jewishness: Trieste and the Jewish Cultural Tradition," *Italian Culture* 50 (1995): 24–47. doi:10.1179/its.1995.50.1.24, and "The Anguish of Assimilation: The Case of Italo Svevo," in *Freud and Italian Culture*, ed. Pierluigi Barrotta, Laura Lepschy, and Emma Bond (Oxford, New York: Peter Lang, 2009), 65–81.

[11] Svevo's father, who is often called Francesco in biographical accounts, in reality signed his name with the German name Franz. From one of Franz's rare letters, Brian Moloney suspects that Franz Schmitz was a native speaker of German and that he spoke Italian with a German accent. See Brian Moloney, *Friends in Exile: Italo Svevo and James Joyce* (Leicester: Troubador Publishing, 2018), 9.

The Aesthetics of Austro-Italian Liminality, 1890–1923   147

downplays Svevo's schooling in Segnitz, near Würzburg, in Germany.[12] In terms of literary taste, Svevo's silence about his abiding love for Goethe and Schiller, and his praise of Carducci, the Italian national poet, rings disingenuous. Published during Fascist rule in Italy, Svevo's tendentious autobiography is obviously cautious to avoid any mention of his heritage as a Habsburg Jew. Svevo himself had officially abjured his Jewish faith. A year after their marriage, he had converted to Catholicism and decided to be baptized in order to alleviate his wife's growing anxiety at having married a Jew, a conversion he privately came to regret. In parallel fashion, *Vita di mio marito*, the biography by his wife Livia Veneziani, who came from a conservative Catholic family that fully embraced Irredentist fervor, similarly depicts the author as the champion of a respectable Italian character. She tries to dispel any possible doubts about Svevo's allegiances, arguing that even his long business trips abroad did not turn the author "at all into a cosmopolitan" and that he always remained a loyal Triestine Italian.[13] Early Svevo criticism took the two biographical accounts at face value. These pages, however, document the rhetorical strategies of an anxiety-ridden double assimilation, namely Svevo's fraught journey from Habsburg Jew to Catholic gentile, and from his nonnational regional patriotism to a never fully accepted Italian national identity.

Like many other Italian-speaking Jews in Trieste, Svevo supported, at least nominally, Irredentism. His allegiances seem to have shifted as his attitude evolved over time. Even though in earlier years Svevo was more sympathetic to Italian cultural Irredentism, he kept himself

---

[12]   A diary entry of Elio Schmitz, Svevo's brother, suggests that the family ascribed a certain degree of alterity to Italian. Elio describes their father's decision to send his young sons to Germany in order to learn the language. He remembers his father remarking that a good businessman must have at least a superficial knowledge of four languages, two of them perfectly in order to be successful in Trieste. Given his Austrian sympathies and the importance of German as a language of commerce and state administration, Mr. Schmitz wished for his children a full immersion into German language and culture, which could be accomplished in the Bavarian boarding school. Italian could be learned in Trieste, he argued, which suggests how, in his opinion, Italian language acquisition did not constitute a natural occurrence in the city. The knowledge of Italian needed to be actively pursued and required an effort. See Carmine di Biase, ed. *The Diary of Elio Schmitz* (Leicester: Troubador Publishing, 2013).
[13]   Veneziani, *Vita*, 71. Livia Veneziani's biography has been translated into English as *Memoir of Italo Svevo* (Evanston, IL: Northwestern University Press, 1990).

always far from the clamour of its political activism.[14] If Svevo at any point in his life genuinely supported Trieste's annexation to Italy, his support did not seem to be willing to sacrifice his sense of belonging to a larger German culture, which he perceived to be an integral and indissoluble component of both his private and public persona.[15] In what appears as a challenge to the exclusionary and divisive logic of monolithic national identifications, Svevo's Germanic Italianness did not conform to the strictures of a national character that demanded absolute and undivided loyalty. Svevo remained committed to a Habsburg Italianness in which these multiple allegiances were not mutually exclusive but could coexist feeding each other. The author presented the bond between his Italian and German backgrounds not as a hierarchical relationship, but rather as a dialogic exchange, a meeting point of the two literary traditions. So, even after the First World War, Svevo's Habsburg Italianness did not suddenly vanish but survived as an aesthetic program that introduced German culture to his new home. Svevo's complex network of loyalties and cultural identifications make any attempt to neatly place him into the narratives of an Italian national literary tradition inadequate. As an author situated in the cultural topography of Central Europe, Svevo better fits the overlapping categorizations of an Austrian novelist and assimilated Jew writing in Italian, thus occupying the interstitial space between national literary traditions. Svevo is an author who is culturally polyvalent, linguistically multilayered, and politically invested in a network of multiple loyalties and transnational allegiances.[16]

---

[14] In Svevo's fiction, the attitude toward Italian Irredentism is ambivalent at best. Telling is the episode in *Further Confessions of Zeno* (1927) in which the protagonist cheers the Italian troops marching in the streets but goes into the office to conduct business as usual with the Austrian enemy. In *A Perfect Hoax* (*Una burla riuscita*), from 1928, the protagonist Mario Samigli reads the novels of Fogazzaro and De Amicis, full of the nationalist enthusiasm so appreciated in Triestine Irredentist circles, to his disabled brother as bedtime stories. Their militarist nationalism is so soporific to Mario's brother that they put him to sleep.

[15] Let me caution against the distorted image of Svevo as a fervent Irredentist, an interpretation supported by an Italian nationalist historiography and literary history invested in finding at all costs a strong and rooted tradition of independence movements in Trieste. See Giuseppe Camerino, *Italo Svevo e la crisi della Mitteleuropa* (Naples: Liguori, 2002) and Elizabeth Schächter, *Origins and Identity: Essays on Svevo and Trieste* (Leeds: Northern Universities Press, 2000), in contrast to the more narrow reading of Enrico Ghidetti, *Italo Svevo: la coscienza di un borghese triestino* (Rome: Riuniti, 1992).

[16] Edouard Roditi was probably the first critic to suggest an Austrian literary background for Svevo, placing the Triestine author in the same literary culture shared by Schnitzler, Musil, and Kafka. As early as 1944, Roditi argued that "It might prove more profitable and conclusive to place Svevo in a context of Austrian literature and compare him to those Austrian novelists whose culture

Svevo's Politics of Literary Style

The uncritical acceptance of Svevo's biographical accounts and their ideological underpinnings informed much of the debate concerning what has been called the "Svevo Affair," *il caso Svevo*, conducted against the background of a literary historiography that imposed upon the modern history of Trieste the narrative of a late *Risorgimento* struggling to unite with the Italian Kingdom. Italian critics largely ignored the Svevo that awkwardly fit the panorama of Italian literary movements until a penniless Irish teacher of English in Trieste encouraged him and resurrected his literary ambitions, performing the "miracle of Lazarus," as Svevo called it.[17] After James Joyce introduced Svevo's works in the literary circles in Paris, Svevo became successful abroad, while Italian critics continued to struggle with the European modernist inspiration of an aesthetic program that introduced Freud's psychoanalysis into Italian letters. For Italian critics, Svevo remained a conundrum: internationally successful but also suspect and questionable at home.[18] While scholars saw him as an ardent Irredentist supporter (for which there has never surfaced any conclusive evidence), he was seen as a writer with a regretfully limited mastery of the language, a novelist whose German-inflected Italian prose, despite the author's continued efforts and multiple revisions, did not conform to the linguistic standards deemed worthy of the Italian literary tradition.

Svevo's adopted bicultural pseudonym signals the intersection of traditions and allegiances as much as it also offers to decode the author's narrative strategies, that never seem to have aimed at linguistic purity. In other words, in the same way that Schmitz's pseudonym eschews purity, the author's stylistic choices bespeak intentional and programmatic contaminations. Below the surface of Svevo's Italian stubbornly hover multiple alloglot substrata. As many Italian critics have lamented in the past, Svevo's Italian prose is rife with semantic and syntactic calques from German and the Triestine dialect, accompanied by occasional Gallicisms of literary origin, an awkwardly employed business Italian, as well as archaic Tuscan expressions

---

was not strictly German and who often wrote in one or the other of the many languages spoken within the polyglot empire" (345). For Roditi, this was possible because the empire, while not possessing the means or the political will to impose a single language on its subjects, nonetheless was able to diffuse a common Austrian culture within its boundaries. "Novelist-philosophers, Italo Svevo" *Horizon* 10 (1944): 342–359.

[17] In 1927, Svevo wrote that Joyce had repeated the miracle of Lazarus in the preface to the second edition of *Senilità*.

[18] See Naomi Lebowitz, *Italo Svevo* (New Brunswick, NJ: Rutgers University Press, 1978), 175.

extrapolated from a dictionary that bring to light Svevo's tendency to overcompensate the uneasiness with the language in which he writes.[19] The recent and felicitous discovery of a portion of Svevo's private library—more than seventy books long believed to be lost—reveals that the author owned the *Dizionario-vocabolario del dialetto triestino e della lingua italiana*, compiled by Ernesto Kosovitz and published in 1889. Svevo actively worked with lexicographic assistance as some underlined entries in the dictionary, among which appear revealing terms such as *cossienza* and *fumo*, unequivocally confirm.[20] Svevo's use of a dictionary betrays the genetic cogitations of a bilingual author struggling with his Italian. Just like Däubler, Svevo seems both incapable but also unwilling to separate his geopoetic vantage point, Habsburg Trieste, from its multilingual fabric. With the adoption of intertwined grammar codes he also suggests the existence of a Triestine literary linguistics which does not take shape around a poetics of contiguous monolingualisms, but instead crystallizes in a literary production governed by a bilingual aesthetics, one that parallels the stylistic techniques of Däubler's linguistic hybridity. Giorgio Voghera described Svevo as a person who usually thought in Triestino, but when the conversation turned to topics related to his writing, Svevo's Triestino became entangled with words, expressions, sentences, and idioms from German. It was difficult for Svevo, according to Voghera, to translate this mixture into Italian, a language he did not completely master.[21] The ideal reader of Svevo's prose is, according to this reconstruction, one who can detect the subterranean German terminology and set of expressions that render Svevo's Italian awkward and almost cacophonic. Voghera disagrees with those commentators, like Umberto Saba, who claimed that Svevo could have written in good German since he did not believe that Svevo's German was perfect either. So, rather than thinking of Svevo as an author at home in two languages, Voghera suggests, perhaps with

---

[19] Giuliana Minghelli comments on Svevo's composite background and the constructed nature of his Italian: "Thus Svevo writes, as an Austrian subject and assimilated Jew, from a constructed and idealized Italian national identity, as a Triestine and German-speaking author, within a constructed Italian language." *Shadow*, 48.

[20] Part of Svevo's library, long believed to have been destroyed during the war, was recently discovered. The findings are presented in Simone Volpato, Riccardo Cepach, and Massimo Gatta, *Alla peggio andrò in biblioteca. I libri ritrovati di Italo Svevo* (Macerata: Biblohaus, 2013).

[21] Voghera writes that Svevo tried to inscribe himself in the Italian literary tradition without much success because his command of Italian was far from perfect, a situation he recognizes, even though to a lesser extent, in many other Triestine writers. Giorgio Voghera, *Gli anni della psicanalisi* (Pordenone: Studio Tesi, 1980), 46.

a bit of pessimism, that one should think of Svevo as a guest in both Italian and German. The best solution for Svevo would have been to write a "mixed-language text."[22] In this discussion of Svevo's language competence, or lack thereof, Giuseppe Camerino argues that Svevo was "more than is usually believed, generally inclined to think in German," a tendency that would suggest that the Triestine author had a native or near-native command of the language.[23] Svevo was comfortable enough with German to write a short philosophical treatise as a young student in Segnitz, an essay that, however, does not survive. While it would be impossible to verify empirically in what language Svevo was inclined to think, one can safely argue that he was inclined to think about his literature in German. This confidence in Svevo's German comes from Umberto Saba, in whose estimation "Svevo could have written well in German; he preferred to write badly in Italian."[24] Saba's implicit assumption is that Svevo did indeed wish to write in what was commonly accepted as good literary Italian. What is absent in Saba's evaluation is a discussion of Svevo's politics of style that questions the notion that Svevo really wanted to write in good Italian. Much of Svevo's reception has operated, and continues to operate, under this erroneous premise. Writing in "corrupt" Italian might have corresponded exactly to Svevo's aesthetic program. Svevo was driven by the ambition to achieve literary fame but also by the aspiration to write in a language that felt legitimate and meaningful to him.[25] For this reason, Svevo was often caught between the painstaking revisions in order to placate his detractors and his determination to maintain a level of linguistic authenticity unencumbered by the dictums of academic purity. His objective was to expose what one might call the rhetoricity of Italian linguistic standardization and to surreptitiously undermine a language ideology that elected literary Florentine as the benchmark of aesthetic quality. Svevo's characters describe Italian by emphasizing its regional

---

[22] Ibid., 49–50.
[23] Camerino, *Mitteleuropa*, 265.
[24] Umberto Saba, *Scorciatoie e Raccontini* (Milan: Mondadori, 1946): 80.
[25] In a letter to Valery Larbaud, written in 1926, Svevo defends his choice of writing what Italian critics considered "bad" Italian: "Ricorda che volevo provarle che avevo ragione di scrivere male? Avevo paura che scoprendomi tanto scalcinato m'avreste voltato le spalle ... Ma in Italia ci sono delle persone incantate nel piacere di trovare dei romanzi scritti male." *Carteggio con James Joyce, Eugenio Montale, Valery Larbaud, Benjamin Crémieux, Marie Anne Comnène, Valerio Jahier*, ed. Bruno Maier (Milan: Dall'Oglio, 1965), 68. Brian Moloney has recently argued that Svevo's point was precisely to write in his own Italian: "If, in the context of the hegemonic Italian culture of his day, authenticity entailed writing 'badly,' Svevo chose to write 'badly' in order to write well." Moloney, *Friends*, 222.

origin, calling it "Tuscan," making the linguistic tensions a question of competition between the centrality of Tuscan and the peripheral position of Triestino. Therefore, critics who have pointed out the author's sense of inadequacy with his own literary language capture only a partial aspect of Svevo's linguistic question. Naomi Lebowitz argues that Svevo had an "evident ... linguistic inferiority complex" and that the author "always knew the hopelessness of writing in a language not his own."[26] More recently, however, Svevo's choices are seen in a different light. Paolo Bartoloni still writes against a deeply rooted prejudice about Svevo's linguistic uncertainties and allegedly inadequate narrative talents, a bias that has accompanied the author's writing since its original reception in Italy. The tacit premise of Bartoloni's argument seems to be Svevo's stable position as an outsider in the Italian literary tradition and thus Svevo's constant need of canonization and rehabilitation. Writing in what sounds like a defense and justification of Svevo's position among the classics of Italian modernism, Bartoloni emphasizes that Svevo's outwardly clumsy prose and Zeno's narrative unreliability in reality conceal shrewd and subtle rhetorical skill, a forcefully manipulative mastermind, operating on both extradiegetic and intradiegetic levels, that is playfully deceptive and intentionally misleading.[27] In a city where Irredentists wanted linguistic choices to smoothly translate into national identification, signaling unwavering loyalty to an Italian cultural and political nation, Svevo knew exactly what he was doing when employing his challenging prose.

Triestino itself was a multilayered linguistic system, not simply because it tended to incorporate the different languages spoken in the empire at large and in the city's polyglot business community. The dialect had an internal layered composition, which was once more the result of specific economic policies dictated by the imperial government. At the beginning of the eighteenth century, before the Habsburgs decided to expand the city, transforming a small fishing town into an imperial port, Friulian, an Eastern Ladino dialect, was spoken in Trieste. With the massive immigration wave of Venetian workers from the surrounding areas, Venetian gradually supplanted Friulian. At the end of the nineteenth century, the inhabitants of the Adriatic city spoke *triestino*, a variation of this *veneziano coloniale*, colonial Venetian. Within the Triestine dialect, there were two recognizable variants. The higher variant was called *triestìn patoco*, spoken and understood in almost all

---

[26] Naomi Lebowitz, *Italo Svevo* (New Brunswick, NJ: Rutgers University Press, 1978), 193.
[27] Paolo Bartoloni, *Sapere di scrivere. Svevo e gli ordigni di La coscienza di Zeno* (Catania: Il Carrubbo, 2015).

social strata, and employed in the poetic production written in dialect; and *triestìn negròn*, literally "darker Triestine," was spoken in the poor and working class neighborhoods of *Cita Vecia* (Old City) and San Giacomo. In Svevo's dialectophone Trieste, Italian was often perceived as a foreign language, a closely related but different and even somewhat alien linguistic system.[28] Italian was known as the language of the *regnicoli*, a term coined by the Italians of Austria to indicate subjects of the Kingdom (*regno*) of Italy. The Tuscan-based standard was by no means a dominant language in terms of usage, but it nevertheless retained the status of a prestige language. It was the language of a celebrated literary tradition to which many writers and intellectuals aspired to belong. The cohabitation of the protean dialect and its formal standardized counterpart can be described in terms of diglossia, in which two related linguistic systems operate in separate societal spheres. One was the language of letters, the other the international vernacular of commerce and thus ultimately a visible sign of the city's economic prosperity.[29] It is important to note that the use of Italian in Trieste constituted an indicator of social class rather than an ethno-national identity marker. Elizabeth Schächter points out that "educated Triestines were trilingual, speaking German, Italian and Triestine dialect."[30] In the case of Svevo, these three linguistic systems submit to a specific usage distribution. Svevo speaks in dialect, thinks in German, and writes in Italian. Given the multiple examples in which German idiomatic expressions and culture-bound terms creep into his Italian, one would be tempted to identify the relationships in this linguistic triangle as composed of a German-Italian bilingualism and a dialect-Italian standard diglossia. Svevo's command of German and Italian was equivalent, even though one should not think that he spoke the languages similarly well but rather that he spoke them in equally bad fashion. Svevo's struggle with Italian and his need of a dictionary to write his novel strongly suggest that Svevo was in no way a balanced bilingual. This is hardly surprising if one considers that bilingual speakers often belong to very heterogeneous groups and linguistic communities, within which language competence and performance can greatly fluctuate. The variables, largely dependent upon psycholinguistic and sociolinguistic factors, include

---

[28] Mario Lavagetto, *La cicatrice di Montaigne. Sulla bugia in letteratura* (Turin: Einaudi, 1992), 191.
[29] Vesna Deželjin describes the linguistic situation of Trieste in terms of a macro-diglossic scenario, in which German represents the high variant, the Triestine dialect a widely spoken middle variant in its function of an urban koine, and Slovene the demotic context. "Reflexes of the Habsburg Empire Multilingualism in Some Triestine Literary Texts," *Jezikoslovje* 13, no. 2 (2012): 419–439.
[30] Schächter, "Assimilation," 65.

manner of eloquence, mode and methods of language acquisition, and order of languages acquired. Svevo's linguistic situation suggests that his native language was a multilayered idiolect, an idiosyncratic parlance that was an inextricable mixture of Triestino, Italian, and German. One could also describe Svevo's situation in terms of what in linguistics is called a diagonal bilingualism, a particular kind of bilingualism that involves a standard language and a dialect. Italian becomes the language of choice for his novels, even though his prose does not conform to the standards of a long-established tradition that elected Tuscan as its measure of literary quality. What prompted his effort of Tuscan enculturation was the wish to acquire those linguistic means that could satisfy Svevo's literary ambitions and his desire to be recognized in intellectual circles. Only his idiolect and its intrinsic code-switching occurring between dialect and Italian, and German and Italian can account for the influences in the author's unique literary prose. The cultural prestige of the Italian literary tradition, combined with the social pressure to assimilate into the "national" culture of Trieste's ethnic majority—an assimilation effort particularly strong in a writer with a Jewish background—was, as we will see below, not the only reason that dictated Svevo's choice to write in Italian. This option was never free from psycholinguistic and sociolinguistic tensions. All major characters in Svevo's novels and short stories record a discomfort that arises from the opposition between Trieste's polyglot vernacular and the cultural prestige of literary Italian. Zeno Cosini, the protagonist of Svevo's third novel, becomes the voice of this conflict when he denounces the asymmetrical power structure that opposes Trieste's dialectophone milieu to the status but also foreignness of the Tuscan-based Italian standard. Before we discuss how Svevo's politics of style governs his novel, we must turn to a different kind of political thinking that will introduce us to Zeno's network of elusive textual subterfuges.

The New Europe in Svevo's Pacifist Essay, 1918–1922

> You are conditioned by European ways of thought.[31]
> —Franz Kafka, *The Penal Colony*

Svevo's "Theory of Peace," an unfinished treatise on pacifism, international commerce, and the League of Nations, falls into a specific textual

---

[31] Franz Kafka, *Complete Stories* (New York: Schocken Books, 1971), 155. "Sie sind in europäischen Anschauungen befangen." Franz Kafka, *Gesammelte Werke in zwölf Bänden. Band 1* (Frankfurt am Main: Fischer, 2004), 180.

category, namely the one that Paul Michael Lützeler has described as the "Europe-essay" (*Europaaufsatz*), an essayistic form that he sees as a genre in its own right at the juncture of historical analysis, cultural-philosophical considerations, and political vision.[32] Drafted during and in the immediate aftermath of the First World War, a war that Svevo considered "the great European tragedy," the document is strongly influenced by Austrian antebellum reform proposals that generally advocated for federalist solutions.[33] Svevo approaches pacifism from the perspective of a businessman intent at minimizing obstacles to commerce and protecting open economic competition. The text also squarely places Svevo within a reformist tradition hailing from the now defunct Habsburg Empire and, in general, within the political philosophy of the German-speaking world.[34] In the absence of other critical writings, Svevo's text offers rare insights into the author's political thought and represents one of the last documents in which one can appreciate a Habsburg regional patriotism before these nonnational modes of identification were replaced by the exclusionary logic of nationalism. In a post–First World War Europe of established nation-states, Svevo tries to carry over and update the intellectual inheritance from the crumbled empire to this new geopolitical context. The text is burdened by a twofold crippling anachronism. On the one hand, Svevo's affinity with the Austro-Marxist version of socialism that envisioned a reorganization of the empire into a European federation could only fit awkwardly in the immediate postbellum scenario of Italy, deaf to any ideas of Austrian imperial heritage. On the other hand, the general interwar support for a future United States of Europe, considered by many Habsburg intellectuals before the war an ideal democratic continuation of the multiethnic empire, was destined to become a workable scenario much later in the future. Svevo's untimeliness is therefore double: too late to propose an updated version of Austro-Europeanism, and too early to be taken seriously with his far-seeing project of a borderless European single market.

---

[32] Lützeler, *Schriftsteller*, 24.
[33] "la grande tragedia europea." Italo Svevo, *Teatro e saggi* (Milan: Mondadori, 2004), 1165. Svevo concludes his short essay "Viaggiando …," dated April 30, 1922, by evoking the image of a dark night that falls upon Europe. Travelling from Karlsruhe to Basel and crossing the Black Forest, the obscurity of the forest becomes a metaphor for the darkness into which Europe has plunged.
[34] Svevo's pacifist text, devoid of a title in the manuscript, has recently been republished by Silvia Buttò and Riccardo Cepach under the title *Italo Svevo. La Lega delle Nazioni [Sulla teoria della pace]* (Trieste: Servizio Bibliotecario Urbano, 2015).

Svevo's lifelong resolve to remain cautious in public discussions of political matters was not vacillating when he decided to begin writing his pacifist essay. Pacifism, especially in the wake of the First World War and later in the interwar years, was not a controversial topic. On the contrary, a European-wide forum of discussion on how to prevent the human and economic cost of warfare had been in existence before the war, and even grew after the events of 1914. Svevo began to write the essay with the intent of expressing his support for an Italian participation in the League of Nations, arguing for a new and democratic Europe. He envisioned an economic union as a single market with porous borders that would permit the free movement of individuals and goods. Brian Moloney suggests that Italy's decision to join the League might have rendered the completion of the essay unnecessary. He appropriately emphasizes Svevo's moving "humanitarian rejection of war and of the jingoistic patriotism" while recognizing the interpretive difficulties the text presents.[35] Moloney argues that the text is a strange document because it suggests that trade agreements granting free passage across national frontiers of goods, people, and ideas could be an alternative to war. Moloney is correct in suggesting a pacifist tradition that reaches back to the eighteenth century as a source for Svevo's article. It would be a misconception, however, to see Svevo's plan as functional only in a despotic political system. What Moloney could not have predicted in the mid-1970s was that Svevo's model for a European Union correctly anticipated such a scenario. The context that Svevo imagines is a European democratic federation of states, similar to today's European economic and political union.

These Europeanist ideas circulated widely in the Habsburg Empire. We know from Livia Veneziani, Svevo's wife, that the author had read the German Neo-Kantian scholar Walther Schücking and the Austrian Jewish pacifist Alfred Hermann Fried. Svevo never explicitly acknowledges his German and Austrian sources in the draft. On the contrary, Schücking and Fried seem to be purposefully concealed from the public he is addressing. The reason for this concealment lies in the circumstance that the essay was meant to support Italy's membership in the League of Nations, which was established in the aftermath of the Treaty of Versailles. Svevo's intended audience is an Italian readership, profoundly wounded in its national pride. The peace negotiations in Paris ignored the secret Treaty of London that had promised Italy significant territorial gains in the Adriatic Sea. The tensions within the government resulting from what the Italians considered a grave diplomatic betrayal

---

[35] Brian Moloney, *Italo Svevo: A Critical Introduction* (Edinburgh: Edinburgh University Press, 1974), 64–65.

would soon fuel the chauvinism of the rising Fascist party. In this politically sensitive context, Svevo cites the one pacifist forerunner on which the Italians could agree, namely Dante Alighieri. Dante's pacifism supposedly serves as a model for Svevo's project: "A complete and perfect theory flowed from Dante's noble mind, although it is not applicable to our present circumstances."[36] Despite the purported completeness and perfection of Dante's theory, Svevo fails to mention specific examples and does not refer to any text in particular. Dante's European Christian Empire of the *De Monarchia* would be a likely candidate, but this hypothesis does not sound convincing in the pages of a Jew who regretted his conversion to Christianity. Dante's presence in the text serves the purpose of convincing Svevo's audience of the Italian character of his pacifist theory.

Svevo further deploys this rhetorical strategy of dissimulation when he argues that for Italians the adherence to the principles of a peaceful community of nations comes as a natural desire: "our people are essentially peaceful. We do not know intolerance or xenophobia."[37] The projection of this utopian essentialism onto Italians should not be read as a naïve enthusiasm dictated by nationalist pride or by a blind faith in the fundamental moral integrity of his fellow citizens. Svevo personally experienced episodes of discrimination because of his Jewish origin, and later carefully tried to eliminate any reference to it in his official papers. What appears as a bland generalization in reality corresponds to a precise tactical move. Addressing a public that believes in the coherent and immutable character of nations, Svevo rhetorically adopts the audience's point of the view, making the claim that the essential peaceful nature of Italians should predispose them to join the League of Nations. Svevo's communicative strategy imposes the obfuscation of the German Austrian sources because an open discussion of his intellectual background would have been met with hostility by his Italian readership.

Svevo's text is clearly inscribed in a larger German pacifist tradition. The echo of Immanuel Kant's 1795 treatise *Perpetual Peace* (*Zum Ewigen Frieden*) is evident in an initial statement in which Svevo justifies the purpose of the League as "an institution that, even if not aiming at a perpetual peace, nevertheless works to postpone the outbreak of other wars."[38] Svevo sets an ambitious goal, aspiring to resume Kant's work

---

[36] "Una teoria completa e perfetta se anche non più applicabile alle nostre circostanze fluì dalla nobile mente di Dante." Italo Svevo, *Teatro e saggi* (Milan: Mondadori, 2004), 860.
[37] "il nostro popolo è per sua essenza pacifico. Non conosce né intolleranze né xenofobie." Ibid.
[38] "un'Istituzione che se anche non sembra mirare ad una pace eterna pure tenta di ritardare lo scoppio di altre guerre." Ibid.

and adjusting its utopian and impractical goal toward a more pragmatic approach that seeks to defer war. The Triestine author makes the proposal of adding a section within the international organization that should study what he calls "the Theory of Peace." Remarkably, he proposes that this subdivision should be composed of scientists and delegates from universities rather than professional diplomats who, in his view, fail to envision political roadmaps that stretch beyond short-term solutions. Svevo suggests taking the destiny of the continent out of the hands of traditional diplomacy in order to find a scientific solution to the question of warfare. In this openly declared distrust in European diplomatic circles, one can also sense an ill-concealed criticism of the Treaty of Versailles itself. The settlement was presented as an agreement regulating the armistice, but because of the harsh and punitive economic terms it imposed on Germany, the treaty was often called a "Carthaginian peace" in the international press, drawing a parallel with how the Romans treated their defeated enemy. Svevo emphasizes the necessity of a new peace treaty, implying that the current one is not satisfactory for all the parties involved: "The men of Europe fight for their happiness and it is this happiness that needs to be offered in order to take them to peace. The next peace treaty must find everyone's happiness, for the winners, the defeated and for those who remained neutral."[39] Against the imposed imbalance of Versailles, Svevo hopes for a compromise, acceptable for all.

Svevo's criticism of Versailles echoes a general dissatisfaction in the German-speaking world. Critical of the agreement, Alfred Hermann Fried (1864–1921) shared the feeling that the peace treaty was unfairly burdening Germany with unreasonably high war reparations. Svevo was convinced of the soundness of Fried's pacifist philosophy because it was primarily based upon the economic cooperation among European nations. A staunch supporter of the League of Nations himself, Fried had played a crucial role in the foundation of the *Deutsche Friedensgesellschaft*, the German Peace Society, in 1892. In 1899, he actively participated in the seminal Peace Conference held in The Hague, the one so ardently admired by the members of Musil's Parallel Campaign. Fried's pacifist effort earned him the Peace Nobel Prize in 1911.

His commitment to continental peace was encouraged by the prominent pacifist Bertha von Suttner (1843–1914), herself a Nobel Peace Prize winner in 1905, and the first woman to receive the prestigious award in this category. Fried was giving a series of six lectures at the

---

[39] "Gli uomini d'Europa combattono oramai tutti per la loro felicità ed è questa che bisogna loro offrire per addurli alla pace. Il prossimo trattato di pace ha da trovare la felicità di tutti, vincitori e vinti e neutrali." Ibid., 874–875.

Wiener Akademischer Friedensverein, when von Suttner suggested to him the publication of his lectures in book form. His *Handbuch der Friedensbewegung*, published in the same year, is a sort of manifesto of the German Austrian peace movement. Fried's main concern in the book was to distance himself from what he considered the naïve and utopian pacifist dilettantes, who were often harmful to their own cause. According to Fried, pacifist debates were still conducted within a militarist paradigm. He dismissed the utopian projects of those who misunderstood the perpetual peace envisioned by Kant as a prolonged armistice between belligerent forces. Instead, a stronger foundation for a structural peace in Europe was grounded in the economic interdependency of European states, so that warfare would become an endeavor that infringed upon the economic and hence strategic interests of governments. He emphasized that the project of a federation of the European world of culture did not overlap with the geographic limits of Europe.[40] He argued that the expression "United States of Europe" originated in a utopian politico-philosophical context that had led to many misconceptions. The political divisions of the First World War had caused the reemergence of European federation projects imagined by Victor Hugo and Garibaldi. Fried argued, however, contrary to a widespread belief in pacifist circles, that international arbitration courts could not represent a sustainable political solution because their legitimacy could be easily undermined within a legal framework of autarchic nation-states. The universal panacea of an international police would cause further disputes among states that were all too unwilling to renounce national sovereignty. The only European unification he could envision was a cooperative of independent states who would limit their own sovereignty only to better represent their shared economic interests. Quite perceptively, he argued that the number of common interests among nation-states was growing, while the ability of single states to effectively operate in a global market was steadily decreasing. A European economic union would grow out of necessity. For Fried, there was no urgent need for a continental political union. General economic partnerships among European states would eventually lead to closer political cooperation, as "the customs union of Western or Central European States" of the past had shown.[41] In *Europäische Wiederherstellung*, published in the English translation as *The Restoration of Europe*, Fried calls this economic and political organism "an organized, a cooperative, a

---

[40] "Föderation der europäischen Kulturwelt." Alfred Fried, *Handbuch der Friedensbewegung* (Vienna: Verlag der Österreichischen Friedensgesellschaft, 1905), 5.
[41] "Zollverband der west- oder mitteleuropäischen Staaten." Fried, *Friedensbewegung*, 88.

self-conscious new Europe."[42] This restoration of Europe had to be an enterprise of interlocking economic interests well before it could aspire to become a viable political project.

In the wake of these ideas, Svevo becomes the advocate for a new and united Europe, in which porous borders permit the free movement of individuals and goods. According to Svevo, "only economic liberalism can guarantee peace."[43] Frontiers within Europe should gradually be abolished; not initially, though, as their function should be to indicate the borders of administrative and legal units that do not obstruct the free flow of persons and goods. Svevo envisions, following the Swiss or American example, the "possibility of minimizing borders so that they do not provoke war and allow for economic competition."[44] Identifying in multilingual Switzerland and American federalism the constitutional models for a future United States of Europe was a common argument of Europeanist thinkers. Border policing in Europe should thus be weakened. In the second part of the manuscript, presumably written later, the author assumes a more radical position: "Sooner or later, the border becomes an obstacle to life," arguing for the complete dissolution of borders.[45] Anticipating a foreseeable opposition to such novelty in a nationalist and protectionist Europe, Svevo wishes that at least an agreement on a "basic program" could be found, one that ensures the fundamental right to appeal against "harmful custom duties" and a generally protected right to travel and cross borders freely.[46] Svevo claims: "This basic program should be applied to the entire world or otherwise, if the application is impractical, in a vast united territory, a Continent."[47] Without specifically mentioning it, Svevo intends the European continent.

This continental dimension of Svevo's pacifism is also found in the writings of the politician and liberal thinker Walther Schücking (1875–1935). Svevo was familiar with the writings of Schücking, who

---

[42] Alfred Fried, *The Restoration of Europe* (New York: Macmillan, 1917), 145.
[43] "il liberismo solo può assicurare la pace." Svevo, *Saggi*, 866.
[44] "possibilità di attenuare i confini perché non provochino la guerra e ammettano la gara." Ibid., 859. He continues, "Per ammettere i popoli alla libera gara che già esiste fra gl'individui queste frontiere dovrebbero ridursi in modo da non essere più neppure tali, semplici segni che avvertono che certe leggi vi regnano e chi le varca deve ottemperarvi, quali quelle p.e. fra' diversi Cantoni della Svizzera o Stati dell'America" Svevo." Ibid., 865.
[45] "E prima o poi la frontiera diventa un impedimento alla vita." Ibid., 876.
[46] "programma minimo" and "dazio lesivo." Ibid., 867.
[47] "Questo programma minimo dovrebb'essere attuato in tutto il mondo e, se non si può fare altrimenti, in un vasto territorio compatto, un Continente." Ibid.

had been one of the German delegates to the Paris Peace Conference, and a negotiator of the Treaty of Versailles. Schücking continued to pursue a successful judicial career, becoming the first German judge at the International Court of Justice in The Hague. An expert in international law, Schücking had published in 1908 *Das Nationalitätenproblem. Eine politische Studie über die Polenfrage und die Zukunft Österreich-Ungarns*, a study of the nationality problem in the Austro-Hungarian Empire. In the study, Schücking reached the conclusion that the oppressive policies in the Habsburg state had only produced social unrest and political turmoil. Whether the elite agreed to it or not, the state was composed of national minorities, and negating their existence was not a productive way of conducting policy. He therefore suggested a larger participation of these national minorities in the political life of the empire. Constitutional amendments were necessary and certainly possible to bring about a general reconciliation and to guarantee justice for all members of the state, regardless of national affiliation.

Schücking had made his own a tradition of constitutional reformists who had been operating in the empire for some time. In the text, he quotes the unpublished essay of the poet Ferdinand Nürnberger who in 1867, the year of the *Ausgleich*, suggested a sociopolitical program based upon the free development of all ethno-national groups in the empire. His proposal was the somewhat hybrid constitutional system of a "federative republic under monarchic rule."[48] While the emperor still dictated a common foreign policy, domestic issues were organized by the self-government of minorities. Schücking's main interlocutor, however, was the already mentioned Aurel Popovici, who two years before had published the proposal for a constitutional reform envisioning a United States of Greater Austria. Both Schücking and Popovici feared that if the constitutional demands of minorities in the empire were not met with reforms, the growing ethnic tensions would eventually lead to an irreparable fragmentation. The two jurists agreed that cohesive and organized ethnolinguistic groups should be recognized as nations, and that their demands for larger cultural autonomy were amply justified.

Popovici's 1906 proposal was an adaptation of the federalist notion of a "United States of Europe" to the Habsburg context, seeking a compromise between the Europeanist movement, the ever-growing nationalist demands of ethnic groups, and the preservation of the imperial

---

[48] "Föderativrepublik mit monarchischer Spitze." Walther Schücking, *Das Nationalitätenproblem. Eine politische Studie über die Polenfrage und die Zukunft Österreich-Ungarns* (Dresden: Von Jahn und Jaentsch, 1908), 65.

state. His suggestion entailed a restructuring of the empire in a federation of fifteen autonomous and nationality-based provinces, and constitutional protections for ethnic and linguistic enclaves within these regions. Popovici compared these ethnically uniform, geographic unities to homogenous nation-states in Europe. Under the proposed reorganization, the emperor would have maintained control of the military, foreign affairs and international diplomacy, commercial and maritime treaties, taxation laws, transportation, and coinage. The fifteen national states would have been granted ample autonomy in domestic affairs and would have been allowed to redact their own constitutions regulating cultural affairs, education, and language policies. Consequently, each nation would have been granted the power to choose its own state language. This measure was meant to correct the insufficient measures outlined in Article XIX of the 1867 Constitution, and would have allowed an even higher degree of language autonomy and preservation. The language of imperial bureaucracy and the intermediary language between national states (*Vermittlungssprache*) would have remained German. The territory of Trieste, including its rural hinterland and the Italian-speaking areas of Gorizia and Istria, would have become one of the fifteen "national-political individualities." Popovici, along with other reformist jurists, became close councilors of the heir to the imperial throne Archduke Franz Ferdinand, who looked upon such reforms with favor.

Despite its equitable character, the proposed reform was considered by many conservatives too radical of a transformation. A first fundamental change within Habsburg state philosophy was the legal recognition of the nationality principle in the empire. Popovoci's proposed reform also entailed a radical redrawing of the traditional borders in the empire, borders that had been in existence for centuries. In 1713, Emperor Karl VI established in the Pragmatic Sanction, an edict regulating female hereditary rights, the principle of indivisibility and inseparability of the Crown Lands in the empire. Staunch opposition to this reformist design came from the Hungarians, who would have lost significant parts of the territory assigned to them with the *Ausgleich*. In the end, it was the premature death of the crown prince that prevented any kind of progress, let alone realization, of this constitutional reform. The assassination of Archduke Franz Ferdinand and the subsequent outbreak of the First World War soon shattered all reformist illusions in the empire.

Despite the war, and perhaps also because of it, the reformist impulse was not lost. Svevo had been sympathetic to these reform proposals and intended in his essay to resume this Habsburg tradition, adapting it to the new geopolitical circumstances in Europe. The Austro-Hungarian Empire had ceased to exist as a political body, and Trieste

The Aesthetics of Austro-Italian Liminality, 1890–1923   163

had now become part of the Italian Kingdom. It would have been a grave *faux pas* to identify in the plans for a Habsburg reorganization a model for a European organization that Italy would join. Once again, Svevo strategically camouflages the theoretical-political sources of his plan. In order to circumvent any political controversy associated with recent events, Svevo identifies a historic precedent for this new Europe in a distant past.

After having proposed a rudimentary prototype for a European single market and established a federalist political paradigm as the most suitable solution for a continental peace, the author moves on to pinpoint in King Alfred the Great a forerunner of a united Europe. The medieval monarch was credited with the unification of a divided England in the ninth century and the restoration of a trade network after the Viking invasions. According to Svevo, the England of King Alfred, thanks to the "blending of various nationalities," was "a small Europe."[49] The Europe that Svevo imagines is an amalgamation of nations and, most importantly, a Europe that promotes its regional identities. Again, the author employs a linguistic example to make a political point. Svevo makes a veiled reference to the status of dialectophone Trieste in Italy when he mentions the successive colonial history of England in Wales. Commenting on the Anglo-Saxon rule of Wales, Svevo notes that the Welsh still give the nation poets and statesmen, even though "in Cornwall the last person that stuttered the dialect of that region died twenty years ago."[50] Svevo associates the nation-state with a cultural colonialism that threatens regional and vernacular cultures. Since its proclamation of independence, the Italian Kingdom adopted language policies that were aimed at imposing a linguistic uniformity based on literary Tuscan in a country that spoke a myriad of dialects. He seems concerned that Trieste's regional dialect might be threatened by this linguistic nationalism, and that Triestino might be completely replaced by Italian, in the way in which English eradicated Welsh and other Gaelic languages, along with the Irish of his friend James Joyce, from the British Isles. The language policies of the Habsburgs, paradoxically, never constituted a menace for the Triestine dialect. Instead of erasing dialectal variety, Svevo reminds his readership, the empire fostered its hybrid composition. As mentioned earlier, the Habsburg expansion of Trieste brought Venetian

---

[49] "fusione delle varie nazionalità" and "piccola Europa." Svevo, *Saggi*, 869.
[50] "nel Cornwall l'ultima persona che balbetta il dialetto di quella provincia morì vent'anni or sono." Ibid.

into the Ladin-speaking city. Svevo asserts that in his day Trieste "speaks Venetian with a rhythm that is suggestive of the ancient vernacular."[51] This linguistic stratigraphy and the local rivalries will not result in interregional conflicts between Friulian-speakers and Venetians now that these regions have been united under Italian hegemony. Selecting once again the Helvetic confederation as a prototype of ethnic cohabitation, Svevo sees an analogy with Switzerland, where Swiss French and Swiss Germans do not quarrel, despite the sworn enmity of neighboring France and Germany. To ward off any suspicion of pro-Austrian sentiments, the author immediately underscores that the healthy competition between different ethnic and linguistic groups is not comparable to the situation of the late Austrian Empire.[52] Yet, he cautiously admits a benefit to the competition among national groups in the defunct Dual Monarchy, where a widespread literacy contributed to heighten the awareness of one's own cultural distinctiveness. Knowing how to read and write in one's own language also had its benefits in terms of employment. Once an ethnic group within the Austrian Empire pushed for the recognition of their language as an officially used idiom, the speakers of that language gained access to service in the administration of the Empire. The paradox for Svevo is that a functioning school system fostered the growth of an exclusionary national consciousness.

Svevo finally reiterates his radical measure, proposing the dissolution of economic boundaries and challenging the nationalist obsession with the border as a protective perimeter of vital space: "Why don't we open the borders of two neighboring countries in order to test the freedom of competition? To avoid rivalries from the very beginning we should grant access to the same liberties to all Nations."[53] Svevo suggests that this opening of state borders should be experimented with

---

[51] "parla il veneto con un ritmo che tuttavia ricorda l'antica parlata." Ibid., 870.
[52] "La gara fra i popoli dell'Austria non appartiene qui perché veramente e consapevolmente preludiava alla guerra. Però si può notare che accanto agli svantaggi (l'odio cieco fra di loro) quella gara apportò qualche beneficio alla cultura delle singole Nazionalità. Non un'alta coltura (esclusa dalla mancanza di libera coscienza nazionale e da un distacco forzato dalla propria più grande nazione che sola questa cultura poteva elaborare) ma una cultura diffussissima. Basti ricorda che fra le reclute della Venezia Giulia in questi anni l'analfabeta mancò del tutto." Ibid.
[53] "Perché non si aprono i confini fra due paesi limitrofi per provare la libertà della gara? Per evitare delle gelosie da bel principio dovrebb'essere aperto l'accesso alla stessa libertà a tutte le Nazioni." Ibid.

in the most hotly contested area in Europe, on the Franco–German border, confident that equal access to resources will bring the territorial disputes between France and Germany to an end. The collaboration of French and Germans should also extend to private matters: another way to prevent belligerent hostilities in Europe is fostering the hybridization of its populations. In the present relationship between French and Germans, Svevo acknowledges the potential for a Nietzschean European hybrid race: "I am not afraid of the fact that the two races intermingle more than they already have."[54] In a text grounded in a German intellectual tradition, it is not surprising that Svevo concludes by invoking Nietzsche's good European. The lesson learned from Austrian pacifists is that economic competition guaranteed by liberalism is the only way to prevent war. Svevo makes it clear that he is no war enthusiast. Warfare remains a repugnant affair, an abomination that cannot be made more tolerable by forms of patriotism or heroism.

Originally intended to be a large essayistic endeavor, the unpublished paper survives in fragmentary form. The manuscript is one of the rare instances in which we can catch, glimpsing through a textual web of shrewd dissimulations and layers of self-imposed censorship, a partial insight into Svevo's Austro-Italian politics and his Europeanist pacifism. One question, however, continues to trouble Svevo scholarship. The author drafts a political philosophy in this Europeanist essay only to abandon the plan and to eventually destroy significant parts of it. The reason for the destruction of this paper remains shrouded in mystery. It is possible that Svevo was not satisfied with his analysis, or that he decided, as Moloney suggests, that Italy's joining of the League of Nations rendered his topic obsolete. One cannot help suspecting that Svevo became increasingly afraid to publish an article that contained ideas that could be judged too radical in Fascist Italy. A change of strategy was in order. Perhaps a different path would be more appropriate and effective. Maybe one could write a novel in which the protagonist was a mischievous charlatan who could underhandedly assert what the author had to suppress in postwar Trieste, namely his Jewishness, his pacifism, and his hybrid identity as an Austro-Italian author. Maybe a Habsburg Phoenician could do the trick. Svevo abandoned the essay so that he could start writing *Zeno's Conscience*.

---

[54] "Non ho paura che le due razze si mescolino più di quanto non lo sieno già." Ibid., 871.

One Last Austrian Cigarette: Zeno, the Habsburg Phoenician, 1923

As readers of Svevo's novel know, the main character, Zeno Cosini, a heavy smoker and an incorrigible hypochondriac, embarks upon a project of psychoanalytic self-scrutiny, written in the form of a diary.[55] The genre conventions of the diary would impose a personal and intimate tone for the narrator's confessions, but Zeno is keenly aware of the fact that his therapeutic autobiography is also a public document open to circulation in medical circles and a manuscript upon which the doctor will build his diagnosis. Zeno is indeed not mistaken about the public dimension of his memoir. Since Zeno is doubtful of the doctor's effectiveness and threatens to quit the sessions, the fictional psychoanalyst—identified by the vaguely Freudian abbreviation of Dr. S.—resorts to rather unorthodox methods and takes revenge on his patient by publishing his patient's diary. Zeno preemptively anticipates his doctor's tactics and prepares the text with a larger audience in mind. With calculated prudence, Zeno constantly reassures his readership of his Italian loyalty, attempting to protect himself from any suspicion that he might be insufficiently Italian. His autobiography is apotropaic rather than simply therapeutic inasmuch as it is a shrewd stratagem to ward off any such suspicion. I argue, however, that at the heart of his autobiography lies a stratagem of resistance aimed instead at destabilizing Italian cultural hegemony and undermining the very cultural politics of Triestine Irredentism to which Zeno allegedly subscribes. Zeno is gifted with what the ancient Greeks called *mêtis*, a polymorphous and adaptive intelligence, capable of managing multiple expectations by addressing diverse audiences simultaneously. He writes his diary to Dr. S, but prepares his autobiography also for an audience of Triestine Irredentists. Manipulative and subversive, he deploys a cunning strategy of resistance to the dominant discourse of national belonging, challenging the political power structures in place and the cultural authority of Italy's literary tradition.

The slowly unfolding self-awareness of the protagonist suggests that Zeno is often a stranger to himself and a stranger to the community

---

[55] The novel is often read as a prime example of Italian modernism, a movement that developed, according to a critical commonplace, at the margins of the Italian peninsula, namely with Italo Svevo in Trieste and with Luigi Pirandello in Sicily. For an extended discussion of Italian modernism, see Luca Somigli and Mario Moroni, ed. *Italian Modernism: Italian Culture between Decadentism and Avant-Garde* (Toronto: University of Toronto Press, 2004); Romano Luperini and Massimiliano Tortora, ed. *Sul modernismo italiano* (Naples: Liguori, 2012); and Mimmo Cangiano, *La nascita del modernismo italiano. Filosofie della crisi, storia e letteratura, 1903–1922* (Macerata: Quodlibet, 2019).

to which he belongs. Zeno's name suggests foreignness, as it derives from the ancient Greek *xénos,* meaning "stranger." Let me suggest that despite the Greek background of his *mêtis,* the ancient genealogy of the protagonist's name is not simply a reference to the pre-Socratic Greek philosopher Zeno of Elea, as commonly assumed, but more importantly also and especially to the Phoenician Zeno of Citium, founder of the Stoic school and one of the main theoreticians of ancient cosmopolitanism.[56] In the novel, Zeno's mendacious autobiography, then, should be read as what the ancient Greeks called "a Phoenician tale," an artfully crafted and persuasive lie, characterized by a deceptive verisimilitude. Rather than a hapless fellow at the mercy of a language he cannot control, Zeno is a shrewd and mischievous master of playful dissimulation, skillful in his conscious and well-crafted deception and his highly choreographed narration, where plausibility and verisimilitude represent the main rhetorical goals. For Zeno, a well-crafted lie is much more persuasive and seductive than the banality of truth.

Zeno's Phoenician origin is embedded in the folds of the character's crypto-Jewishness. Although Zeno never explicitly mentions his Semitic background, he embodies a particular kind of Jewishness, one that Joyce identified in Svevo himself, namely a Jewishness that is "secular, introspective, humane, and idiosyncratically clever."[57] Since the Phoenicians were construed as the Semites behind the Jews, Zeno embodies a Jewishness that is twice removed. At the same time, Zeno allows Svevo to foreground a Jewishness that is not completely obscured but rather is hiding in plain sight. This Jewishness is only part of Zeno's larger and more inclusive Semitic character that is not exclusively Jewish but also and especially Phoenician. It is possible, indeed likely, that Svevo's Phoenician Zeno was inspired by Freud's identification with Hannibal. Svevo's debt to Freudian psychoanalysis is well known. He was introduced to Freud's writings around 1908 by Edoardo Weiss, who was destined to become a prominent psychoanalyst in Italy.

---

[56] Most commentators focus on the philosopher of Elea and ignore the Phoenician context of the name. Gatt-Rutter acknowledges that the name Zeno implies a double reference to both to the Greek and Phoenician Zeno, but leaves the Phoenician Zeno as a passing remark without further investigating the significance of this ambiguity. Gatt-Rutter, *Double,* 315.

[57] Neil Davison was the first to suggest that Zeno may be Jewish in *James Joyce, Ulysses, and the Construction of Jewish Identity: Culture, Biography, and "the Jew" in Modernist Europe* (Cambridge: Cambridge University Press, 1996), 171. Deborah Amberson also makes a convincing case for Zeno's Jewishness by discussing the character's failed attempt to become a violinist in the context of Wagner's accusations of Jewish cacophony. "Zeno's Dissonant Violin: Italo Svevo, Judaism, and Western Art Music," *Italian Studies* 71, no. 1 (2016): 98–114. doi:10.1080/007 51634.2015.1132608.

168 Modernism in Trieste

Svevo read Freud habitually in German and knew Freud's *Interpretation of Dreams* very well. In "Soggiorno londinese," Svevo recalls with his usual self-mockery that with the writing of *Zeno's Conscience* he had introduced Freudian psychoanalysis into Italian aesthetics, indulging in the fantasy that Freud himself would one day telegraph him a note of gratitude for such service.[58] Svevo even undertook a translation of one of Freud's texts on dreams into Italian with the help of his nephew Aurelio Finzi.[59] Like Freud's Hannibal, Svevo's Zeno is the assertion of an alternative Judaism. But while Freud's Punic general embodies the physical prowess of an assertive Jewishness, the heroism of Svevo's character lies in his rhetorical dexterity. Svevo's Zeno is a modern Phoenician by virtue of his skillful fabrications, his cosmopolitanism, and Stoic acceptance of fate. At the end of the novel, Zeno comes to accept his lot and his diseases like a Stoic. His disposition is mirrored by biographical accounts of Svevo. Eugenio Montale described Svevo with a characteristic "intimate Stoicism," an opinion echoed by Bruno Maier. Svevo's daughter Letizia reports that when Svevo realized on his deathbed that his life was coming to an end, he greeted his death with Stoic acceptance, asking for the very last cigarette. He accepted death like "an ancient Stoic philosopher."[60] In the scholarship, it is widely accepted that Svevo creates with Zeno his own fictional alter ego, in the same way that Svevo's literary persona was the double of the businessman Ettore Schmitz.[61] I am not suggesting a straightforward and unproblematic autobiographical reading of Zeno. Rather, Zeno is a fictional projection of an authorial double that carefully chooses his strategies of self-representation.

In order to fully appreciate the cultural politics of Svevo's choice to name his protagonist after the Phoenician founder of Stoicism, it is useful to remember that the philosophical speculations of Zeno of Citium were considered alien to the spirit of the Greeks. He was the author of *The Republic*, a work now lost that was written in opposition to Plato's *Republic*. German classicists in the 1930s and 1940s stressed

---

[58] Svevo, *Saggi*, 686.
[59] The *Profilo autobiografico* is vague about which text is translated, simply stating that the two men started on an Italian version of Freud's work on dreams. Phillip Furbank in *Italo Svevo: The Man and the Writer* (Berkeley: University of California Press, 1966) argues that the work in question is *On Dreams* while Lebowitz in *Svevo* takes for granted that it is *The Interpretation of Dreams*.
[60] Montale, *Carteggio Svevo-Montale. Con gli scritti di Montale su Svevo*. (Milan: Mondadori, 1976), 78. Maier, *Italo Svevo e la critica straniera* (Trieste: La Editoriale Libraria, 1956), 62. Letizia Svevo Fonda Savio, *Italo Svevo* (Pordenone: Edizioni Studio Tesi, 1981), 133.
[61] See Giovanni Palmieri, *Schmitz, Svevo, Zeno: storia di due biblioteche* (Milan: Bompiani, 1994).

The Aesthetics of Austro-Italian Liminality, 1890–1923   169

the fundamentally "un-Hellenic" character of the Stoic school. Max Pohlenz, an authority on Stoicism, wrote of Zeno as a *Vollblutphöniker*, a "full-blooded Phoenician."[62] In the early decades of the twentieth century, Phoenician Stoicism was largely associated with cosmopolitan citizenship, a racially destructive force that compromised ethnic purity. A fundamental tenet of Stoic cosmopolitanism was that all humans were equal in a universal fellowship. Membership of this cosmopolitan community was not determined by any particular blood lineage or affiliation with an ethnic or racial group, but by the role individuals played within a meritocratic society, a worldview that disqualified Stoicism in the eyes of nationalist racism. Svevo's Habsburg Phoenician has to be read in the context of these widespread anti-Phoenician sentiments.

In his own search of lost time, Zeno tries to recover long-forgotten memories, recalling the very inception of his nicotine dependence. While much has been written about Zeno's smoking habit, little attention has been dedicated to the origin of these cigarettes. Zeno realizes that "The cigarettes I first smoked are no longer on the market. Around 1870 in Austria there was a brand that came in cardboard boxes stamped with the two-headed eagle."[63] Zeno's memories crystallize around the heraldic image of the double-headed Habsburg bird of prey. He is smoking the cigarettes produced by the Imperial Austrian Tobacco Monopoly, the *Kaiserlich-Königliche Tabakregie*, founded in 1784 by Emperor Joseph I. Smoking was a thoroughly politicized affair in the last decades of the Austro-Hungarian Empire.[64] By emphasizing the Austrian origin of these cigarettes, Svevo entangles his character in the cultural and economic politics of the Habsburgs. The monopoly established that only the Austrian state was entitled to raise, manufacture, and sell tobacco. Joseph I is the same monarch who promulgated the Edict of Tolerance, promoting the integration of ethnic minorities in the empire, allowing the demographic and economic expansion of Trieste and ultimately the prosperity of Habsburg Jews like Svevo himself. In 1870, the Austrian Tobacco Monopoly had expanded its initial scant

---

[62]   Max Pohlenz, "Die Stoa: Geschichte einer geistigen Bewegung," in *Das Neue Bild der Antike. Band 1 Hellas*, ed. Helmut Berve (Leipzig: Koehler und Amelang, 1942), 356.
[63]   Italo Svevo, *Zeno's Conscience*, 7. In the original Italian the text goes: "Oggi scopro subito qualche cosa che più non ricordavo. Le prime sigarette ch'io fumai non esistono più in commercio. Intorno al '70 se ne avevano in Austria di quelle che venivano vendute in scatoline di cartone munite del marchio dell'aquila bicipite." *Zeno*, 628.
[64]   Richard Klein argues that Zeno's cigarette consumption is a political gesture since smoking represents the most direct intervention of the state into the intimate pleasure of the individual. Richard Klein, *Cigarettes Are Sublime* (Durham, NC: Duke University Press, 1993), 84–85.

offerings. In addition to the *Ordinäre Doppel-Zigarette*, a long cigarette that needed to be broken in two before smoking, initially sold only in Trieste under the name *Moro*, the state monopoly now sold a variety of cigarettes that included *Damen, Baffra, Samsun, Trebinje, Gemischte, Salon, Stambul, Sultan*, and *Jenidge*. The names in this cigarette assortment suggest a marketing strategy that presents smoking as an exotic, Orientalist pleasure. Georg Thiel has shown that Zeno smokes the *Jenidge* variety, named after the area in Macedonia where the tobacco was grown.[65] The text also seems to exploit the association between state-produced cigarettes and constructions of Habsburg masculinity. In Austrian First World War propaganda, it was popular belief that an army that smoked well, also fought well. Given the scarcity of supply, the Austrian populace donated cigarettes and other tobacco products to the soldiers in the trenches. But Zeno is not telling the whole story. Conspicuously absent from Zeno's account of his smoking habit are the matches with which he lit the cigarettes, a detail that is far from constituting a trivial matter. At the beginning of the century, matchbox labels became the passionately contested arena of increasingly polarizing nationalist attitudes in Trieste. The German cultural society *Verein Südmark* started selling matches, called *Südmark-Zünder*, that were literally and metaphorically incendiary with their explicit pan-Germanist propaganda. The commerce of these matches was an important source of income for the association. Lighting your cigarettes meant not only showing ideological espousal for the cause but also supporting the organization financially. The *Lega Nazionale* in Trieste responded with matchboxes that featured patriotic messages. In particular, there was one matchbox label that featured a quote from *Risorgimento* hero Vincenzo Gioberti whose words gravely admonished patriots that "the death of languages is the death of nations."[66] Reading Zeno's proclamation about the expressive possibilities of Italian against Gioberti's linguistic nationalism shows how Svevo's novel could be perceived as extremely unpatriotic.

The coat of arms of the Austrian Empire on Zeno's beloved pack of cigarettes initiates the flow of memories and thus the narration of

---

[65] Georg Thiel, "Letzte Fragen-Ultime domande" in *Lastricato di buoni propositi. Il centocinquantenario della nascita di Italo Svevo 1861–2011*, ed. Riccardo Cepach (Trieste: Comunicarte Edizioni, 2012), 72–75.

[66] The green and white labels read "la morte delle lingue è la morte delle nazioni." According to Triestine author and journalist Giulio Caprin (1880–1958), Gioberti's admonishment on these matchboxes was successful in preserving the purity of Italian, despite the looming threats of contamination and corruption represented by non-native speakers, who spoke a Germanized Habsburg Italian and worked for the Austrian bureaucracy. *Paesaggi e spiriti di confine* (Milan: Treves, 1915), 67–70.

the protagonist's clandestine smoking itself. The doctor forbids him to smoke, and the protagonist remembers how as a young man he already smoked, against the wishes of his father. Zeno pledges not to smoke ever again, except for one, intensely enjoyed and endlessly deferred, last cigarette. In Svevo's comic parody of psychoanalytic treatment, the doctor attempts to break Zeno's smoking habit with rather unconventional methods. One of these techniques consists in putting Zeno in a prison-like clinic. His prison warden Giovanna is persuaded to provide him with alcoholic beverages and cigarettes but delivers, much to Zeno's dismay, instead of his beloved Austrian cigarettes cheap Hungarian smokes, which he finds nauseating. One cannot help but notice the political overtones of Zeno's preference of Austrian over cheap Hungarian cigarettes in a novel set in the Austro-Hungarian Empire.

Giving up smoking is what triggers Zeno's autobiographic and allegedly therapeutic writing, through which he records a number of last cigarettes. Zeno's secret smoking habit is often associated with the clandestine writing that accompanied Svevo's life. The author's early literary aspirations were kept a secret from his strict and business-oriented father Franz.[67] Likewise, the Veneziani family, especially his mother-in-law Olga, disapproved of Svevo's artistic ambitions because she perceived literature as a frivolous distraction from the industriousness that a successful family-run company required. After the bitter failure of *As a Man Grows Older (Senilità)* and his commitment to dedicate his energies fully to business activities, Svevo solemnly vowed to definitively renounce writing, which the Triestine author in a diary entry of 1902 defined "that ridiculous and noxious thing they call literature."[68] Despite the temporary resolve to stop engaging in unhealthy writing activities, Svevo continues to be drawn to writing in secret. For this reason, Zeno's smoking is usually read as a metaphor for writing itself, an embedded commentary on Svevo's literary activity. His cigarette becomes, in the words of Fabio Vittorini, a "degeneration of the pen."[69] In the way Zeno is forever smoking one "last" Austrian cigarette, he is forever writing a "last" page of Austrian literature. If we accept this scriptural transfiguration of the protagonist's Austrian cigarette, Zeno's combined smoking and writing becomes the signature of Svevo's own inscription in a literary tradition that now defiantly

---

[67] Gatt-Rutter, *Double*, 26.
[68] "Io, a quest'ora e definitivamente ho eliminato dalla mia vita quella ridicola e dannosa cosa che si chiama letteratura." Svevo, *Opera Omnia* (Milan: Dall'Oglio, 1968), 818.
[69] Fabio Vittorini, *Svevo: Guida alla Coscienza di Zeno* (Rome: Carocci, 2003), 91.

reaches beyond the fall of the empire. Zeno's elusive identity, revealing a subject shrouded in the misty smoke of an intangible and impalpable self, suggests Svevo's own distinctiveness as an Italian novelist with a Habsburg pen. And while I caution against the slippery slope of reading Zeno's account as a fictional projection of Svevo's own autobiography, I would like to suggest that among Zeno's multiple confessions in his memoir, the admission to his clandestine smoking of Austrian cigarettes looms as Svevo's own meta-narrative confession of being, quite clandestinely now, a Habsburg Italian novelist, a confession that signals the liminality of Svevo's Austro-Italian novel within the literary landscape of European modernism. Once again, one detects a recurring strategy in Svevo's writing, where self-censorship combines with censurable ideas that boldly hide in plain sight. Svevo's Austrian character is not a particularly secretive or coded message. With the heraldic image of the Austrian double-headed eagle, the author offers his readership an unmistakable key of interpretation. This Austro-Italian character of the novel, then, plays an important role in understanding Svevo's language question. Svevo's Italian is not the language of the Kingdom of Italy or the language of Italian literary tradition, but the author's own Italian written with an Austrian accent. This Habsburg-inflected Italian is Svevo's language of choice, as opposed to the dialect, since for him the Triestine vernacular remained the language of international commerce in Trieste, and not the language of literature.

Literature and the Language of Lies

An underlying tension between standard Italian and the Triestine dialect is a veritable leitmotif in Svevo's three novels, which one could read as one longer book about Trieste that narrates the vicissitudes of Alfonso, Emilio, and Zeno who are unlikely to ever meet.[70] The narrator in *A Life* makes a mordant mockery of a pedantic Italian teacher. Alfonso Nitti, the protagonist, attempts to teach Italian to Lucia Lanucci, the daughter of the family with whom he lives, by asking her to read the entries of a dictionary so that she can finally "conquer" the Italian language. Nitti falls in love with his boss's daughter, Annetta Maller, who is receiving private lessons from a certain Mr. Spalati, an elderly professor of Italian language and literature. Alfonso describes him as a self-professed intellectual who ostensibly subscribes to the claims of linguistic authenticity promoted by *verismo*, the Italian literary realist tradition of another peripheral Italian, namely the Sicilian

---

[70] In a letter to Enrico Rocca, from April 1924 (the exact date is uncertain), Svevo says: "Forse si accorgerà ch'io non ho scritto che un romanzo solo in tutta la mia vita." Svevo, *Epistolario*, 846.

novelist Giovanni Verga. Professor Spalati's reading of Italian authors, however, transpires to be a nitpicking investigation of word choices not legitimized by Petrarch's vocabulary. The obvious irony here is that if the professor were truly a follower of Italian *verismo* he would certainly not castigate literary terms outside the Petrarchan tradition, but value a literary language that heavily borrows from quotidian linguistic expressions and from the dialect. He evidently subscribes to the literary trends of his time only formally but cannot resist the urge to emphasize the need for a unified Tuscan-based Italian legitimated by tradition. Embedded in the narrator's attempt to expose Spalati's contradictions looms a larger commentary on the literary history of the Italian language. In his *Prose della Volgar Lingua* (1525) the Renaissance scholar and philologist Pietro Bembo proposed a codification of the Italian literary standard by maintaining that the linguistic model for prose and poetry should be the fourteenth-century Tuscan authors Giovanni Boccaccio and Francesco Petrarca respectively. Bembo's insistence on the Tuscan tradition will later also include the language of Dante's *Divine Comedy*. These rigid codifications established what terms were to be considered proper Italian and excluded the unacceptable influence from the various regional dialects. Famous are Alessandro Manzoni's rewritings of his influential novel *The Betrothed*, whose earlier drafts had to be painstakingly Tuscanized for the definitive version of the work. This Tuscan linguistic model inspired the standardization of Italian when the country became an independent and sovereign state in 1861. Spalati's pedantic corrections and his adhesion to a strict Petrarchan vocabulary are the expression of an engrained cultural nationalism in which good and acceptable Italian should be devoid of influences from the dialect.

Svevo's main protagonists—Alfonso, Emilio, and Zeno—living in dialectophone Trieste resent this pressure to conform to a model of linguistic purity, which they perceive as an imposition of cultural hegemony. It is important to note that all of Svevo's characters speak Triestino in the novels. On multiple occasions, the narrators remind their readership that the conversations between characters, even when relayed in Italian direct speech by the narrator, occur in dialect. Toward the end of *A Life*, Alfonso tries to console the wife of an English colleague who is desperately trying to find her husband. Although all direct and indirect speech is rendered in Italian, Alfonso remarks that this English woman speaks the dialect perfectly, surreptitiously suggesting that all exchanges have to be imagined as spoken in dialect, unless otherwise noted.[71] Such is the case in *As a Man Grows Older*, where the protagonist Emilio Brentani

---

[71] Italo Svevo, *Romanzi e continuazioni* (Milan: Mondadori, 2004), 336.

falls in love with Angiolina Zarri. For all his infatuation with Angiolina, Emilio strongly dislikes an affected mannerism in her speech with which she imitates Tuscan diction and expressions. The narrator recalls Angiolina's *toscaneggiare*, her parroting of Tuscan.[72] In her salon meetings with the Triestine upper crust Angiolina boasts social prestige by trying to speak Tuscan-based Italian, but her attempts are, according to Emilio, rather unsuccessful because her accent sounds more like English than Italian. In a delightfully comic and ironic scenario, the artificiality of Angiolina's pretentious speech is closer to the effort required in the speaking of a foreign language, which once again depicts Trieste's difficulties with the "national" language of Italy. Italian is not only the idiom of a flaunted social prestige but also of the language of seduction. Emilio's friend Stefano Balli flirts with Angiolina quite impertinently. Commenting on his impudent expressions, the narrator notes that Balli first employs sweet and aspirated Tuscan expressions that she sees as caresses but later, when he also resorts to expressions in "good, harsh, and vulgar Triestino," Angiolina is far from offended.[73] The narration here stages common sociolinguistic perceptions of those members of the upper class in turn-of-the-century Trieste that were sympathetic to Irredentism. Tuscan is associated with a pleasant inflection, while the local dialect assumes the features of an unrefined drawl.

Zeno's Conscience frames questions of linguistic acceptability in terms of social class division and political allegiances. Zeno himself is often plagued by doubts about whether dialect or standard is more suitable in given social situations. His anxiety over correct language use affects his interpersonal relationships and romantic encounters, and assumes wider social and political implications in his public interactions. An example of Zeno's sociolinguistic concerns is the interaction with his mentor Mr. Malfenti, the successful businessman who will become his father-in-law in the course of the novel. When Zeno decides to ask Malfenti for the hand of his daughter Ada, he wonders in what kind of

---

[72] "Ella toscaneggiava con affettazione e ne risultava un accento piuttosto inglese che toscano. 'Prima o poi' – diceva Emilio, – 'le leverò tale difetto che m'infastidisce.'" Svevo, *Romanzi*, 431. "She used to try and talk the Tuscan dialect, but in such an affected manner that her accent was more English than Tuscan. 'Sooner or later,' said Emilio, 'I must cure her of that habit; it is beginning to irritate me.'" Svevo, *As a Man Grows Older*, 34–35.

[73] "Dapprima s'era accontentato di dirgliele in toscano, aspirando e addolcendo, e a lei erano sembrate carezze, ma anche quando le capitarono addosso in buon triestino, dure e sboccate, ella non se ne adontò." Svevo, *Romanzi*, 469. "At first he used to come with them in Tuscan, in such softly breathed accents that they seemed to her a caress; but even when they came pouring forth in the Triestine dialect, in all their harsh obscenity, she showed no sign of offence." Svevo, *Man Grows Older*, 76.

language he should propose. To Zeno, the language choice seems to be an even greater concern that the marriage proposal itself: "I had only to inform him of my resolve to marry his daughter ... Yet I was troubled by the problem of whether, on such an occasion, I should speak to him in dialect or standard Italian."[74] The reasons for his doubts are connected to the social space in which he plans to propose. Triestino comes naturally to Zeno, but he also associates the dialect with lower education and lower class status. Zeno indicates this belief when he argues, rather unconvincingly, that he has difficulties understanding the slurred speech of Giovanna, his prison warden, who speaks pure Triestino. Given the formality of the present occasion, Zeno ponders whether Italian is more appropriate since the two men meet at the Café Tergesteo, where the younger Zeno tries to elicit from the older Malfenti some business secrets that might later be helpful in his own commercial activities. The Tergesteo was a favorite meeting place for Irredentists, and speaking Italian there assumes a further meaning, as it would have been interpreted as indicative of nationalist political leanings.

Zeno's political allegiances are shrewdly staged: he pretends to subscribe to Italian Irredentism, but this posture is clearly determined to deceive his doctor. The scene in which Zeno is first introduced to Guido Speier, his rival and future brother-in-law, reveals much of the identity politics and its underlying social mechanisms that govern the interactions in the novel. Zeno, who is more at ease with the dialect, is jealous of Guido's mastery of Italian and immediately develops a dislike for him. To offend Guido, Zeno intimates that he may be German.[75] Zeno is fully aware of the anti-Austrian sentiment of the Irredentists and consequently mimics their social strategies. Guido replies to Zeno's offensive remark with suspiciously calculated aplomb. His gracious answer sounds as though it has been rehearsed repeatedly. While

---

[74] Svevo, *Conscience*, 97. "Bastava dirgli la mia determinazione di sposare sua figlia ... Mi preoccupava tuttavia la quistione se in un'occasione simile avrei dovuto parlare in lingua o in dialetto." Svevo, *Romanzi*, 723.
[75] "Si chiamava Guido Speier. Il mio sorriso si fece più spontaneo perché subito mi si presentava l'occasione di dirgli qualche cosa di sgradevole: - Lei è tedesco? Cortesemente egli mi disse che riconosceva che al nome tutti potevano crederlo tale. Invece i documenti della sua famiglia provavano ch'essa era italiana da varii secoli. Egli parlava il toscano con grande naturalezza mentre io e Ada eravamo condannati al nostro dialettaccio." Svevo, *Romanzi*, 735. "His name was Guido Speier. My smile became more spontaneous because I was immediately offered the opportunity of saying something disagreeable to him: 'You are German?' He replied politely, admitting that because of his name, one might believe he was. But family documents proved that they had been Italian for several centuries. He spoke Tuscan fluently, while Ada and I were condemned to our horrid dialect." Svevo, *Conscience*, 109.

admitting that it would be reasonable to assume that he is German, he seeks refuge in an alleged bureaucratic evidence of his century-long Italian character. Documents prove that his family has been Italian for several centuries. Without probably realizing it, Guido's justification is an implicit admission that his family is indeed of German stock. His last name, a toponym that refers to the German city of Speyer, also suggests a Jewish background. To compensate his lack of a pure Italian identity, Guido has learned perfect Tuscan, and now he eagerly shows it off. Later, the reader learns that Guido in fact speaks German very well, just as Zeno speaks it, too. In narrating the episode, Zeno opposes Guido's competence with standard Italian to the "horrid" dialect to which Ada and he are condemned. In denigrating the dialect and wishing for better competence in Italian, Zeno is adopting a dissimulating strategy similar to Guido's. Zeno knows that he is writing his confessions upon his doctor's request and that his private diary is really a public document, subject to the scrutiny of official medical discourse. This explains his circumspect treatment of the nationality question and his careful avoidance of politics in his dairy. Zeno stages himself as a self-loathing Triestine, constantly sick, condemned to speak an ugly drawl, longing to speak better Italian and to implicitly prove his political allegiance to Italy. Despite Zeno's antagonistic feelings toward his brother-in-law, he shares with Guido a well-calculated agenda that is on display in their social interactions. Guido's attempt to hide his German background bears a striking resemblance to Zeno's own strategy of social assimilation.

It is within this context of social and political anxieties that one needs to read the oft-quoted passage in *Zeno's Conscience* in which the protagonist transfers his linguistic angst onto an epistemological level. The passage is often seen as exemplary of Svevo's unreliable narrator, where the arbitrariness of Italian as the language of narration is exposed, and the very moment in which Svevo unveils the unsettling interpretative coordinates that radically undermine the centrality of the very language in which the novel is written. Zeno's startling confession is the following:

> The doctor puts too much faith also in those damned confessions of mine, which he won't return to me so I can revise them. Good heavens! He studied only medicine and therefore doesn't know what it means to write in Italian for those of us who speak the dialect but can't write it. A confession in writing is always a lie. With our every Tuscan word, we lie! If only he knew how, by predilection, we recount all the things for which we have the words at hand, and how we avoid those things that would oblige us to turn to the dictionary! This is exactly how we choose, from

our life, the episodes to underline. Obviously our life would have an entirely different aspect if it were told in our dialect.[76]

In Zeno's fictional autobiography, written in standard Italian, the assertion according to which every Italian word presupposes a mendacious statement radically undermines any presumption of truthfulness in the novel. Near the end, the reader is told that the entire narration is based on a language that cannot possibly express any truth. What is said in Italian is a lie, and the truth can only be spoken, and not be written, in the Triestine dialect. The discrepancy between the expressive capabilities of Zeno's writing and his oral communication in the dialect points to a paradoxical situation, which may suggest that the character embodies a parody of the paradoxes of Zeno of Elea. The linguistic nature of the paradox, however, turns Zeno's autobiography into what the ancient Greeks called a "Phoenician tale," a well-crafted lie. Zeno, then, embodies the prejudice of Greeks and Romans who believed the Phoenicians to be inveterate liars.

The unavoidable lies of Zeno, the Habsburg Phoenician, perform a disruptive deterritorialization of language and channel all of Svevo's subversive force of what Gilles Deleuze and Felix Guattari have called a "minor literature," i.e., a literature written in a major language by a member of an ethnic or linguistic minority who represents some kind of outsider to the majority culture.[77] Deleuze and Guattari's theorization of minor literature occurs in the context of Kafka's linguistic morphologies of resistance and certainly applies to Svevo, too. The Prague of Kafka, Brod, and Hašek and the Trieste of Däubler, Kosovel, and Svevo were both multilingual cities that interrogated the monolingualism of national literary traditions. Writing required a choice, electing one language over the other, which in turn determined different audiences and different subject matters. What can be or should be said varies from one language to another. Like the Prague German of the Czech Jew Kafka, the Trieste Italian of the Austrian Jew Svevo posits the irreducible

---

[76] Svevo, *Conscience*, 404. "Il dottore presta una fede troppo grande anche a quelle mie benedette confessioni che non vuole restituirmi perché le riveda. Dio mio! Egli non studiò che la medicina e perciò ignora che cosa significhi scrivere in italiano per noi che parliamo e non sappiamo scrivere il dialetto. Una confessione in iscritto è sempre menzognera. Con ogni nostra parola toscana noi mentiamo! Se egli sapesse come raccontiamo con predilezione tutte le cose per le quali abbiamo pronta la frase e come evitiamo quelle che ci obbligherebbero di ricorrere al vocabolario! È proprio così che scegliamo dalla nostra vita gli episodi da notarsi. Si capisce che la nostra vita avrebbe tutt'altro aspetto se fosse detta nel nostro dialetto." Svevo, *Romanzi*, 1050.
[77] Gilles Deleuze and Felix Guattari, *Kafka: Toward a Minor Literature* (Minneapolis: University of Minnesota Press, 1986).

conundrum of the inability of writing in the majority language and the concomitant impossibility of not writing in it. Underneath the surface of the majority language dwells a subterranean and undomesticated dialect without a proper grammar, filled with an unstable vocabulary of migrating terms spoken, approximated, and mispronounced with different accents and inflections. This vernacular, inextricably interconnected with a Habsburg multilingualism, raises anxieties over questions of linguistic purity. Svevo can only write a novel via an act of sweeping disturbance that irremediably alters the possibilities of the Italian literary canon.

Deleuze and Guattari's notion of minor literature conveys a particular attitude toward this literary canon that disarticulates the presumed homogeneity of the majority culture. Zeno's attribution of truthfulness to the spoken language at the expense of the written medium is particularly significant for a language such as Italian. For many centuries, Italian existed as a written literary language that lacked an oral dimension.[78] Zeno implicitly casts a retrospective judgment onto the history of an entire literary tradition. He calls attention to a paradoxical history in which the production of literary texts in Italian is an artificial imitation of a linguistic model that is not spoken by the people who write in it, emphasizing in this way the insincere and deceitful nature of his own literary endeavor in Italian. Yet, his autobiography is not much different from authors who did not speak Italian, but nonetheless imitated a literary model that was later adopted as the Italian national language. Zeno perceives the language he chooses as artificial for his autobiographical narration, and for him it becomes the most pertinent means to deceive the credulous doctor, a naïve and incompetent reader who is unable to grasp Zeno's literary artifice and uncritically accepts the fiction upon which he builds his medical diagnosis. Zeno's unreliability introduces an epistemological instability into the narrative apparatus, revealing a profound psycholinguistic dilemma that marks the impossibility of speaking the truth in writing. Since dialect is his sole adequate expressive medium, Zeno can grasp the truth only

---

[78] In 1861, the year in which Svevo was born and Italy became politically unified, only about 2.5 percent of Italians spoke what could be called Italian. In the same year, illiteracy was as high as 78 percent. Italian began to be spoken very late in the Italian peninsula. The initial and slow diffusion of Italian began with a struggling primary education program and with the compulsory military service in the Italian Kingdom. Italian became a widely spoken language as late as the twentieth century with the gradual spread of radio and television in Italian households. See Tullio de Mauro, *Storia linguistica dell'Italia unita* (Bari: Laterza, 1976), 43 and Bruno Migliorini, *Storia della lingua italiana* (Florence: Sansoni, 1989), 603.

through a vernacular epistemology. He cannot be truthful unless a dictionary is at hand, an idea that after the discovery of Svevo's annotated terms in his dictionary suggests the author's own misgivings about the expressive possibilities of Italian. Both Zeno and Svevo can only articulate their story in the same way one writes in a foreign language, the mastery of which is far from being satisfactory. The question nevertheless does not solely lie with their inadequate mastery of Italian but also with the structural inability of the standard language to operate as a unifying social and political medium. Zeno's regionalism calls into question the unity of the Italian linguistic community, and in addition to the communicative failures of Italian on a synchronic level, his statement has far-reaching implications, once again, in the diachronic dimension of the language. Zeno challenges the language of Dante and Manzoni, upon which Italian cultural and political unity was substantially constructed.

Zeno's confession that his autobiography could have been written in German or in Triestino applies to Svevo's project, too. His novels are not written in Italian by virtue of an inescapable national destiny. They could have been written in a different linguistic medium, which would not have been a translation of the Italian version we are reading. A version of *Zeno's Conscience* in the Triestine dialect would have told the protagonist's life from a different perspective. It would have been an autobiography in which other episodes would have determined a different personal profile for Zeno. Consequently, with the choice of different episodes to narrate, a choice determined by different linguistic media, we would have known a different Zeno. This is why Zeno's account does not correspond to an absolute truth, but to a linguistically and culturally determined account of reality. Imagining his diary in a multiplicity of versions, for instance in Italian, dialect, or German, opens up the possibility of parallel universes that exist simultaneously. This implication is certainly the starkest contradiction to what his psychoanalyst says at the beginning of the novel, when he recommends writing the diary so that Zeno can feel "whole" again. Instead, Zeno writes the diary and discovers exactly the opposite. His life is fragmented as a result of the different cultural allegiances that defy any stable commitment. The pathological insecurity and psychosomatic manifestations of a hypochondriac constitute much of a liberating lack of purpose in this man without qualities. The reader is invited to accept, together with Zeno, this alternative and experimental mode of existence in which disease loses its negative connotation.[79]

---

[79] See Elena Coda, 'Between Borders: Reading Illness in Trieste' (PhD Diss., University of California, 1998), 219.

Zeno shares this diglossic dissonance with James Joyce's Stephen Dedalus, who in *A Portrait of the Artist as a Young Man* expresses a conspicuously analogous inner linguistic turmoil. Joyce's Stephen famously laments his own difficult relationship with English when, prompted by a conversation with the dean of his school, he realizes what colonial dynamics underlie the social perception of lexical differences between Hiberno-English and the language spoken by the English conqueror. Stephen is surprised to hear the word "funnel," while the dean had never heard of the corresponding Irish English term "tundish." Initially confounded by the divergent word choice, Stephen is finally struck by a disconcerting linguistic epiphany:

> The language in which we are speaking is his before it is mine. How different are the words *home, Christ, ale, master* on his lips and on mine! I cannot speak or write these words without unrest of spirit. His language, so familiar and so foreign, will always be for me an acquired speech. I have not made or accepted its words. My voice holds them at bay. My soul frets in the shadow of his language.[80]

The adoption of the language of the Anglo-Saxon conqueror causes, according to Stephen, a profound cultural and linguistic aphasia in which English is an incongruous linguistic vehicle that cannot adequately express the specificity of Irish Gaelic genius. As we will see in the next chapter, Joyce develops these ideas in Trieste. In one of his articles on Ireland entitled "La Cometa dell'Home Rule," published in December 1910 in the evening edition of the Triestine daily *Il Piccolo della Sera*, Joyce decries that Ireland "abandoned her own language almost entirely and accepted the language of the conqueror without being able to assimilate the culture or adapt herself to the mentality of which this language is the vehicle."[81] Joyce reformulates this critique in one of Stephens's harsh tirades against his fellow Irish compatriots. There are striking parallels between Stephen and Zeno. Both characters denounce the alien nature of the majority language they employ and denounce the colonial imposition of a hegemonic linguistic standard. Svevo's construction of Zeno clearly owes some debt of recognition to Joyce's Stephen. Even though the whimsical and daydreaming Zeno displays a different temperament from the arrogant and acrimonious

---

[80] James Joyce, *A Portrait of the Artist as a Young Man* (New York: Penguin Books, 2003), 205.
[81] James Joyce, *Occasional, Critical, and Political Writing* (Oxford: Oxford University Press, 2000), 159. Joyce, *Portrait*, 205– 206.

Stephen, their linguistic recalcitrance is governed by the same paradox. Like Stephen, Zeno the stranger is the native speaker of a foreign tongue.

One important question remains: If Zeno, and by extension also Svevo, perceives hegemonic Italian standard as a cultural-colonial imposition, why does he choose to write in Italian? The answer lies in a political strategy that one could describe with Brett Levinson's words when he writes, "the subaltern can only break into the master's house with the master's keys."[82] In other words, in order to effectually subvert the hegemonic discourse, Zeno/Svevo must necessarily employ the instruments offered by the dominant culture. Precisely through his writing in Italian, Svevo dismisses a linguistic and literary model of a national project based on a Tuscan centrality that relegates dialects to an inferior social status. In the novel, Zeno stages with a subtle ventriloquism of Italian cultural patriotism what the social and cultural anthropologist Arjun Appadurai calls a "Trojan nationalism." Appadurai proposes via complex structures of "Trojan nationalisms" a theory of internal subversions within the ethnically and linguistically monolithic nation-state:

> Such nationalisms actually contain transnational, subnational links and, more generally, nonnational identities and aspirations. Because they are so often the product of forced as well as voluntary diasporas, of mobile intellectuals as well as manual workers, of dialogues with hostile as well as hospitable states, very few of the new nationalisms can be separated from the anguish of displacement, the nostalgia of exile, the repatriation of funds, or the brutalities of asylum seeking.[83]

The complex network of emotional attachments to different communities present in Habsburg Trieste is articulated through the three main forces that coexist along with Italian nationalism. First of all, there is a strong local dialectophone culture, which identifies itself with the local community and regional dialect as opposed to the Tuscan-based Italian standard. Second, one can observe the city's transnational identity illustrated by a set of multiple attachments to German, Italian, and Slovenian cultures. Third, Triestine intellectuals around the turn of the century subscribed to a supranational project, a United States of

---

[82] Brett Levinson, *Market and Thought: Meditations on the Political and Biopolitical* (New York: Fordham University Press, 2004), 28.
[83] Arjun Appadurai, "Patriotism and Its Futures." *Public Culture* 5, no. 3 (1993): 417. doi:10.1215/08992363-5-3-411.

Europe. This set of local, transnational, and supranational attachments, while existing alongside Triestine Irredentism, was often employed as a means to undermine or circumvent the logic of the nation-state. These nonnational identities function through circumvention since subnational allegiances are ideally located beneath the nation, while supranational attachments are above it. While regional and supranational attachments operate as vertical vectors, transnationalism, on the other hand, operates horizontally by establishing links between national communities.

Appadurai's Trojan nationalism has crucial implications for Zeno's stratagem. The siege of Troy proved unsuccessful until Odysseus devised the subtle ruse of the horse, presented as a gift to the Trojans. Once within the walls of Troy, the Greek soldiers that had hidden in the hollow structure of the horse exited overnight to take military control of the city. Odysseus's scheme operates on two semiotic levels. First, through mimicry he intends to flatter the Trojans and pretends to pay homage to their local tradition of horse taming. Secondly, what motivates Odysseus' gesture is a logic of substitution, in which the horse functions as a symbolic, fetishistic compensation for the loss of prince Hector who, as Homer's epithet goes, is the quintessential "breaker of horses." Svevo's Zeno reminds us of Homer's Odysseus, since both tell very persuasive "Phoenician tales." Just like for Zeno, the reader of the Homeric text can never be sure whether Odysseus tells the truth.[84] Analogous to its function in classical Greek mythology, the image of the Trojan horse in Appadurai represents an internal threat that is not immediately perceived as such by the host community. Exploiting the isomorphism between regional and national loyalties, Appadurai's notion of Trojan nationalism functions through mimicry, i.e., through an imitation of allegiance to the nation-state, a strategy that Zeno deploys masterfully. Trojan nationalisms are intrinsic to the structure of nations, and their subversive mimicry can be understood as the intersection of two axes of similarity and difference. Their similarity rests upon the fact that regional patriotism and supranational allegiances often pre-exist or develop in national contexts. Their difference, on the other hand, originates in their claims to transculturation, *métissage*, and hybrid cultures. Eroding the nation-state from within, local and transnational loyalties have the potential to subvert monolithic and essentialist conceptions of race and ethnicity, redirect political desire, and deploy a complex

---

[84] Odysseus's master narrative at the court of the Phaeacians is probably the best example of this doubt. In the episode, the goal of the Homeric hero is to convince his hosts to give him a ship that can take him home. In order to win them over, he tells fantastical tales that no one can corroborate as all of his crew members have perished.

network of parallel allegiances, eventually leading to a political configuration in which the nation-state becomes obsolete. Appadurai's tripartite schema of subnational, national, and supranational contexts echoes Benedict Anderson's known collocation of the nation as an "imagined community" between a regional framework and a broader context above the nation. Anderson famously maintains that "national consciousness" comes as the result of a linguistic intervention, specifically of "print-capitalism," which bestowed language with a "new fixity" and thus created "unified fields of exchange and communications below Latin and above the spoken vernaculars."[85] Reading Appadurai's notion of Trojan nationalism through the lens of Anderson's linguistic agency, it is clear that the major operational factor in the subversion of the nation is the deconstruction of a hegemonic, standardized language.

The paradoxical linguistic alterity of Italian defies the idealist ontologies of a national project in Trieste. As if this were not enough, Zeno's pragmatism takes aim at the Irredentist rhetoric of deliverance also via a materialist approach. He returns to the notion of Italian mendacity, arguing that the use of the standard language would be harmful to the local economy tied to international commerce. In Trieste, Zeno argues, what counts is not who we are but what we do. He does so with his usual humorous remarks that tend to deescalate any tensions, and yet his analysis sounds dead serious. He considers his omission to report to the psychoanalyst that he and Guido own a lumberyard close to the doctor's office yet another proof that a confession made in Italian could be neither comprehensive nor truthful. The numerous varieties of timber in the lumberyard have "barbarous names" derived from the dialect, Croat, German, and French. Since nobody in Trieste has knowledge of the Italian translations corresponding to the technical terms of this specialized vocabulary, should he in his old age seek employment with a lumber dealer from Tuscany?[86] The rhetorical question has the advantage of leaving the answer implied, but Zeno's underlying economic analysis is clear. A political annexation to Italy would negatively affect Trieste's commercial infrastructures. Zeno, once again, walks a fine line. He uses the term "barbarous," which has a negative

---

[85] Benedict Anderson, *Imagined Communities: Reflections on the Origin and Spread of Nationalism* (London, New York: Verso, 1991), 44.
[86] Svevo, *Conscience*, 414. "Quest'eliminazione non è che la prova che una confessione fatta da me in italiano non poteva essere né completa né sincera. In un deposito di legnami ci sono varietà enormi di qualità che noi a Trieste appelliamo con termini barbari presi dal dialetto, dal croato, dal tedesco e qualche volta persino dal francese (zapin p.e. non equivale mica a sapin). Chi m'avrebbe fornito il vero vocabolario? Vecchio come sono avrei dovuto prendere un impiego da un commerciante in legnami toscano?" Svevo, *Romanzi*, 1060–1061.

connotation, in lieu of the more neutral term "foreign" to describe the languages of his trade. Faking a sympathetic attitude toward Italian Irredentism, Zeno raises a point that even the most fervent nationalist in Trieste could not ignore.

In the midst of Svevo's tactics of concealment, the author offers the reader a glimpse into his own sympathies when he briefly introduces Nilini, a minor character, inconsequential for the further development of the plot. Nilini's name is obviously a pun on the Latin word *nihil*, meaning "nothing," and a variation on Zeno's last name Cosini that indicates "small things." Nilini takes pleasure in educating Zeno in the matters of international politics, in which he was deeply versed thanks to his activity on the stock exchange. He introduces Zeno to the politics of the Great Powers, explaining shifts between peaceful relations and sudden warfare in international diplomacy. Svevo constructs a character whose ideas about international relations are deeply informed by economic transactions. Zeno and Nilini share a social ineptness, a profound clumsiness in matters of interpersonal relationships. More importantly, however, Zeno befriends Nilini because he smuggles the protagonist's beloved cigarettes.[87] Here Svevo's aesthetics of liminality comes full circle. The references to smoking at the beginning and at the end of the novel act as a narrative frame that contains Zeno's life and encapsulate Svevo's literary activity at the border between Habsburg Austrian and Italian traditions. While Zeno's Austrian cigarettes at the beginning of the novel can be read as a metaphor of Svevo's status as a Habsburg author, now the contraband cigarettes are again associated with his status of a transnational writer. With a few, masterly strokes Svevo paints in the brief characterization of Nilini what appears like his own self-portrait. An idiosyncratic Socialist, Nilini adores Germany and the punctuality of German trains.[88] Zeno divines that Nilini is "an Italian of suspect coloration," one who holds the outrageous belief that

---

[87] "Mi procurava delle sigarette di contrabbando e me le faceva pagare quello che gli costavano, cioè molto poco." Svevo, *Romanzi*, 1002. "He procured contraband cigarettes and charged me only what they had cost him, namely very little." Svevo, *Conscience*, 358.

[88] Svevo nurtured Socialist sympathies, by aligning himself with a Socialist tradition in Italy, in this way strategically avoiding participation in the local debate. Svevo publishes the parable "La tribù" (1897) in Filippo Turati's magazine *Critica Sociale*. It would have been unwise for him to publish in the other Socialist newspaper *Il Lavoratore*, which in 1895 had officially become the mouthpiece of the Triestine Socialists who were opposed to Irredentism. One should not mistake Svevo's approval of Socialist ideas as a subscription to militant proletarian class struggle. He adhered to a utopian anti-war Socialism that would eventually predispose him to European pacifism.

"Trieste would be better off remaining Austrian."[89] The narrator adds a comic twist to the episode, mocking the trite stereotype, also widely popularized under Italian Fascism, of trains arriving on time.

Although not straightforwardly autobiographic, Zeno's apprehension with the shipyard lumber echoes those business concerns in Svevo's life that make an appearance in the novel. Once again, the novel's genealogy is intertwined with Phoenician history. The Levantine Phoenicians were known for their precious timber on Mount Lebanon, where the abundant cedar forests also provided many byproducts that could be exported in the Mediterranean. Cedar resin became a significant article because the Greeks employed it to make cough syrup and the Egyptians used a variety of resins to make ointments used in their embalming techniques. In general, resin was used as a waterproof varnish to caulk the joints and hulls of ships. When the Phoenicians established colonies in the Mediterranean, they often settled in areas with an abundance of forests, including pine and fir, to use for their production and trade of resin. Svevo seemed to have this history in mind when in 1900 he relates a dream to his wife, in which he set up a branch of the Veneziani firm, opening a factory to produce turpentine, a resin that was necessary in the production of the anti-fouling compound. He narrates: "Of course I became the factory manager and without telling anyone at home of this new enterprise I was able to purchase maritime pine forests. These forests were enormously profitable and with the profits I would always buy more ... In my brain there must be a wheel that cannot stop making novels that no one wants to read."[90] In addition to the connection between the dream and the writing of novels, what is striking is Svevo's obsession with maritime commerce. A large share of Habsburg Trieste's Mediterranean economy was represented by naval mercantilism and shipping insurance companies like the Lloyd Triestino. Two years into his marriage, Svevo joins the Veneziani family business, becoming an important player in the city's commercial activities and in Austria's maritime business. The Veneziani family made its fortune with the chemical formula for a powerful

---

[89] Svevo, *Conscience*, 358–359. "Potei accorgermi ch'egli era un italiano di color dubbio perché gli pareva che per Trieste fosse meglio di restare austriaca. Adorava la Germania e specialmente i treni ferroviarii tedeschi che arrivavano con tanta precisione. Era socialista a modo suo e avrebbe voluto fosse proibito che una singola persona possedesse più di centomila corone" (1002–1003).

[90] "Naturalmente il capo fabbrica divenivo io e lentamente senza scriverne a casa con economie sulle spese di fabbrica comperavo dei boschi di pino marittimo. Tali boschi fruttavano enormemente e coi guadagni ne comperavo sempre di nuovi ... Deve esserci nel mio cervello qualche ruota che non sa cessare di fare quei romanzi che nessuno vuole leggere." Svevo, *Epistolario*, 196.

anticorrosive paint for ships. When applied on the iron hulls of naval vessels, the dye kept rust away, as well as marine flora and fauna that attached to the ship's keel and that would eventually foul on it. Once the thick dye hardened on the hull, it improved the ship's structural integrity and dramatically decreased overall maintenance costs. The lack of detritus on the undercarriage also meant less resistance in the water and thus enhanced speed. The Veneziani business had developed the latest improvement in the long history of naval technology innovations. Svevo and the Veneziani family were operating in the tradition of Phoenician shipbuilders, who were credited with the refinement of seafaring conditions. Among the celebrated modifications the Phoenicians had introduced in the ancient Mediterranean was the weighting of their ships' keels to improve stability at sea and the skillful caulking of the ships' hulls to make vessels watertight. The new naval technology of the Veneziani firm attracted business on a global scale, allowing them to hold a virtual monopoly on antifouling and anticorrosive agents in the shipping industry. The company started supplying customers such as the German and British navies. During the Russo–Japanese War in 1904–1905, the company took pride in having contributed to Japan's victory. The Japanese navy treated their ships with the Veneziani antifouling compound, which maintained the maneuverability of the vessels after long periods at sea. Among the international clientele were the Austrian Lloyd shipping company and the Austrian Navy even after Austria-Hungary and Italy were formally at war.[91] One of Svevo's ironies is that his family business made naval warfare more efficient and deadly, a circumstance that he must have been aware of but that he never explicitly addresses in his pacifist essay. For all of Svevo's alleged Irredentism, his business interests could not afford the patriotic idealism that came with the Triestine separatist movement.

---

[91] Given the success of the family business, Svevo spends some time in England, where the Veneziani Company opens a subsidiary. Svevo's letters from England are available in "*This England is so different ...*" *Italo Svevo's London Writings*, eds. John Gatt-Rutter and Brian Moloney (Leicester: Troubador Publishing, 2003).

Four Habsburg Hybrid: James Joyce and the Ethnolinguistics of Hiberno-Punic Mythography, 1904–1939

Italo Svevo was among the first to emphasize the Triestine inspiration of James Joyce's work. In the mid-1920s, Svevo was pleased to point out with a mixture of pride and gratitude that there was much of Trieste and a little bit of Svevo in the novels of the now famous Irish author.[1] Joyce's artistic direction and aesthetic maturity indeed owe much to the formative years he spent in Habsburg Trieste. Joyce lived here from 1904 to 1915, where he conceived and wrote much of his work. He was particularly struck by the cosmopolitan lives of many of his Triestine friends and acquaintances, who, like Svevo, were often simultaneously at home in several languages and inhabited multiple cultural realms. This Habsburg transculturalism became the matrix of the border-crossing and transhistorical intersubjectivity of many of his characters such as Bloom in *Ulysses* or the multiplying avatars of *Finnegans Wake*. Attentive to the linguistic variety with which the city's diverse population spoke Triestino, Joyce also envisaged the multilingualism of Habsburg Trieste as the blueprint for the polyglot cross-fertilizations of the literary language of the *Wake*, a text written and published long after Joyce left the

---

[1] Svevo's "Triestinità di un grande scrittore irlandese: James Joyce" was first published on May 1, 1926 in "Il Popolo di Trieste." Svevo then delivered a talk in Milan on March 8, 1927 titled "Conferenza su James Joyce." The texts are now reprinted in *Teatro e Saggi*, 1166–1170 and 911–960. In Trieste, Joyce wrote *Stephen Hero* (1904–1906), the greater part of the stories that comprise *Dubliners* (1914), *Giacomo Joyce* (1914 but published posthumously in 1968) as well as *A Portrait of the Artist as a Young Man* (1916), *Exiles* (1918), and important sections of *Ulysses* (1922).

city.² This chapter argues, moreover, that the public discussions about language, ethnicity, and nationality in Trieste triggered in Joyce a reflection about what place his native Ireland should occupy in a modern Europe, suggesting to the author that the Europeanization of Ireland would represent a way to escape the stifling yoke of English colonialism. The debates about a possible Phoenician origin in Trieste, in particular, informed Joyce's adoption of the comparative ethnolinguistics of Gaelic antiquarianism that posited a Phoenician ancestry for the Irish. This largely discredited genealogy provided Joyce with the matrix of creative misappropriations in the *Wake*, where he builds an anatomy of Irish culture based upon constant dislocations. Through this "aesthetics of error," Joyce adopts an anti-colonial cultural politics through which he inscribes Irish history into the archive of a more inclusive vision of classical antiquity.³ Joyce's literary invention of Europe is thus a Hiberno-Punic mythography of origins, through which he rewrites the history of Ireland, severing its connection with the British Empire and placing Irish identity in a wider European context, one of "Iro-European ascendances" (*FW* 37.26). In the *Wake*, the idiosyncratic lineage exploits the intrinsic colonial subtext underlying *Metamorphoses'* rape of Europa. Joyce, drawing a parallel between the Roman colonization of Phoenicia and the English colonization of Ireland, molds Jupiter's ethnic rape of the Phoenician maiden into a foundational myth for Ireland.

What Is in a Name? Italo Svevo and Giacomo Joyce

Among Joyce's texts, *Giacomo Joyce* is the author's only work set in Trieste. Svevo once prompted Joyce to write about the city, but we have no evidence that this text is indeed a response to this appeal.⁴

---

[2] John McCourt, who describes the local dialect of Trieste as "a living encyclopaedia of the cultures, nations and languages that had been assimilated in the city," has suggested that the language of *Finnegans Wake* is "an exaggerated, exploded version of *Triestino* ... which itself was used and misused, understood, half-understood, sometimes misunderstood at all." *The Years of Bloom. James Joyce in Trieste, 1904–1920* (Madison: University of Wisconsin Press, 2000), 52–53. For Trieste as a blueprint for the *Wake*, see Cary, *Ghost*, 10. For Joyce's years in Habsburg Trieste, see, among others, Renzo Crivelli, *James Joyce: Itinerari Triestini / Triestine Itineraries* (Trieste: MGS Press, 1996) and Franz Stanzel, *James Joyce in Kakanien 1904–1915* (Würzburg: Königshausen und Neumann, 2019).
[3] Building on Stephen's aphorism, "A man of genius makes no mistakes. His errors are volitional and are the portals of discovery" (*U* 9.90), Tim Conley argues that Joyce devises an "aesthetic of error" that is crucial for the *Wake*. See *Joyces Mistakes: Problems of Intention, Irony, and Interpretation* (Toronto: University of Toronto Press, 2003).
[4] Cfr. Svevo, *Epistolario*, 692. Brian Moloney has suggested that the work is indebted to Svevo because it employs a "lexical cluster that derives from *Senilità*." Moloney, *Friends in Exile*, 74.

Published from Joyce's handwritten pages, the plot of the short prose poem revolves around the aesthetic sublimation of the protagonist's erotic desire for a confident and elegant young woman who belongs to the Triestine upper class.[5] Beyond the vicissitudes of the penniless language teacher and his spurned infatuation with the wealthy Jewish student, *Giacomo Joyce* interests us for the protagonist's perspective on the multicultural and polyglot composition of Habsburg Trieste, where imperial subjects speak "in boneless Viennese Italian" (*GJ* 1) and are "rounded by the lathe of intermarriage and ripened in the forcing-house of the seclusion of [their] race" (*GJ* 2). Irredentists are likened to depressed bugs that hide in houses covered by roofs that recall tortoise shells: "Trieste is waking rawly: raw sunlight over its huddled browntiled roofs, testudoform; a multitude of prostrate bugs await a national deliverance" (*GJ* 8). The protagonist's mocking commentary on such hope of deliverance is accompanied by the equally sarcastic exposure of the fragile and ever-shifting definition of patriotism: "They love their country when they are quite sure which country it is" (*GJ* 9). In a text in which definite meanings are erotically concealed and playfully withheld, the value of "when" adds to a temporal deferral the fluidity of cultural commitments and political allegiances in Trieste.

There is one other important feature in *Giacomo Joyce* that interests us. In the previous chapter, I proposed that the semantic quandary of Joyce's Stephen served as a model for the linguistic dilemma of Svevo's Zeno. Now, let me suggest that the Triestine's election of the hybrid pseudonym of "Italo Svevo" exerted a crucial influence on Joyce's choice to adopt a similar pseudonym in *Giacomo Joyce* through which the Irish author Italianized his name.[6] Both "Italo Svevo" and "Giacomo Joyce" reveal a strategy of self-representation in a state of cultural liminality. They assert the hybrid identity of European authors who write across languages and literary traditions. Like

---

[5] After its publication, critics debated about the textual categorization of *Giacomo Joyce*, with suggestions covering a wide range of literary genres. The interpretations extended from highly polished prose poem to short novelette, while it was often considered an unpretentious notebook to be ransacked for Joyce's allegedly more important works.

[6] Richard Ellmann suggests that Svevo might have given Joyce the idea for a work set in Trieste in the summer of 1914. See James Joyce, *Giacomo Joyce*, (New York: Viking Press, 1968), xvi. McCourt proposes a slightly different timeframe, suggesting that the work might have been written sometime between 1911 and 1914, which would exclude Joyce's response to Svevo's prompting but does not negate a direct influence in the choice of the name. Even if Svevo's suggestion to write about Trieste came after Joyce had jotted down notes for *Giacomo Joyce*, the Triestine writer, who had adopted his pseudonym long before they first met, might very well have been the inspiration for Joyce.

Svevo, Joyce stages himself as a *Homo Europaeus habsburgensis*, a European subject of the Austro-Hungarian Empire. John McCourt has argued that with the choice of a hybrid Italian-Irish title for his volume Joyce decided to offer a more complex representation of himself, suggesting the image of an Italianized Irishman at home in Trieste and immersed in Italian culture, literature, and language.[7] The adoption of this Habsburg Italian identity never occurs at the expense of Joyce's Irishness. The playful dimension of this onomastic metamorphosis, documented in Joyce's letters, returns in *Finnegans Wake*, where Joyce's fictional projection takes the name of Shem, the Irish version of James: "Shem is as short for Shemus as Jem is joky for Jacob" (*FW* 169.1). In the novel, the act of writing is Shem's main activity, as his epithet "Penman" suggests. In one of the many transpersonal migrations, Shem the Penman assumes a Slavic identity, becoming "Shem Skrivenitch," who annoys his brother Shaun by "always cutting my prhose to please his phrase" (*FW* 423.15–16). Shem Skrivenitch is based on Alois Skrivanich, a Croatian student of Joyce in Trieste. Here again, Joyce reshapes his literary alter ego in the image of a Habsburg subject. The epithet "Skrivenitch" is, of course, parallel to "Penman," since it suggests the English term "scribbling," the Irish "scríobh," and the Italian "scrivere." Such cultural and historical translations are common in the text. Anna Livia Plurabelle, also known as ALP and the mother figure of the two brothers, undergoes a similar Slavification when she becomes "Annushka Lutetiavitch Pufflovah" (*FW* 207.8–9). While her last name suggests a German brothel, her Slavic patronymic puns on Lutetia, the Gallo-Roman name of an early settlement on the river Seine that will later become Paris. James, Giacomo, and Shem are respectively the English, Italian, and Irish transcultural embodiments of Joyce's composite literary identity. Through this tripartite nomenclature, Joyce projects a self-portrait that responds to the Cubist logic of juxtaposition of fragmented "multiple Mes" (*FW* 410.12).

Joyce and the "United States of Europe of the Future"

Joyce's playful juggling with the multiple iterations of his name was a way to suggest in his fiction a dynamic relationship between Ireland and Europe. His public statements about Irish and European politics were quite infrequent, and when he sometimes took a public stance on matters of policy and legislation, he expressed his opinions not in

---

[7] John McCourt, "The Importance of Being Giacomo," *Joyce Studies Annual* 11 (Summer 2000): 4–26. www.jstor.org/stable/26285212.

English, but only on occasions that required his use of Italian.[8] Joyce produced his critical writings—including lectures, essays, and newspaper articles—in Habsburg Trieste, a city that in many ways shaped his political views. Conversely, Joyce's fictional characters, often politically outspoken figures, are anything but cautious in their pronouncements. Take, for instance, the eponymous character of Joyce's first novel, *Stephen Hero*, an unfinished project started in 1903 in Dublin and abandoned around 1906 after Joyce tried to complete it in Trieste. Plagued by a deep-seated inferiority complex, Stephen laments the marginal status of Ireland, merely an "afterthought of Europe" (*SH* 53). Ireland is located in a double periphery, an island beyond an island, relegated to the "farthest remove from the centre of European culture" (*SH* 194). To compensate for this perceived inadequacy, he embraces a literary Europeanism that celebrates the figures of Dante and Ibsen, Shakespeare and Goethe. When his classmates accuse him of a traitorous xenophilia, Stephen Hero is confronted with the demands of Irish cultural and political nationalism. He is described as a "renegade from the Nationalist ranks," having professed "cosmopolitanism" (*SH* 103). An artist without national loyalties cannot be trusted since, "a man that was of all countries was of no country—you must first have a nation before you have art" (*SH* 103). The nation occupies the first position in an allegedly natural hierarchy of identity markers: all other personal traits, aspirations, and loyalties are secondary and subordinate to it. This hegemony of the nation forces a series of impositions on individual choices that to an artist and free spirit like Stephen, entangled in the elaborate definitions of an aesthetic theory, remain unacceptable. Already in this early and immature text, Joyce considers the political slogans that put nation first with the same suspicion with which Musil and Svevo, Däubler and Kosovel stage the process by which national identification demands supremacy among all other modes of social bonding.

The failure of Irish nationalists to involve the protagonist in their cultural interests is preserved in *A Portrait of the Artist as a Young Man*. Stephen famously endeavors to escape in a self-imposed exile from the burdens of nationality, language, and religion. His classmate McCann, a political activist and pacifist, reproaches the skeptical protagonist, declaring proudly: "Dedalus, you are an anti-social being, wrapped up

---

[8] See Eric Bulson, "An Italian Tongue in an Irish Mouth: Joyce, Politics, and the Franca Langua," *Journal of Modern Literature* 24, no. 1 (Fall 2000): 63–79. https://www.jstor.org/stable/3831700. Bulson points out the hyphenation of Joyce's identity in the Irish press that described the author as an "Irish-Italian journalist" from Trieste.

in yourself. I am not. I'm a democrat: and I'll work and act for social liberty and equality among all classes and sexes in the United States of the Europe of the future" (*P* 181). In McCann's fruitless attempt to convert the pacifist but aloof Stephen, invested in "forging in the smithy of [his] soul the uncreated conscience of [his] race" (*P* 253), to social and political activism is embedded an implicit commentary on the failed pacifism of W. T. Stead's *The United States of Europe on the Eve of the Parliament of Peace*, a work Joyce knew. The trajectory McCann describes for Ireland is nevertheless configured in a contextual transition from a monarchic and imperial-colonial England to a democratic and federal Europe. Whatever position on the political future of Ireland and Europe that Joyce's characters develop, at this point their opinions are shaped by the debates about nationalism and cosmopolitanism that Joyce witnessed in Trieste.

Joyce develops this aesthetic and political program in Richard Rowan and Robert Hand, the male protagonists of *Exiles*, Joyce's play published just a few months before the end of the First World War, who attempt to divine the geopolitical future of Ireland. Richard, a loose fictional projection of Joyce's authorial self, has just returned to Dublin from a self-imposed exile in Italy. His best friend Robert, modelled upon Roberto Prezioso, the vice-director of the local newspaper in Trieste *Il Piccolo della Sera* where Joyce published, seems to provide a summary for the political convictions that the Irish author had at that point reached in Trieste. Lighting a Virginia cigar, Robert claims: "These cigars Europeanize me. If Ireland is to become a new Ireland she must first become European. And that is what you are here for, Richard. Some day we shall have to choose between England and Europe. I am a descendant of the dark foreigners: that is why I like to be here" (*PE* 158). In this somewhat deservedly less celebrated work in the Joycean canon, Robert's prediction about the future of Ireland rings quite prophetic.[9] Ireland will indeed gain independence from England four years after the publication of the play, and will subsequently become a member of European-wide institutions. The mission of the Irish intellectual is, according to Robert, to engender a process of Europeanization, a cultural revolution whimsically launched by the lighting of the cigars, incidentally the same that Zeno's father liked to smoke.[10] Striking is Joyce's use of the term "Europeanize," at this point a relatively recent neologism in the English language, which occurs in one other instance of Joyce's works, namely in the expression "Europasianised Afferyank" (*FW* 191.4),

---

[9] Jean-Michel Rabaté, *1913: The Cradle of Modernism* (Malden, MA: Blackwell Publishing, 2007), 100.
[10] Joyce enjoyed smoking the long, Italian Virginia cigars, incidentally the same that Svevo's Zeno steals from his father.

one of the many insults that the chauvinist Shaun hurls at Shem, his cosmopolitan brother and "national apostate" (FW 171.33) in *Finnegans Wake*.[11] The Europeanized Robert acknowledges that he remains the descendant of darker-skinned foreigners but does not specify the origin or cultural composition of this group of immigrants. The other question that Joyce leaves unanswered in *Exiles*, a work much more interested in the interpersonal dynamics governing romantic entanglements, concerns the very nature of this future relationship between a postcolonial Ireland and an anticolonial Europe. What would this Europeanization of Ireland look like? Which social, cultural, and political forces would reshape this new Ireland? Modeled on Henrik Ibsen's dramaturgy and largely inspired by Joyce's network of intellectuals in Trieste, the play revolves around the issue of women's social and sexual emancipation, experimenting with the questions of exile and betrayal.

The Metamorphosis of Irish History

The text that best outlines Joyce's discursive triangulations that involve his country of origin, his city of residence, and Europe remains "Ireland: Island of Saints and Sages," a lecture he gave at the Università Popolare in Trieste on April 27, 1907. Delivered shortly after Joyce abandons the project of *Stephen Hero*, the lecture marks a crucial turning point for him. The author considered the long draft of his novel a failed experiment still largely informed by his Dublin upbringing. Now that he had started to take in the rich impressions offered in Trieste, this was an important occasion to change course. The address reads like an extended manifesto of his aesthetic and political priorities that he will develop in his later works. In his critique of Irish nationalism, an attitude that characterized both *Stephen Hero* and *A Portrait*, Joyce did not engage one of the most prominent tropes employed to assert cultural autonomy—the alleged Phoenician origin of Ireland. "Ireland: Island of Saints and Sages" shows that only after Joyce starts absorbing the culture of Trieste do the Phoenicians appear in his discussion of Irish identity. This is not a straightforward and uncritical acceptance of the propositions of Gaelic antiquarians. Joyce's Phoenicians are of a distinctly Triestine brand, that is, denationalized and transmuted into a figure of his own cosmopolitanism.

Still speaking in a somewhat shaky and bookish Italian, Joyce was eager to exhibit his erudition, offering his audience a rich and detailed history of Ireland. He addressed a sizeable crowd in the conference hall

---

[11] This was a recently coined term in the English language. The *Oxford English Dictionary* indicates the first recording of the term in 1849, some sixty years before the publication of *Exiles*.

of the Chamber of Commerce, seeing the speech as a contribution to the intellectual life in the city and, more importantly, as a welcome opportunity to promote and disseminate a different view of Ireland, all too often the object of racial ridicule in the colonial propaganda of the Victorian and Edwardian press. In the popular cartoons of the time, caricatures depicted the Irish with simian features mocking them as irrational and savage brutes.[12] Against the stereotype of a barbaric backwater promoted by the English, Joyce wished to defend Ireland's long tradition of scholarly endeavors, an Ireland holding high the banner of learning and writing during the European Middle Ages. The country Joyce presents to his Triestine audience is an important focal point of a flourishing academic network, an "enormous seminary" (*OCPW* 108) and "true centre of intellectualism and sanctity" (*OCPW* 108) that scholars from all over Europe visited for their studies. At the same time, an Irish monastic intelligentsia embarked upon a civilizing mission on the European continent, "carrying the torch of knowledge" (*OCPW* 108) during a dark age of ignorance and widespread loss of literacy. Joyce hence attributes Ireland's contemporary cultural isolation not to its peripheral geographic location, but to a marginalization imposed by English imperialism, determined to enclose Ireland in its sphere of political influence and to sever Irish connections with Europe. It is important to note here that in denouncing the imperial oppression of England, Joyce refuses to adopt a rhetoric of victimhood by emphasizing Irish collusion in its own colonization. Instead, his mission is to contribute to Irish efforts "to renew in a modern form the glories of a past civilization" (*OCPW* 111), reestablishing the interrupted connection between an Irish and a European cultural and literary tradition. "Ireland: Island of Saints and Sages" is particularly revealing of Joyce's aesthetic trajectory because many of the ideas expressed here, far from constituting fleeting opinions in an emerging artistic program, will become solid positions that Joyce will continue to embrace over the years. Joyce's lecture outlines important questions about language and politics to which Joyce will repeatedly return in his later texts, in *Ulysses* first and especially *Finnegans Wake* later.

Rhetorical complexity and argumentative density are defining features of "Ireland: Island of Saints and Sages," both characteristics

---

[12] These cartoons appeared in English periodicals like *Punch* and *Judy*. Here, the "Simian Irish Celt" was depicted with facial features suggestive of gorillas or baboons. Along the same lines, the American magazine *Harper's Weekly* described Irish-American immigrants as beastly and degenerate, employing the same racist rhetoric of dehumanization used for the depiction of African-Americans. For Joyce's knowledge of English imperial propaganda and the history of colonial representations of the Irish as dehumanized apes, see Vincent J. Cheng, *Joyce, Race, and Empire* (Cambridge: Cambridge University Press, 1995).

that are easy to underestimate if one were to assess the lecture solely in the context of Anglo-Irish politics. While Joyce is indeed opposing English imperialism, rejecting Irish nationalism, and distancing himself from the provincialism of the Gaelic Revival, he is at the same time addressing very specific local concerns in Trieste. In April 1907, Joyce had just made the acquaintance of Svevo and had already met many prominent intellectuals in the city, Irredentists, and politically engaged journalists such as Silvio Benco, Roberto Prezioso, and Theodor Mayer. Upon his return from an unsuccessful stay in Rome, he was happy to start his work as a journalist in Trieste, reporting on the cultural and political life in Ireland. Particularly with this lecture, the first of three proposed talks at the Università Popolare, Joyce makes a conscious attempt at establishing his role as public intellectual and political commentator in Trieste. As a result, "Ireland: Island of Saints and Sages" is not simply a lecture concerning Irish history and culture; I suggest that the address reveals much about Trieste as it mirrors concerns and expectations of its listeners. Joyce engages a politically heterogeneous crowd, participating in broader citywide conversations, and although he almost never openly mentions contemporary Trieste, several topics he discusses clearly and effectively resonate with his audience.

Indicative of Joyce's oratorical dexterity and rhetorical strategies is the treatment of the national question. Speaking to an audience that has been debating about questions of nationhood and nonnational identities, cultural and political affiliations, Joyce opens his lecture addressing this very debate, comparing the nation's self-centeredness to an individual's egoism. Joyce argues here that nations act in their self-interest, attributing to themselves glorious qualities. This attribution necessarily occurs in the context of cultural and political institutions that promote such a self-image. Joyce acknowledges that he is participating in such a promotion, even though via strategies that are far from the xenophobic provincialism of the Gaelic League and likewise of the parochialism of Irredentist organizations in the city. Dismantling the idea that national groups are homogeneous monoliths, Joyce presents Irish civilization as fundamentally composite, absorbing and assimilating different social and cultural practices in the course of a long history that witnessed several populations disembarking on Irish shores, from Phoenicians and Romans to Vikings and Anglo-Saxons. Joyce describes Ireland as "an immense woven fabric in which very different elements are mixed" and in which "it is pointless searching for a thread that has remained pure, virgin, and uninfluenced by other threads nearby" (*OCPW* 118). Joyce's strategy is to draw implicit but forceful parallels between Ireland and Trieste. Given the dynamics of social, cultural, and ethnic amalgamation that Joyce sees occurring in both places, he uses Ireland as a rhetorical catalyst in a crescendo of arguments that build up from the idea of a hybrid Ireland, extends to the equally mixed Trieste, and moves from these particular case studies to a more general assertion about the nature of populations and languages. Joyce invites his audience to contemplate the question of national identity as a fundamentally hybrid phenomenon when he adds the rhetorical question, "What race or language ... can nowadays claim to be pure?" (*OCPW* 118). But more than exposing the idea of ethnic purity as a myth to debunk, Joyce argues that "nationality" is a "useful fiction" (*OCPW* 118). Joyce presents himself as Nietzsche's "good European" borrowing, like Musil, the Nietzschean treatment of the nation as *Einbildung*, as the product of a necessary imagination.[13] His historical excursus is a learned refutation of ideas of ethnic purity, one that had the force of a slap in the face for any die-hard nationalists in the audience. His words, however, remain beyond reproach. After all, he is just speaking about Ireland.

The question of nationality is not the only topic through which Joyce signals his desire to engage in a larger conversation with his Triestine audience. The other pressing issue Joyce addresses is the question of the Phoenicians, a thematic thread that runs from the beginning to the end of the speech. Joyce envisions the future of Ireland as a modern sea power, as a "rival, bilingual, republican, self-centered and enterprising island next to England, with its own commercial fleet and its ambassadors in every port throughout the world" (*OCPW* 125). Inspired by a Phoenician mercantilism, this Ireland with its own commercial fleet resonates with his Triestine audience. Despite the imagined continuity between the Phoenicians of the past and the Irish of the future, Joyce does not shy away from using tropes from Roman anti-Phoenician propaganda. When he explains recent Irish emigration patterns as the result of the misery and famine caused by brutal English rule, Joyce argues that the Treaty of Limerick was broken by the "Punic faith of the English" (*OCPW* 123), associating the stereotypical Carthaginian treachery with English colonialism.

Joyce knows that challenging deep-seated prejudices against the Irish requires a profound reexamination of the assumptions handed down from ancient and medieval European history. He therefore invokes the authority of some unnamed German historians, who have offered a better understanding of Celtic lore but have failed to satisfactorily explain Europe's Mediterranean past. The cornerstone of Joyce's understanding of the classical world remains the Italian historian Guglielmo Ferrero (1871–1945), a respected intellectual in Trieste known for his new

---

[13] Sam Slote sees in Joyce's speech a Nietzschean origin: "Joyce's conception of national identity is one of evolving, mingling hybridities." Sam Slote, *Joyce's Nietzschean Ethics* (New York: Palgrave Macmillan, 2013), 85.

approach to Roman history: "Ferrero now tells us that the discoveries of these good German professors, as far as concerns the ancient history of the Roman republic and of the Roman Empire, are mistaken from beginning to the end, or almost" (*OCPW* 109). Joyce's reference to Ferrero, only ostensibly in passing, is not simply an attempt to capture the audience's benevolence, as it signals, more importantly, an introduction to Ferrero's historical revisionism, a fitting methodological paradigm for Joyce's subsequent linguistic ethnography that identifies a Phoenician origin of the Irish. By the time Joyce was delivering his lecture, he might not have read Ferrero's massive five-volume history of Rome in its entirety, but certainly significant portions of it. Just a few lines down from his reference to Ferrero, Joyce argues for a linguistic, ethnic, and cultural continuity between the Phoenicians and the Irish:

> This language [Irish] is eastern in origin and has been identified by many philologists with the ancient language of the Phoenicians, the discoverers, according to historians, of commerce and navigation. With their monopoly over the sea, this adventurous people established a civilization in Ireland, which was in decline and had almost disappeared before the first Greek historian took up his quill. It jealously guarded the secrets of its science, and the first mention of the island of Ireland in foreign literature is to be found in a Greek poem of the fifth century before Christ in which the historian reiterates the Phoenician tradition. The language that the comic dramatist Plautus puts in the mouth of the Phoenicians in his comedy *Poenula* is virtually the same language, according to the critic Vallancey, as that which Irish peasants now speak (*OCPW* 110).

Reminding his audience that the Phoenicians are credited with inventing the alphabet, Joyce asserts with this Orientalist genealogy Ireland's long-lost cultural prestige.[14] However peculiar this Hiberno-Punic ethnography may sound today, the notion of a Phoenician origin represented an important *topos* in the cultural politics of Irish Revivalists, invested in demonstrating ethnic otherness and cultural superiority with respect to the English colonizer. Since the seventeenth and eighteenth

---

[14] In *Ireland's Others: Ethnicity and Gender in Irish Literature and Popular Culture* (Notre Dame, IN: University of Notre Dame Press, 2001), Elizabeth Butler Cullingford argues that for many Irish authors, the opposition between Rome and Carthage operated as origin legend and anti-colonial parable that fueled Irish nationalism. Her valuable discussion of Joyce and the Phoenicians ignores how this association made its way into *Finnegans Wake*.

centuries, Irish antiquarians and historians used this Phoenician and Carthaginian origin of Ireland as a way to advance a political agenda rather than exploring historical truth. Joyce's association is grounded in the more recent comparative historical linguistics of the nineteenth century that erroneously identified a Semitic derivation of ancient Gaelic.[15] Today, there is archeological evidence suggesting Phoenician contacts with populations in the British islands, but the postulation of linguistic derivation remains unfounded. A linguistics focused largely on etymology rather than comparative grammar afforded a certain degree of interpretive flexibility in the efforts to prove ancient connections. Coincidental phonetic similarities between unrelated languages could easily be exploited to demonstrate genetic affiliations between languages.[16] Joyce knew that these ideas were largely discredited, but was more than willing to suspend his beliefs, or pretend to do so, if this meant he could establish a deeper connection with his audience. Part of a carefully constructed and shrewdly deployed strategy, the imagined Phoenician genealogy of the Irish was less a question of historical accuracy than it was of anti-colonial cultural politics. Joyce must have been aware of Gaelic Phoenicianism before he arrived in Trieste, but it is only here, where a Phoenician myth of origin is circulating, that it is worth mentioning. He does so to establish an ethnic kinship with maritime Trieste, implying that Joyce and his Triestine audience members are some sort of distant cousins who plotted different itineraries at sea and disembarked on different shores.

Joyce was an enthusiastic reader of Ferrero's work, in particular *Militarism* (*Militarismo*), *The Greatness and Decline of Rome* (*Grandezza e decadenza di Roma*), and *Young Europe* (*L'Europa giovane*), works he read around 1905 and 1906. Ferrero, who was reaching his peak in popularity around the turn of the century, was a household name in the city, where he enjoyed the friendship of many leading intellectuals including Silvio Benco and Umberto Saba. The historian published in the local newspaper *Il Piccolo della Sera* and gave public lectures at the *Circolo di studi sociali*, the cultural center of the city's Austro-Marxists, as well as

---

[15] Joseph Lennon sees Irish Orientalism as a rhetorically multifaceted phenomenon closer to cultural mythology than historiography, developing in both imperial and anti-colonial directions. According to Lennon, when more rigorous historical research replaced this tradition, the shift "pushed Oriental-Celtic connections into more legendary, literary, and racial realms." Joseph Lennon, *Irish Orientalism: A Literary and Intellectual History* (Syracuse, NY: Syracuse University Press, 2004), 135.

[16] This attitude was widespread even after the monogenetic model, which identified in ancient Hebrew the source of all modern European languages, had been abandoned. See Lennon, *Irish Orientalism*, 65–69.

at the *Società di Minerva*, where the city's antiquarians gathered. Ferrero never wrote a dedicated monograph about the Phoenicians, but he attributed to them a foundational role, an idea that resonated with many intellectuals in the city. Like many of his Triestine colleagues, he believed that the origin of Western civilization was to be found not only in the Greco-Roman tradition but in the Phoenician thalassocracy as well. His position is summed up in his comparative study *Ancient Rome and Modern America*, where the historian underscored the fundamental role of the Phoenician contribution to ancient Mediterranean history and modern European identity. In his comparison between antiquity and modernity, the Italian historian maintains that together with Roman militarism, Christian morality, and Greek philosophy, the Phoenician economy is one of the four founding pillars of Western civilization: "In war, we fight like the Romans, and in peace, we turn our eyes away from bloody spectacles. We should hold the gladiatorial games in no whit less horror than the most pious of Christian monks. We trade like the Phoenicians and we love knowledge like the Greeks."[17] Ferrero argued that Phoenician trade with the Greeks and Romans opened up possibilities of exchange that went beyond mere economic transactions. In the first volume of *The Greatness and Decline of Rome*, he maintained that early Roman trade was exclusively entertained with Etruscans and Phoenicians, importing ivory ornaments, perfumes for funerals, and especially the fine purple robes used as ceremonial attire of the magistrates.[18] The establishment of an economy of luxury products implies for Ferrero the institution of cultural values and practices that in turn affect sexual mores.

The association between Phoenician sexual mores and ancient politics had occupied Ferrero's mind since the beginnings of his career. Thanks to his training as a classical historian, Ferrero contributed with his knowledge to the influential *Criminal Woman, the Prostitute, and the Normal Woman*, co-authored with his future father-in-law Cesare Lombroso. As a promising but inexperienced intellectual, Ferrero was little more than a research assistant to the more experienced Lombroso. The authors offer some historical background for their interdisciplinary investigation of female criminology and prostitution. According to their reconstruction of Mediterranean and Near Eastern history, ancient sexual customs entailed a tripartite socio-behavioral pattern, articulated

---

[17] Guglielmo Ferrero, *Ancient Rome and Modern America: A Comparative Study of Morals and Manners* (New York: G. P. Putnam's Sons, 1914), 112.
[18] "Perciò Roma comprava poco fuori: Ceramiche per le costruzioni pubbliche e metalli in Etruria; ninnoli artistici, punici o fenici; gingilli di avorio; profumi per i funerali e porpore per gli abiti da cerimonia dei magistrati." Guglielmo Ferrero, *Grandezza e decadenza di Roma* (Milan: Treves, 1902–1906), 1:4.

in secular, hospitable, and sacred prostitution. The two latter forms of prostitution were a phenomenon that could be observed in Phoenician culture. Citing Herodotus, the two authors argue that similar to the Babylonians, the Phoenicians prostituted their virgin daughters to foreigners to demonstrate their hospitality. The payment they received from the foreigners became sacred money.[19] Ferrero's historical contribution to Lombroso's study in criminology must not have escaped Joyce, always eager to acquaint himself with Phoenician lore. Motivated by a keen interest in the history of sexuality and sexual degeneracy, Joyce was familiar with Lombroso's theories, which partially intersected with Ferrero's early positions. Already in *Militarism*, a main source for Joyce's early works, Ferrero described how Phoenicians established colonies and trading posts on the Greek mainland, associating military action with erotic desire. The merchant seafarers were greeted by "troops of women and girls" who developed a "desire" to purchase luxury items.[20] Temptation and satisfaction continue to frame the commercial transaction in which the display of exotic goods produces a drive to purchase from the merchant's "inexhaustible treasure-bag."[21] For Ferrero, female sexual desire appeared as an economic drive regulating the contacts among different populations in the ancient world.

Ferrero developed further this association between sexuality and militarism in *Young Europe*. In his study, the Italian historian maintained

---

[19] Cesare Lombroso and Guglielmo Ferrero, *Criminal Woman, the Prostitute, and the Normal Woman*, eds. and trans. Nicole Hahn Rafter and Mary Gibson (Durham, NC: Duke University Press, 2004), 102. "Secondo Erodoto, tra i Babilonesi le donne nate nel paese erano obbligate, una volta almeno nella vita, ad andare al tempio di Venere, ed ivi abbandonarsi a uno straniero; né potevano tornarsene a casa se prima qualche forestiero non avesse loro gettato danaro sulle ginocchia e non le avesse invitate al coito fuori del luogo sacro: questo danaro diventava sacro. Tra i Fenici esisteva la prostituzione ospitale e sacra; essi, secondo le affermazioni di Eusebio, prostituivano le figliuole vergini ai forestieri a maggior gloria dell'ospitalità." Cesare Lombroso and Guglielmo Ferrero, *La donna delinquente: la prostituta e la donna normale* (Turin: Bocca, 1903), 220–221.

[20] Guglielmo Ferrero, *Militarism. A Contribution to the Peace Crusade* (Boston, MA: Paige & Company, 1903), 299. "Il mercante fenicio sbarca sulla costa greca; trae dalla nave molte mercanzie del suo paese e le espone sulla spiaggia: ecco allora dai villaggi vicini vengono donne e fanciulle a guardare, e intorno ai campioni di una industria più raffinata i primi bisogni di un lusso più eletto nascono negli spiriti semplici dei barbari." Guglielmo Ferrero, *Il Militarismo: dieci conferenze di Guglielmo Ferrero* (Milan: Treves, 1898), 421.

[21] Ferrero, *Militarism*, 300. "poi tutti se ne sono invogliati e hanno comperato, credendo di soddisfare senza danno un desiderio innocente. Ma il sacco del mercante era inesauribile; ogni giorno ne usciva qualche cosa nuova, qualche sorpresa più strana, e intorno ai nuovi oggetti le voglie resistevano sempre meno alle tentazioni rinnovate." Ferrero, *Il Militarismo*, 422.

that the male tradition of belligerent nationalism envisions sexual encounters as dominated by brutal violence and conquest instead of the courteous gallantry expected by the female counterpart. Joyce employed these ideas in *Dubliners*, particularly in "Two Gallants" and "The Dead." Ferrero argued that this connection between sex and war is particularly evident in the ancient world, where one can observe in the sexual politics of rape a deep analogy to the imperial politics of conquest. Examples in classical literature, Ferrero believes, support this argument. The narrative nuclei of both *The Iliad* and *The Odyssey* associate sexual violence with the art of war. The rape of Helen will have military consequences, as it becomes the reason or excuse for Greeks and Trojans to wage war against each other. The quarrel over Briseis between Agamemnon and Achilles responds to the same logic. Similarly, when Odysseus finally returns to Ithaca, he has to fight the suitors who intend to usurp his nuptial bed along with his throne.

Besides having an interest in the interlocking dynamics of sexual violence and colonial politics, Joyce paid particular attention to Ferrero's other lines of argumentation, especially Irish affairs and the case of Parnell. Ferrero saw an affinity between Italian and Irish emigration patterns, an affinity that he could exploit by drawing a parallel between the Irish claim to independence and Irredentism in Trieste. Ferrero was a Dreyfusard, and his pages on anti-Semitism were conceived as an intervention in the debates around the *Affaire*. Joyce was struck by Ferrero's examination of Jewish identity contributing to a European cultural transnationalism and the implicit assumption that anti-Semitic hatred was one of the factors that made a more just Europe realizable only in the future. Joyce elaborated the vital role the Jewish community played in the definition of European identity later in the construction of Bloom.

Joyce's Mediterranean Classicism

In *Ulysses*, Joyce's "epic of two races, (Israel-Ireland)" (*Letters* 1: 146), Leopold Bloom, the son of a Hungarian Jew who settled in Dublin, embodies the modern-day parody of the Homeric Odysseus. As readers of Joyce know, Joyce models his protagonist on Victor Bérard's understanding that Homer was indeed Greek but that Odysseus was a Phoenician, albeit Hellenized, seafarer. The close association between Ferrero's revisionism and Joyce's discussion of the Phoenicians, however, suggests that Joyce's combined readings of Ferrero contributed substantially to the author's construction of Bloom. Very much a product of Joyce's years in Habsburg Trieste, Leopold Bloom is largely inspired by Italo Svevo and Theodor Mayer, another Triestine acquaintance, and named after Habsburg emperors. In the "Circe" episode of the novel, Joyce's idealized vision of Trieste fuels the urban cosmopolitanism of his character's visionary "new Bloomusalem," capital of the "Nova Hibernia of the future" (*U* 15.1544–45), a postcolonial utopia of religious freedom and tolerance, interethnic marriages, social justice and equality, free of nationalist excesses where people speak Esperanto.[22] Bloom's advocacy of Esperanto is indicative of the Habsburg genesis of the character. The invention of the artificial language was the product of a typically Habsburg anxiety over a peaceful coexistence of different linguistic groups. Esperanto combined a simplified grammar with a Greco-Latin substratum and Germanic, Romance, and Slavic vocabulary, and was an explicitly cosmopolitan enterprise aimed at uniting Europe linguistically.

Bloom's hallucinatory manifesto gives expression to his messianic and utopian political reformism, but it offers in the context of the novel a most lucid parody of several Habsburg-inspired reform proposals. His delirium as a benign dictator performs a therapeutic function after his marginalization during the nationalist tirade of the garrulous Citizen in the "Cyclops" episode. When prompted to offer a definition of the nation, his response only ostensibly produces clumsy results. Beleaguered and intimidated by a derisive crowd, Bloom manages nonetheless to offer a concise definition with his flustered response: "A nation is the same people living in the same place" (*U* 12. 1422–23). Bloom's nation does not correspond to the classical criteria that nineteenth-century nationalism had proposed and thus meets the mockery of his interlocutors at the pub who expect the recourse to biological racism or some sort of blood-and-soil rhetoric. While critics recognize that Joyce contrasts Bloom's dialogic vision to the monocular short-sightedness of the cycloptic Citizen, Bloom's response has baffled commentators who dismiss his definition as uncertain and vague.[23] Nevertheless, if one takes the specifically Austrian genesis of Bloom's pragmatic cosmopolitanism into account, his often-quoted formulation loses much of

---

[22] Joyce developed his interest in Esperanto in Trieste. Nico Israel appropriately argues that "on the level of the line, the word, and the phoneme, what Joyce tried to accomplish in *Finnegans Wake* was, in many ways, like Dr. Zamenhof's Esperanto, precisely the creation of a new, 'invented' language made up of a network of already-existing other ones" (10). More in general, Israel continues, "Joyce's novels do truly seem to reflect Esperantists' hope that a critically cosmopolitan outlook can engender progressive, indeed revolutionary political change" (12). See Nico Israel, "Esperantic Modernism: Joyce, Universal Language, and Political Gesture," *Modernism/modernity* 24, no. 1 (2017): 1–21.

[23] The question that the Citizen asks Bloom is "What is a Nation"? Walkowitz reads Bloom's response as a "platitude." Walkowitz, *Cosmopolitan*, 76. Davison maintains that Bloom does not know the answer to the question, offering a response that is "contradictory" or "presumptive." Davison, *Construction of Jewish Identity*, 217.

its alleged naïveté. Bloom's "nation" is highly reminiscent of the kind of urban *Landespatriotismus* Joyce encountered in Habsburg Trieste. Much like Kosovel's ethics of mediation, Bloom's political program implies a citizenship of residence that decouples ethnic nationality from the full participation in civic life. The formulation of the nation as "the same people living in the same place" stresses territoriality without the recourse to ethnic or racial uniformity, a geographically defined administrative unit capable of accommodating the matrix of primary identifications and multiple belongings of its inhabitants. Bloom's definition thus suggests a culturally heterogeneous and more inclusive alternative to exclusionary models of nationhood, one that integrates difference in a transcultural context where race and ethnicity, language, and religious beliefs are not priorities in the entitlement to citizenship rights. Joyce recreates this model of urban or regional multiethnicity also in Bloom and Molly's reminiscence of Gibraltar, another microcosm of a Mediterranean Europe.[24] These Dubliners have their eyes set on the Mediterranean.

In the "Eumaeus" chapter, Joyce parodies the Phoenician undercurrent of the Homeric counterpart of the episode. The Gilbert schema indicates "sailors" as the symbol for episode, while the art is "navigation." Both categories in the reading grid need to be understood as specifically Phoenician. In Homer, Odysseus has just arrived in Ithaca, after having convinced the Phaeacians, Homer's transfiguration of the Phoenicians, with his tear-jerking story to bring him back home on one of their infallible ships. Once disembarked on native soil, Odysseus, still going incognito, relates the false account of how he, a Cretan pirate, was tricked by a Phoenician. The story is supposed to resonate with Eumaeus, Odysseus' loyal swineherd, who was kidnapped as a child by his Phoenician nurse, seduced by a merchant from Sidon. Joyce's continuous reference to the Phoenicians in "Eumaeus" remains implicit, but the allusions are anything but subtle. In the intertextual network of asymmetrical parallels and skewed correspondences, Bloom is unable to hitch a ride because a cab ignores his beckoning. The taxi is parked in front of the North Star Hotel, a clear reference to the Phoenician Star, as Polaris was called in antiquity. The other protagonist of the episode

---

[24] Gayle Rogers has shown how Molly's Gibraltar is a Europe "of multiethnic, multilingual subject formation portable to his European Dublin." Rogers has argued that Joyce tried to "renovat[e] the category of 'Europe' not by submitting to its hegemony but by infusing it with their locally grounded cosmopolitanisms" with places like Gibraltar, where Joyce connects Hispanicity with a Mediterranean dimension of Arab, Jewish, and Hellenic traditions that came to Ireland through Spain. *Modernism and the New Spain: Britain, Cosmopolitan Europe, and Literary History* (New York: Oxford University Press, 2012), 92–93.

is W. B. Murphy, a red-bearded mariner, who spins his seaman's yarn to an increasingly doubtful audience of late-night city wanderers. The less-than-convincing and hence failing Phoenician tales of this drunken sailor include the story of a murder he allegedly witnessed in the notorious port of Trieste. The story of the fatal knifing is, on the surface, believable given the precedent of Winckelmann's death, to which Joyce is probably referring. Pressed to offer details, Murphy remains evasive on questions that may expose his lies, such as Bloom's inquiry on whether he has seen Europa Point in Gibraltar. Joyce will explore on a grander scale the nocturnal fantasies that Bloom produces in "Circe" and the Phoenician lore of "Eumaeus" in the oneiric world of *Finnegans Wake*, the dark book of the night, where a subversive sequence of dreams challenges the official syntax and grammar of daytime life, as well as the repressive authority of nations and empires.

Europe Minor

In *Finnegans Wake*, young Europe embodies one of the many semantically cloaked and morphologically blurred dramatis personae of the narration. Ferrero's discussion of the interconnection between sexual violence and colonial conquest in *Young Europe* informs Joyce's construction of the maiden. At the very inception of the work, the semantic coordinates of young Europe oscillate between geographic expression and fictional character. The opening lines introduce a seafaring Tristan, embarked upon a quest of dubious romance and warfare: "Sir Tristram, violer d'amores, fr'over the short sea, had passencore rearrived from North Armorica on this side the scraggy isthmus of Europe Minor to wielderfight his penisolate war" (*FW* 3.4–6). Tristan's epithet is indicative of an amorous violator. Sexual violence is also suggested in the image of a recurrent (German *wieder*) wielding of a penis, the male member brandished like a sword in battle. The *Wake* constantly envisions the human body as an inscribable map, which makes it possible to read "Europe Minor" as a geographic expression and its own personification at the same time. Europa's oscillation between onomastics and geography appears to be analogous to Homeric Greek and its "anthropomorphic interpretation of Phoenician toponymy" that Stuart Gilbert identifies in his early commentary on *Ulysses*.[25] In fact, while Europe indicates a young maiden in Greek mythology, its etymology derives from the Phoenician term *ereb*, "the land of the setting sun," thus indicating the West. Joyce was aware of the Phoenician toponymic etymology of Europa: "The phaynix rose a sun before Erebia sank his

---

[25] Stuart Gilbert, *James Joyce's Ulysses: A Study* (New York: Vintage, 1952), 223.

smother!" (*FW* 473.16) "Europe Minor" also indicates the region of Asia Minor, associated with the expression "Phenicia or Little Asia" (*FW* 68.29) that occurs later in the text. The expression also cues the maiden Europa as a transfiguration of ALP/Issy/Iseult. In the text, the erotic tension between land and sea reaches its climax in the archetypical violence perpetrated on Europe's raped and colonized body. In physical geography, an isthmus is a thin strip of land in a larger body of water that connects two territories. The "scraggy isthmus of Europe Minor," the place where the sexual warfare is waged, is evocative of Europa's hymen, the very locus of male sexual violence.

Ferrero's *Europa giovane* materializes as Europe Minor, and returns in Shaun's vilification of his brother Shem. Shaun accuses his sibling "Shem Skrivenitch" (*FW* 423.15) of having contracted a disease: "Then he caught the europicolas and went into the society of jewses. With Bro Cahlls and Fran Czeschs and Bruda Pszths and Brat Slavos" (*FW* 423.36–424.1). The "europicolas" are an allusion to Ferrero's work, but also a pun on *Il Piccolo*, the Triestine daily newspaper in which the Italian historian, and also Joyce, published a series of articles. The "society of jewses" mixes Jesuits and Jews, pointing at the religious diversity of Habsburg Trieste. Shaun's accusation of European internationalism is framed as an infectious disease, a syndrome that makes Shem an outcast. Shem joins the "European family" (*U* 12.1202) presented as an interethnic brotherhood. The prefixes "Fra-(n)," "Bro," "Brud," and "Brat" are all variations on the Indo-European root *bhrā́ter, meaning brother. The expression "Fran Czeschs" is suggestive of the Italian *francese* and also Czech brother. "Bruda Pszths" and "Brat Slavos" are a pun on a Slavic brotherhood and the Habsburg cities of Budapest and Bratislava.

To Ferrero, Ovid was not only the "poet of rakes and mistresses" but also the literary interpreter of Rome's rise to geopolitical prominence in the Mediterranean.[26] Joyce was receptive to this political reading of the Latin poet. In Books 2 and 3 of the *Metamorphoses*, Ovid places the mythical account within a frame of Rome's military history.[27] Ovid's source for the Europa episode was the abovementioned Sicilian Greek poet Moschus, who thematized in a short poem the early encounter between Greeks and Phoenicians. Moschus was drawing inspiration from contemporary exchanges between the Greek colonial settlements

---

[26] Ferrero, *Grandezza* 5: 303.
[27] R. J. Schork stresses how many of the undetected references to Ovid in *Finnegans Wake* are "highly camouflaged," requiring an "exercise in literary archaeology." R. J. Schork, *Latin and Roman Culture in Joyce* (Gainesville: University of Florida Press, 1997), 154–158.

in Eastern Sicily and Phoenician trading posts located in the Western part of the island. Similarly, Ovid gave mythical and poetic substance to Rome's colonization of Ptolemaic Egypt that included Phoenician territories. The victory at the Battle of Actium (31 BCE) secured these territories for Rome. In addition, the Punic wars against the Phoenician city Carthage, waged two centuries before Ovid's time, were still a vivid part of the cultural imagination in Rome. As we have already seen, some thirty years before Ovid's poem, Vergil had fictionalized the Roman-Phoenician encounter through Aeneas and Dido of Carthage in the *Aeneid*. Given their status as economic and military archenemy, capable of threatening the geopolitical integrity of the Empire, the presence of Phoenician figures in Ovid's poem constitutes a political subtext for discourses associated with colonial dominance.

Let us briefly recall the myth. According to Ovid, Europa is the daughter of Agenor, the Phoenician king of Tyre. She is a beautiful maiden whose comeliness attracts the attention of Jupiter. One day, as the virgin is playing along the shore, the god metamorphoses into a snow-white bull and browses around her. The girl is struck by the docility of the handsome bull, and once she overcomes her initial diffidence she pets the animal, plays with it, and adorns its horns with flowers. While playing, the tame bull reclines and invites the princess to mount its back. In a sudden move, bovine-shaped Jupiter runs off with the virgin on his back and swims to Crete. There, according to various other mythographers, she will bear him two (Minos and Rhadamanthus) or three sons (including Sarpedon).

Ovid's poetic narration of the divine abduction, however, does not terminate at Europa's seizure, but continues to recount the aftermath of the rape, which coincides with the Phoenician foundation of Thebes. In Ovid's seamless narrative continuum, Cadmus's colonization represents an episode in its own right, but also serves as an explicatory appendix to the rape of Europa, providing an interpretative key to Jove's abduction in the preceding episode. Agenor sends out Europa's brother Cadmus in order to find her, admonishing his son that if he fails to find his sister, he will be banished into exile. Cadmus' search is fruitless, and given his status of expatriate, he looks for a land to colonize. The oracle of Phoebus Apollo advises him to look for a heifer, one that has not yet known the yoke and has not penetrated the earth with a curved plow. According to the oracle, he should follow the young cow and build his home where she finally rests. When the heifer at last lies down, Cadmus kisses the foreign earth and honors the unknown landscape. He promptly discovers a virgin timber that conceals a cave with an underground source of fresh water. With the swift narrative pace of Ovid's poem, the following episode already leads into the process of colonization of Thebes. The heifer that Cadmus follows is clearly a mythic transfiguration, an implicit and tacit metamorphosis of Europa herself. Both are virgins and both are mates for a bull. When Cadmus finds the heifer, he symbolically accomplishes his mission since, after all, finding the mate for a bull was the ultimate goal of his explorative journey. Cadmus's quest is described through a pervasive sexual imagery. The heifer is explicitly described as not having borne the yoke, one that has "not broken up the earth with a curved plow" (*Met.* 3, 14–15). The earth is coded as a female body, as he kisses the ground and the underground cave, a uterine symbol, conceals water, an image of vaginal liquid and one more generally signifying the fertility of the soil. The plow breaking up the earth is highly suggestive of sexual violence. The image of the yoke, similarly, unambiguously suggests colonial subjugation. Agenor and Cadmus proceed according to a misogynist and colonial logic that operates in a fashion parallel to Jupiter's ethnic rape of Phoenician Europa. Her impregnation will give life to Greek individuals, not to barbarians.

A close reader of Ovid, Joyce exploited the colonial subtext of this myth in order to draw a Viconian parallel, a historic *ricorso*, between Phoenician and Irish colonial histories. In the *Wake*, the episode is placed within the context of a parody of the *Annals of the Four Masters*, who undergo a textual metempsychosis and reappear in the Mamalujo quartet, the novel's version of the four canonical Evangelists. In *Criminal Woman*, Ferrero indicated Herodotus as a source for sexual mores in antiquity. Not surprisingly, then, the source for Joyce's poetic history is the "herodotary Mammon Lujius in his grand old historiorum" (*FW* 13.20–21). The term "herodotary" conflates the ancient historian Herodotus with notions of heredity and erudition. Herodotus's historiography famously chronicled the introduction of Egyptian and Phoenician civilization to Greece. The ancient historian recognizes a factual event behind the myth of Europa's rape: "Some Greeks landed at Tyre in Phoenicia and abducted the king's daughter Europa. The Persian sources are not in a position to name these Greeks, but they were presumably Cretans."[28] This episode is part of Herodotus' introduction to the Persian wars, in which the abduction of four mythical women constitutes the origin of military conflicts. The four abducted women were Io of Argos by Phoenician traders, the Phoenician princess Europa by Cretans, Medea at the hands of a crew led by Jason, and Helen by the Trojan prince Paris. From the note sheets that Joyce prepared for the composition of *Ulysses*, we know that Joyce had taken notes from the initial pages of Herodotus' *Histories* interpreting the abduction theme

---

[28] Herodotus, *The Histories* (Oxford: Oxford University Press, 1998), 3.

as a Phoenician version of the rape of Helen.[29] The association between rape and colonial conquest is central to the annals passage, worth quoting at length:

> 1132 A.D. Men like to ants or emmets wondern upon a groot hwide Whallfisk which lay in a Runnel. Blubby wares upat Ublanium.
>
> 566 A.D. On Baalfire's night of this year after deluge a crone that hadde a wickered Kish for to hale dead turves from the bog lookit under the blay of her Kish as she ran for to sothisfeige her cowrieosity and be me sawl but she found hersell sackvulle of swart goody quickenshoon and small illigant brogues, so rich in sweat. Blurry works at Hurdlesford.
>
> (Silent.)
>
> 566 A.D. At this time it fell out that a brazenlockt damsel grieved (*sobralasolas!*) because that Puppette her minion was ravisht of her by the ogre Puropeus Pious. Bloody wars in Ballyaughacleeaghbally.
>
> 1132 A.D. Two sons at an hour were born until a goodman and his hag. These sons called themselves Caddy and Primas. Primas was a santryman and drilled all decent people. Caddy went to Winehouse and wrote o peace a farce. Blotty words for Dublin. (*FW* 13.33–14.15)

Devoid of a distinct and linear chronology, the quadripartite structure of the chronicle indicates the record of four different versions of the same mytho-historical event. The chiastic disposition of the narration stages two competing versions of the respectively consensual and forced sexual encounters. The first and fourth vignettes appear to function as a prologue, signaling the arrival of the foreigner, and the aftermath, i.e., the birth of offspring, to the coitus proper.

The dates 1132 and 566 AD, while alluding to events in Irish history, provide clues to a blurry and uncertain time continuum, suspended between competing chronologies, gaps in the timeline, and numerical symbology. Throughout the text the number 1132 is associated with

---

[29] See R. J. Schork, *Greek and Hellenic Culture in Joyce* (Gainesville: University of Florida Press, 1998), 20. Joyce's treatment of the Phoenicians in *Finnegans Wake* is usually studied in the context of Joyce's reception of the classical world. When scholars discuss the *Wake* in conjunction with contemporary racial thought and Fascism, the Phoenicians are rarely, if at all, mentioned. See, for instance, Len Platt, *Joyce, Race and Finnegans Wake* (Cambridge: Cambridge University Press, 2007).

virility and its numeric half 566 stands for a female principle. For all their symbolic meaning, the dates provide important thematic clues. The setting is clearly Dublin, as each of the four versions of the toponym indicates. "Ublanium" evokes the ancient settlement of Eblana, but also suggests the notion of oblivion. "Ballyaughacleeaghbally" indicates the ancient Gaelic name of the city, Baile Átha Cliath, meaning Town of the Ford of Hurdles. 566 AD is the year in which the Irish High Kings Domnall and Forggus mac Muirchertaig, who reigned jointly, die in a battle close to the Liffey. Laurence O'Toole, the patron saint of Dublin, was born in 1132. In 1132, Diarmaid mac Murchadha, also known as Dermot Macmurrough, Irish king of the province of Leinster, burned the abbey at Kildare and ordered the rape of the abbess. In his attempt to become High King of Ireland, Dermot sought English help. Taking advantage of the political and military instability of Ireland, the English king Henry II was convinced to invade Ireland. Traditional readings consider Dermot responsible for the English invasion and thus a betrayer of the Irish cause. Catholic defenders of Dermot took a more moderate stance, emphasizing his association with Church reform. In fact, in the same year St. Malachy is consecrated archbishop of Armagh, with the intent to impose Roman liturgy on the independent Irish Church. 1132 is the year in which Ireland becomes "servant of two masters ... an English and an Italian" (*U* 1.638).

Vico's archetypical family articulates the cyclical recurrence of these historical patterns associated with patriarchy, incest, and misery in the vicissitudes of Humphrey Chimpden Earwicker, aka HCE, and ALP, Issy, Shem, and Shaun. This historical chronicle narrates "cycles of events grand and national" (*FW* 13.31–32) assuming the features of a creative storytelling, constantly playing a variation on the themes in a spiral timeline, always producing "another tellmastory repeating yourself" (*FW* 397.7–8). The *Wake*'s poetic chronicle is not solely indebted to Vico's philosophy of history based on the cyclical returns of social configurations. Ferrero's historiographic methodology, in evident conversation with Vico, emphasizes the recognition of parallel patterns between the present and the past as a crucial instrument for the deeper understanding of contemporary history.[30] Joyce's reading of Ferrero reinforces the status of Vico in the *Wake*. The archetypical coitus occurs between a male principle, associated through HCE with patriarchal and colonial violence, and a female principle, embodied by the "daughter-wife" (*FW* 627.2) cluster of ALP/Issy. Underneath the morpho-semantic encrustations of the language and a family structure of systematically

---

[30] For Joyce's view of the cyclical nature of history in the episode, see Thomas Hofheinz, *Joyce and the Invention of Irish History: Finnegans Wake in Context* (Cambridge: Cambridge University Press, 1995), 106.

metamorphosing characters, one can extrapolate yet another underlying narrative nucleus. The mythical rape of Hiberno-Punic Europa, perpetrated by the ogre and placed in the prehistory of Ireland, foreshadows the sexual union of an Irish woman with a foreign master. In the annals passage, Europa is associated with both Issy and ALP: the former inasmuch as she represents a young maiden, the latter for her childbearing attribute.

Joyce, however, is far from simply lamenting Ireland's status of colonial victim. The two sections dated 566 AD describe the same scene (hence the same date) but from different perspectives. Joyce introduces a double vision of Irish history, presenting his own annals as a mythopoetic record that puts into focus two competing interpretations. The term "silence" represents the axis of symmetry and functions like a mirror between the two sections. In the first section, one can observe a Europa seeking out the sexual encounter, a Europa willing to be done, probably a female version of the Duke of Willingdone. The following section is indeed a mirror-like distortion of the preceding narrative. Joyce places Ireland's collaboration first, giving in this way priority to a revisionist approach to Irish history. The author depicts the complicity of Ireland in its own colonization before he emphasizes the rape of Europa.

In the expression "Baalfire's night" Joyce inserts a Nordic layer in an already existing context of cultural and religious syncretism between the Phoenician and Roman worlds. Baal is a Semitic fertility god and the name of several kings of the Phoenician city Tyre, home city of Europa. In Heliopolis of Phoenicia, today the Lebanese city of Baalbek, a temple dedicated to the syncretic deity Jupiter-Baal, also known as the Heliopolitan Zeus, was built when the Romans colonized the city in the first century CE.[31] The nexus linking Roman Jupiter to Phoenician Baal is the common tradition of their auxiliary bovine nature, a common characteristic among bull-worshipping cultures in ancient Mediterranean traditions.[32] The vowels in the term "Baal" suggest the Hebrew letter aleph, the pictographic image of which is the bull or ox. The association between the letter aleph and the bull reappears later in the character of "Olaph the Oxman" (*FW* 132.17–18), a spin on the Northern "Oxman" (*FW* 15.6) and the metonymic toponomy of "Oxmanstown" (*FW* 47.24), suggestive of North Bull Island in Dublin Bay. "Baalfire's night" also suggests Walpurgis Night, the Northern European fertility rite celebrated at the beginning of spring with nightly bonfires.

---

[31] In the *Wake*, the city of Baalbek figures as "Bullbeck" (*FW* 627.2).
[32] Besides the Greek and Roman traditions, bull cults are present in Egyptian, Minoan, Mesopotamian, and Ugaritic cultures. In Ugaritic mythology, particularly, Baal lies with his sister Anat, a virgin goddess of fertility, who bears him a son in the form of an ox.

It is probable that Joyce was aware of William Betham's comparative analysis of Gaels and Phoenicians. A member of Irish antiquarianism to which Vallancey also belonged, Betham proposed one of the bizarre Gaelic-Semitic etymologies. He argued that the term Baal had the exact same meaning in Gaelic and Phoenician, namely "lord of heaven."[33] Baal is thus presented as an Irish-Semitic god, the "bog," Slovenian for god, to whose sexual prowess the "Kish," from the Hungarian adjective *kis* meaning "little," succumbs.

The annals continue to record the sexual encounter between Europa and the foreigner. Ferrero's account of hospitable and sacred prostitution, described as a customary practice among the Phoenicians in *Criminal Woman*, provides the cultural coordinates for the characters' behavior in this first section, dated 566 AD. The crone is pushing her daughter to hail and welcome the divinity, suggesting that the mother looks favorably upon her daughter's sexual encounter. The alteration of "herself" into "hersell" strongly reinforces the notion of ritualized prostitution. Europa is eager to offer her sexual favors, for which she receives a dowry of shoes and elegant robes. This version symbolically represents an Ireland cooperative in its own colonization, receiving only a meager compensation in the economic transaction. The outcome of this sexual encounter is a pregnancy: "she found hersell sackvulle" indicating that she was full of seed from his scrotum (*Hodensack* in German), but also gifted with a dowry, in the form of a sack full of black (swart from the German *schwarz*) and elegant shoes. The sack of goods she receives alludes to Ferrero's passage in *Militarism*, in which the Phoenician women buy a specimen of the merchant, believing, in the words of Ferrero, that they satisfied an innocent desire. Since the merchant's treasure-bag was inexhaustible, always producing new items to purchase, the temptation to indulge in them grew continuously.[34] "Shoon" is an archaic plural for shoes, whereas brogues were heavy leather shoes worn in Ireland. The term "brogue" also indicates a strong Irish accent in English, indicative of the Gaelic substratum of the Hibernian dialect. In the "Finnegan's Wake" ballad, Tim Finnegan is said to have "a beautiful brogue, so rich and sweet."[35] The Hiberno-English intonation is another clue suggesting a colonial dynamic.

---

[33] William Betham, *The Gael and Cymbri: Or an Inquiry into the Origin and History of the Irish Scoti, Britons, and Gauls* (Dublin: W. Curry, 1834), 226.
[34] Ferrero, *Militarism*, 300.
[35] There are several versions of the ballad that slightly differ from each other. In the version quoted by Patricia Hutchins, Tim Finnegan has "a beautiful brogue, so rich and sweet." Patricia Hutchins, *James Joyce's World* (London: Methuen, 1957), 214. Richard Ellmann, and with him the majority of Joyce scholars, rely on a version that reads, "He had a tongue both rich and sweet." Richard Ellmann, *James Joyce* (New York: Oxford University Press, 1982), 543.

For their intercourse, the maiden approaches the bull in order to "sothisfeige her cowrieosity" (*FW* 14.2–3). This portmanteau registers a confluence of manifold meanings. McHugh's annotations suggest that Sothis is the Egyptian name of Sirius, the star of Isis. The cow would consequently be the cow that is sacred to Isis.[36] More meanings, however, can be extracted. First of all, the expression is a phonological distortion suggesting the phrase "to satisfy her curiosity," while at the same time indicating her bovine nature. The phrase again emphasizes her active role in the sexual encounter. It is likely that Joyce had also read about Europa taking the initiative in Wilhelm Roscher's encyclopaedia of classical mythology, which the author had consulted. In Roscher, the entry concerning Europa stresses her audacity, depicting her as courageous and daring: "Europa, the most beautiful and audacious of all, [who] even dares to sit on the back of the handsome animal."[37] The term "cowrieosity" can be glossed in two ways, indicating a cow and at the same time a cowrie. Her bovine nature makes Europa the appropriate match for the bull, with whom she can satisfy her curiosity and sexual appetite. I shall discuss Europa's cowlike reappearance in the text shortly. For now, suffice it to say that the maiden's characterization as a cowrie is yet another element that identifies her as Phoenician Europa. As discussed in previous chapters, the Phoenicians produced their highly priced purple dye from a cowrie—the marine gastropod *Murex brandaris*. Accordingly, Issy/Europa later makes another veiled appearance in the text as the "purple cardinal's princess" and "cowmate" (*FW* 243.30 and 32).

In the section described as "annadominant" (*FW* 14.17), Europa is described as a "brazenlockt damsel." This marks a shift from her bold initiative. Chastity takes the place of her audacity if we take the expression as suggestive of brass-locked, the description of the closing mechanism of a chastity belt. The term damsel is evocative of medieval courtly love and the ideal of a distant and unreachable lady. She expresses her grief *sobre las olas*, "above the waves," another reference to the ancient myth in which Europa is taken across the sea to the island of Crete. In this passage, Joyce masterfully stages the paradox of multiplying the identities of the god and the girl while at the same time stripping them of any secondary traits, attaining a minimalist reduction to their sexual

---

[36] Roland McHugh, *Annotations to Finnegans Wake* (Baltimore, MD: Johns Hopkins University Press, 2016), 14.
[37] My translation. "Europa, die schönste und übermütigste von allen, [welche] es sogar wagt, sich auf den Rücken des reizenden Tieres zu setzen." Wilhelm Heinrich Roscher et al., eds. *Ausführliches Lexikon der griechischen und römischen Mythologie*, 6 vols (Leipzig: B. G. Teubner, 1884–1937), 1: 1410.

organs. Rapist and victim, the "ogre Puropeus Pious" and "her minion" are reduced to a penis (*peos* in Greek) and a vulva (*mouni* in Greek).

The raping god is presented as "Puropeus Pious," a pun that signals the convergence of Vico and Nietzsche as primary sources. The pure and pious qualities of the god hint at Vico's religious wars of the Heroic Age, characterized with the Latin formula *pura et pia bella* in the *New Science*.[38] This reference to Vico, however, is a successive layer that Joyce added. The earliest version of this passage reads "Europeus Pius," an allusion to Nietzsche's notion of the "good European" echoed in the "goodman and his hag" (*FW* 14.11–12).[39] Their union produces the birth of Caddy and Primas, mythic precursors of Shem and Shaun and embodiments of the tension between Ireland and its colonial masters. Once again, Joyce makes a Phoenician character prefigure an Irish one. The prehistoric Caddy—whose name is a diminutive for Cadmus, Europa's mythological brother—appears as a pacifist author and thus foreshadows the later appearance of Shem the Penman. Shem's rival brother Shaun undergoes a dual characterization as a belligerent archbishop—the Primate drilling all decent people—who personifies Ireland's two masters, in the form of English military aggression and the ecclesiastical power of the Catholic Church.

In a text rich with transhistorical and interpenetrating personalities, where everyone has their own "multiple Mes" (*FW* 410.12), the Phoenician/Irish maiden undergoes a "doublin" (*FW* 3.8, 578.14), a metamorphosis from a female and ravished Europa into a male ravisher Europe. In this way, young Europa is paradoxically ravished by her own masculine double, by that "Puropeus Pious" who epitomizes the colonial imagination of a European imperial project. The masculine metamorphosis of Europa into Europe occurs via a transgendering process. Since the Phoenicians are associated with the ancient clothing trade, this transformation occurs through transvestitism. The maiden puts on different clothes; Europe becomes "Newrobe" (*FW* 155.5), a new Europe through a new robe. Cross-dressing constitutes an underlying subtext in different episodes of the *Wake*, a recurrent leitmotif whose overtones are associated with Europe's double characterization as male and female. Ferrero's description of Phoenician religious sexuality provided Joyce with the historical background of this transformation. The historian recounts how in the major Phoenician cities, including Tyre and Sidon, the temples of the goddess Astarte were consecrated

---

[38] Gimbattista Vico, *The New Science. Principles of the New Science concerning the Common Nature of Nations* (New York: Penguin Classics, 2001), 958.
[39] James Joyce, *A First-Draft Version of Finnegans Wake* (Austin: University of Texas Press, 1963), 53.

to the practice of sacred prostitution. Her statues depicted the goddess with both male and female sexual organs to signify the cross-dressing of men into women, and women into men, during the celebration of the goddess's nocturnal festivals.[40] In the "Burrus and Caseous" episode, which will be discussed in more detail shortly, Europe the "new robe," despite being a *"seducente infanta,"* is unable to "conceal her own more mascular personality by flaunting frivolish finery over men's inside clothes, for the femininny of that totamulier will always lack the musculink of a verumvirum" (*FW* 166.23–26). The ambiguous status of Europa's androgynous character cluster is suspended between the poles of a masculine and aggressive militarism associated with the bull and a feminine, pacifist anti-colonialism associated with the image of the cow. Depending on her dress code, Europa can assume a more feminine personality to hide the masculine aspects of her character, even though as a total woman she lacks true virility. Clothes and militarism are also associated in ALP's letter. The envelope of ALP's letter "exhibits only the civil or military clothing of whatever passionpallid nudity or plaguepurple nakedness may happen to tuck itself under its flap" (*FW* 109.10–13). ALP's letter, clothed by a semitransparent envelope, is an overwritten palimpsest from which only fragments of Europa's tale can be recognized. The "military clothing" and "plaguepurple nakedness" are the vestigial traces of the rape of Phoenician Europa.

The bull and the cow make a systematic return in the text. The metempsychotic reincarnation of archetypes in history associates the figure of the bull with colonial conquest as can be seen with "Ivaun the Tauribble" (*FW* 138.17), a condensation of Ivan the Terrible and a *taurus*, which is Greek and Latin for bull. Another association between military conquest and a bull is made in the passage that introduces "Ussur Ursussen of the viktaurious onrush," described "as bold and as madhouse a bull in a meadows" (*FW* 353.12–13). A few lines down, this "viktaurious bull" is described as "Deo Jupto" (*FW* 353.18), as the raping Jupiter/ Zeus. In the archetypical bull one cannot help but also recognize a zoomorphic adaptation of John Bull, the personification of England in late nineteenth- and early twentieth-century propaganda, as well as a comment on the papal bull *Laudabiliter* that in 1155 sanctioned the English invasion of Ireland. In that year, Ireland was "bulledicted" (*FW* 458.3) to English rule.

---

[40] "I templi della dea Astarte a Tiro, a Sidone e nelle principali città della Fenicia, erano consacrati alla prostituzione: Astarte nelle sue statue scolpiva gli organi maschili e femminili a significare il travestirsi degli uomini in donna, e delle donne in uomini, allorchè celebravansi le notturne feste della Dea." Lombroso and Ferrero, *Donna delinquente*, 221.

Next to the recurrent image of the bull, the cow makes several appearances in the course of the text. Europa has to be "Playing bull before shebears" (*FW* 522.15), meaning that she has to become a bull before she can bear his children. Later, the theme of a young Europe, carried over the sea and bearing the offspring of a bull, returns in a passage in which a sympathetic narrative voice says, "Poor little tartanelle, her dinties are chattering, the strait's she's in, the bulloge she bears!" (*FW* 583.3–4). The "cowrymaid" (*FW* 164.8) appears as a maternal figure for later appearances such as "Sweet Margareen" (*FW* 164.19) and the brothers "Burrus and Caseous" (*FW* 165.12).[41] The offspring of the cow-maid, respectively butter and cheese, are personified dairy products. These multifaceted names combine matrilineal genealogy with a patrilineal logic of descent. While the children retain maternal characteristics in their names, Europa's union with the Ovid-inspired Jupiter produces avatars of Brutus and Cassius, markedly Roman offspring. Burrus is presented as "full of natural greace" and quite paradoxically also as "obsoletely unadulterous" (*FW* 161.16 and 17). Burrus is full of grease—as well as full of grace like the Virgin—and absolutely unadulterated. But then, this unadulterated state appears to also be obsolete. This adulterating mixture of butter with grease is already foreshadowed by the accusations made to HCE in chapter 1.3. Among the 111 allegations figures the claim that he mixes butter with grease: "*Grease with the Butter*" (*FW* 71.13). When the rumors about HCE's transgressions attain international scope in the "Casaconcordia" (*FW* 54.10), he is accused of dishonest business practices that take the form of "cowhaendel" (*FW* 54.27). The term suggests the German *Kuhhandel*, literally "cow-business," that indicates devious bartering exchanges. Burrus's sibling Caseous is "obversely the revise" (*FW* 161.18) of his brother. The Phoenician origin of the offspring of Europa as a "cowrymaid" is emphasized twice in the "Burrus and Caseous" episode. First in the sentence: "The older sisars (Tyrants, regicide is too good for you!) become unbeurrable from age" (*FW* 162.1–2). The two Caesars become Tyrants and unbearable, with a pun of the French *beurre*, "butter." The term "Tyrants" is to be understood in two ways: in the sense of oppressor, but also in the sense of being citizens of the Phoenician city Tyre, legendary birthplace of Europa. The same concept is reiterated shortly afterwards, in the passage "Caseous, the brutherscutch or puir tyron" (*FW* 163.8–9). These references to the Phoenician city Tyre conveniently overlap with Tyrone, one of the traditional counties of Ireland. In this

---

[41] This morphological reconstruction contradicts Schork's assertion, according to which "[it] would be pushing allusions to the limits to claim that 'cowrymaid' ... refers to the metamorphosis of Io." Schork, *Greek*, 2.

expression, Joyce makes Phoenicia and Ireland overlap again. At this point it is probably useful to bear in mind that the etymology of the term "butter" mediated through Germanic languages derives from the Latin *butyrum*, borrowed from the Greek *boutyron*, which appears to be a combination of *bous*, "ox, cow," and *tyros*, "cheese." Joyce must have been aware of this etymology and exploited it for the construction of the children and Shem, Shaun, and Issy that here become Burrus, Caseous, and the mother/sister Margareen (*FW* 164.14).

This "emended food theory" (*FW* 163.35–36) that regulates the interpersonal dynamics of the family with a pronounced "eatusup complex" (*FW* 128.36) is linked to the Habsburg Empire and Europe. The Austro-Hungarian monarchy becomes "old Auster and Hungrig" (*FW* 464.27–28), Joyce's own comment on his precarious life in Trieste and the meager food supply in the early years of his stay on the Adriatic. Given that in Trieste Joyce and his partner and future wife Nora lived well beyond their means, at the expense of his brother Stanislaus, it seems likely that the oysters (German *Austern*) mentioned refer to the lavish spending the couple indulged in whenever the possibility arose. The ghostly appearance of the crumbled Habsburg Empire is regulated by a recurrent cycle of destruction and Phoenix-like resurrection, since history "moves in vicous cicles yet remews the same" (*FW* 134.16–17). Joyce's last work is not only the wake for Finnegan, but also "the wrake of the hapspurus" (*FW* 557.6). While the expressions cues Henry Longfellow's poem "The Wreck of the Hesperus," it also suggests the "wake of the Hapsburgs," in terms of a funeral, or "funforall" (*FW* 458.22), and the wreckage of the Austrian monarchy. After the demise of imperial Habsburg, Joyce envisions the possibility of a resurrection of the multicultural and polyglot state, as becomes clear in the expression "Osterich, the U.S.E." (*FW* 70.1). Here Joyce makes the explicit connection between *Österreich*, i.e., Austria, and the United States of Europe. Joyce's stay in Central Europe, or "Zentral Oylrubber" (*FW* 69.36), has informed Shem's preference to "far sooner muddle through the hash of lentils in Europe than meddle with Irrland's split little pea" (*FW* 171.5–6). Joyce's description of the European empire and Ireland in terms of victuals suggests an association with the basic alimentary concerns of a writer who had lived through days without food in Trieste.

The Phoenician Wakes

The Irish-Phoenician Europa myth represents a foundational episode in Joyce's Wakean history, an archetypical *figura* that cast a long shadow in the text. Joyce indeed conceives of *Finnegans Wake* as the textual locus where "the Phoenician wakes" (*FW* 608.32). In the archeology of myths that builds the narrative foundation of the text, Joyce's Phoenician-Irish genealogy does not simply inform the numerous subterranean plots of the novel. Excavating the multiple textual layers reveals a buried architecture that systematically supports and organizes the development of the narration, a structural framework whose prominence matches the importance of other constitutional fundaments of the book, from Dublin's topography to Vico's philosophy of history, from the Western literary canon to Freudian and Jungian psychoanalysis, from ancient Egyptian funerary rites to the sacred texts of world religions.[42] The *Wake* insists on the Semitic substratum of Irish Gaelic lore, a lineage that makes its appearance in all key episodes of the text, from foundational myths and events to historical figures and places to the point in which the ethnic and geographic distinctions between Ireland and Phoenicia are intertwined, blurred, and often become undistinguishable. One such figure is "Hannibal mac Hamiltan the Hegerite" (*FW* 274. 9–10), a Phoenician-Irish archetypical warrior-navigator.[43] In this spirit, Joyce rewrites the mythical Tír na nÓg, the Celtic otherworld and home of the Irish pantheon of the Tuatha Dé Danann, as "Tyre-nan-Og" (*FW* 91.25–26), fashioning the legendary land of youth and bounty into Europa's Phoenician hometown. In medieval Irish literature, the Tír na nÓg was a realm west of Ireland, located underneath the water. Access was possible via navigation or by diving underwater, which in the *Wake* becomes "to return to the atlantic and Phenitia proper" (*FW* 85.20), a formula that also indicates Tristan's recurrent homecoming to Dublin. His vessel reemerges at later stages both as a "punic judgeship" (*FW* 90.36) and the "gran Phenician rover" (*FW* 197.31).

Joyce presents the Semitic ancestors of the Irish according to a tripartite configuration as Canaanite, Phoenician, and Carthaginian. These three phases replicate the three stages of civilization of Vico's cyclical history: the divine, the heroic, and the human. The Irish represent the fourth age, the *ricorso*. This means that we should read the references to Canaanites, Phoenicians, and Carthaginians in the text as indications of a pervasive writing of Irish history. Not surprisingly, this threefold identity appears early on, in the section that details the story of how the protagonist Humphrey Chimpden Earwicker received his name. In an episode rich in references to nautical matters, HCE appears in front of King William IV, called here by his nickname "Our sailor king"

---

[42] John Bishop, who explores the nocturnal and oneiric dimension of the *Wake*, sees a parallel between Vico's "Poetic Wisdom" and Freud's unconscious. In the same way that Vico describes the logic of irrational and animalistic humans who gave rise to the subsequent evolution of history and human consciousness, Bishop argues, Freud employs psychoanalysis to gauge the irrational drives that shape personal history. John Bishop, *Joyce's Book of the Dark: Finnegans Wake* (Madison: University of Wisconsin Press, 1986), 185.

[43] In the night lessons, Issy's footnote suggests that he is a "gnative of Genuas" (*FW* 274.34). This Genoese origin conflates him with another famous navigator, namely Christopher Columbus.

(*FW* 31.11), an epithet the monarch earned as Lord High Admiral of the Royal Navy. As readers of Joyce know, in the episode HCE explains to the king that he carries a pot to catch earwigs. Amused and smiling under "his walrus moustaches" (FW 31.13), the king addresses two members of his entourage, one of whom is "an Italian excellency named Giubilei according to a later version cited by the learned scholarch Canavan of Canmakenoise" (FW 31.21–22). The figure of the erudite and majestic sage, the scholar-monarch, explicitly links Canaanites with the Irish monastery of Clonmacnoise while associating Trieste with the Phoenicians. Canavan clearly signals Canaan (and caravan) but also renders, via metathesis, Cavana, the old and rowdy neighborhood in downtown Trieste, home to the red-light district in the city, where Joyce spent many a night drinking among sailors and prostitutes, and where the family lived for a while.

On a number of occasions, Earwicker is identified with the mythical Phoenix, the bird that cyclically dies and rises again. He is the "phoenix in our woodlessness, haughty, cacuminal, erubescent" with roots that are "asches" (*FW* 55.28–30). His travels are "the vaguum of the Phoenix" (*FW* 136.34–35), the wanderings (*vagus* in Latin) of the Phoenician. In the trial discussed below, we are able to recognize HCE because the initials of the following name spell out "Here Comes Everybody": "And with tumblerous legs, redipnominated Helmingham Erchenwyne Rutter Egbert Crumwall Odin Maximus Esme Saxon Esa Vercingetorix Ethelwulf Rupprecht Ydwalla Bentley Osmund Dysart Yggdrasselmann? Holy Saint Eiffel, the very phoenix!" (*FW* 88.20–24). In chapter 1.6, the long-winded answer in the first riddle associates HCE and the Irish mythological hero Finn MacCool with a flaming "phoenix" (*FW* 128.35 and 136.35). In the course of the first chapters, various figures accuse HCE of having committed an unnamed crime, an offence that may include an act of voyeurism, a sexual or incestuous transgression, indecent exposure, or possibly urination or defecation in public. The alleged and undefined transgression takes place in Phoenix Park, and the protagonist is described as a "foenix culprit" (*FW* 23.16), an ambiguous expression that puns on the Christian theological concept of the *felix culpa*, theorized by St. Augustine of Hippo, a city in the vicinity of Carthage.[44] In the economy of the text, the wrongdoing in Phoenix Park

---

[44] In her study of Joyce's use of Dante's linguistic and literary theories, Lucia Boldrini connects Phoenix Park with the theology of sin. The culpa undergoes a metonymic transformation into the "culprit," Adam and HCE, while Phoenix Park is assimilated to the Garden of Eden where the first, original sin was committed. Lucia Boldrini, *Joyce, Dante, and the Poetics of Literary Relations: Language and Meaning in Finnegans Wake* (Cambridge: Cambridge University Press, 2001), 73.

is a felicitous, albeit sinful, fault as it functions as a narrative catalyst. Precisely in the name of Phoenix Park, an estate located in the heart of Dublin, appears a serendipitous occasion of Phoenician and Celtic confluences. The origin of the term "Phoenix" in Phoenix Park derives from a mispronunciation of the Irish expression *fionn uishge*, meaning "clear water," from a pool of limpid water on site. Since 1747, the park has featured a prominent monument, a Phoenix rising from its ashes, elevated on a Corinthian column. Joyce was aware of the etymological corruption behind the park's name, as a letter to Harriet Shaw Weaver, dated August 14, 1927, shows. When Joyce asked the early readers of his work in progress to guess the title of what would develop into *Finnegans Wake*, Weaver speculated it would be "Phoenix Park." He told Weaver that her guess was "rather close" (*Letters* 3: 161), pointing to the association between the park and the novel as a whole. In antiquity, the Phoenix was often associated with the Phoenicians because of the phonetic similarities between the two terms and thus imagined as a purple-feathered bird. As a symbol of death and rebirth, the ever-renewing Phoenix is obviously a fitting representation of a textual universe governed by Vico's cyclical history. Joyce found the convergence of Phoenician-Gaelic etymologies amusing and was happy to exploit the defective translation of the Irish toponym for the *Wake*'s comedy of errors and mistakes, humanity's fall from divine grace, and the characterization of his much-maligned hero.

The slanderous rumors about HCE's alleged misconduct spread quickly, but the malevolent gossip is reportedly "as punical as finikin" (*FW* 32.6), as puny as it is finicky, hence inconsequential for the determination of his true character. The two terms, however, also suggest the exact opposite, as they point to a critical methodology of reading the *Wake*'s Phoenician subtext.[45] Events concerning the origin of Ireland are both Punic and Phoenician, a correspondence implying that we should regard Punic, i.e., Carthaginian, matters for what they really are, namely Phoenician and thus, by proxy, Irish. What is puny, and hence of little importance, is the difference between Phoenicians and their colony Carthage. Joyce plays again with Giordano Bruno's coincidence of opposites conflating the Phoenicians, peaceful traders in the

---

[45] Commenting on the wordplay of "pun" and "Punic," John Paul Riquelme attributes to the phrase great importance for the economy of the text: "Finnegan is not only a pun but Punic ... And that is why the name 'Finnegan' occurs as a plural as well as an implied possessive in Joyce's title. The awakening involves many Finnegans, many Phoenicians and their avatars, not just one, whom the author commands to arise." John Paul Riquelme, *Twists of the Teller's Tale in Joyce's Fiction: Oscillating Perspectives* (Baltimore, MD: The Johns Hopkins University Press, 1983), 32.

Mediterranean, with their more belligerent colony. The *Wake* seems to imply that what Phoenician Carthage was to the Roman Empire, Phoenician Ireland is to the British Empire. HCE's subsequent fall is in part ascribable to a certain belligerence in his character since he is "attracted by the norse of guns playing Delandy is cartager" (*FW* 64.2–3), a Nordic noise of gunshots playing, like an orchestra, a military march whose title replicates Cato the Elder's motto "Carthago delenda est," with which he campaigned for the destruction of Carthage.

The Punic Wars continue to figure prominently during HCE's trial, in chapter 1.4, a section rich in references to Carthaginian history. HCE falls asleep and rests in a sort of comatose slumber suggestive of his own death and interment in a vast burial ground that extends to include battlefields covered with fallen soldiers from different wars. In this underworld, he is faced with various forms of judgment. First, Humphrey Chimpden Earwicker is transfigured into "first pharoah, Humpheres Cheops Exarchas" (*FW* 62.20–21), defending himself with funerary spells and magic incantations from the chthonic adversaries of the ancient Egyptian afterlife. Then, the reader is invited, as we have seen, to "return to the atlantic and Phenicia proper" (FW 85.20), where the pharaonic HCE morphs into Festy King, standing trial in a chaotic court of law that fails to convict him, given the rambling and contradictory testimony of drunken plaintiffs. His struggle with untrustworthy accusers is reminiscent of the slander and defamation that was part of the psychological warfare in the conflict between Rome and Carthage. When his adversaries, "nuptial eagles [who] sharped their beaks of prey" (*FW* 80.21), allege that HCE has been sighted in "Phornix Park" (*FW* 80.6), a place of fornication, the narrator deems the rumors a question of "propagana fidies" (*FW* 80.20–21), an instance of the infamous *Punica fides*, as well as a perfidious propaganda that is disseminating a Christian faith corrupted to become a pro-pagan agenda. A whole crowd of rowdy detractors shouts at Festy in the courtroom, supporters of "local congsmen and donalds" who appear "in the shape of betterwomen with bowstrung hair of Carrothagenuine ruddiness, waving crimson petties and screaming from Isod's towertop" (*FW* 87.25–28). It is unclear whether these women are indeed Carthaginian citizens or if they are merely posing as townswomen of the city, shrewdly mimicking their appearance, to further discredit the Phoenician Festy. They appear "in the shape" of red-haired women, whose color, the reader is suspiciously reassured, is genuinely Carthaginian, despite and maybe perhaps because of the fact that they are shouting from Isod's Tower, a fortified stronghold along the walls of Dublin that was demolished in 1675. The scene alludes to the Third Punic War, when the Roman siege of Carthage was so relentless that the women in the city cut their hair and braided it into bowstrings in a last, desperate attempt of resistance before the city was razed to the ground. The opposition to Festy is thus likened to a staunch and unwavering obstruction, from a city that rightfully fears its ultimate annihilation. Irish-Phoenician history blends once again with a reference to Joyce's years in Trieste. The red hair reminds us of Joyce's model for ALP. Joyce was inspired by Italo Svevo's wife, Livia Veneziani, whose long auburn hair became the model for both Anna Livia Plurabelle's luscious red locks and the flowing movement of the River Liffey in Dublin.

The legal proceedings culminate in a mistrial not only because the plaintiffs' accusations are prejudiced and unreliable but also because judges and jurors are unable to deliver a verdict, given the multiple distractions that divert their attention. Their thoughts are elsewhere, since "they might talk about Markarthy or they might walk to Baalastartey or they might join the nabour party" (*FW* 91.13–15). If an anti-Carthaginian prejudice motivates the plaintiffs against HCE, the Carthaginian pantheon comes to the rescue of the protagonist who leaves the trial with impunity. Melqarth, literally "god of the city," is the protector of Carthage, and in Pseudo-Gaelic guise (Mark and McCarthy) intervenes in a defensive distraction that benefits HCE. The joining of Baal, the supreme god of the Phoenicians, and Astarte, the moon goddess, has to be understood as the sexual union in an ancient fertility rite, whose offspring is the very Melqarth. HCE walks away from the trial scot-free thanks to divine intervention: "If this was Hannibal's walk it was Hercules' work" (*FW* 81.3). Once again, Joyce demonstrates his profound knowledge of Phoenician and Carthaginian lore.[46] In the religious syncretism characteristic of ancient Mediterranean cultures, the Carthaginian Melqarth was often associated with the Greco-Roman Herakles/Hercules. Joyce's connection of Hannibal's marching troops with Herculean labors is a reference to the Second Punic War, when the Carthaginian general famously crossed the Alps accompanied by his war elephants, accomplishing the spectacular deed of building with his civil engineers a viable passageway through the formerly impervious mountain range. The shrewd Hannibal knew how to capitalize on this stunning logistical success, a feat of almost mythical proportions, by turning it into a cornerstone of his war propaganda. In his march toward Rome, Hannibal claimed that

---

[46] Joyce's education at Clongowes Wood College and Belvedere College focused heavily on the ancient world. At Clongowes, pedagogical strategies required students to divide into two groups that would compete against each other in a grammar contest revolving around noun declensions and verb conjugations. The two camps would represent Rome and Carthage during the Punic Wars, which added a historical lesson to the exercise. See Bruce Bradley, *James Joyce's Schooldays* (New York: Saint Martin's Press, 1982), 41–43.

he was walking in the footsteps of Herakles/Hercules, boasting that his military exploits were assisted by divine favor. His military progression largely overlapped with what in antiquity was known as the Heraklean Way, a coincidence he knew well to manipulate in his intimidation campaign of the Romans. According to a widely circulating mythological tale, in his Tenth Labor Herakles/Hercules had stolen the cattle of the giant Geryon on the island of Erytheia, west of the Iberian Peninsula, and brought them to the Mycenaean city of Argos, breaking his path through Italy and crossing the Alps.

The following chapter is a prolonged inquiry into the form and content of ALP's letter, a widely circulating document that tries to exonerate HCE but that ultimately ends up implicating him even further. ALP's mysteriously letter is a motherly manifesto, a "mamafesta" (*FW* 104.4), that bears resemblance to "the littleknown periplic bestteller popularly associated with the names of the wretched mariner ... a Punic admiralty report ... had been cleverly capsized and saucily republished as a dodecanesian baedeker" (*FW* 123.22–27). Professor Tung-Toyd, a tongue-tied scholar combining Jung and Freud, echoes the positions of Victor Bérard who argued for a Phoenician prehistory of Homer's Greek *Odyssey*.[47] In the background of Odysseus' wanderings lies a long tradition of *periploi*, travel logs that functioned as navigation guides and sailing routes, which ancient Phoenician merchants used for their voyages in the known world. Concealed under etymological encrustations and anthropomorphic interpretations of physical geography, the Greek explorations of the Mediterranean conceal a Semitic matrix. The original document is written in "what is known as Hanno O'Nonhanno's unbrookable script" (*FW* 123.32–33), a mysterious lettering and an unbreakable code of Phoenician origin, penned by Hanno, the Carthaginian explorer who, according to Pliny, successfully completed a circumnavigation of Africa and recorded his explorations.[48]

Joyce would have undoubtedly appreciated the description of *Finnegans Wake* as a novel written in a highly elaborate "purple prose," to borrow an expression derived from Horace's condemnation of extravagantly ornate writing styles in the *Ars Poetica*.[49] Horace calls this style

---

[47] The chapter also suggests methods and approaches for reading and understanding *Finnegans Wake* in which the narrator mocks any attempt at literary criticism, especially psychoanalytic readings of the *Wake*.

[48] John Paul Riquelme argues, "As a Carthaginian, and therefore a Phoenician, Hanno, along with the other Carthaginians mentioned in the *Wake*—including Hannibal, Hamilcar, and Hasdrubal—is an avatar of Odysseus as the wandering Phoenician." Riquelme, *Twists*, 36.

[49] Horace, *Satires, Epistles, and Ars Poetica* (Cambridge, MA: Harvard University Press, 1978).

a *pannus purpureus*, a patch of purple cloth, associating text with textile, and once again Roman fastidiousness with Phoenician traditions. In the *Wake*, the color purple remains an important marker of identity politics. In the same way in which in the ancient world Tyrian purple became synonymous with Phoenicia, the land of the purple cloth, in *Finnegans Wake* purple signals the Phoenician subtext of the multiple plotlines, as well as the hidden history of a "violet indigonation" (*FW* 23.2). Tyrian purple was a darker reddish variant of purple that over time would not easily fade on dyed clothes but would instead turn brighter if exposed to the sun. This means that Tyrian purple appeared along a narrow range of gradations along the chromatic spectrum, deep and intense on newer clothes, shiny and brilliant on more weathered garments. In the *Wake*, purple is systematically present, endowed with a prismatic quality that reflects and refracts the color in a myriad of shades if viewed from different perspectives. Purple appears in manifold manifestations such as "ruddyberry" (*FW* 27.16) and "lavender" (*FW* 41.26); tints "of gingerine hue" (*FW* 52.26); the deep reddish "crimson" (*FW* 87.28–29), already mentioned in connection with Carthage; the warm mulberry color of the "oakmulberryeke" (*FW* 221.33); the pale variant of purple "mauve" (*FW* 253.17) and tones of "turkiss indienne mauves" (*FW* 215.21); and "violaceous" (*FW* 612.11), among many others.

In the very beginning, when Sir Tristan returns to Armorica in his quest to fight his peninsular war he is described as a "violer d'amores" (*FW* 3.4) a rapist who also arrives *viola d'amore*, Italian for "purple with love," an indication both of a reddened face caused by physical exertion—martial and sexual—and of the damsel's loss of virginity. The young and virginal ALP is later described as the "vierge violetian" (*FW* 203.29). The violet of the opening scene reappears in Shaun's sermon where he admonishes an avatar of Issy, now with indigo/violet eyes, not to become the nude model for reprobate and voyeuristic artists. Abundant with sexual innuendos, the passage introduces a group of gaudily erotic painters in a parody of great masters of tradition: "left to right the party comprises, to hogarths like Bottisilly and Titteretto and Vergognese and Coraggio with their extrahand Mazzaccio, plus the usual bilker's dozen of dowdycameramen" (*FW* 435.6–9). The Italian artists mentioned here—Botticelli, Tintoretto, Veronese, Caravaggio, and Masaccio—are painters who, like Titian, have painted the rape of Europa or other scenes of sexual violence.[50]

---

[50] Finn Fordham shows how "violet and violation reveal their root in the word 'viol', the rape, and beyond that in the power of desire ... This move inverts the sequence of colour in the first page where we move from 'violer' and end with the orange of the sun going down." Finn Fordham, *Lots of Fun at Finnegans Wake: Unravelling Universals* (New York: Oxford University Press, 2007), 82.

Since purple signals the convergence of military might and sexual violence, it should come as no surprise that the color is on full display in the Willingdone Museum, a locus of memorialization of warfare.[51] The tour of the museum is intended as a celebration of Arthur Wellesley, the Irishman and British Army Officer who defeated Napoleon at Waterloo, assuming the title of Duke of Wellington. Joyce took notes for the museum scene while visiting famous battle fields in Belgium, in particular Waterloo but also Flanders Fields where, in John McCrae's famous poem, red poppies grew after the fallen soldiers were buried ["This is Canon Futter with the popynose" (FW 9.19–20)]. In the museum, the Duke of Wellington appears "grand and magentic in his goldtin spurs and his ironed dux" (FW 8.18–19). Blending with Mussolini, self-proclaimed leader of Fascist Italy with the Latin term *dux*, "leader," the figure of the Duke is both majestic and magnetic, but also colored magenta. The origin of the color magenta, an alkaline dye first produced in nineteenth-century industrial chemistry, is indeed inscribed in a history of warfare and bloodshed. The pigment takes its name from the famous Battle of Magenta, fought in 1859 between the French and the Austrians in the context of what became Italy's Second War of Independence. During the combat, the carnage was so extensive that the color of the battlefield turned purplish dark red, on account of the soldiers' blood soaking the brown earth.

As the result of a bold literary experiment that tests the limits of readability, *Finnegans Wake* constantly interrogates the nature of its own writing. Obsessively self-reflexive, the text makes the act of writing a most pressing and recurring question. In order to realize his ambition to write a universal history, Joyce conceives of the text as a history of writing that features annals and chronicles, manuscripts and transcripts, typescripts and postscripts, and in which *Finnegans Wake* figures as the culmination of the history of the book. The penning of this archive of letters and epistles, languages and alphabets, often appears as dictated by a "Haunted Inkbottle" (FW 182.21), exercising its own "excellent inkbottle authority" (FW 263.23–24), written in a language that "porpurates" (FW 185.10) an idiom that tinges everything purple (*purpura* is Latin for purple). In the context of this Hiberno-Punic palimpsest, the ink with which many of the inscriptions are penned could obviously be only of the color that defined the Phoenicians in the ancient Mediterranean and that gave them their name, namely Tyrian purple, but also the many different and derivative hues and gradations of the color. ALP's

---

[51] Vincent Cheng calls the Museyroom scene "a Joycean case study of colonial power politics and of the responses that such politics engender from the margins of empire." Cheng, *Race and Empire*, 266.

letter is contained in "a huge chain envelope written in seven divers stages of ink, from blanchessance to lavaindette" (*FW* 66.13–15), suggesting that the writing on the envelope follows a gradation that culminates in lavender, a shade of purple, the final color on the chromatic spectrum of the rainbow. Purple ink is no novelty in human history. In late antiquity, Roman Emperors used the "sacrum encaustum," a very durable reddish-purple ink, to sign their documents. It was prepared with the same purple dye that the Phoenicians produced from shellfish. The Code of Justinian prohibited any alternative use of the encaustum; any utilization by common people or for uses other than imperial signatures was punishable by death and could trigger a state confiscation of goods. The purple encaustum turns to blue ink when Shem the Penman—writer, alchemist, and forger—endeavors to inscribe a universal history onto his own skin. He is "making encostive inkum out of the last of his lavings and writing a blue streak over his bourseday shirt" (*FW* 27.10–11), writing blue on his naked body, his birthday suit. Purple was also the color of the Philosopher's Stone, the substance sought by the alchemists that would turn base metals into gold. Shem the "alshemist" (*FW* 185.35) is invested in finding that particular "brand of scarlet" (*FW* 185.11). He produces the ink from a mixture of his own bodily fluids after cooking and refrigerating the blend, making an indelible ink, in an alchemic process described in Latin as "*encaustum sibi fecit indelibile*" (*FW* 185.25, italics in the original). Shem's bodily engraving, a kind of tattooing, retains the etymological origin of the encaustum, which in ancient Greek meant "burned in," suggesting that Shem writes as much as burns world history onto his skin, his own bodily parchment. Shem's production of this world history ink, made from feces and urine, is compatible with ancient dyeing techniques. The color purple could be produced with shellfish but also with fermented urine, used as a source of ammonia.

The Mime of Mick, Nick, and the Maggies in the first chapter of Book 2 is both a guessing game played by Shem, Shaun, and Issy and her friends, the 28 little girls, and a performance staged in "Feenichts Playhouse" (*FW* 219.2), an establishment that cues the Elizabethan Phoenix Theater and that here does not require an entrance fee. The guessing game is juvenile entertainment but also a veiled ritual of courtship and seduction, initiating the slow growth into sexual maturity of the siblings and their playmates. The secret word that Shem has to guess is "heliotrope," a term that carries multiple meanings. A heliotrope is technically any plant that turns toward the sun (like sunflowers); it is also a fragrant flower that is light purple or lavender in color; and as a pigment it is the color of Issy's underwear. The section is, again, rich in references to Phoenician and Carthaginian history. In a letter to Harriet Shaw Weaver, Joyce explains that he imagined the Maggies, buds on the verge of blossoming, as the "wild flowers on the ruins of Carthage, Numancia etc. [that] have survived the political rises and falls of Empires" (*Letters* 1, 295). After Shem fails twice to guess the secret word, Issy offers a hint to the solution, conjuring a fantastic scenario of seduction: "In the house of breathings lies that word, all fairness. The walls are of rubinen and glittergates of elfinbone. The roof herof is of massicious jasper and a canopy of Tyrian awning rises and descends to it" (*FW* 249.6–9). The description of the house and garden is, with its lavish building materials, clustered grapes, and smell of roasted meat, highly reminiscent of the opening scene in Flaubert's *Salammbô*, where the garden of the Carthaginian general Hamilcar, father of Hannibal, contains a "gold-fringed purple awning" and hosts a rich banquet.[52] The word to be guessed is described, misleadingly, "with consonantia and avowals" (*FW* 249.13), in a fashion typical of Semitic languages since the Phoenician abjad expressed consonants but not vowels. Furnishings for this building were described at the beginning of the televised burlesque, when the actors were introduced and the choreography was outlined, and include "Phenecien blends and Sourdanian doofpoosts" (*FW* 221.32), Venetian blinds and Sardinian doorposts, in what appears to be a silent movie (*sourd* and *doof* mean "deaf" in and French and Dutch respectively).

The echoes of Flaubert here are not casual. As I have argued, Joyce's knowledge of the Phoenicians grows in Trieste, where besides becoming familiar with the works of Ferrero, he also reads Flaubert. Joyce proudly said that he had read every single word Flaubert had ever written, and could recite whole pages from Flaubert's work by heart. Joyce owned a copy of *Salammbô* in the original French while he lived in Trieste.[53] While, as Scarlett Baron emphasizes, "*Finnegans Wake*

---

[52] Gustave Flaubert, *Salammbô*, 3. Schork reads the passage as a parody that perfectly imitates Flaubert's descriptions of Punic furnishings in the novel. R. J. Schork, "Awake, Phoenician Too Frequent," *James Joyce Quarterly* 27, no. 4 (1990): 767–776.

[53] Joyce's Triestine library also contained Flaubert's *Premières Œuvres*, *La Tentation de Saint Antoine*, and *Madame Bovary* in the English translation by Henry Blanchamp. See Michael Gillespie, *James Joyce's Trieste Library: A Catalog of Material at the Harry Ransom Humanities Research Center* (Austin, TX: Harry Ransom Humanities Research Center, 1986). In her authoritative reading of the two authors, Scarlett Baron shows how Flaubert remains a constant and pervasive presence throughout all of Joyce's writings, not exclusively or necessarily as a direct influence but rather as a part of a wider web of intertextual references. While allusions to Flaubert are relatively easy to identify, references to *Salammbô* in Joyce's works seem harder to detect. See Scarlett Baron, *'Strandentwining Cable': Joyce, Flaubert, and Intertextuality* (Oxford: Oxford University Press, 2012).

arguably marks the climax of Joyce's Flaubertian intertextuality," tracing allusions, echoes, and quotations of Flaubert in Joyce's last work may prove quite challenging given that clearly recognizable references are obviously in short supply.[54] Details from Flaubert's historical novel, however, appear to constitute the background of a plot twist in the "Haveth Childers Everywhere" section of Book 3.3. In the episode HCE continues to defend himself from the charges leveled against him, professing his innocence and general moral integrity. He tries to project an image of himself as an honest and incorruptible man who would never accept sexual or monetary bribes, rejecting the allegations that he may have had a part in the English slave trade, trying to sell a black slave mistress in an auction. In a passage rich in references to trade and credit, he swears by the goddess "Juno Moneta" (*FW* 538.1), the admonishing Juno, in whose temple the ancient Romans minted their coins. If anyone were to approach him for an extramarital affair, he continues, he would obviously be "tradefully unintiristid" (*FW* 538.3), an expression that cues the Phoenician Tyre, *Tiro* in Italian, and that indeed indicates his interest in trading sexual favors. In a sentence particularly difficult to decipher, HCE seems to reject the notion that he has received gold in the transaction: "Or to have ochtroyed to resolde or borrough by exchange same super melkkaart, means help" (*FW* 538.7–8), a passage that might also conceal, perhaps unintentionally, a brutally honest admission. HCE seems to suggest that money assists those who garner the power to levy octroy, a local entry tax on goods introduced into cities or municipalities. He denies that the privilege granted by the octroy authorizes him to resell or borrow by exchange both sexual and divine favor, in particular the one of Carthaginian god Melqarth, as well as some extraordinary milk cart, suggestive of payment in kind. Such sexual exploitation would be a "honnibel crudelty" (*FW* 538.10) equivalent to the the ritualized collective prostitution "we devour about in the mightyevil roohms of encient cartage" (*FW* 538.11–12).[55] HCE refers to the material construction of Carthage, its rooms and boundary walls, *murs d'enceinte* in French, walls that surround the city like a belt (*ceinture* in French). The circular structure of the city walls becomes HCE's wedding ring for his future wife. In the following pages, amidst courtship

---

[54] Baron, *Strandentwining*, 245.
[55] James Atherton already suspected a generic reference to *Salammbô* in the passage without explaining the deeper significance of the Phoenician subtext. See James Atherton, *The Books at the Wake. A Study of Literary Allusions* (London: Faber and Faber, 1959). Later, Schork engages in a much more systematic reading of the Phoenician and Carthaginian allusions to *Salammbô* in the passage, suggesting that Joyce is referring to the mass orgies performed by the Carthaginians. See Schork, "Phoenician," 771.

and conquest, he will declare his love for ALP, assuring her of his marital faithfulness until the two become the wedded couple "Big Maester Finnykin" and "Phenicia Parkes" (*FW* 576.28–29).

HCE the pontifex, builder of bridges and founder of cities, can thus count Carthage among the cities he has erected, a doomed city that here is also pregnant (French *enceinte*)—ready to produce offspring, giving life to other cities, in turn destined to rise and fall. In the *Wake*, where identities are transpersonal and events are transhistorical, the destiny of cities follows a similar pattern of interchangeability in which the rise and fall of ancient cities prefigure the checkered vicissitudes of the modern city. In particular, the destruction of Carthage, the capture of Rome, and the fall of Troy mark the end of entire civilizations with their social infrastructures and systems of cultural values. This recurrent and paradigmatic collapse of the ancient city foreshadows what Joyce saw as the fall of Habsburg Trieste, whose annexation to Italy coincided with the demise of an entire epoch. In the eyes of the author, Trieste had lost its appeal once the Austro-Hungarian Empire crumbled. It is worth remembering that Joyce moved back to Trieste after his interim sojourn in Zurich, where he stayed for the duration of the First World War, only to find, upon his return, a city that was fundamentally changed. The Joyce family returned in October 1919, when Joyce was supposed to resume his teaching post at the Revoltella Institute, now restructured to be included in the Italian university system. Much to his dismay, however, he soon realized that the vibrant cosmopolitan Trieste he had left behind, a city that had stimulated him and provided much of his literary inspiration, had now irremediably vanished. Adjusting to live in the shadow of a city he once considered his second home was too much to tolerate for Joyce. Ezra Pound, in the meantime, was endeavoring to convince Joyce to move with his family to Paris, an invitation they ultimately accepted, leaving for the French capital in July 1920. In a letter to his brother Stanislaus, dated August 29, 1920, Joyce calls himself a Triestine exile, "Exul Tergestinus" (*SL*, 268). An expatriate from Tergeste, the Habsburg Italian author of Irish origin was ready to start a new chapter in Paris.

The *Wake* records the fall of the Adriatic city in a textual tangle where Troy and Trieste overlap. When rumors about HCE's fall continue to resound and the scandal spreads, his fall is likened to the tragic destiny of the House of Atreus: "The house of Atreox is fallen indeedust (Ilyam, Ilyum! Maeromor Mournomates!)" (*FW* 55.3–4). The House of Atreus is indeed fallen in the dust after the conquest of Troy. Ilium is Latin for Troy, but the mourning mates, a male version of the ancient profession of wailing women mentioned in connection with the killing of Agamemnon, lament the death of the fallen victim in Miramare, in the outskirts of Trieste, where the Habsburg castle of the slain brother of the Emperor, Maximillian, is located. When these Miramare mourning mates grieve for the end of Atreus, they also mourn the fall of Atreox, a city that combines Troy and the Adriatic. This Adriatic Troy stands for Joyce's vision of a Trojan Trieste, "his citadear of refuge," where he lived "beyond the outraved gales of Atreeatic" (*FW* 62.1–2). These windstorms of the Adriatic refer to the Bora, the strong and chilly wind blowing in Trieste, and make their appearance in the "Boraborayellers, blohablasting tegolhuts up to tetties and ruching sleets off the coppeehouses, playing ragnowrock rignewreck" (*FW* 416.34–36). The destructive force of the Bora wind, propelling into the air shingles off the roofs and huts and Trieste's famous coffeehouses causes wreckage comparable to the legendary Ragnarök, marking the end of time in Norse mythology. In another instance, Trieste is described as the "Troia of towns and Carmen of cities" (*FW* 448.11–12), with a clear reference to Bizet's opera. It was easy for Joyce to exploit the alliteration between Troy and Trieste, but the intermingling of phonetic similarities involves three cities and includes the Phoenician Tyre. Vergil had already exploited the consonance of Tyre and Troy in Dido's reassurance that descendants of the two cities would receive the same treatment: "Tros Tyriusque mihi nullo discrimine agetur" (Aen. 1, 574), Tyre and Troy make no difference to Dido since her experience as an exile from Tyre predisposes her to a sympathetic welcome of the Trojan refugees.[56] It is important to note how Joyce saw many parallels between Troy and Trieste. Windy metropoles, both cities were important transnational commercial hubs, located at the crossroads of much-travelled trading routes. Troy was located on the Strait of the Dardanelles, connecting the Black Sea with the Eastern Mediterranean, and hence Asian markets with European mercantile centers. Destructive wars ended up definitively altering their previous role in the Mediterranean and beyond.

Joyce's last and arguably most important novel, *Finnegans Wake* represents the culmination of many interconnected narrative threads about language and politics that he spun in his earlier works. As the ambitious attempt to inscribe Ireland into the matrix of European history and its literary tradition, the text also tries to prophetically divine its position in a future institution of the United States of Europe. What started as a strategic anti-colonial tactic to liberate Ireland from the stifling yoke of English imperialism in *A Portrait* and in *Ulysses* turns into a more

---

[56] Joyce's quotes and adaptations of Vergil are so precise that R. J. Schork doubts that Joyce could recall the passages from memory, as well versed as the Irish author was in Vergil's poems. Schork has argued that Joyce took notes for these passages with Vergil's original Latin text in front of him, using the copies of the *Aeneid* and the *Georgics* that he owned in Trieste. See Schork, *Latin and Roman Culture in Joyce*, 266n and Gillespie, *Trieste Library*, 246–248.

nuanced literary invention of Europe that allowed Joyce to imagine an alternative to the dreadful contours assumed by contemporary history. If Stephen is trying to awake from the nightmare of history, the *Wake* plunges the reader into a nocturnal and oneiric text in which this history can be rewritten. Structurally circular and self-reflexive, the text suggests that the future of Europe is *Finnegans Wake*, since it also represents its prehistory. Joyce is fully aware that his Hiberno-Punic mythography of origins was based on a faulty ethnolinguistic kinship between Phoenician seafarers and Irish islanders, but it provides the powerful rhetorical and literary tools to challenge the established epistemologies of colonial historiography that viewed Irish subalternity as a natural fact of Anglo-Saxon Britain. Joyce's investigation of the literary origins of the concept of Europe further allowed him to inscribe Ireland within a larger Mediterranean dimension of the classical tradition. Through the *Wake*'s rape of Phoenician-Irish Europa, Joyce is able to connect Ireland's colonial past to Europe's imperial mission, craftily exposing the problematic question of what it means to consider a tale of sexual and colonial violence the foundational myth for European civilization. The subtle political commentary embedded in the passage suggests that the sexual politics intrinsic to imperial conquest has shaped the very notion of Europe, evoking a critique of European imperialism. In the annals passage, the tension between Ireland's status as imperial victim and the image of eager collaborator in its own colonization subsumes a highly ambiguous role for Europe, suspended between the old imperial paradigm and the promise of an anti-colonial future. For Joyce, this future nonnational and anti-colonial Europe is a multicultural state where primary modes of identification are not subsidiary of a colonizing national identity. The source of this Europeanization is Habsburg Trieste, which he remembered fondly years after he had left the Adriatic city. The *Wake* is the textual endeavor to capture in memory the multilingual fabric of the city, an attempt to "regain that absendee tarry easty, his città immediata" (*FW* 228.22–23), the absent Trieste, a city he very much felt his own. The reference to the Austrian bureaucratic lingo of the *reichsunmittelbare Stadt* emphasizes once again Joyce's point that it was the Austro-Italian culture of the city that inspired him. In a letter to Mary Colum, Joyce famously said, "They called the Austrian Empire as a ramshackle empire ... I wish to God there were more such empires."[57] It is worth noting that Joyce's recollections of Habsburg Trieste did not translate into any particular fondness for the imperial administration of Austria-Hungary, nor for the Irredentists in Trieste. Alien to any form of colonial sympathy, Joyce is not indulging in any imperial nostalgia here

---

[57] Mary Colum, *Life and the Dream* (Doubleday & Company, 1947), 383.

but recalling affectionately memories of his formative years as a writer, years that stimulated his generous glottological creativity.

Joyce's lack of sympathy for any colonial-imperial project stems from his awareness of the linguistic trauma that comes with the loss of a native tongue. Stephen's denunciation of the loss of Irish Gaelic and a subsequent cultural aphasia anticipates many linguistic anxieties of Samuel Beckett's characters, who are often at a loss for words or whose linguistic abilities wane and completely disappear. While Beckett's linguistic strategies were geared toward a distancing from English and self-translation, Joyce's substitute for Irish in *Finnegans Wake* is the multilingualism of Habsburg Trieste. Rather than writing in an Esperanto-like mélange of European languages, Joyce devises an open-ended machine of meaning production that breaks down semantic delimitations in a process of multiplication where alternate and opposite meanings are included. As a resounding echo of the Triestine dialect, a local vernacular that absorbed the manifold accents and vocabularies of its multilingual speakers, Joyce's protean language of the *Wake* is a bold textual strategy of modernist cosmopolitanism and the expression of a Habsburg transculturalism. In the semantic and morphological hybridity of the text's interlingual puns and portmanteaux, a radical openness invites surreptitious contaminations from additional idioms. The mechanics of this multiplication of meanings depends upon an echo that hails from across a linguistic divide. Joyce's language in the *Wake* is always the language of otherness. This linguistic transculturalism is intrinsic to the experimental epistemology of the *Wake*'s vernacular language, the text's "epistlemadethemology" of the "vermicular" (*FW* 374.17 and 82.12), a sort of secular theology of the epistle preached in the vernacular. Joyce's vernacular epistemology undermines and destabilizes hegemonic regimes of canonical representation while radically deconstructing traditional narrative conventions. It is made up of worms—the Italian *verme* and the German *Made*—that bore holes into traditional structures of meaning. In the same way in which Svevo's dialect disrupts the expressive possibilities of the Italian standard language, Joyce attempts to "unenglish" (*FW* 160.22–23) his language. The idiom of the *Wake* is a "slanguage" (*FW* 421.17), suggesting slang and slander, and a "sinscript" (*FW* 421.18), a language coded as a transgression of moral authority. In its ambition to become a textual microcosm of the Western literary tradition, the *Wake* forces its intended collective European readership to learn how to read anew. Written in the shadow of wars, the text is the harbinger of a cyclical renewal, whereby a future united Europe will rise like a Phoenix out of its ashes. Still far from its political realization, *Finnegans Wake* is a playful rehearsal, the textual and linguistic performance of this young Europe.

Conclusion: The Danube Flows into the Mediterranean

On December 16, 1934, Musil delivered a lecture in Vienna to the Society for the Protection of German Writers in Austria with the title "The Serious Writer in Our Time."[1] The address was one of his now rare public appearances. Adolf Hitler had been in power for almost two years in Germany, and Chancellor Engelbert Dollfuss, the champion of an Austrian version of Fascism, had been assassinated earlier that year in a failed Nazi coup that was a prelude to the *Anschluss*. As intellectuals are increasingly feeling the pressure of an overbearing state apparatus, Musil argues that even in times like the present, the values of humanity, freedom, internationalism, and objectivity are intrinsic to the work of an author. Cautious in his pronunciations but firm in resolve, Musil speaks with his usual complexity of thought. The independence of the writer from the capricious whims of everyday politics, he argues, remains a necessary condition for the shaping and renewing of the realm of culture. He concedes that although the work of an individual artist is influenced by historical contingencies, culture is fundamentally transhistorical as it transcends the rise and fall of nations and the boundaries of their state institutions. Musil's professed individualism dismayed those who misinterpreted his distance from current ideological camps as a lack of political commitment.[2] Equally mystifying to his audience must have been the argument he made when he placed German culture in the tradition of the ancient Mediterranean world

---

[1] Musil, "Der Dichter in dieser Zeit," in *Gesammelte Werke*, 8: 1243–1258.
[2] Musil earned his reputation as an apolitical intellectual also thanks to the unfavorable reception he received at the International Congress for the Defense of Culture, held in Paris in June 1935, where he made a speech. The Paris Congress was officially not affiliated with any political party, but was organized under the auspices of Communist intellectuals who saw in the Soviet Union the only valid opposition to Nazi Germany. In his speech, Musil warned about the perils of totalitarian regimes, and his critique was applicable to Communism and National Socialism alike. His equal distrust of both Communism and Nazi-Fascism was interpreted as an unwillingness to make a political choice.

and its hinterlands. He postulates that elements of the German soul can be found in the romantic missive of a Phoenician maiden: "The serious writer is not only the expression of a momentary attitude of mind, even should it herald a new age. His tradition is not decades old, but millennia. The love letter of a Phoenician girl could have been written today."[3] In Egyptian sculpture, Musil continues, one can find a deeper expression of the German soul than in all German art expositions. The reference to Egyptian culture is perhaps less surprising given that Musil considered his 1923 "Isis and Osiris" poem the narrative nucleus of the sibling incest of Ulrich and Agathe in *The Man without Qualities*. The rhetorical power of the Phoenician girl, on the contrary, lies in her unexpected appearance as a figure of defiance. Emerging from the Mediterranean culture that invented alphabetic writing in the Western world, this young Phoenician woman, not a Greek or Roman author, marks the beginning and becomes the leader of a tradition of intellectual resistance against authoritarianism. This is a stark departure from Musil's passing remark in the novel, where she is at the mercy of the divine bull. Here, she has become the protagonist of a mythical struggle against the colonial and sexual violence of an overbearing power. Her imagined letter suggests yet another aspect in this rewriting of the ancient tale. Embedded in Musil's Phoenician girl expressing her romantic preference in writing is a Nietzschean interpretation of the classical Europa myth, where the assertive maiden takes on a proactive active role in her longing for Zeus/Jupiter. By explicitly blurring the distinctions between ancient and modern, between Phoenician letters and German literary tradition, Musil aligns himself with the young Europa, establishing a continuity between her bold writing and the author's own Austro-European modernism. The literate Europa is the herald of a literary Europe that defies the authoritarianism of Fascism.

In Musil's lecture about the imaginative freedom of the writer, the figure of young Europa embodies the temporality of a present perfect, of an unfinished past whose effects continue to shape current state of affairs. In similar fashion, the literary invention of Europe described in *Modernism in Trieste* casts a shadow in a successive legacy of contemporary writers and thinkers. Claudio Magris and Jacques Derrida continue to interrogate what they see as the liquid nature of identities and the porous boundaries of Europe. In the 1986 novel *Danube*, Magris's narrator reflects on the legacies of the former polyglot and

---

[3] Musil, *Precision and Soul*, 256. "Der Dichter ist nicht nur der Ausdruck einer augenblicklichen Geistesverfassung, mag sie selbst eine neue Zeit einleiten. Seine Überlieferung ist nicht Jahrzehnte, sondern Jahrtausende alt. Der Liebesbrief eines phönikischen Mädchens könnte heute geschrieben sein." Musil, *Gesammelte Werke*, 8:1250.

multicultural Habsburg Empire while Derrida's 1991 essay *The Other Heading* envisions a Mediterranean Europe that is inclusive of alternative, Afro-Semitic points of origin that canonical narratives about Europe have long suppressed. Magris and Derrida, both attentive readers of modernism, emphasize once again the literary dimension of the European project.

In Magris's essay-novel, the Danubian riverscape constitutes the spiritual geography against which the narrator maps the cultural history of Mitteleuropa. Despite the purportedly apolitical tone of the narration, the narrator's rhetorical strategies reveal a complex network of subterranean discursive streams, a fluid system of allusions, hints, and insinuations that not only addresses Cold-War anxieties about the geopolitical conformation of contemporary Europe, but also revisits the ambivalence of the Habsburg legacy. Magris insists on the "Europeanness of Danubian civilization" but also invites caution against the almost ubiquitous temptations of the nostalgic sentimentalism he had identified decades earlier in the Habsburg myth.[4] Magris's conception of Mitteleuropean culture focusses on the idea of a continually imminent ending that never fully materializes, a totality that is never fully realized, one that signifies the precariousness and fragility of identity constructs. The inability to reach a complete synthesis does not lead to the dissolution of the subject but becomes a defense of marginality, of the peripheral, and of the transient.[5] We should not mistake Magris's notion of Mitteleuropa as a mourning of the past that endlessly defers closure. Like Musil, he is more attuned to historical processes that aim at a renewal of culture. In other words, the Danubian narrator wonders whether somewhere in this postimperial periphery it is possible to find the beginnings of a reconceptualization of Europe as an anti-colonial, nonhegemonic space.

The narrator identifies Europe in the border-crossing inherent in the historical encounter between the Roman Empire and Germanic tribes. The Roman *limes germanicus*, the sturdy stone wall that worked as the frontier between the civilized empire and the barbarians, was

---

[4] In *The Works of Claudio Magris: Temporary Homes, Mobile Identities, European Borders* (New York: Palgrave Macmillan, 2015), Nicoletta Pireddu suggests that Magris's characterization of the Mitteleuropean culture of irony should be read as "an instrument of moderation" and "a counterdiscourse to the Eurocentrism of the past but also as a warning against the persisting risks of discrimination and hegemony within Europe itself." In Pireddu's view, Magris aims to "transcend both the acritically celebratory approach to the Mitteleuropean search for order and unity and the equally tendentious denigration of its discovery of fragmentation and chaos." Pireddu, *Magris*, 52–53.

[5] Ibid., 56.

designed to contain the migratory flux of Germanic populations. In the description of the *limes*, the narrator does not simply insist on the materiality of the fortified barrier, but emphasizes also its aura of impenetrability and its psychological function as a sharp line of separation between one world and system of beliefs and another. And yet, the frontier failed to hold back the barbaric invasions, the Roman Empire crumbled, and then "the despised barbarians became the forgers of the new Europe."[6] The narrator of *Danube* emphasizes the connection between borders and historical transience when she adds, "Our history, our civilization, our Europe are the daughters of that Limes."[7] For the narrator, borders are necessary because they provide delimitations and offer form. But the border is, for the narrating voice, also a threshold, a doorstep of sorts that delimits the familiar and domestic from what is alien and foreign. In the novel, the physical geography of the river, a natural border that divides, invites the crossing necessary in a process of transculturation that dissolves the dichotomies of identity and alterity. Earlier in the text, the narrator had clarified the stages of this metamorphosis: "To acquire a new identity does not mean to betray the first one, but to enrich one's person with a new soul."[8] The border, be it a physical boundary or a conceptual barrier, is constantly trespassed. Published on the thirtieth anniversary of the armed Soviet invasion of Budapest, *Danube* presents the Hungarian capital as suggestive of the political potential that Europe could and should have. The narrator reclaims what the Czech novelist and critic Milan Kundera provokingly called the "European Orient" as an integral and indivisible part of the historical, cultural, and literary legacy of Europe. In reimagining the cultural and sociopolitical coordinates of the Danube region, Magris conceives of a polycentric Europe made of local identities and heterogeneous microcosms.

While denouncing the perils of imperial nostalgia inherent in the Habsburg myth, Magris's narrator nonetheless believes that if there is one aspect of the failed Habsburg experiment worth saving it is the nonnational matrix of personal allegiances, one that literature has

---

[6] "I disprezzati barbari sono diventati i fabbri della nuova Europa." Magris, *Danubio*, 113.

[7] "La nostra storia, la nostra civiltà, la nostra Europa sono figlie di quel Limes." Magris, *Danubio*, 113.

[8] "Acquistare una nuova identità non significa tradire la prima, ma arricchire la propria persona di una nuova anima." Magris, *Danubio*, 45. The narrator in *Microcosmi* will return to the necessity of a border in the definition of identity: "Ogni identità è anche orribile, perché per esistere deve tracciare un confine e respingere chi sta dall'altra parte." Claudio Magris, *Microcosmi* (Milan: Garzanti, 1997), 43.

tried to preserve and history endeavored to forget.[9] In the narrative engagement with the Europeanist legacy of the Habsburg Empire, the narrator offers a crucial distinction when she explains in the first chapter: "Writers tend to see almost exclusively the *hinternational* Danube, while historians also account for the German character of Danubian Austria."[10] Magris evokes Urzidil's portmanteau *hinternational*, so aptly descriptive for much of the political culture of the empire. Literature and historiography are at odds here: authors of literary texts tend to perceive the multiethnic Danube region as a Europe behind the nations, whereas historians tend to focus their attention on the hegemonic presence of the German Austrian elite. Since "the European spirit feeds on books ... gnawing on volumes of historiography," literary representations seek to take the place of historical analysis.[11] The idea of Europe appears as a literary creation, not simply as a utopia but constructed to provide an alternative paradigm to the monolithic and monolingual nation. The flow of the Danube is verbose, and this Europe-to-come exists on a paper, in a literary construction that challenges the pages of history.

Derrida's *L'autre cap*, translated into English as *The Other Heading: Reflections on Today's Europe*, was first published in book form in January 1991. This was a written version of a lecture he had given on May 20, 1990 in Turin, during a colloquium on European cultural identity. Derrida's Europe is primarily a Mediterranean Europe.[12] As such, the goal of Derrida's text is to embark upon a reimagined European journey, a project that needs a new captain, in a process that decapitates traditional phallocratic authority, and that needs a new course toward an-other heading, *l'autre cap*. In this process, Derrida reflects on his own critical

---

[9] Magris is certainly suspicious of the Austro-Hungarian legacy, one that can easily lead to imperial nostalgia of the Habsburg myth. Robert Menasse is less cautious: "Maybe it's not a fiction at all, but rather, the 2.0 version of the Josephinian bureaucracy which in its multicultural reach can, on a certain level, be considered a precursor to the present European administration. With all due criticism of the Habsburg monarchy and with all the due mistrust of its subsequent idealization, the merits of Josephinism and the Habsburg bureaucracy are still evident, even in the former Crown lands—almost a century after the demise of the multi-ethnic state." Robert Menasse, *Enraged Citizens, European Peace, and Democratic Deficits; Or Why the Democracy Given to Us Must Become One We Fight For* (Chicago: Seagull, 2016).

[10] "I letterati tendono a vedere quasi soltanto il Danubio hinternazionale, gli storici fanno anche i conti con la tedeschità dell'Austria danubiana." Magris, *Danubio*, 30.

[11] Magris, *Danubio*, 265.

[12] "The European Community ... is predominantly Mediterranean." Jacques Derrida, *The Other Heading: Reflections on Today's Europe* (Bloomington: Indiana University Press, 1992), 23.

position, the metaphorical locus from which he speaks and writes that in turn outgrows from the very physical location of his origin. He confesses to "a somewhat weary feeling of an old European," one who is "not quite European by birth."[13] Derrida was born into a Sephardic Jewish family in Algeria, a family whose origins, like those of many other Algerian Jews, were steeped by language and customs in Arabic culture. Derrida comes from "the southern coast of the Mediterranean" and sees himself more and more as an "over-acculturated, over-colonized European hybrid."[14] For Derrida, this Semitic point of origin is important when he addresses the writings of Paul Valéry, whose works Derrida sees as "those of a European from the Greco-Roman Mediterranean world."[15] Speaking in Turin, close to the Italian seaboard of the northern Mediterranean, Derrida says: "[T]his Mediterranean shore interests me—coming as I do from the other shore if not from the other heading (from a shore that is principally neither French, nor European, nor Latin, nor Christian)."[16] This position is the premise of the two axioms Derrida establishes in the early stages of his text. The first axiom hinges on the aporia that Europe is both old, outdated, anachronistic and yet, at the same time, young and youthful. The second axiom declares, *"what is proper to a culture is not to be identical to itself,"* which does not mean to renounce identity but to acknowledge the alterity, the radical otherness in oneself.[17] Culture, in this case European culture, is not only transhistorical but also and especially pluricentric and polycratic, a culture for which it is proper and necessary to negotiate between that which it constructs as identity and its intrinsic alterity. An internal otherness always exists because culture never has a single origin and thus a single genealogy.[18] Arguing otherwise would amount to a mystification of culture.

There is much of Joyce's *Finnegans Wake* in Derrida's Europe. The philosopher appreciated in Joyce's text the very idea that cultures have multiple origins and that they contain a radical internal difference, a notion encapsulated in the Irishness of what Derrida called the novel's "Finno-Phoenician motif."[19] In *The Other Heading*, Derrida never explicitly mentions the literary inspiration for his thinking, even though his discussion is clearly built around a mythical female protagonist who

---

[13] Ibid., 6–7.
[14] Ibid., 7.
[15] Ibid., 35.
[16] Ibid., 35–36.
[17] Ibid., 9. Italics in the original.
[18] Ibid., 9–11.
[19] Jacques Derrida, *The Post-Card: From Socrates to Freud and Beyond* (Chicago: The University of Chicago Press, 1979), 240.

needs to take the helm of this new Europe. Embedded in the historical legacy of Europe are obviously the crimes of xenophobia and racism, anti-Semitism and genocide, sexism and homophobia, as well as religious and nationalist violence. For Derrida, what is proper is to imagine a new Europe, the Europe of the other heading, a Europe that does not yet exist but whose promise is worth pursuing, a Europe that we do not see clearly but barely make out on the horizon in our uncertain Mediterranean navigation. This young girl, both the old Europe and the new captain, is no other than the mythological Europa, the maiden raped by Zeus/Jupiter in Greco-Roman antiquity. Like Derrida himself, this Europa is Semitic in origin and hails from the other heading, from the coast opposite of what supposedly is Europe. To Derrida, the "very old subject of European identity ... retains a virgin body."[20] He also wonders whether "its name mask[s] something that does not yet have a face?"[21] The virginal body and the girl's countenance are clear indications that Derrida has the mythological Europa in mind. There are two possible etymologies for the term Europa: one is εὐρύς, eurys, and ὤψ, ops, an expression that indicates a "broad face" or a "broad eye." Another etymological suggestion indicates the Semitic root *erebu*, attested in Akkadian as carrying the meaning of "setting or going down," with reference to the sun, or the Phoenician *ereb*, which correspondingly signifies "evening" and hence the "west." Similar to Derrida, Jean-Luc Nancy reads the European project as a combination of these two etymologies, a Europe whose glance sees far in the distant future but whose eyes also see the obscurity of the evening, Europe's own darkness.[22] In this recognition of its history of colonial and genocidal violence and the ethical commitment to self-critique lies Derrida's idea of a Europe that needs to rise once again, almost like a Phoenix born out of its own ashes.

Now, speaking of Derrida and the European project might sound like a contradiction in terms. He is, after all, the philosopher who undermined the hegemony of Eurocentric epistemologies. Here, however, he attempts to write beyond the dichotomies that oppose Eurocentrism to an anti-Eurocentrism.[23] Derrida clarified his position on Europe in his last interview given to *Le Monde*, where he declared that deconstruction, even when directed against a European intellectual tradition, remains "European, is a product of Europe, a reflection of Europe on itself as experience of a radical otherness." Rejecting with unconcealed

---

[20] Derrida, *Other Heading*, 5.
[21] Ibid., 5–6.
[22] Jean-Luc Nancy, "Euryopa: le regard au loin," *Cahiers d'Europe* (Spring/Summer 1997): 82–94.
[23] Derrida, *Other Heading*, 13.

indignation the idea that Europe is exclusively defined by its historical crimes, he continues that Europe has been in a permanent state of self-critique since the Enlightenment. This ethical "tradition of perfectibility" remains for Derrida a beacon of hope for the future.[24]

Derrida shares the belief in Europe's ability to interrogate its own notions of morality and justice with Jürgen Habermas, inheritor of the Frankfurt School who is invested in salvaging those aspects of the Enlightenment tradition that oppose the instrumental use of reason. In 2003, Derrida and Habermas published an article together in *Die Frankfurter Allgemeine Zeitung*, entitled "Plädoyer zu einer Wiedergeburt Europas" in which the two philosophers argue for the necessity of a European Renaissance of sorts, a Europe beyond Eurocentrism. Necessary in such an overhaul lies a radical denationalization of European life. After all, Eurocentrism presents itself as a nationally inflected ethnocentrism. Against the pyramidal structure of national loyalty that subordinates all sorts of allegiances, this is a democratic, polycentric, and nonhegemonic model of Europe that exists within what Habermas envisions as a postnational constellation.[25] Anchored in a constitutional patriotism and a public ethics of inclusion, Habermas's postnational political geography defies the constant mechanism of recolonization that excludes foreigners or migrants from the privileges and entitlements that come with the belonging to a community of citizens. Magris is the thinker who recognizes in this citizenship not based on nationality and in the multiple networks of horizontal, nonhierarchical loyalties and allegiances a legacy of the Habsburg experiment that is worth preserving.[26] Habermas, with Derrida and Magris, challenges the idea that the nation is the only way for us to find a home in the world, arguing that democracy and human rights are possible in contexts that are not national.

The current refugee crisis and other forced migrations from the global South suggests that Europe may need to return to one of its many origins—the literary invention of Europe, the product of an unlikely Habsburg southern thought—to imagine its future. The multiple cultural and emotional allegiances of the authors and their characters described in this book are a reminder of the very human ability to

---

[24] Jacques Derrida, *The Last Interview*. www.studiovisit.net/SV.Derrida.pdf. 2004. See also Michael Peters, "Derrida as a Profound Humanist." in ed. Michael Peters and Gert Biesta, *Derrida, Deconstruction, and the Politics of Pedagogy* (New York: Peter Lang, 2009), 39–58.

[25] See Jürgen Habermas, *The Postnational Constellation. Political Essays* (Cambridge, MA: MIT Press, 2001).

[26] For Magris's proximity to Habermas's idea of a post-national Europe, see Pireddu, *Magris*, 55.

The Danube Flows into the Mediterranean   241

inhabit different homes and communities, an ability that the nationalization of private and public lives has opposed, condemned, and pathologized. In a nonnational Europe, one can be European without having to regard race and ethnicity, class, sex, gender, regional, linguistic, or religious affiliation as an impediment to the full participation of civic life. Therefore, yes, a brown-skinned, Arabic-speaking Muslim woman from Syria arriving in Trieste as a refugee should be able to become, if she ever so wishes, European, with all the political rights and social privileges appertaining thereunto. After all, is she not one of the daughters of Europa, ignored by history, but whose love letter could be written today? If the image of this foreign and yet familiar woman, modern offspring of Phoenician Europa, may seem a stretch, let us conclude by considering what authoritarian and book-burning regimes of the past have feared the most: the potential of literary fiction to become historical reality.

Contemporary Austrian fiction continues to be fascinated and haunted by Trieste's literary modernism. Walter Grond's *Absolut Homer* revives many of the images and tropes employed by the authors described in the previous chapters, most notably among them the notion that Trieste, the city with a long Habsburg past, is solidly anchored in a Phoenician Mediterranean. The text attempts to rewrite *The Odyssey*, accepting Joyce's belief that the ancient epic poem was based on sea routes recorded in a Phoenician periplus. In one of the many journeys along the Adriatic littoral, the modern travelers fly with an aircraft over the Istrian and Dalmatian coasts. During the flight, worlds collide: they spot in the distance the most powerful symbol of the Habsburg Mediterranean, the Miramare Castle, the "little castle of Sissi," right next to Scheria, home of the Phaeacians.[27] The novel suggests that Trieste is a city whose modern vicissitudes continue to be discoverable; its ancient history, however, remains as mysterious and elusive as the Homeric transfigurations of the Phoenicians. In a text that follows an alleged Phoenician circumnavigation of the globe, the maps of the ancient and modern worlds overlap: Trieste is the Ithaca of this postmodern odyssey, the implausible *omphalos* from which and to which bold navigations and forced migrations begin and end.

---

[27] "Hinaus aus dem Golf von Triest, flogen wir entlang der istrischen Küste … Wir flogen weiter die dalmatinische Küste entlang ins Ionische Meer. Scheria-die-phönizische-Handels-hebräische-Schacher-Phäakenland-Insel" and "Sissis Schlößchen." Walter Grond, *Absolut Homer. Ein Roman* (Vienna, Graz: Literaturverlag Droschl, 1995), 46.

Bibliography

Abulafia, David. *The Great Sea: A Human History of the Mediterranean*. New York: Oxford University Press, 2011.
Amann, Klaus. *Robert Musil, Literatur und Politik: mit einer Neuedition ausgewählter politischer Schriften aus dem Nachlass*. Hamburg: Rowohlt, 2007.
Amberson, Deborah. "Zeno's Dissonant Violin: Italo Svevo, Judaism, and Western Art Music." *Italian Studies* 71, no. 1 (2016): 98–114. doi:10.1080/00751634.2015.1132608.
Anderson, Benedict. *Imagined Communities: Reflections on the Origin and Spread of Nationalism*. London, New York: Verso, 1991.
Apih, Elio. *Trieste*. Bari: Laterza, 2015.
Appadurai, Arjun. "Patriotism and Its Futures." *Public Culture* 5, no. 3 (1993): 411–429. doi:10.1215/08992363-5-3-411.
Appiah, Kwame Anthony. *Cosmopolitanism: Ethics in a World of Strangers*. New York: Norton & Norton, 2006.
Appiah, Kwame Anthony. *The Lies That Bind: Rethinking Identity, Creed, Country, Color, Class, Culture*. New York: Norton & Norton, 2018.
Ara, Angelo. *Fra nazione e impero. Trieste, gli Asburgo, la Mitteleuropa*. Milan: Garzanti, 2009.
Ara, Angelo, and Claudio Magris. *Trieste. Un'identità di frontiera*. Turin: Einaudi, 1982.
Arens, Katherine. *Vienna's Dreams of Europe: Culture and Identity beyond the Nation-State*. London and New York: Bloomsbury Academic, 2015.
Aristotle. *Politics*. Oxford: Oxford University Press, 1995.
Armand, Louis, and Clare Wallace, eds. *Giacomo Joyce: Envoys of the Other*. Dublin: Maunsel, 2002.
Arthurs, Joshua. *Excavating Modernity: The Roman Past in Fascist Italy*. Ithaca, NY: Cornell University Press, 2013.
Atherton, James. *The Books at the Wake: A Study of Literary Allusions in James Joyce's Finnegans Wake*. London: Faber and Faber, 1959.
Attridge, Derek, and Marjorie Elizabeth Howes, eds. *Semicolonial Joyce*. Cambridge: Cambridge University Press, 2000.
Aubet, Maria Eugenia. *The Phoenicians and the West: Politics, Colonies, and Trade*. Cambridge: Cambridge University Press, 2001.
Bahr, Hermann. *Dalmatinische Reise*. Frankfurt am Main: Fischer Verlag, 1909.
Ballinger, Pamela. *History in Exile: Memory and Identity at the Borders of the Balkans*. Princeton, NJ: Princeton University Press, 2003.

Baron, Scarlett. *'Strandentwining Cable': Joyce, Flaubert, and Intertextuality*. Oxford: Oxford University Press, 2012.
Bartoloni, Paolo. *Sapere di scrivere. Svevo e gli ordigni di La coscienza di Zeno*. Catania: Il Carrubo, 2015.
Bauer, Otto. *Die Nationalitätenfrage und die Sozialdemokratie*. Vienna: Brand, 1907.
Bauman, Zygmunt. *Europe: An Unfinished Adventure*. Malden, MA: Polity Press, 2004.
Beer, Marina. "Alcune note su Ettore Schmitz e i suoi nomi: per una ricerca sulle fonti di Italo Svevo." In *Contributi sveviani*, with an introduction by Riccardo Scrivano, 11–30. Trieste: Lint, 1979.
Benussi, Bernardo. *L'Istria sino ad Augusto: Studi*. Trieste, 1883.
Bérard, Victor. *Les Phéniciens et l'Odyssée*. 2 vols. Paris: Colin, 1902.
Berman, Jessica. *Modernist Commitments: Ethics, Politics, and Transnational Modernism*. New York: Columbia University Press, 2011.
Bernal, Martin. *Black Athena: The Afroasiatic Roots of Classical Civilization*. Vol. 1. New Brunswick, NJ: Rutgers University Press, 1987.
Bernardi, Amy. *L'Istria e la Dalmazia*. Bergamo: Istituto di Arti Grafiche, 1915.
Betham, William. *The Gael and Cymbri: Or, An Inquiry into the Origin and History of the Irish Scoti, Britons, and Gauls, and of the Caledonians, Picts, Welsh, Cornish, and Bretons*. Dublin: W. Curry, 1834.
Bishop, John. *Joyce's Book of the Dark: Finnegans Wake*. Madison: University of Wisconsin Press, 1986.
Blaschke, Bernd. *Der homo oeconomicus und sein Kredit bei Musil, Joyce, Svevo, Unamuno und Céline*. Munich: Wilhelm Fink, 2004.
Boldrini, Lucia. *Joyce, Dante, and the Poetics of Literary Relations: Language and Meaning in Finnegans Wake*. Cambridge: Cambridge University Press, 2001.
Boss, Ulrich. "Eine bemerkenswerte Einzelheit. Arnheims phönikischer Schädel im Kontext antisemitischer Rassendiskurse." *Musil-Forum. Studien zur Literatur der klassischen Moderne* 31 (2009/2010): 64–83. doi:10.1515/9783110271218.64.
Boss, Ulrich. *Männlichkeit als Eigenschaft: Geschlechterkonstellationen in Robert Musils Der Mann ohne Eigenschaften*. Berlin: de Gruyter, 2013.
Bradley, Bruce. *James Joyce's Schooldays*. New York: Saint Martin's Press, 1982.
Braudel, Fernand. *The Mediterranean and the Mediterranean World in the Age of Phillip II*, vol. 1. Berkeley: University of California Press, 1995.
Bressan, Marina. "Theodor Däubler: A Mediator between Florentine Futurism and German Modernism." *International Yearbook of Futurism Studies* 4 (2014): 450–476.
Brubaker, Rogers. *Nationalism Reframed: Nationhood and the National Question in the New Europe*. New York: Cambridge University Press, 1996.
Bulson, Eric. "An Italian Tongue in an Irish Mouth: Joyce, Politics, and the Franca Langua." *Journal of Modern Literature* 24, no. 1 (Fall 2000): 63–79. www.jstor.org/stable/3831700.
Bury, J. B. *A History of Greece to the Death of Alexander the Great*. London: Macmillan, 1914.
Camerino, Giuseppe Antonio. *Italo Svevo e la crisi della Mitteleuropa*. Naples: Liguori, 2002.
Campanile, Anna. "The Torn Soul of a City: Trieste as a Center of Polyphonic Culture and Literature." In *History of the Literary Cultures of East-Central Europe: Junctures and Disjunctures in the 19th and 20th Centuries*, edited by Marcel Cornis-Pope and John Neubauer, 145–161. Herndon: John Benjamins Publishing Company, 2006.

Cangiano, Mimmo. *La nascita del modernismo italiano. Filosofie della crisi, storia e letteratura, 1903–1922*. Macerata: Quodlibet, 2019.
Caprin, Giulio. *Paesaggi e spiriti di confine*. Milan: Treves, 1915.
Carducci, Giosuè. *Tutte le poesie*. Rome: Newton & Compton, 1998.
Cary, Joseph. *A Ghost in Trieste*. Chicago: University of Chicago Press, 1993.
Cassano, Franco. *Southern Thought and Other Essays on the Mediterranean*. Edited by Norma Bouchard and Valerio Ferme. New York: Fordham University Press, 2012.
Catenazzi, Flavio. *L'italiano di Svevo. Tra scrittura pubblica e privata*. Florence: Leo S. Olschki, 1994.
Cattaruzza, Marina. "Slovenes and Italians in Trieste, 1850–1914." In *Ethnic Identity in Urban Europe. Comparative Studies on Governments and Non-dominant Ethnic Groups in Europe, 1850–1940*, edited by Max Engman, F. W. Carter, A. C. Hepburn, and C. G. Podey. Vol. 8, 189–217. New York: New York University Press, 1991.
Chamberlain, Houston Stewart. *Die Grundlagen des neunzehnten Jahrhunderts*. Munich: Bruckmann, 1915.
Chambers, Ian. *Mediterranean Crossings: The Politics of an Interrupted Modernity*. Durham, NC: Duke University Press, 2008.
Chapoutot, Johann. *Greeks, Romans, Germans: How the Nazis Usurped Europe's Classical Past*. Oakland: University of California Press, 2016.
Cheng, Vincent. *Joyce, Race, and Empire*. Cambridge: Cambridge University Press, 1995.
Coda, Elena. 'Between Borders: Reading Illness in Trieste.' PhD Diss., University of California, 1998.
Costa, Heinrich von. *Der Freihafen von Triest, Österreichs Hauptstapelplatz für den überseeischen Welthandel*. Vienna, 1838.
Colum, Mary. *Life and the Dream*. Garden City, NY: Doubleday & Company, 1947.
Conley, Tim. *Joyces Mistakes: Problems of Intention, Irony, and Interpretation*. Toronto: University of Toronto Press, 2003.
Contini, Gabriella. *Il quarto romanzo di Svevo*. Turin: Einaudi, 1980.
Corino, Karl. "Robert Musil. Aus der Geschichte eines Regiments." *Studi Germanici* 11 (1973): 109–115.
Corino, Karl. *Robert Musil. Eine Biographie*. Hamburg: Rowohlt, 2003.
Crispi, Luca, and Sam Slote, eds. *How Joyce Wrote Finnegans Wake. A Chapter-by-Chapter Genetic Guide*. Madison: The University of Wisconsin Press, 2007.
Crivelli, Renzo S. *James Joyce: Itinerari Triestini / Triestine Itineraries*. Trieste: MGS Press, 1996.
Cullingford, Elizabeth Butler. *Ireland's Others: Ethnicity and Gender in Irish Literature and Popular Culture*. Notre Dame, IN: University of Notre Dame Press, 2001.
Cüneyt, Arslan. *Der Mann ohne Eigenschaften und die wissenschaftliche Weltauffassung. Robert Musil, die Moderne und der Wiener Kreis*. Vienna: Springer, 2014.
Curci, Roberto, and Gabriella Ziani, eds. *Bianco, rosa e verde: scrittrici a Trieste fra '800 e '900*. Trieste: Lint, 1993.
Dainotto, Roberto Maria. *Europe (In Theory)*. Durham, NC: Duke University Press, 2007.
Dainotto, Roberto Maria. *Place in Literature: Regions, Cultures, Communities*. Ithaca, NY: Cornell University Press, 2000.
Däubler, Theodor. *Das Nordlicht*. Leipzig: Insel Verlag, 1921.
Däubler, Theodor. *Der Fischzug*. Hellerau: Hegner, 1930.
Däubler, Theodor. *Der neue Standpunkt*. Dresden: Hellerauer Verlag, 1916.

Däubler, Theodor. *Dichtungen und Schriften*. Edited by Friedhelm Kemp. Munich: Kösel, 1956.
Däubler, Theodor. *Lucidarium in Arte Musicae: Des Ricciotto Canudo aus Gioja del colle*. Leipzig: Insel Verlag, 1917.
Däubler, Theodor. *Päan und Dithyrambos. Eine Phantasmagorie*. Leipzig: Insel Verlag, 1924.
Däubler, Theodor. *Wir wollen nicht verweilen. Autobiographische Fragmente*. Leipzig: Insel Verlag, 1915.
Davison, Neil R. *James Joyce, Ulysses, and the Construction of Jewish Identity: Culture, Biography, and "the Jew" in Modernist Europe*. Cambridge: Cambridge University Press, 1996.
Debenedetti, Giacomo. *Saggi Critici*. Milan: Mondadori, 1955.
De Cauwer, Stijn. *A Diagnosis of Modern Life: Robert Musil's Der Mann ohne Eigenschaften as a Critical-Utopian Project*. Brussels: Peter Lang, 2014.
Deleuze, Gilles, and Felix Guattari. *Kafka: Toward a Minor Literature*. Minneapolis: University of Minnesota Press, 1986.
De Mauro, Tullio. *Storia linguistica dell'Italia unita*. Bari: Laterza, 1976.
Demetz, Peter. *Mein Prag. Erinnerungen 1939 bis 1945*. Vienna: Paul Zsolnay Verlag, 2008.
Derrida, Jacques. *The Last Interview*. www.studiovisit.net/SV.Derrida.pdf. 2004.
Derrida, Jacques. *The Other Heading: Reflections on Today's Europe*. Bloomington: Indiana University Press, 1992.
Derrida, Jacques. *The Post-Card: From Socrates to Freud and Beyond*. Chicago: The University of Chicago Press, 1979.
Dethurens, Pascal. *De l'Europe en littérature. Création littéraire et culture européenne au temps de la crise de l'esprit (1918–1939)*. Geneva: Droz, 2002.
Deželjin, Vesna. "Reflexes of the Habsburg Empire Multilingualism in Some Triestine Literary Texts." *Jezikoslovje* 13, no. 2 (2012): 419–439. https://hrcak.srce.hr/91471.
DiBernard, Barbara. *Alchemy and Finnegans Wake*. Albany, NY: The State University of New York Press, 1980.
Dimino, Mariaelisa, Elmar Locher, and Massimo Salgaro, eds. *Oberleutnant Robert Musil als Redakteur der Tiroler Soldaten-Zeitung*. Paderborn: Wilhelm Fink, 2019.
Di Biase, Carmine, ed. *The Diary of Elio Schmitz: Scenes from the World of Italo Svevo*. Leicester: Troubador Publishing, 2013.
Dommelen, Peter van. "Punic Identities and Modern Perceptions in the Western Mediterranean." In *The Punic Mediterranean: Identities and Identification from Phoenician Settlement to Roman Rule*, edited by Josephine Crawley Quinn and Nicholas C. Vella, 42–57. Cambridge: Cambridge University Press, 2014.
Dougherty, Carol. *The Raft of Odysseus: The Ethnographic Imagination of Homer's Odyssey*. Oxford: Oxford University Press, 2001.
Dović Marija. "From Autarky to 'Barbarian' Cosmopolitanism: The Early Avant-Garde Movements in Slovenia and Croatia." In *Mediterranean Modernism: Intercultural Exchange and Aesthetic Development*, edited by Adam J. Goldwyn and Renée M. Silverman, 233–250. New York: Palgrave Macmillan, 2016.
Dubin, Lois. *The Port Jews of Habsburg Trieste: Absolutist Politics and Enlightenment Culture*. Stanford, CA: Stanford University Press, 1999.
Duffy, Andre Endaw. *The Subaltern Ulysses: Mapping an Aesthetics of Post-Colonial Literature*. Minneapolis: University of Minnesota, 1994.

Eisenstädter, Guglielmo. "L'antichissima Trieste ed i fenici." *L'Osservatore triestino* 82 (April, 12, 1870): 653–654.
Eisenstädter, Guglielmo. *Le scomparse dieci tribù di Israele*. Trieste, 1870.
Eliot. T. S. *The Complete Plays and Poems, 1909–1950*. New York: Harcourt Brace, 1950.
Ellmann, Richard. *James Joyce*. New and revised edition. New York: Oxford University Press, 1982.
Epstein, Edmund Lloyd. *A Guide through Finnegans Wake*. Gainesville: University Press of Florida, 2009.
Feichtinger, Johannes, Ursula Prutsch, and Moritz Csáky, eds. *Habsburg Postcolonial: Machtstrukturen und kollektives Gedächtnis*. Innsbruck: Studienverlag, 2003.
Ferrero, Guglielmo. *Ancient Rome and Modern America: A Comparative Study of Morals and Manners*. New York: G. P. Putnam's Sons, 1914.
Ferrero, Guglielmo. *L'Europa giovane. Studi e viaggi nei paesi del nord*. Milan: Treves, 1897.
Ferrero, Guglielmo. *Grandezza e decadenza di Roma*. 5 vols. Milan: Treves, 1902–1906.
Ferrero, Guglielmo. *The Greatness and Decline of Rome*. 5 vols. Translated by Alfred E. Zimmern. New York: G. P. Putnam's Sons, 1909–1910.
Ferrero, Guglielmo. *Il Militarismo: dieci conferenze di Guglielmo Ferrero*. Milan, 1898.
Ferrero, Guglielmo. *Militarism. A Contribution to the Peace Crusade*. Boston: Paige & Company, 1903.
Ferris, Paul. *Dr. Freud: A Life*. Washington, DC: Counterpoint, 1997.
Flaubert, Gustave. *Salammbô*. New York: Penguin Classics, 1977.
Fogu, Claudio. "We Have Made the Mediterranean; Now We Must Make Mediterraneans." In *Critically Mediterranean: Temporalities, Aesthetics, and Deployments of a Sea in Crisis*, edited by Yasser Elhariry and Edwige Tamalet Talbayev, 181–197. New York: Palgrave MacMillan, 2018.
Fölkel, Ferruccio. *Trieste, provincia imperiale: splendore e tramonto del porto degli Asburgo*. Milan: Bompiani, 1983.
Fordham, Finn. *Lots of Fun at Finnegans Wake: Unravelling Universals*. New York: Oxford University Press, 2007.
Frank, Alison. "Continental and Maritime Empires in an Age of Global Commerce." *East European Politics and Societies* 25, no. 4 (2011): 779–784. doi:10.11 77/2F0888325411399123.
Frauer, Emilio. "L'Istria semitica." *Archeografo triestino* 13, no. 2 (1887): 351–355. www.google.com/books/edition/Archeografo_triestino/ZI4BAAAAYAAJ?hl= en&gbpv=0.
Freed, Mark. *Robert Musil and the NonModern*. New York: Continuum, 2011.
Freud, Sigmund. *The Interpretation of Dreams*. New York: Avon Books, 1965.
Freud, Sigmund. *Jugendbriefe an Eduard Silberstein 1871–1881*. Frankfurt am Main: Fischer Verlag, 1989.
Freud, Sigmund. *The Letters of Sigmund Freud to Eduard Silberstein, 1871–1881*. Translated by Arnold J. Pomerans and edited by Walter Boehlich. Cambridge, MA: Harvard University Press, 1990.
Fried, Alfred. *Handbuch der Friedensbewegung*. Vienna: Verlag der Österreichischen Friedensgesellschaft, 1905.
Fried, Alfred. *The Restoration of Europe*. New York: Macmillan, 1917.
Furbank, Philip N. *Italo Svevo: The Man and the Writer*. Berkeley: University of California Press, 1966.

Furness, Raymond. *Zarathustra's Children: A Study of a Lost Generation of German Writers*. Rochester, NY: Camden House, 2000.
Gandolfi, Laura. "Freud in Trieste: Journey to an Ambiguous City." *Psychoanalysis and History* 12, no. 2 (2010): 129–151. doi:10.3366/pah.2010.0002.
Gatt-Rutter, John. *Italo Svevo: A Double Life*. Oxford: Clarendon, 1988.
Gatt-Rutter, John, and Brian Moloney, eds. *"This England is so different …" Italo Svevo's London Writings*. Leicester: Troubador Publishing, 2003.
Gay, Peter. *Freud: A Life for our Time*. New York: Norton, 1988.
Generini, Ettore. *Trieste antica e moderna ossia descrizione e origine dei nomi delle sue vie, androne e piazze: curiosità triestine*. Trieste, 1884.
Gere, Cathy. *Knossos & the Prophets of Modernism*. Chicago: The University of Chicago Press, 2009.
Ghidetti, Enrico. *Italo Svevo: la coscienza di un borghese triestino*. Rome: Riuniti, 1992.
Gibson, Andrew. *Joyce's Revenge: History, Politics, and Aesthetics in Ulysses*. Oxford: Oxford University Press, 2002.
Gibson, Andrew. *The Strong Spirit: History, Politics and Aesthetics in the Writings of James Joyce 1898–1915*. Oxford: Oxford University Press, 2013.
Gilbert, Stuart. *James Joyce's Ulysses: a Study*. New York: Vintage, 1952.
Gillespie, Michael Patrick. *James Joyce's Trieste Library: A Catalog of Materials at the Harry Ransom Humanities Research Center*. Austin, TX: Harry Ransom Humanities Research Center, 1986.
Giovannini, Elena. "Der Parallel-Krieg. Zu Musils Arbeit in der *Soldatenzeitung*." *Musil-Forum. Studien zur Literatur der klassischen Moderne* 13/14 (1987/88): 88–99.
Godina-Verdéljski, Josip. *Opis in zgodovina Tersta in njegove okolice z uverstitvijo kratkega geografičnega in zgodovinskega pregléda starih in sadanjih slavjanov*. Trieste, 1872.
Grafenauer, Ivan. *Lepa Vida. Študija o izvoru, razvoju in razkroju narodne balade o Lepi Vidi*. Ljubljana: Akademija znanosti in umetnosti, 1943.
Grill, Genese. *The World as Metaphor in Robert Musil's The Man without Qualities: Possibility as Reality*. Rochester, NY: Camden House, 2012.
Grillparzer, Franz. *Tagebücher und Reiseberichte*. Edited by Klaus Geissler. Berlin: Verlag der Nation, 1980.
Grond, Walter. *Absolut Homer. Ein Roman*. Vienna, Graz: Literaturverlag Droschl, 1995.
Guagnini, Elvio, ed. *Scipio Slataper. L'inquietudine dei moderni*. Trieste: Edizioni Ricerche, 1997.
Habermas, Jürgen. *The Postnational Constellation: Political Essays*. Translated by Max Pensky. Cambridge, MA: MIT Press, 2001.
Hametz, Maura. *Making Trieste Italian, 1918–1954*. Rochester, NY: Boydell Press, 2005.
Hametz, Maura. "Presnitz in the Piazza: Habsburg Nostalgia in Trieste." *Journal of Austrian Studies* 47, no. 2 (2014): 131–154. doi:10.1353/oas.2014.0029.
Hametz, Maura. "Zionism, Emigration, and Anti-Semitism in Trieste: Central Europe's Gateway to Zion 1896–1943." *Jewish Social Studies* 13, no. 3 (2007): 103–134. https://muse.jhu.edu/article/230679.
Harrison, Thomas. *1910: The Emancipation of Dissonance*. Berkeley: University of California Press, 1996.
Harrison, Thomas. *Essayism: Conrad, Musil and Pirandello*. Baltimore: Johns Hopkins University Press, 1992.

Hartshorn, Peter. *James Joyce and Trieste*. Westport, CT: Greenwood, 1997.
Healy, Maureen. *Vienna and the Fall of the Habsburg Empire: Total War and Everyday Life in World War I*. New York: Cambridge University Press, 2004.
Herodotus. *The Histories*. Edited by Carolyn Dewald and translated by Robin Waterfield. Oxford: Oxford University Press, 1998.
Hesse, Hermann. "Die Brüder Karamasow oder Der Untergang Europas." In *Gesammelte Werke*, vol. 12, 320–337. Frankfurt am Main: Suhrkamp, 1970.
Hickman, Hannah. *Robert Musil & the Culture of Vienna*. La Salle, IL: Open Court Publishing, 1984.
Hofheinz, Thomas. *Joyce and the Invention of Irish History: Finnegans Wake in Context*. Cambridge: Cambridge University Press, 1995.
Horace. *Satires, Epistles, and Ars Poetica*. Translated by H. Rushton Fairclough. Cambridge, MA: Harvard University Press, 1978.
Hroch, Miroslav. *Social Preconditions of National Revival in Europe: A Comparative Analysis of the Social Composition of Patriotic Groups among the Smaller European Nations*. New York: Columbia University Press, 2000.
Humphreys, Susan L. "Ferrero Etc: Joyce's Debt to Guglielmo Ferrero." *James Joyce Quarterly* 16 (Fall 1978 / Winter 1979): 239–251. www.jstor.org/stable/25476189.
Hutchins, Patricia. *James Joyce's World*. London: Methuen, 1957.
Isaac, Benjamin. *The Invention of Racism in Classical Antiquity*. Princeton, NJ: Princeton University Press, 2014.
Israel, Nico. "Esperantic Modernism: Joyce, Universal Language, and Political Gesture." *Modernism/modernity* 24, no. 1 (2017): 1–21.
Jameson, Frederic. *A Singular Modernity: Essay on the Ontology of the Present*. London: Verso, 2002.
Janik, Allan, and Stephen Toulmin. *Wittgenstein's Vienna*. London: Weidenfeld and Nicholson, 1973.
Jelnikar, Ana. *Universalist Hopes in India and Europe: The Worlds of Rabindranath Tagore and Srečko Kosovel*. New Delhi: Oxford University Press, 2016.
Jonsson, Stefan. *Subject without Nation: Robert Musil and the History of Modern Identity*. Durham, NC: Duke University Press, 2000.
Joyce, James. *A First-Draft Version of Finnegans Wake*. Edited by David Hayman. Austin, TX: University of Texas Press, 1963.
Joyce, James. *Finnegans Wake*. Edited by Robbert-Jan Henkes, Erik Bindervoet, and Finn Fordham. Oxford: Oxford University Press, 2012.
Joyce, James. *Dubliners*. Edited by Margot Norris. New York: Norton & Norton, 2006.
Joyce, James. *Giacomo Joyce*. With an introduction and notes by Richard Ellmann. New York: Viking Press, 1968.
Joyce, James. *The Letters of James Joyce*. 3 vols. Edited by Stuart Gilbert. New York: Viking Press, 1957.
Joyce, James. *Occasional, Critical, and Political Writing*. Edited with an introduction by Kevin Barry. Translations from the Italian by Conor Deane. Oxford: Oxford University Press, 2000.
Joyce, James. *Poems and Exiles*. Edited with an introduction and notes by J. C. C. Mays. New York, Penguin Classics, 1992.
Joyce, James. *A Portrait of the Artist as a Young Man*. New York: Penguin Classics, 2003.
Joyce, James. *Selected Letters of James Joyce*. Edited by Richard Ellmann. London: Faber and Faber, 1975.
Joyce, James. *Stephen Hero*. Norfolk, CT: New Directions, 1963.

Joyce, James. *Ulysses*. The Corrected Text. Edited by Hans Walter Gabler. New York: Vintage, 1986.
Judson, Pieter. *Guardians of the Nation: Activists on the Language Frontiers of Imperial Austria*. Cambridge, MA: Harvard University Press, 2007.
Judson, Pieter. *The Habsburg Empire: A New History*. Cambridge, MA: Harvard University Press, 2016.
Kafka, Franz. *Complete Stories*. New York: Schocken Books, 1971.
Kafka, Franz. *Gesammelte Werke in zwölf Bänden*. Frankfurt am Main: Fischer, 2004.
Keller, Thomas. "Fremdheit ohne Alterität. Die Nordlicht-Mythologie Theodor Däublers." In *Interkulturelle Lebensläufe*, edited by Bernd Thum and Thomas Keller, 191–234. Tübingen: Stauffenburg, 1998.
King, Jeremy. *Budweisers into Czechs and Germans: A Local History of Bohemian Politics, 1848–1948*. Princeton, NJ: Princeton University Press, 2002.
Kirchner Reill, Dominique. *Nationalists Who Feared the Nation: Adriatic Multi-Nationalism in Habsburg Dalmatia, Trieste, and Venice*. Stanford, CA: Stanford University Press, 2012.
Kosovel, Srečko. *The Golden Boat: Selected Poems of Srečko Kosovel*. Translated by Bert Pribac and David Brooks with the assistance of Teja Brooks Pribac. Norfolk: Salt Publishing, 2008.
Kosovel, Srečko. *Zbrano Delo*. Vol. 3.1. Ljubljana: Državna Založba Slovenije, 1964.
Klein, Richard. *Cigarettes are Sublime*. Durham, NC: Duke University Press, 1993.
Klopp, Charles, ed. *Bele Antiche Stòrie: Writing, Borders, and the Instability of Identity. Trieste, 1719–2007*. New York: Bordighera, 2008.
Knowles, Sebastian, Geert Lernout, and John McCourt. *Joyce in Trieste: An Album of Risky Readings*. Gainesville: University of Florida Press, 2007.
Lavagetto, Mario. *La cicatrice di Montaigne. Sulla bugia in letteratura*. Turin: Einaudi, 1992.
Lavagetto, Mario. *La gallina di Saba*. Turin: Einaudi, 1974.
Lebowitz, Naomi. *Italo Svevo*. New Brunswick, NJ: Rutgers University Press, 1978.
Leigh, Matthew. *Comedy and the Rise of Rome*. New York: Oxford University Press, 2004.
Leja, M. von. "Die Austrofizierung der Triester Staatsbeamten." *Österreichische Rundschau* 36 (1913): 385–389.
Lemon, Robert. *Imperial Messages: Orientalism as Self-Critique in the Habsburg Fin-de-siècle*. Rochester, NY: Camden House, 2011.
Lennon, Joseph. *Irish Orientalism: A Literary and Intellectual History*. Syracuse, NY: Syracuse University Press, 2004.
Levinson, Brett. *Market and Thought: Meditations on the Political and Biopolitical*. New York: Fordham University Press, 2004.
Lewis, Pericles. *Modernism, Nationalism, and the Novel*. New York: Cambridge University Press, 2000.
Le Rider, Jacques. *Modernity and Crises of Identity: Culture and Society in fin-de-siècle Vienna*. Malden, MA: Polity Press, 1993.
Libardi, Massimo, and Fernando Orlandi. "La «Soldaten-Zeitung». Una palestra per *L'uomo senza qualità*." *Studi Germanici* 12 (2017): 291–311.
Ličen, Daša. "The Vagaries of Identification in the *Società di Minerva* in Trieste (1810–1916)." *Traditiones* 46, nos. 1–2 (2017): 35–54. doi: 10.3986/Traditio2017460403.
Lombroso, Cesare. *Criminal Woman, the Prostitute, and the Normal Woman*. Translated and with a new introduction by Nicole Hahn Rafter and Mary Gibson. Durham, NC: Duke University Press, 2004.

Lombroso, Cesare, and Guglielmo Ferrero. *La donna delinquente, la prostituta e la donna normale*. Turin: Bocca, 1903.
Luft, David. *Hugo von Hofmannsthal and the Austrian Idea: Selected Essays and Addresses, 1906–1927*. West Lafayette, IN: Purdue University Press, 2011.
Luft, David. *Robert Musil and the Crisis of European Culture, 1880–1942*. Berkeley: University of California Press, 1980.
Lunzer, Renate. *Irredenti redenti. Intellettuali giuliani del '900*. Trieste: Lint Editoriale, 2011.
Luperini, Romano, and Massimiliano Tortora, eds. *Sul modernismo italiano*. Naples: Liguori, 2012.
Lützeler, Paul Michael. *Kontinentalisierung: Das Europa der Schriftsteller*. Bielefeld: Aisthesis, 2007.
Lützeler, Paul Michael. *Plädoyers für Europa. Stellungnahmen deutschsprachiger Schriftsteller 1915–1949*. Frankfurt am Main: Fischer Verlag, 1987.
Lützeler, Paul Michael. *Die Schriftsteller und Europa: von der Romantik bis zur Gegenwart*. Munich: Piper, 1992.
Macmillan, Margaret. *Paris 1919: Six Months That Changed the World*. New York: Random House, 2002.
Magris, Claudio. *Danube*. Translated by Patrick Creagh. New York: Farrar Straus Giroux, 2008.
Magris, Claudio. *Danubio*. Milan: Garzanti, 1986.
Magris, Claudio. *Lontano da dove. Joseph Roth e la tradizione ebraico-orientale*. Turin: Einaudi, 1977.
Magris, Claudio. *Microcosmi*. Milan: Garzanti, 1997.
Magris, Claudio. *Il mito asburgico nella letteratura austriaca moderna*. Turin: Einaudi, 1963.
Magris, Claudio. "Svevo e la cultura tedesca a Trieste." In *Il Caso Svevo*, edited by Giuseppe Petronio, 37–55. Palermo: Palumbo Editore, 1988.
Mahaffey, Vicki. *States of Desire: Wilde, Yeats, Joyce, and the Irish Experiment*. New York: Oxford University Press, 1998.
Maier, Bruno. *Italo Svevo e la critica straniera*. Trieste: La Editoria Libraria, 1956.
Mameli, Goffredo, and Michele Novaro. *Inno di Mameli (Il canto degli italiani)*. Milan: Ricordi, 1948.
Manganiello, Dominic. *Joyce's Politics*. London: Routledge and Kegan Paul, 1980.
Marinetti, Filippo T. *Teoria e invenzione futurista*. Milan: Mondadori, 1983.
Matvejević, Predrag. *Mediterranean: A Cultural Landscape*. Berkeley: University of California Press, 1999.
McBride, Patrizia. *The Void of Ethics: Robert Musil and the Experience of Modernity*. Evanston, IL: Northwestern University Press, 2006.
McCourt, John. "The Importance of Being Giacomo." *Joyce Studies Annual* 11 (Summer 2000): 4–26. www.jstor.org/stable/26285212.
McCourt, John. *The Years of Bloom: James Joyce in Trieste, 1904–1920*. Madison: University of Wisconsin Press, 2000.
McCrea, Barry. *Languages of the Night: Minor Languages and the Literary Imagination in Twentieth-Century Ireland and Europe*. New Haven, CT: Yale University Press, 2015.
McGrath, William. "Freud as Hannibal: The Politics of the Brother Band." *Central European History* 7, no. 1 (1974): 31–57. www.jstor.org/stable/4545692.
McHugh, Roland. *Annotations to Finnegans Wake*. Fourth Edition. Baltimore: Johns Hopkins University Press, 2016.

Menasse, Robert. *Enraged Citizens, European Peace, and Democratic Deficits; Or Why the Democracy Given to Us Must Become One We Fight For*. Translated by Craig Decker. Chicago: Seagull, 2016.
Migliorini, Bruno. *Storia della lingua italiana*. Florence: Sansoni, 1989.
Miles, Richard. *Carthage Must Be Destroyed: The Rise and Fall of an Ancient Civilization*. New York: Viking, 2011.
Millo, Anna. *L'elite del potere a Trieste: Una biografia collettiva, 1891–1928*. Milan: Franco Angeli, 1989.
Minghelli, Giuliana. *In the Shadow of the Mammoth: Italo Svevo and the Emergence of Modernism*. Toronto: University of Toronto Press, 2002.
Moloney, Brian. *Friends in Exile: Italo Svevo and James Joyce*. Leicester: Troubador Publishing, 2018.
Moloney, Brian. *Italo Svevo: A Critical Introduction*. Edinburgh: Edinburgh University Press, 1974.
Moloney, Brian. "Svevo as a Jewish Writer." *Italian Studies* 28 (1973): 52–65.
Mommsen, Theodor. *Römische Geschichte*. Band 1. Berlin, 1861.
Montale, Eugenio. *Carteggio Svevo-Montale. Con gli scritti di Montale su Svevo*. Milan: Mondadori, 1976.
Morris, Jan. *Trieste and the Meaning of Nowhere*. New York: Simon & Schuster, 2001.
Moscati, Sabatino, ed. *The Phoenicians*. London: I. B. Tauris Publishers, 1999.
Müller-Funk, Wolfgang, Peter Plener, and Clemens Ruthner, eds. *Kakanien Revisited: Das Eigene und das Fremde (in) der österreichisch-ungarischen Monarchie*. Tübingen: Francke, 2001.
Musetti, Gabriella, ed. *Oltre le parole: scrittrici triestine del primo Novecento*. Trieste: Vita Activa, 2016.
Musil, Robert. *Briefe*. 2 vols. Edited by Adolf Frisé. Hamburg: Rowohlt, 1981.
Musil, Robert. *Gesammelte Werke in neun Bänden*. Edited by Adolf Frisé. Hamburg: Rowohlt, 1978.
Musil, Robert. *Klagenfurter Ausgabe: kommentierte Edition sämtlicher Werke, Briefe und nachgelassener Schriften; mit den Transkriptionen und Faksimiles aller Handschriften*. Edited by Walter Fanta, Klaus Amann, and Karl Corino. Klagenfurt: Drava, 2009. DVD-ROM.
Musil, Robert. *The Man without Qualities*. Translated by Sophie Wilkins and Burton Pike. New York: Vintage, 1996.
Musil, Robert. *Der Mann ohne Eigenschaften*. Edited by Adolf Frisé. Hamburg: Rowohlt, 2006.
Musil, Robert. *Precision and Soul. Essays and Addresses*. Edited and translated by Burton Pike and David S. Luft. Chicago: The University of Chicago Press, 1990.
Musil, Robert. *Tagebücher*. 2 vols. Edited by Adolf Frisé. Hamburg: Rowohlt, 1983.
Musil, Robert. *Tagebücher, Aphorismen, Essays und Reden*. Edited by Adolf Frisé. Hamburg: Rowohlt, 1955.
Nancy, Jean-Luc. "Euryopa: le regard au loin." *Cahiers d'Europe* (Spring/Summer 1997): 82–94.
Nietzsche, Friedrich. *Beyond Good and Evil: Prelude to a Philosophy of the Future*. Translated and with a commentary by Walter Kaufmann. New York: Vintage, 1989.
Nietzsche, Friedrich. *Human, All Too Human: A Book for Free Sprits*. Translated by Marion Faber with Stephen Lehmann. Lincoln: University of Nebraska Press, 1996.

Nietzsche, Friedrich. *Werke: Kritische Gesamtausgabe*. Edited by Giorgio Colli, Mazzino Montinari, Wolfgang Müller-Lauter, and Karl Pestalozzi. 40 vols. Berlin, New York: de Gruyter, 1967–.

Nübel, Birgit. *Robert Musil. Essayismus als Selbstreflexion der Moderne*. Berlin, New York: de Gruyter, 2006.

Nübel, Birgit, and Norbert Christian Wolf, eds. *Robert-Musil-Handbuch*. Berlin: de Gruyter, 2016.

Österreichische Adria-Ausstellung Wien 1913. Offizieller Catalog mit einem Plan. Herausgegeben von der Ausstellungs-Kommission. Vienna: Elbemühl, 1913.

Ovid. *Metamorphoses*. Translated by Charles Martin. New York: W. W. Norton & Company, 2004.

Pahor, Boris. *Necropolis*. Translated by Michael Biggins. Champaign, IL: Dalkey Archive Press, 2010.

Pahor, Boris. *Srečko Kosovel: pričevalec zaznamovanega stoletja*. Ljubljana: Znanstvena založba Filozofske fakultete, 2008.

Palmieri, Giovanni. *Schmitz, Svevo, Zeno: storia di due biblioteche*. Milan: Bompiani, 1994.

Passerini, Luisa. *Europe in Love, Love in Europe: Imagination and Politics in Britain between the Wars*. London, New York: I. B. Tauris, 1999.

Payne, Philip. *Robert Musil's "The Man without Qualities": A Critical Study*. Cambridge: Cambridge University Press, 1988.

Perloff, Marjorie. *Edge of Irony: Modernism in the Shadow of the Habsburg Empire*. Chicago: The University of Chicago Press, 2016.

Pervanoglù, Pietro. "Attinenze dei metalli colla mitologia e colla paletnologia delle terre della penisola balcanica e italica." *Archeografo triestino* 14, no. 1 (1888): 192–210. www.google.com/books/edition/L_Archeografo_triestino/Zw8vAAAAYAAJ?hl=en&gbpv=0

Pervanoglù, Pietro. "Corcira nelle attinenze con la colonizzazione delle coste del Mare Adriatico." *Archeografo triestino* 11, no. 3–4 (1885): 344–359. www.google.com/books/edition/Archeografo_triestino/-A4vAAAAYAAJ?hl=en&gbpv=0.

Pervanoglù, Pietro. "Dell'origine del nome Italia." *Archeografo triestino* 11, no. 1–2 (1885): 119–130. www.google.com/books/edition/_/oY0BAAAAYAAJ?hl=en&gbpv=1.

Pervanoglù, Pietro. "Delle colonie greche sulle coste dell'Illirio." *Archeografo triestino* 10, no. 1–2 (1884): 20–28. www.google.com/books/edition/_/GjIxAQAAIAAJ?hl=en&gbpv=0.

Pervanoglù, Pietro. "La Leggenda di Ulisse sulle rive del mare Adriatico." *Archeografo triestino* 10, no. 3–4 (1884): 328–338. www.google.com/books/edition/_/GjIxAQAAIAAJ?hl=en&gbpv=0.

Pervanoglù, Pietro. "Sull'origine del nome del Mare Adriatico." *Archeografo triestino* 7, no. 4 (1881): 290–301. www.google.com/books/edition/Archeografo_Triestino/vUcxAQAAIAAJ?hl=en&gbpv=0.

Peters, Michael A. "Derrida as a Profound Humanist." In Michael A. Peters and Gert Biesta, *Derrida, Deconstruction, and the Politics of Pedagogy*, 39–58. New York: Peter Lang, 2009.

Pireddu, Nicoletta. "On Hercules' Threshold: Epistemic Pluralities and Oceanic Realignments in the Euro-Atlantic Space." In *Imperialism in the Wider Atlantic: Essays on the Aesthetics, Literature, and Politics of Transatlantic Cultures*, eds. Tania Gentic and Francisco LaRubia-Prado, 19–46. Cham: Palgrave Macmillan, 2017.

Pireddu, Nicoletta. *The Works of Claudio Magris: Temporary Homes, Mobile Identities, European Borders*. New York: Palgrave Macmillan, 2015.
Pizzi, Katia. *A City in Search of an Author: The Literary Identity of Trieste*. London: Sheffield Academic Press, 2001.
Pizzi, Katia. "A Modernist City Resisting Translation? Trieste between Slovenia and Italy." In *Speaking Memory: How Translation Shapes City Life*, edited by Sherry Simon, 45–57. Montreal: McGill-Queen's University Press, 2016.
Pizzi, Katia. "Gender, Confession and Ethnicity: Women Writers and Trieste." *Journal of Romance Studies* 7, no. 1 (Spring 2007): 71–78. doi:10.3828/jrs.7.1.71.
Pizzi, Katia. "Triestine Literature between Slovenia and Italy: A Case of Missed Transculturalism?" *Primerjalna književnost* 36, no. 1 (2013): 145–155.
Platt, Len. *Joyce, Race and Finnegans Wake*. Cambridge: Cambridge University Press, 2007.
Pohlenz, Max. "Die Stoa: Geschichte einer geistigen Bewegung." In *Das Neue Bild der Antike*. Band 1 *Hellas*, ed. Helmut Berve, 354–368. Leipzig: Koehler und Amelang, 1942.
Popovici, Aurel. *Die Vereinigten Staaten von Groß-Österreich: politische Studien zur Lösung der nationalen Fragen und staatsrechtlichen Krisen in Österreich-Ungarn*. Leipzig: Verlag von B. Elischer Nachfolger, 1906.
Quinn, Josephine Crawley. *In Search of the Phoenicians*. Princeton, NJ: Princeton University Press, 2018.
Quinn, Josephine Crawley, and Nicholas C. Vella, eds. *The Punic Mediterranean: Identities and Identification from Phoenician Settlement to Roman Rule*. Cambridge: Cambridge University Press, 2014.
Rabaté, Jean-Michel. *1913: The Cradle of Modernism*. Malden, MA: Blackwell Publishing, 2007.
Rabaté, Jean-Michel. *James Joyce and the Politics of Egoism*. Cambridge: Cambridge University Press, 2001.
Radossi, Giovanni, ed. *Il Carteggio Pietro Kandler-Tomaso Luciani (1843–1871)*. Rovigno: Centro di Ricerche Storiche, 2014.
Rafael, Vicente. *Motherless Tongues: The Insurgency of Language amid Wars of Translation*. Durham, NC: Duke University Press, 2016.
Rathenau, Walther. *Gesammelte Schriften in fünf Bänden*. Band 1. *Zur Kritik der Zeit*. Berlin: Fischer Verlag, 1918.
Rathenau, Walther. *Zur Mechanik des Geistes*. Berlin: Fischer Verlag, 1913.
Rawlinson, George. *History of Phoenicia*. London: Longmans, 1889.
Reidel-Schrewe, Ursula. "Freud's Debut in the Sciences." In *Reading Freud's Reading*, edited by S. L. Gilman, J. Birmele, J. Geller, and V. D. Greenberg, 1–22. New York: New York University Press, 1993.
Reitani, Luigi. "Das Italienbild Robert Musils in seiner Kriegserfahrung." *Musil-Forum. Studien zur Literatur der klassischen Moderne* 34 (2016): 177–185. doi:10.1515/9783110520453-009.
Rietzschel, Thomas. *Theodor Däubler. Eine Collage seiner Biographie*. Leipzig: Phillip Reclam, 1988.
Rindler Schjerve, Rosita, ed. *Diglossia and Power: Language Policies and Practice in the 19th Century Habsburg Empire*. Berlin: de Gruyter, 2003.
Riquelme, John Paul. *Twists of the Teller's Tale in Joyce's Fiction: Oscillating Perspectives*. Baltimore: The Johns Hopkins University Press, 1983.
Roditi, Edouard. "Novelist-Philosophers, Italo Svevo." *Horizon* 10 (1944): 342–359.

Rogers, Gayle. *Modernism and the New Spain: Britain, Cosmopolitan Europe, and Literary History*. New York: Oxford University Press, 2012.
Rosen, Georg. *Juden und Phönizier. Das antike Judentum als Missionsreligion und die Entstehung der jüdischen Diaspora*. Tübingen: Mohr, 1929.
Roscher, Wilhelm Heinrich et al., eds. *Ausführliches Lexikon der griechischen und römischen Mythologie*. 6 vols. Leipzig: B. G. Teubner, 1884–1937. https://archive.org/stream/Roscher/Roscher1AH#page/n3/mode/2up
Roth, Joseph. *The Wandering Jews*. Translated by Michael Hofmann. New York, London: W. W. Norton & Company, 2001.
Roth, Joseph. *Werke. Romane und Erzählungen, 1930–1936*. 5 vols. Frankfurt am Main: Büchergilde Gutenberg, 1994.
Robinson, Richard. *Narratives of the European Border: A History of Nowhere*. New York: Palgrave Macmillan, 2007.
Saba, Umberto. *Scorciatoie e Raccontini*. Milan: Mondadori, 1946.
Saba, Umberto. *Songbook. The Selected Poems of Umberto Saba*. Translated by George Hochfield and Leonard Cathen. New Haven, CT: Yale University Press, 2008.
Said, Edward. *Orientalism*. New York: Vintage Books, 1978.
Sauer, August. *Adalbert Stifters Sämmtliche Werke*. Vol. 19, *Briefwechsel*. Prague: Gesellschaft zur Förderung deutscher Wissenschaft, Kunst und Literatur in Böhmen, 1901–1927.
Schächter, Elizabeth. "The Anguish of Assimilation: The Case of Italo Svevo." In *Freud and Italian Culture*, edited by Pierluigi Barrotta, Laura Lepschy, and Emma Bond, 65–81. Oxford, New York: Peter Lang, 2009.
Schächter, Elizabeth. "The Enigma of Svevo's Jewishness: Trieste and the Jewish Cultural Tradition." *Italian Culture* 50 (1995): 24–47. doi:10.1179/its.1995.50.1.24.
Schächter, Elizabeth. *Origin and Identity: Essays on Svevo and Trieste*. Leeds: Northern Universities Press, 2000.
Schaunig, Regina. *Der Dichter im Dienst des Generals. Robert Musils Propagandaschriften im Ersten Weltkrieg. Mit zwei Beiträgen von Karl Corino und 87 Musil zugeschriebenen Zeitungsartikeln*. Klagenfurt: Kitab, 2014.
Scherber, Peter. "Regionalism versus Europeanism as Leading Concepts in the Works of Srečko Kosovel." *Slovene Studies* 13, no. 2 (1991): 155–165. doi:10.7152/ssj.v13i2.14296.
Schlipphacke, Heidi. "The Temporalities of Habsburg Nostalgia." *Journal of Austrian Studies* 47, no. 2 (2014): 1–16. doi:10.1353/oas.2014.0023.
Schloss, Max. *Deutschösterreich und die Zukunft von Triest*. Vienna: Verlag der Danzer Armee-Zeitung, 1919. https://archive.org/details/deutschsterrei00schl.
Schneider, Erik Holmes. *Zois in Nighttown: Prostitution and Syphilis in the Trieste of James Joyce and Italo Svevo (1880–1920)*. London: Ashgrove Publishing, 2015.
Schneider, Oliver. *Triest: Eine Diskursanalyse*. Würzburg: Königshausen & Neumann, 2003.
Schork, R. J. "Awake, Phoenician Too Frequent." *James Joyce Quarterly* 27, no. 4 (1990): 767–776. www.jstor.org/stable/25485093.
Schork, R. J. *Greek and Hellenic Culture in Joyce*. Gainesville: University of Florida Press, 1998.
Schork, R. J. *Latin and Roman Culture in Joyce*. Gainesville: University of Florida Press, 1997.
Schorske, Carl. E. *Fin-de-siècle Vienna: Politics and Culture*. New York: Random House, 1979.

Schücking, Walther. *Das Nationalitätenproblem. Eine politische Studie über die Polenfrage und die Zukunft Österreich-Ungarns*. Dresden: Von Jahn und Jaentsch, 1908.
Simon, Sherry. *Cities in Translation: Intersections of Language and Memory*. New York: Routledge, 2012.
Simon, Sherry, ed. *Speaking Memory: How Translation Shapes City Life*. Montreal: McGill-Queen's University Press, 2016.
Simmons, Laurence. *Freud's Italian Journey*. Amsterdam: Rodopi, 2006.
Slataper, Scipio. *Il mio Carso*. Milan: Rizzoli, 2007.
Slataper, Scipio. *Scritti politici*. Milan: Mondadori, 1954.
Slataper, Scipio. *Alle tre amiche: lettere*. Edited by Giani Stuparich. Milan: Mondadori, 1958.
Slote, Sam. *Joyce's Nietzschean Ethics*. New York: Palgrave Macmillan, 2013.
Sluga, Glenda. *The Problem of Trieste and the Italo–Yugoslav Border: Difference, Identity, and Sovereignty in Twentieth-Century Europe*. Albany: The State University of New York Press, 2001.
Somigli, Luca, and Mario Moroni, eds. *Italian Modernism: Italian Culture between Decadentism and Avant-Garde*. Toronto: University of Toronto Press, 2004.
Sorrels, Katherine. *Cosmopolitan Outsiders: Imperial Inclusion, National Exclusion, and the Pan-European Idea, 1900–1930*. New York: Palgrave Macmillan, 2016.
Spencer, John Malcolm. *In the Shadow of Empire: Austrian Experiences of Modernity in the Writings of Musil, Roth, and Bachmann*. Rochester, NY: Camden House, 2008.
Spoo, Robert. "'Una Piccola Nuvoletta': Ferrero's *Young Europe* and Joyce's Mature *Dubliners* Stories." *James Joyce Quarterly* 24, no. 4 (Summer 1987): 401–410. www.jstor.org/stable/25476827.
Stanzel, Franz Karl. *James Joyce in Kakanien 1904–1915: Mit erzähltheoretischen Analysen des "Ulysses" im Anhang*. Würzburg: Königshausen und Neumann, 2019.
Stead, W. T. *The United States of Europe on the Eve of the Parliament of Peace*. New York, 1899.
Strutz, Josef. *Politik und Literatur in Musils Mann ohne Eigenschaften: am Beispiel des Dichters Feuermaul*. Königstein: Hain, 1981.
Stuparich, Giani. *Trieste nei miei ricordi*. Milan: Garzanti, 1948.
Stuparich, Giani. "La realtà di Trieste." *Il ponte* 10, no. 4 (1954): 549–556.
Svevo Fonda Savio, Letizia. *Italo Svevo*. Pordenone: Edizioni Studio Tesi, 1981.
Svevo, Italo. *A Life*. Translated by Archibald Colquhoun. London: Pushkin Press, 2018.
Svevo, Italo. *As a Man Grows Older*. Translated by Beryl de Zoete. New York: New York Review of Books, 2002.
Svevo, Italo. *Carteggio con James Joyce, Eugenio Montale, Valery Larbaud, Benjamin Crémieux, Marie Anne Comnène, Valerio Jahier*. Edited by Bruno Maier. Milan: Dall'Oglio, 1965.
Svevo, Italo. *Epistolario*. Milan: Dall'Oglio, 1966.
Svevo, Italo. *La lega delle nazioni. (Sulla teoria della pace)*. Edited by Simone Buttò and Riccardo Cepach. Trieste: Servizio Bibliotecario Urbano, 2015.
Svevo, Italo. *Opera omnia*. Milan: Dall'Oglio, 1968.
Svevo, Italo. *Racconti e scritti autobiografici*. Milan: Mondadori, 2004.
Svevo, Italo. *Romanzi e continuazioni*. Milan: Mondadori, 2004.
Svevo, Italo. *Teatro e saggi*. Milan: Mondadori, 2004.
Svevo, Italo. *Zeno's Conscience: a Novel*. Translated by William Weaver. New York: Vintage, 2003.
Thaler, Peter. *The Ambivalence of Identity: the Austrian Experience of Nation-Building in a Modern Society*. West Lafayette, IN: Purdue University Press, 2001.

Thiel, Georg. "Letzte Fragen - Ultime domande." In *Lastricato di buoni propositi. Il centocinquantenario della nascita di Italo Svevo 1861–2011*, edited by Riccardo Cepach, 72–75. Trieste: Comunicarte Edizioni, 2012.
Thompson, Mark. *The White War: Life and Death on the Italian Front 1915–1919*. New York: Basic Books, 2009.
Tihanov, Galin. "Robert Musil in the Garden of Conservatism." In *A Companion to the Works of Robert Musil*, edited by Philipp Payne, Graham Bartram, and Galin Tihanov, 117–148. Rochester, NY: Camden House, 2007.
Tomasin, Pietro. "Del nome Istria. Origini fenicie." *Archeografo triestino* 2 (1870–1871): 153–156. https://books.google.fr/books?id=5Ze6aZ-3dVMC&source=gbs_navlinks_s.
Urbaner, Roman. "Schriftführer Musil. Der Jahrhundertschriftsteller als Chefredakteur der *Soldaten-Zeitung*." *Quart Heft für Kultur Tirol* 5 (2005): 54–67.
Urzidil, Johannes. *Prager Triptychon*. Munich: Wilhelm Heyne, 1960.
Valente, Joseph. *James Joyce and the Problem of Justice: Negotiating Sexual and Colonial Difference*. Cambridge: Cambridge University Press, 1995.
Vego, Milan. *Austro-Hungarian Naval Policy, 1904–1914*. New York: Routledge, 1996.
Veneziani Svevo, Livia. *Memoir of Italo Svevo*. Translated by Isabel Quigly with a preface by P. N. Furbank. Evanston, IL: Northwestern University Press, 1990.
Veneziani Svevo, Livia. *Vita di mio marito*. Trieste: Edizioni dello Zibaldone, 1950.
Vico, Gimabattista. *The New Science. Principles of the New Science concerning the Common Nature of Nations*. Translated by David Marsh with an introduction by Anthony Grafton. New York: Penguin Classics, 2001.
Vittorini, Fabio. *Svevo: Guida alla Coscienza di Zeno*. Rome: Carocci, 2003.
Vivante, Angelo. *Irredentismo adriatico. Contributo alla discussione sui rapporti austro-italiani (1912); Dal covo dei traditori: note triestine (1914)*. Genoa: Graphos, 1997.
Voghera, Giorgio. *Gli anni della psicanalisi*. Pordenone: Studio Tesi, 1980.
Volpato, Simone, Riccardo Cepach, and Massimo Gatta. *Alla peggio andrò in biblioteca. I libri ritrovati di Italo Svevo*. Macerata: Biblohaus, 2013.
Walkowitz, Rebecca L. *Cosmopolitan Style: Modernism beyond the Nation*. New York: Columbia University Press, 2006.
Wallace-Hadrill, Andrew. "Afterword." In *The Punic Mediterranean: Identities and Identification from Phoenician Settlement to Roman Rule*, edited by Josephine Crawley Quinn and Nicholas C. Vella, 299–304. Cambridge: Cambridge University Press, 2014.
Winkler, Eduard. *Wahlrechtsreformen und Wahlen in Triest 1905–1909. Eine Analyse der politischen Partizipation in einer multinationalen Stadtregion der Habsburgermonarchie*. Munich: Oldenburg Verlag, 2000.
Wolf, Michaela. *Die vielsprachige Seele Kakaniens. Übersetzen und Dolmetschen in der Habsburgermonarchie 1848–1918*. Vienna: Böhlau Verlag, 2012.
Wolf, Norbert Christian. *Kakanien als Gesellschaftskonstruktion. Robert Musils Sozioanalyse des 20. Jahrhunderts*. Vienna: Böhlau Verlag, 2011.
Zahra, Tara. *Kidnapped Souls: National Indifference and the Battle for Children in the Bohemian Lands 1900–1948*. Ithaca, NY: Cornell University Press, 2008.
Ziolkowski, Saskia Elizabeth. "Svevo's Uomo senza Qualità: Musil and Modernism in Italy." In *Gender and Modernity in Central Europe*, edited by Agatha Schwartz, 83–102. Ottawa: University of Ottawa Press, 2010.

Ziolkowski, Saskia Elizabeth. "Trieste and the Migrations of Modernism: Fin-de-siècle Austria in the Italian Literary Landscape." PhD Diss., Columbia University, 2009.
Ziolkowski, Theodore. *Classicism of the Twenties: Art, Music, and Literature*. Chicago: University of Chicago Press, 2014.
Ziolkowski, Theodore. *Minos and the Moderns: Cretan Myth in Twentieth-Century Literature and Art*. New York: Oxford University Press, 2008.
Zisselsberger, Markus. "Cultural Nationalism in the Twilight of History: Robert Musil's Austrian ImagiNation." *Modern Austrian Literature* 37 no. 1–2 (2004): 21–45. www.jstor.org/stable/24649082.
Zweig, Stefan. *Die Welt von Gestern. Erinnerungen eines Europäers*. Frankfurt am Main: Fischer Verlag, 2003.

Index

Alexander the Great 50
Alfred the Great 163
Alighieri, Dante 144, 157, 173, 179, 191
Amari, Michele 11, 12
Appian 55

Bahr, Hermann 92
Bambič, Milko 80
Barca, Hamilcar 59, 68, 69, 226
Barca, Hannibal 39, 42, 44, 48, 54, 55, 59, 65–69, 74, 130–135, 167, 168, 217, 221, 226
Barthélemy, Jean-Jacques 58
Bartol, Vladimir 80
Bauer, Otto 20, 21
Beckett, Samuel 231
Bembo, Pietro 173
Benco, Silvio 195, 198
Benussi, Bernardo 63
Bérard, Victor 201, 222
Bernardi, Amy 47, 48, 79, 80
Betham, William 211
Beulé, Charles E. 59
Bizet, Georges 229
Boccaccio, Giovanni 173
Bonaparte, Napoleon 116, 224
Botticelli, Sandro 223
Brod, Max 177
Bruno, Giordano 219

Caesar, Julius 48
Cankar, Ivan 84

Caravaggio (Michelangelo Merisi) 223
Carducci, Giosuè 16, 48, 147
Carniel, Luisa (Gigetta) 17, 72
Cato the Elder 55, 220
Černigoj, Avgust 80
Cesari, Giulio 146
Chamisso, Adelbert von 17, 143
Colum, Mary 230
Conti Luzzatto, Emma 17
Corneille, Pierre 57
Coudenhove-Kalergi, Richard 111

D'Annunzio, Gabriele 7, 16, 28, 60
Däubler, Theodor 6, 38, 39, 42, 45, 70–79, 82, 85, 88, 103, 150, 177, 191
Derrida, Jacques 45, 234–241
Dias, Willy 28
Dollfuss, Engelbert 233
Doolittle, Hilda 39

Eisenstädter, Guglielmo / Wilhelm 61–64
Eliot, T. S. 10, 39
Elisabeth (Sissi) (Empress of Austria) 241
Elizabeth I (Queen of England) 225
Evans, Arthur 59

Ferdinand Maximilian (Archduke) 92, 229

Ferrero, Guglielmo 196–201,
    204–213, 226
Fichte, Johann Gottlieb 41
Finzi, Aurelio 168
Finzi, Ida (*see* Haydée)
Flaubert, Gustave 59–61, 226, 227
Franz Ferdinand (Archduke) 20,
    95, 162
Franz Joseph I (Emperor) 92, 95,
    116, 122, 125, 128, 229
Frauer, Emilio 63
Frederick II von Hohenstaufen 144
Freud, Sigmund 42, 44, 64–69, 70,
    74, 131, 149, 166, 167, 168,
    217, 222
Fried, Alfred Hermann 43,
    156–160
Fritsch, Johann Ritter von 91

Gandhi, Mohandas Karamchand
    83
Garibaldi, Giuseppe 159
Gervasio Macina, Luisa 17
Gesenius, Wilhelm 58
Gilbert, Stuart 203, 204
Gioberti, Vincenzo 170
Godina-Verdéljski, Josip 62, 80
Goethe, Johann Wolfgang von 17,
    38, 57, 93, 147, 191
Grafenauer, Ivan 84
Grillparzer, Franz 91–92
Grond, Walter 241
Gruden, Igo 80

Habermas, Jürgen 41, 240
Hanno 52, 222
Hašek, Jaroslav 177
Haydée 28
Hebbel, Friedrich 143
Heine, Heinrich 17
Henry II 209
Herod 143, 145
Herodotus 52, 84, 200, 207
Herder, Johann Gottfried von 41

Hesse, Hermann 113
Himilco 53
Hitler, Adolf 36, 37, 233
Hofmannsthal, Hugo von 13, 128
Hohenlohe-Schillingsfürst,
    Konrad zu 94, 95, 103–106,
    119
Homer 55, 57, 76, 182, 201, 203,
    204, 222, 241
Horace 55, 222
Horvàt, Heinrich 141
Hugo, Victor 159

Ibsen, Henrik 191, 193
Ivičević, Stipan 18

Jarnach, Philip 88
Joseph I 169
Joseph II 132
Joyce, James 5, 6, 14, 27, 38, 40, 41,
    44, 45, 88, 149, 163, 167, 180,
    187–231, 238, 241
Joyce, Nora (née Barnacle) 216
Joyce, Stanislaus 216, 228
Jung, Carl Gustav 217, 222
Junker, Carl 92
Justinian 225
Juvenal 55

Kafka, Franz 154, 177
Kandler, Pietro 60–62
Kant, Immanuel 11, 156, 157, 159,
    160
Karl VI 162
Kaznačić, Ivan August 18
Kolb, Annette 10
Kosovel, Srečko 6, 38, 42, 79–89,
    177, 191, 203
Kosovitz, Ernesto 150
Kundera, Milan 236

Larbaud, Valery 141
Leja, M. von 106
Libesny, Kurt 101–103, 134, 137

Livy (Titus Livius) 55
Löffler, Bertold 99, 100, 102
Lombroso, Cesare 199, 200
Longfellow, Henry 216

Mac Muirchertaig, Forggus 209
Mac Muirchertaig, Domnall 209
Mac Murchadha, Diarmaid 209
Magris, Claudio 1, 45, 234–241
Maier, Bruno 168
Malachy of Armagh 209
Mameli, Goffredo 48
Mann, Thomas 10, 93, 129
Manzoni, Alessandro 173, 179
Marcianus of Heraclea 49
Marinetti, Filippo Tommaso 16
Martelanc, Vladimir 81
Martinuzzi, Giuseppina 18
Masaccio (Tommaso di Ser Giovanni di Simone) 223
Masaryk, Tomáš 21
Matvejević, Predrag 34
Mayer, Theodor 195, 201
McCrae, John 224
Metternich, Klemens von 116
Moeller van den Bruck, Arthur 71
Mommsen, Theodor 58, 60
Montale, Eugenio 168
Montesquieu (Charles Louis de Secondat) 11
Morpurgo, Fortuna (see Willy Dias)
Moschus 74, 85, 205
Musil, Robert 5, 6, 38–44, 69, 88, 91–139, 141, 142, 158, 191, 196, 233, 234, 235
Musil, Martha (née Heinemann) 105
Mussolini, Benito 36, 37, 142, 224

Nancy, Jean-Luc 239
Necho II 52
Nietzsche, Friedrich 44, 70, 73, 77, 78, 79, 110, 111, 117, 133, 165, 196, 213, 234

Nordau, Max 69
Novalis (Georg Philip Friedrich von Hardenberg) 38
Nürnberger, Ferdinand 161

Oberdank Wilhelm / Oberdan Guglielmo 122
Oblath, Elody 17, 29
Ovid (Publius Ovidius Naso) 74, 188, 205, 206, 207, 215
O'Toole, Laurence 209

Pahor, Boris 79, 80, 84, 85
Parnell, Charles Stewart 201
Pascoli, Giovanni 7
Pastrone, Giovanni 59
Pericles 57
Pervanoglù, Pietro 63
Petrarca, Francesco 173
Pittoni, Anita 29
Plato 54, 55, 99, 128, 168
Plautus (Titus Maccius Plautus) 56, 197
Pliny, the Elder (Gaius Plinius Secundus) 49, 52, 222
Plutarch, 55
Pohlenz, Max 169
Pope, Alexander 57
Popovici, Aurel 20, 21, 161, 162
Popper, Amalia 17
Posidonius of Rhodes 55
Pound, Ezra 39, 228
Prešeren, France 84
Prezioso, Roberto 192, 195
Prezzolini, Giuseppe 17
Pulitzer, Anna 17
Pytheas of Massalia 53

Racine, Jean-Baptiste 57
Rathenau, Walther 129–133
Rebula, Alojz 80
Renan, Ernest 58, 59, 61
Renner, Karl 20, 21
Richter, Jean Paul 67

Index 261

Rilke, Rainer Maria 92
Riefenstahl, Leni 36
Rimini, Pia 28
Roscher, Wilhelm 212
Rossetti, Domenico 60, 66
Roth, Joseph 27, 33, 34

Saba, Umberto 19, 150, 151, 198
St Laurence see O'Toole, Laurence
Šanda, Dragan 86
Schiller, Friedrich 38, 57, 147
Schlegel, Karl Wilhelm Friedrich 38
Schlegel, August Wilhelm 38
Schliemann, Heinrich 59
Schmitz, Aron Hector (*see* Italo Svevo)
Schmitz, Franz 171
Schücking, Walther 43, 156, 160, 161
Scipio (Publius Cornelius Scipio Africanus) 48
Shakespeare, William 145, 191
Silberstein, Eduard 65–67
Skrivanich, Alois 190
Slataper, Scipio 17–20, 35, 70, 72, 82, 87, 88, 144
Soliman, Angelo 132
Spengler, Oswald 86, 113
St. Augustine of Hippo 218
Stead, W. T. 192
Stifter, Adalbert 91, 92
Stuparich, Carlo 17, 19, 20, 70
Stuparich, Giani 17, 19, 20, 70
Stürgkh, Karl von 95, 105
Suttner, Bertha von 10, 128, 158, 159
Svevo, Italo 5, 6, 27, 38, 40, 41, 43, 44, 69, 72, 88, 127, 141–186, 187–191, 195, 201, 221
Svevo Fonda Savio, Letizia 168
Swift, Jonathan 57

Tavčar, Zora 80
Tiepolo, Giambattista 74, 75
Tintoretto (Jacopo Robusti) 223
Titian (Tiziano Vecellio) 74, 223
Tomasin, Pietro 63
Tommaseo, Niccolò 18, 23
Trampus, Clelia 17

Unamuno, Miguel de 10
Urzidil, Johannes 31, 237

Valerio, Alfonso 95
Valéry, Paul 10, 238
Vallancey, Charles 197, 211
Valussi, Pacifico 18
Veneziani, Olga 171
Veneziani, Livia 147, 156, 221
Verga, Giovanni 173
Vergil (Publius Vergilius Maro) 37, 56, 206, 229
Veronese, Paolo 74, 223
Vico, Giambattista 207, 209, 213, 216, 217, 219
Vivante, Angelo 15–18
Voghera, Giorgio 150

Weaver, Harriet Shaw 219, 225
Weiss, Edoardo 167
Wellesley, Arthur (Duke of Wellington) 224
Werfel, Franz 128
Wilhelm II 125
William IV 217
Wilson, Woodrow 24
Winckelmann, Johann Joachim 38, 48, 66–68, 93

Zeno of Elea 44, 167, 177
Zeno of Citium 44, 167, 168, 169, 177
Zweig, Stefan 13, 20, 29, 128, 137

www.ingramcontent.com/pod-product-compliance
Lightning Source LLC
Chambersburg PA
CBHW072130290426
44111CB00012B/1851